NetWare 5 Advanced Administration
The Cram Sheet

This Cram Sheet contains the distilled, key facts about NetWare 5 Advanced Administration. Review this information right before you enter the test room, paying special attention to those areas where you feel you need the most review. You can transfer any of these facts from your head onto a blank sheet of paper before beginning the exam.

UPGRADING AND MIGRATING TO NETWARE 5

1. In-Place Upgrade is performed with INSTALL.BAT.
2. Across-the-wire migration is configured with projects in Novell Migration Wizard.

NETWARE VOLUMES

3. The two types of NetWare volumes are:
   - **Traditional NetWare volumes** The SYS volume must be this type.
   - **NSS volumes** These are very large volumes with a maximum size of 8TB, unlimited number of files, no memory overhead, fast mounts, and enhanced CD-ROM support.
4. The components of a NSS volume are the provider, consumer, and storage group.

NETWARE 5 SERVER STARTUP FILES

5. The three types of server startup files are:
   - **SERVER.EXE** This file is located on the DOS partition in C:\NWSERVER.
   - **STARTUP.NCF** This file is found in C:\NWSERVER. It contains storage device drivers and some **SET** parameters.
   - **AUTOEXEC.NCF** This file is found in SYS:\SYSTEM. It contains time zone information, server name, server ID, protocol configuration, and bindery context information.

FILE SYSTEM DESIGN

6. The DOS partition has to be a minimum of 50MB and is found in C:\NWSERVER\SERVER.EXE.
7. The SYS:\PUBLIC\WIN32 directory contains common administrative utilities.
8. The SYS:\SYSTEM directory contains NLMs and AUTOEXEC.NCF.

QUEUE-BASED PRINTING

9. Print Queue is a subdirectory under QUEUES at the root of the specified volume. It stores users' print jobs until they're serviced by the print server.
10. The term *printer* correlates to a physical device. A printer can be either:
    - **Manual load** A printer that isn't attached to the server running PSERVER.
    - **Auto load** A printer that is attached to the server running PSERVER. NPRINTER.NLM is auto loaded for each attached printer.

NETSCAPE FASTTRACK SERVER

59. Netscape FastTrack Server is a Hypertext Transport Protocol (HTTP) or Web server.
60. NSWEB.NCF is executed at the server console to start Web services.
61. NSWEBDN.NCF is executed at the server console to stop Web services.
62. ADMSERV.NLM is executed at the server console to start the Administrative server.
63. The Netscape FastTrack Server is administered through a Web browser on the workstation. You can stop and start the server from the main Administrative page.
64. You can also use the Server Manager page to start and stop the Web server with the Server Off and Server On buttons.
65. The default primary Web content document directory is SYS:\NOVONYX\SUITESPOT\DOCS. This can be configured for another location.
66. The Netscape FastTrack Server system can be secured by binding to NDS. Access to Web content is then controlled through NDS.

FTP SERVICES

67. Configuration and administration of FTP services is done through a server-based utility called UNICON.NLM.
68. A workstation browser can upload and download files to the FTP server.

NIAS REMOTE ACCESS

69. NIAS can be configured to support dial-in and remote access to the network.
70. Connections can be IP and/or IPX with security.

GROUPWISE

71. GroupWise provides email, messaging, scheduling, and calendaring features.

MANAGEWISE

72. ManageWise is used for network and server monitoring, hardware inventory, and workstation remote control.
73. NetExplorer is used to discover network entities.
74. LANalyzer is used to monitor network traffic.

BORDERMANAGER

75. BorderManager is a firewall product for controlling services and traffic between intranets.

NDS FOR NT

76. NDS for NT is used for managing NT domains in NDS.
77. Novell created the SAMSRV.DLL file for running NDS on NT primary domain controllers (PDCs) and backup domain controllers (BDCs).
78. NDS for NT administration is done through NetWare Administrator.

Certification Insider™ Press
© 1999 The Coriolis Group. All Rights Reserved.

35. The property rights are divided into two types:
    - **All Properties** Rights assigned apply to all properties of that object.
    - **Selected Properties** Rights assigned apply just to those properties.
36. If a user has the Supervisor object right on the Server object or the Write right on the server's Object Trustees (ACL) property, that user has all file system rights to that server.
37. Container Administrators control local administrative activities for container objects, such as modifying user accounts and configuring access to objects in the container.
38. Enterprise Administrators control the tree name, partition and replication strategies, and time synchronization.

NDS PARTITIONS

39. Partitions are logical divisions of the NDS tree.
40. The partition root object is the topmost object in the partition, which is either a container or [Root] object.
41. Reasons for partitioning include performance and fault tolerance.

NDS REPLICAS

42. Replicas are copies of data corresponding to an NDS partition (with the exception of subordinate reference replicas).
43. The master replica is an original copy of the partition that's used for authentication and is needed for merging.
44. The read/write replica is a complete copy of the partition. You can have several read/write replicas, and they can be used for authentication.
45. The read-only replica is a complete copy of the partition that cannot be used for authentication.
46. The subordinate reference replica is not a complete copy of the partition. It's created automatically on servers that have a complete replica of a parent partition and not its children. It cannot be used for authentication.

NDS MAINTENANCE AND TROUBLESHOOTING

47. The NDS Manager is a workstation utility that can be used to perform partition continuity, synchronization, and NDS version comparison, and to determine replica locations and partition boundaries. It contains a repair menu that's a subset of features found in DSREPAIR.
48. DSREPAIR.NLM is server-based utility that's used to obtain NDS information and status and to initiate repair actions.
49. Load **DSREPAIR -A** at the server console for more advanced options.
50. NDS inconsistencies appear as question marks in yellow circle icons in NetWare Administrator. The first action to take is to let the system run for a few hours while you monitor NDS.
51. Examples of NDS errors include:
    - -625 TRANSPORT FAILURE
    - -621 TTS DISABLED
    - -701 SYNCHRONIZATION DISABLED
52. DSTRACE.NLM is server-based utility used to monitor and interact with NDS events.

DNS AND DHCP SERVICES

53. Installation extends the schema. You can install DNS and DHCP Services during installation with DNINST.NLM or after, using Install in ConsoleOne.
54. Three default DNS and DHCP objects are created, and only one instance per tree can exist:
    - RootServerInfo Zone object
    - DSN-DHCP GROUP Group object
    - DNSDHCP Locator object
55. DNS/DHCP Management Console is a Java-based workstation utility used to configure and monitor DNS and DHCP Services.
56. DHCPSRVR.NLM is executed at the server console to start DHCP Services.
57. NAMED.NLM is executed at the server console to start DNS services.
58. For information to be imported into DNS, the file must be in BIND format.

11. The print server sends print jobs from the print queue to the printer.
12. PSERVER.NLM can service up to 254 printers.
13. You configure and monitor printers with NetWare Administrator.
14. The default print queue user is the container in which the print queue resides.
15. The default print server and print queue operator is the User object that created the objects.

BACKING UP AND RESTORING INFORMATION

16. SBCON is a server-based utility.
17. NWBACK32 is a workstation-based utility.
18. SBCON and NWBACK32 are used to back up and restore file systems, Novell Directory Services (NDS), workstations, and GroupWise.

CONSOLE COMMANDS AND UTILITIES

19. Common console commands include:
    - **CONFIG**
    - **VOLUMES**
    - **DOWN**
    - **RESTART SERVER**
20. Common console utilities include:
    - DSREPAIR
    - DSTRACE
    - INETCFG
    - MONITOR
    - NSS
    - NWCONFIG
    - SCRSAVER
    - VRPAIR

NETWARE GUI

21. STARTX.NCF loads the Java-based NetWare 5 GUI.
22. C1START.NCF loads Java, if it's not already running, and then loads ConsoleOne.

REMOTE CONSOLE ACCESS

23. To access Remote Console on an IP network, type "RCONAG6.NLM <*password*> TCP *port#* IPX *port#*".
24. To access Remote Console on an IPX network, type "REMOTE.NLM <*password*>". (The REMOTE.NLM is loaded when you load the RSPX.NLM.)
25. Both RCONAG6.NLM and REMOTE.NLM can be loaded with the **-E** (encrypt) option.

SECURING THE NETWARE 5 SERVER

26. Limit physical access to the NetWare 5 server.
27. SCRSAVER.NLM includes options to lock the server console.
28. The **SECURE CONSOLE** command prevents users from changing the server's time and date and prevents them from loading NLMs in directories other than the SYS:\SYSTEM directory.

MONITOR.NLM

29. The server parameters allow you to view and modify **SET** parameters and values.
30. When the Long Term Cache Hits value is less than 90 percent, you need to add memory to the server.

NETWARE 5 VIRTUAL MEMORY

31. The **SWAP** command is used to view and set virtual memory parameters.
32. If your server is running very low on memory, disk thrashing may occur.

NDS SECURITY REVIEW

33. The object rights are:
    - Supervisor
    - Browse
    - Create
    - Delete
    - Rename
    - Inheritable
34. The property rights are:
    - Supervisor
    - Compare
    - Read
    - Write
    - Add Self
    - Inheritable

EXAM CRAM™

for Advanced NetWare 5 Administration CNE

Melanie Hoag

CORIOLIS

Exam Cram for Advanced NetWare 5 Administration CNE
© 1999 The Coriolis Group. All Rights Reserved.

This book may not be duplicated in any way without the express written consent of the publisher, except in the form of brief excerpts or quotations for the purposes of review. The information contained herein is for the personal use of the reader and may not be incorporated in any commercial programs, other books, databases, or any kind of software without written consent of the publisher. Making copies of this book or any portion for any purpose other than your own is a violation of United States copyright laws.

Limits Of Liability And Disclaimer Of Warranty
The author and publisher of this book have used their best efforts in preparing the book and the programs contained in it. These efforts include the development, research, and testing of the theories and programs to determine their effectiveness. The author and publisher make no warranty of any kind, expressed or implied, with regard to these programs or the documentation contained in this book.

The author and publisher shall not be liable in the event of incidental or consequential damages in connection with, or arising out of, the furnishing, performance, or use of the programs, associated instructions, and/or claims of productivity gains.

Trademarks
Trademarked names appear throughout this book. Rather than list the names and entities that own the trademarks or insert a trademark symbol with each mention of the trademarked name, the publisher states that it is using the names for editorial purposes only and to the benefit of the trademark owner, with no intention of infringing upon that trademark.

The Coriolis Group, LLC
14455 N. Hayden Road, Suite 220
Scottsdale, Arizona 85260

480/483-0192
FAX 480/483-0193
http://www.coriolis.com

Library of Congress Cataloging-in-Publication Data
Hoag, Melanie
   Exam cram for advanced NetWare 5 Administration CNE / by Melanie Hoag
      p. cm.
   Includes index.
   ISBN 1-57610-352-8
   1. Electronic data processing personnel--Certification. 2. Novell software--Examinations Study guides. 3. NetWare (Computer file) I. Title.
QA76.3.H63   1999
005.7'1369--dc21   99-25866
                                                                      CIP

Printed in the United States of America
10 9 8 7 6 5 4 3 2 1

Publisher
Keith Weiskamp

Acquisitions Editor
Shari Jo Hehr

Marketing Specialist
Cynthia Caldwell

Project Editor
Melissa D. Olson

Technical Reviewer
Cory Merritt

Production Coordinator
Wendy Littley

Cover Design
Jody Winkler

Layout Design
April Nielsen

Coriolis: The Training And Certification Destination™

Thank you for purchasing one of our innovative certification study guides, just one of the many members of the Coriolis family of certification products.

Certification Insider Press™ has long believed that achieving your IT certification is more of a road trip than anything else. This is why most of our readers consider us their *Training And Certification Destination*. By providing a one-stop shop for the most innovative and unique training materials, our readers know we are the first place to look when it comes to achieving their certification. As one reader put it, "I plan on using your books for all of the exams I take."

To help you reach your goals, we've listened to others like you, and we've designed our entire product line around you and the way you like to study, learn, and master challenging subjects. Our approach is *The Smartest Way To Get Certified*™.

In addition to our highly popular *Exam Cram* and *Exam Prep* guides, we have a number of new products. We recently launched Exam Cram Live!, two-day seminars based on *Exam Cram* material. We've also developed a new series of books and study aides—*Practice Tests Exam Crams* and *Exam Cram Flash Cards*—designed to make your studying fun as well as productive.

Our commitment to being the *Training And Certification Destination* does not stop there. We just introduced *Exam Cram Insider*, a biweekly newsletter containing the latest in certification news, study tips, and announcements from Certification Insider Press. (To subscribe, send an email to **eci@coriolis.com** and type "subscribe insider" in the body of the email.) We also recently announced the launch of the Certified Crammer Society and the Coriolis Help Center—two new additions to the Certification Insider Press family.

We'd like to hear from you. Help us continue to provide the very best certification study materials possible. Write us or email us at **cipq@coriolis.com** and let us know how our books have helped you study, or tell us about new features that you'd like us to add. If you send us a story about how we've helped you, and we use it in one of our books, we'll send you an official Coriolis shirt for your efforts.

Good luck with your certification exam and your career. Thank you for allowing us to help you achieve your goals.

Keith Weiskamp
Publisher, Certification Insider Press

About The Author

Melanie Hoag, Ph.D., holds MCNI, MCNE, MCT, and MCP certifications. She is a senior technical training consultant for Productivity Point International, Inc., (PPI) in Austin, Texas. Melanie began her computer career in 1983 at Drexel University in Philadelphia. She was involved in activities and projects ranging from software design and construction, courseware development, technical presentations, and consulting. Between her time at Drexel and PPI, Melanie ran a small software development company with her husband. Currently, Melanie teaches Novell authorized courses covering the entire NetWare 5 and NetWare 4.11 CNE and CNA certification tracks and selected MCNE courses. In addition to teaching, she's also involved in network-related issues and projects within PPI. When not associated with networking "things," Melanie and her family run a small ranch near Hutto, Texas. They raise and show prize-winning purebred Longhorn cattle.

Acknowledgments

Several people have helped me in the development of this book, and without them, it would not have been possible.

First, a very special thanks and love to my family—my husband and partner, Bob Bliss, and our daughter, Lee Ann Bliss. Putting together this book has put a burden on our lives together, and I thank you both for your understanding, help, and encouragement. I would also like to thank my parents, Bill and Doris, who taught me that "you'll never know if you can do it, until you have tried." And to my brother, David, your skills as a screenwriter inspired me to take the plunge into writing. Thanks also to all my friends who constantly lend a helping hand, and always when it's needed the most.

I would like to offer a special thanks to Mary Burmeister whose wonderful editing skills produce smooth and polished products. Mary was also an efficient project manager; she kept me in line, before I drifted too far away. Also, thanks to Ed Tittel and the rest of the crew at LANWrights for giving me the opportunity to do this book. And, thanks to Joel Stegall and Cory Merritt whose contributions and comments helped make the book possible.

Finally, a big thanks to all my fellow instructors and employees at Productivity Point International, Inc., (PPI). Being both friends and coworkers makes PPI a fun place to work and to share our "geekdom."

And, I must not forget all of my students, both past and future, who make teaching fun. Sharing your experiences, both good and bad, enhances all our skill sets and makes for lively discussions.

God bless.

—*Melanie Hoag*

Contents At A Glance

Chapter 1	Novell Certification Exams
Chapter 2	Upgrading To NetWare 5
Chapter 3	Migrating To NetWare 5
Chapter 4	Traditional NetWare Volumes
Chapter 5	NSS Volumes
Chapter 6	File System Design
Chapter 7	Queue-Based Printing
Chapter 8	Backing Up And Restoring Files And NDS
Chapter 9	NetWare Operating System And Configuration Basics
Chapter 10	The NetWare GUI And Java
Chapter 11	ConsoleOne, Remote Access, And Server Security
Chapter 12	Server Management
Chapter 13	Managing Server Memory
Chapter 14	Other Optimization Options
Chapter 15	NDS Security Review
Chapter 16	NDS Security Implementations
Chapter 17	NDS Partitions And Replicas
Chapter 18	NDS Preventive Maintenance And Utilities
Chapter 19	NDS Troubleshooting And Recovery
Chapter 20	DHCP Services
Chapter 21	DNS Services
Chapter 22	Netscape FastTrack Server
Chapter 23	FTP Services
Chapter 24	NIAS Remote Access
Chapter 25	Additional Novell Services
Chapter 26	Sample Test
Chapter 27	Answer Key
Appendix A	**SET** Parameters
Appendix B	Commands And Utilities Tables
Appendix C	Sample Configuration Files

Table Of Contents

Introduction .... **xix**

Self-Assessment .... **xxxi**

Chapter 1
Novell Certification Exams **1**
    Assessing Exam-Readiness   2
    The Exam Situation   3
    Exam Layout And Design   5
    Test-Taking Strategy For Form And Adaptive Tests   7
    Test-Taking Basics   8
    Question-Handling Strategies   9
    Mastering The Inner Game   9
    Additional Resources   10

Chapter 2
Upgrading To NetWare 5 .... **15**
    Upgrade Options   16
    Requirements   17
    Protocol Options   18
    In-Place Upgrade Procedures   18
    Practice Questions   22
    Need To Know More?   28

Chapter 3
Migrating To NetWare 5 .... **29**
    Migration Options   30
    Requirements   32
    Upgrade Wizard   32
    Post-Upgrade Procedures   38
    Practice Questions   39
    Need To Know More?   45

Chapter 4
Traditional NetWare Volumes 47

Features Of Traditional NetWare Volumes 48
Advantages Of Traditional NetWare Volumes 53
Practice Questions 54
Need To Know More? 59

Chapter 5
NSS Volumes 61

Features Of NSS Volumes 62
Advantages Of NSS Volumes 66
Limitations Of NSS 68
Creating A NSS Volume 69
Practice Questions 72
Need To Know More? 80

Chapter 6
File System Design 81

Features Of The Traditional NetWare File System 82
Creating System And Custom Volumes 83
System-Created Directories 84
Custom Directories 87
Possible Directory Structures 89
Practice Questions 91
Need To Know More? 95

Chapter 7
Queue-Based Printing 97

Queue-Based Printing Process 98
Configuring Print Objects 100
Starting Queue-Based Print Services 107
Configuring Network Printers 108
Managing Print Services 109
Configuring Usage Rights For The User 112
Practice Questions 113
Need To Know More? 118

Chapter 8
Backing Up And Restoring Files And NDS 119
Strategies For Information Backup And Restore   120
SMS Components And Guidelines   125
Backing Up A NetWare 5 Server   127
Backing Up A Windows Workstation   130
Restoring Data   131
Practice Questions   134
Need To Know More?   139

Chapter 9
NetWare Operating System And Configuration Basics 141
NetWare Operating System Overview   142
The Server Console   145
Server Configuration Files   147
Server Script Files   149
Practice Questions   151
Need To Know More?   154

Chapter 10
The NetWare GUI And Java 155
NetWare 5 Java Support   156
Java Classes And Java Applets   157
NetWare GUI Support   159
Using The NetWare GUI   160
Practice Questions   163
Need To Know More?   165

Chapter 11
ConsoleOne, Remote Access, And Server Security 167
ConsoleOne   168
Remote Access   180
Server Security   183
Practice Questions   185
Need To Know More?   189

Chapter 12
Server Management 191
    MONITOR.NLM 192
    Practice Questions 198
    Need To Know More? 202

Chapter 13
Managing Server Memory 203
    NetWare 5 Memory Architecture Key Components 204
    Virtual Memory Basics 205
    Protected Memory Basics 207
    Optimizing Available Memory 208
    Monitoring Memory Usage 208
    Practice Questions 210
    Need To Know More? 213

Chapter 14
Other Optimization Options 215
    Hardware Issues 216
    Optimizing Disk Usage 217
    SET Parameters 222
    Packet Burst 224
    Large Internet Packets (LIP) 225
    Practice Questions 226
    Need To Know More? 231

Chapter 15
NDS Security Review 233
    Object And Property Rights 234
    Trustees 235
    Effective Rights 238
    Changing And Blocking Inherited Rights 239
    Supervisor Object Right To A Server Object 241
    Object Trustees Property 242
    Comparison Of NDS And File System Security 243
    Practice Questions 245
    Need To Know More? 252

Chapter 16
NDS Security Implementations 253
    NDS Default Rights   254
    Configuring Access To Network Resources   256
    NDS Security Guidelines   257
    Administration   260
    Guidelines For Creating Container Administrators   263
    Practice Questions   267
    Need To Know More?   275

Chapter 17
NDS Partitions And Replicas 277
    Partitions And Replicas In A New Tree   278
    Partitioning NDS   280
    Practice Questions   283
    Need To Know More?   287

Chapter 18
NDS Preventive Maintenance And Utilities 289
    NDS Replication And Synchronization   290
    Utilities   291
    Preventive Maintenance Procedures   293
    Planned Server Downtime   297
    Practice Questions   299
    Need To Know More?   305

Chapter 19
NDS Troubleshooting And Recovery 307
    NDS Inconsistencies   308
    Unplanned Server Downtime   311
    Examples Of Some NDS Errors   312
    Fixing NDS   314
    Practice Questions   318
    Need To Know More?   325

Chapter 20
DHCP Services 327
    Overview Of DHCP   328
    DHCP And DNS Services Installation   330

Configuring DHCP   334
Global DHCP Options   341
Importing And Exporting DHCP Databases   342
Practice Questions   344
Need To Know More?   351

Chapter 21
DNS Services 353

Overview Of DNS   354
Installing DNS   357
DNS Configuration   358
Importing And Exporting DNS Databases   361
Practice Questions   363
Need To Know More?   367

Chapter 22
Netscape FastTrack Server 369

Defining The Function Of A Web Server   370
Netscape FastTrack Server Installation   371
FastTrack Server Basics   374
Securing The FastTrack Server   377
Practice Questions   379
Need To Know More?   382

Chapter 23
FTP Services 383

Defining The File Transfer Protocol (FTP)   384
FTP Services Installation   385
FTP Configuration And Management Using UNICON   386
Securing FTP Services   390
Using FTP Services   390
Practice Questions   392
Need To Know More?   395

Chapter 24
NIAS Remote Access 397

Features And Requirements Of NIAS   398
Overview Of Technologies For Remote Access
  Data Transmission   399
Installing And Configuring NIAS   401

NIAS Remote Access Security   404
Using NIAS Remote Access   406
Practice Questions   408
Need To Know More?   411

Chapter 25
Additional Novell Services 413
GroupWise   414
ManageWise   418
BorderManager   421
NDS For NT   424
Practice Questions   429
Need To Know More?   437

Chapter 26
Sample Test 439
Questions, Questions, Questions   440
Picking Proper Answers   441
Decoding Ambiguity   441
Working Within The Framework   442
Deciding What To Memorize   443
Preparing For The Test   444
Taking The Test   444

Chapter 27
Answer Key 477

Appendix A
SET Parameters 493

Appendix B
Commands And Utilities Tables 499

Appendix C
Sample Configuration Files 505

Glossary 509

Index 523

Introduction

Welcome to *Exam Cram for Advanced NetWare 5 Administration CNE*! This book aims to help you get ready to take—and pass—Novell certification Test 050-640, titled "NetWare 5 Advanced Administration." This Introduction explains Novell's certification programs in general and talks about how the *Exam Cram* series can help you prepare for Novell's certification tests.

Exam Cram books help you understand and appreciate the subjects and materials you need to pass Novell certification tests. *Exam Cram* books are aimed strictly at test preparation and review. They do not teach you everything you need to know about a topic, such as using the Novell Upgrade Wizard to upgrade a 3.x or 4.x server to NetWare 5, or all of the low-level details about how to install and configure Domain Name System (DNS) and Dynamic Host Configuration Protocol (DHCP) services for NetWare 5. Instead, we (the authors) present and dissect the questions and problems we've found that you're likely to encounter on a test. We've worked from Novell's own training materials, preparation guides, and tests, and from a battery of third-party test preparation tools. Our aim is to bring together as much information as possible about Novell certification tests.

Nevertheless, to completely prepare yourself for any Novell test, we recommend that you begin by taking the Self-Assessment immediately following this Introduction. The Self-Assessment will help you evaluate your knowledge base against the requirements for a CNE under both ideal and real circumstances.

Based on what you learn from that exercise, you might decide to begin your studies with some classroom training or by reading one of the many study guides available from Novell Press (an imprint of IDG Books Worldwide) or third-party vendors. We strongly recommend that you install, configure, and use any software that you'll be tested on—especially NetWare 5 itself—because nothing beats hands-on experience and familiarity when it comes to understanding questions you're likely to encounter on a certification test. Book learning is essential, but hands-on experience is the best teacher of all.

Novell Professional Certifications

Novell's various certifications currently encompass six separate programs, each of which boasts its own special acronym (as a would-be certificant, you need to have a high tolerance for alphabet soup of all kinds):

➤ **CNA (Certified Novell Administrator)** This is the least prestigious of all the certification tracks from Novell. Candidates can demonstrate their skills in any of a number of areas of expertise. This certification requires passing one test in any of five tracks (three are specific to NetWare versions 3.x, 4.x, and 5; two are specific to GroupWise versions; for the purposes of this book, we assume the NetWare 5 track is the one for you). Table 1 shows the required test for the CNA certification. For more information about this program and its requirements, visit **http://education.novell.com/cna/**.

➤ **CNE (Certified Novell Engineer)** This is the primary target for most people who seek a Novell certification of one kind or another. Candidates who wish to demonstrate their skills in installing and managing

Table 1 Novell CNA And CNE Requirements*

CNA

Only 1 test required	
Test 050-639	NetWare 5 Administration

CNE

All 5 of these tests are required	
Test 050-639	NetWare 5 Administration
Test 050-632	Networking Technologies
➤ Test 050-640	NetWare 5 Advanced Administration
Test 050-634	NDS Design and Implementation
Test 050-635	Service and Support
Choose 1 elective from this group	
Test 050-629	Securing Intranets with BorderManager
Test 050-628	Network Management Using ManageWise 2.1
Test 050-641	Network Management Using ManageWise 2.6
Test 050-636	intraNetWare: Integrating Windows NT
Test 050-618	GroupWise 5 Administration
Test 050-633	GroupWise 5.5 System Administration

* This is not a complete listing. We have included only those tests needed for the NetWare 5 track. If you are currently a CNE certified in NetWare 4, you need only take the CNE NetWare 4.11 to NetWare 5 Update test (Test 050-638) to be certified in NetWare 5.

NetWare networks make up its primary audience. This certification is obtained by passing six or seven tests, including five or six (depending on which track you pursue) required core tests and a single elective. Table 1 shows the required and elective tests for CNE certification in the NetWare 5 track. For more information about this program and its requirements, visit **http://education.novell.com/cne/**.

▶ **MCNE (Master CNE)** Candidates for this certification program must first prove their basic expertise by obtaining CNE certification. To obtain MCNE status, candidates must pass four to six additional tests in any of seven specialized areas. This is Novell's most elite certification. For more information about this program and its requirements, visit **http://education.novell.com/mcne/**.

▶ **CIP (Certified Internet Professional)** This certification program is designed for individuals who seek to step into one or more of a variety of professional Internet roles. These roles include that of Certified Internet Business Strategist, Certified Web Designer, Certified Web Developer, Certified Internet Manager, and Certified Internet Architect. To qualify, candidates must pass anywhere from one to five required tests, depending on which role they seek to fill. For more information about this program and its requirements, visit **www.netboss.com**.

▶ **CNI (Certified Novell Instructor)** Candidates who wish to teach any elements of the Novell official curriculum (and there's usually an official class tied to each of the Novell certification tests) must meet several requirements to obtain CNI certification. They must take a special instructor training class, demonstrate their proficiency in a classroom setting, and take a special version of the test for each certification topic they wish to teach to show a higher level of knowledge and understanding of the topics involved. For more information about this program and its requirements, visit **http://education.novell.com/cni/**.

Novell also offers a Master CNI (MCNI) credential to exceptional instructors who have two years of CNI teaching experience, and who possess an MCNE certification as well.

▶ **CNS (Certified Novell Salesperson)** This is a newer Novell certification and focuses on the knowledge that sales professionals need to master to present and position Novell's various networking products accurately and professionally.

To obtain this certification, an individual must pass a self-study class on sales skills and Novell products, as well as take regular product update training when it becomes available. This level of certification is intended to demonstrate a salesperson's ability to position and represent Novell's many products accurately and fairly. For more information about this program and its requirements, visit **http://education.novell.com/powersell/**.

Certification is an ongoing activity. Once a Novell product becomes obsolete, Novell certified professionals typically have 12 to 18 months during which they may recertify on new product versions. If individuals do not recertify within the specified period, their certifications become invalid. Because technology keeps changing and new products continually supplant old ones, this should come as no surprise to anyone. Certification is not a one-time achievement, but rather a commitment to a set of evolving tools and technologies.

The best place to keep tabs on Novell's certification program and its various certifications is on the Novell Web site. The current root URL for all Novell certification programs is **http://education.novell.com/certinfo/**. But if this URL doesn't work, try using the Search tool on Novell's site with "certification" or "certification programs" as a search string. You will then find the latest, most up-to-date information about Novell's certification programs.

Taking A Certification Exam

Alas, testing is not free. Each computer-based Novell test costs $95, and if you don't pass, you may retest for an additional $95 for each try. In the United States and Canada, tests are administered by Sylvan Prometric and by Virtual University Enterprises (VUE). Here's how you can contact them:

➤ **Sylvan Prometric** Sign up for a test through the company's Web site at **www.slspro.com**. In the United States or Canada, call 800-233-3382; outside that area, call 612-820-5706.

➤ **Virtual University Enterprises** Sign up for a test or get the phone numbers for local testing centers through the Web page at **www.vue.com**. In the United States or Canada, call 800-511-8123 or 888-834-8378; outside that area, call 612-897-7370.

To sign up for a test, you need a valid credit card, or contact either company for mailing instructions to send them a check (in the United States.). Only when payment is verified, or a check has cleared, can you actually register for a test.

To schedule a test, call the number or visit either of the Web pages at least one day in advance. To cancel or reschedule a test, you must call before 7 P.M. pacific standard time the business day before the scheduled test time (or you may be charged, even if you don't show up for the test). To schedule a test, please have the following information ready:

➤ Your name, organization, and mailing address.

➤ Your Novell Test ID. (Inside the United States, this means your Social Security number; citizens of other nations should call ahead to find out what type of identification number is required to register for a test.)

➤ The name and number of the test you wish to take.

➤ A method of payment. (As we've already mentioned, a credit card is the most convenient method, but alternate means can be arranged in advance, if necessary.)

Once you sign up for a test, you'll be informed as to when and where the test is scheduled. Try to arrive at least 15 minutes early. You must supply two forms of identification—one of which must be a photo ID—to be admitted into the testing room.

All tests are completely closed-book. In fact, you will not be allowed to take anything with you into the testing area, but you will be furnished with a blank sheet of paper and a pen or, in some cases, an erasable plastic sheet and an erasable pen. We suggest that you immediately write down all the information you've memorized for the test. In *Exam Cram* books, this information appears on a tear-out sheet inside the front cover of each book. You'll have some time to compose yourself, to record this information, and even to take a sample orientation test before you begin the real thing. We suggest you take the orientation test before taking your first test, but because they're all more or less identical in layout, behavior, and controls, you probably won't need to do this more than once.

When you complete a Novell certification test, the software will tell you whether you've passed or failed. Results are broken into topical areas that map to the test's specific test objectives. Even if you fail, we suggest you ask for—and keep—the detailed report that the test administrator should print for you. You should use this report to help you prepare for another go-round, if needed.

If you need to retake a test, you'll have to schedule a new test with Sylvan Prometric or VUE and pay another $95.

> The first time you fail a test, you can retake the test the next day. However, if you fail a second time, you must wait 14 days before retaking that test. The 14-day waiting period remains in effect for all retakes after the first failure.

Tracking Novell Certification Status

As soon as you pass one of the applicable Novell tests, you'll attain Certified NetWare Administrator (CNA) status. Novell also generates transcripts that indicate which tests you have passed and your certification status. You can check (or print) your transcript at any time by visiting the official Novell site for certified professionals through its login page at **http://certification.novell.com/pinlogin.htm**. As the name of the Web page (pinlogin) is meant to suggest, you need an account name and a Personal Identification Number (PIN) to access this page. You'll receive this information by email about two weeks after you pass any exam that might qualify you for CNA or CNE status.

At the Novell certification site, you can also update your personal profile, including your name, address, phone and fax numbers, email address, and other contact information. You can view a list of all certifications that you've received so far and check a complete list of all exams you've taken.

Benefits Of Novell Certification

Once you pass the necessary set of tests (one for CNA, six or seven for CNE, four to six more for the MCNE), you'll become certified (or obtain an additional certification). Official certification normally takes anywhere from four to six weeks, so don't expect to get your credentials overnight. When the package for a qualified certification arrives, it includes a set of materials that contain several important elements:

➤ A certificate, suitable for framing, along with an official membership card.

➤ A license to use the appropriate Novell certified professional logo, which allows you to use that logo in advertisements, promotions, and documents, and on letterhead, business cards, and so on. As part of your certification packet, you'll get a logo sheet, which includes camera-ready artwork. (Note that before using any artwork, individuals must sign and return a licensing agreement that indicates they'll abide by its terms and conditions.)

➤ A subscription to the *NetWare Connection* magazine, which provides ongoing data about testing and certification activities, requirements, and changes to the program.

➤ Access to a special Web site, commensurate with your current level of certification, through the **http://certification.novell.com/pinlogin.htm**

login page. You'll find more than your own personal records here—you'll also find reports of new certification programs, special downloads, practice test information, and other goodies not available to the general public.

Many people believe that the benefits of Novell CNA or CNE certification go well beyond the perks that Novell provides to newly anointed members of these elite groups. For years, job listings have included requirements for CNA, CNE, and so on, and many individuals who complete the program can qualify for increases in pay and/or responsibility. As an official recognition of hard work and broad knowledge, any of the Novell certifications is a badge of honor in many IT organizations, and a requirement for employment in many others.

How To Prepare For An Exam

Preparing for any NetWare-related test (including "NetWare 5 Advanced Administration") requires that you obtain and study materials designed to provide comprehensive information about the product and its capabilities that will appear on the specific test for which you are preparing. The following list of materials will help you study and prepare:

➤ The objectives for the course that relates to Test 050-640 appear in the information that Novell provides for Course 570: NetWare 5 Advanced Administration. You can read these objectives on the Novell Web site at **http://education.novell.com/testinfo/objectives/570tobj.htm**. These will also define the feedback topics when you take the test, so this document should be an essential part of your planning and preparation for the exam. You might even want to print a copy and use it along with your other study materials.

➤ General information about Novell tests is also available, including what type of test will be delivered for each topic, how many questions you'll see on any given test, the minimum passing score (which Novell calls a *cut score*) for each test, and the maximum amount of time allotted for each test. All this information is compiled in a table called "Test Data" that you can read at **http://education.novell.com/testinfo/testdata.htm**.

In addition, you'll probably find any or all of the following materials useful as you prepare for the "NetWare 5 Advanced Administration" test:

➤ **Novell Course 570: NetWare 5 Advanced Administration** Novell Education offers a five-day class that covers the materials for this test at a level intended to permit anyone who's taken the 560 class (NetWare 5 Administration) and the 565 class (Networking Technologies) to completely master this material.

- **Novell Press Study Guide** Novell Press offers a book titled *Novell's CNE Study Guide for NetWare 5*, by David James Clarke IV (ISBN 0-7645-4543-4) that covers all the objectives for Test 050-640, plus tests 050-639, NetWare 5 Administration, and 050-632, Networking Technologies, in complete detail. The Novell study guides complement this book well, and we highly recommend them.

- **The Novell Support Connection CD** This monthly CD-based publication delivers numerous electronic titles on topics relevant to NetWare and other key Novell products and topics, primarily, "Monthly Update" CDs (there are two at the time of this writing). Offerings on these CDs include product facts, technical articles and white papers, tools and utilities, and other information.

  A subscription to the Novell Support Connection costs $495 per year, (a $100 discount is available to all CNEs and MCNEs as one of the benefits of certification), but it is well worth the cost. Visit **http://support.novell.com/** and check out the information under the "Support Connection CD" menu entry for details.

- **Classroom Training** Although you'll find Novell Authorized Education Centers (NAECs) worldwide that teach the official Novell curriculum, unlicensed third-party training companies (such as Wave Technologies, American Research Group, Learning Tree, Data-Tech, and others) offer classroom training on NetWare 5 Advanced Administration as well. These companies aim to help you prepare to pass Test 050-640. Although such training runs upwards of $350 per day in class, most of the individuals lucky enough to partake (including your humble authors, who've even taught such courses) find them to be quite worthwhile.

- **Other Publications** You'll find direct references to other publications and resources in this book, but there's no shortage of information available about NetWare 5 Advanced Administration. To help you sift through the various offerings available, we end each chapter with a "Need To Know More?" section that provides pointers to more complete and exhaustive resources covering the chapter's subjects. This should give you some idea of where we think you should look for further discussion and more details, if you feel like you need them.

By far, this set of required and recommended materials represents a nonpareil collection of sources and resources for NetWare 5 Advanced Administration and related topics. We anticipate that you'll find that this book belongs in this company. In the following section, we explain how this book works, and we give you some good reasons why this book counts as a member of the required and recommended materials list.

About This Book

Each topical *Exam Cram* chapter follows a regular structure, along with graphical cues about important or useful information. Here's the structure of a typical chapter:

➤ **Opening Hotlists** Each chapter begins with a list of the terms, tools, and techniques that you must learn and understand before you can be fully conversant with that chapter's subject matter. We follow the hotlists with one or two introductory paragraphs to set the stage for the rest of the chapter.

➤ **Topical Coverage** After the opening hotlists, each chapter covers a series of topics related to the chapter's subject title. Throughout this section, we highlight topics or concepts likely to appear on a test using a special Exam Alert layout, like this:

> This is what an Exam Alert looks like. Normally, an Exam Alert stresses concepts, terms, software, or activities that are likely to relate to one or more certification test questions. For that reason, we think any information found offset in Exam Alert format is worthy of unusual attentiveness on your part. Indeed, most of the information that appears on The Cram Sheet appears as Exam Alerts within the text as well.

Pay close attention to any material flagged as an Exam Alert. Although all the information in this book pertains to what you need to know to pass the exam, we flag certain items that are especially important. You'll find what appears in the meat of each chapter to be worth knowing, too, when preparing for the test. Because this book's material is highly condensed, we recommend that you use this book along with other resources to achieve the maximum benefit.

In addition to the Exam Alerts, we have provided tips that will help you build a better foundation for NetWare 5 Advanced Administration knowledge. Although the information may not be on the exam, it's certainly related and will help you become a better test-taker.

> This is how tips are formatted. Keep your eyes open for these, and you'll become a NetWare 5 Advanced Administration expert in no time!

➤ **Practice Questions** Although we talk about test questions and topics throughout each chapter, this section presents a series of mock test questions and explanations for both correct and incorrect answers. We also try to point out especially tricky questions by using a special icon, like this:

Trick! question

Ordinarily, this icon flags the presence of a particularly devious inquiry, if not an outright trick question. Trick questions are calculated to be answered incorrectly if not read more than once, and carefully, at that. Although they're not ubiquitous, such questions make occasional appearances on the Novell tests. That's why we say test questions are as much about reading comprehension as they are about knowing your material inside out and backwards.

➤ **Details And Resources** Every chapter ends with a "Need To Know More?" section, which provides direct pointers to Novell and third-party resources offering more details on the chapter's subject. In addition, this section tries to rank or at least rate the quality and thoroughness of the topic's coverage by each resource.

If you find a resource you like in this collection, use it, but don't feel compelled to use all the resources we cite. On the other hand, we recommend only resources we use on a regular basis, so none of our recommendations will waste your time or money. But purchasing them all at once probably represents an expense that many network administrators and would-be CNAs, CNEs, and MCNEs might find hard to justify.

The bulk of the book follows this chapter structure slavishly, but there are a few other elements that we'd like to point out. Chapter 26 includes a sample test that provides a good review of the material presented throughout the book to ensure you're ready for the exam. Chapter 27 is an answer key to the sample test that appears in Chapter 26. We suggest you take the sample test when you think you're ready for the real thing, and that you seek out other practice tests to work on if you don't get at least 75 percent of the questions correct. In addition, you'll find a Glossary, which explains terms, and an index that you can use to track down terms as they appear in the text.

Finally, the tear-out Cram Sheet attached next to the inside front cover of this *Exam Cram* book represents a condensed and compiled collection of facts and tips that we think you should memorize before taking the test. Because you can dump this information out of your head onto a piece of paper before taking the exam, you can master this information by brute force—you need to remember it only long enough to write it down when you walk into the test room. You might even want to look at it in the car or in the lobby of the testing center just before you walk in to take the test.

Novell Terms

While studying for your NetWare 5 Advanced Administration test, you may come across terms that we represent a certain way in our material, but that are represented differently in other resources. Some of these are as follows:

- **Across-the-wire migration** You may see this referred to as an across-the-wire upgrade, and migrating "across-the-wire." Regardless of what it's called, it's the process that moves the user accounts, data, printers, and rights to a new server across the network.

- **NetWare Administrator** You may see this referred to as NWAdmin in some resources; however, NWAdmin is not acknowledged by Novell as a copyrighted term. Try not to confuse NetWare Administrator with NETADMIN, which is the text-based version of NetWare Administrator.

- **Network board** A network board is also called a network interface card (NIC), network adapter, network card, and network interface board. Novell uses the term *network board* most often. However, the network board vendors usually refer to network boards as NICs.

- **Application Launcher** You may see this called the Novell Application Launcher and sometimes abbreviated as NAL.

- **Novell Directory Services (NDS)** You may also see this service referred to as NetWare Directory Services (it even appears as such on Novell's own Web site, www.novell.com). However, the official trademark name is Novell Directory Services.

- **NDS tree** The NDS tree is also called the Directory tree and sometimes it's simply referred to as the Directory (with a capital D).

- **Object Trustees property** This is also called the ACL, and you'll sometimes see it referred to as the Object Trustees (ACL) property.

One general source of confusion (as is the case with NDS) is that sometimes an "N" in an acronym is thought to stand for "NetWare" when it really stands for "Novell." As long as you know how to work the utility, you should be okay—the name isn't a huge issue.

How To Use This Book

If you're prepping for a first-time test, we've structured the topics in this book to build on one another. Therefore, some topics in later chapters make more sense after you've read earlier chapters. That's why we suggest you read this book from front to back for your initial test preparation. If you need to brush up on a topic or you have to bone up for a second try, use the index or table of contents to go straight to the topics and questions that you need to study. Beyond helping you prepare for the test, we think you'll find this book useful as a tightly focused reference to some of the most important aspects of the "NetWare 5 Advanced Administration" test.

Given all the book's elements and its specialized focus, we've tried to create a tool that will help you prepare for—and pass—Novell Test 050-640, "NetWare 5 Advanced Administration." Please share your feedback on the book with us, especially if you have ideas about how we can improve it for future test-takers. We'll consider everything you say carefully, and we'll respond to all suggestions.

Send your questions or comments to us at **cipq@coriolis.com** or to our series editor, Ed Tittel, at **etittel@lanw.com**. He coordinates our efforts and ensures that all questions get answered. Please remember to include the title of the book in your message; otherwise, we'll be forced to guess which book you're writing about. And we don't like to guess—we want to *know*! Also, be sure to check out the Web pages at **www.certificationinsider.com** and **www.lanw.com/examcram**, where you'll find information updates, commentary, and certification information.

Thanks, and enjoy the book!

Self-Assessment

Based on recent statistics from Novell, as many as 400,000 individuals are at some stage of the certification process but haven't yet received a CNA, CNE, or other Novell certification. We also know that easily twice that number may be considering whether to obtain a Novell certification of some kind. That's a huge audience!

The reason we included a Self-Assessment in this *Exam Cram* book is to help you evaluate your readiness to tackle CNE (and even the MCNE) certification. It should also help you understand what you need to master the topic of this book—namely, Exam 050-640, "NetWare 5 Advanced Administration." But before you tackle this Self-Assessment, let's talk about concerns you may face when pursuing a CNE and what an ideal CNE candidate might look like.

CNEs In The Real World

In the following section, we describe an ideal CNE candidate, knowing full well that only a few real candidates will meet this ideal. In fact, our description of that ideal candidate might seem downright scary. But take heart: Although the requirements to obtain a CNE may seem pretty formidable, they are by no means impossible to meet. However, you should be keenly aware that it does take time, requires some expense, and consumes substantial effort to get through the process.

More than 160,000 CNEs are already certified, so it's obviously an attainable goal. You can get all the real-world motivation you need from knowing that many others have gone before, so you'll be able to follow in their footsteps. If you're willing to tackle the process seriously and do what it takes to obtain the necessary experience and knowledge, you can take—and pass—all the certification tests involved in obtaining a CNE. In fact, we've designed these *Exam Crams* to make it as easy on you as possible to prepare for these exams. But prepare you must!

The same, of course, is true for other Novell certifications, including:

➤ **MCNE (Master CNE)** This certification is like the CNE certification, but it requires a CNE, plus four to six additional exams, across eight different tracks that cover topics such as network management, connectivity, messaging, Internet solutions, and a variety of hybrid network environments.

➤ **CNA (Certified Novell Administrator)** This entry-level certification requires passing a single core exam in any one of the five possible NetWare tracks, which include NetWare 3, NetWare 4/intraNetWare, and NetWare 5, plus GroupWise 4 and GroupWise 5.

➤ **Other Novell certifications** The requirements for these certifications range from two or more tests (Certified Novell Instructor, or CNI) to many tests, plus a requirement for the minimum time spent as an instructor (Master CNI).

The Ideal CNE Candidate

Just to give you some idea of what an ideal CNE candidate is like, here are some relevant statistics about the background and experience such an individual might have. Don't worry if you don't meet these qualifications or even don't come that close—this is a far from ideal world, and where you fall short is simply where you'll have more work to do:

➤ Academic or professional training in network theory, concepts, and operations. This includes everything from networking media and transmission techniques through network operating systems, services, protocols, routing algorithms, and applications.

➤ Four-plus years of professional networking experience, including experience with Ethernet, token ring, modems, and other networking media. This must include installation, configuration, upgrade, and troubleshooting experience, plus some experience in working with and supporting users in a networked environment.

➤ Two-plus years in a networked environment that includes hands-on experience with NetWare 4.x and, hopefully, some training on and exposure to NetWare 5 (which only started shipping in August 1998, so nobody outside Novell has years of experience with it—yet). Some knowledge of NetWare 3.x is also advisable, especially on networks where this product remains in use. Individuals must also acquire a solid understanding of each system's architecture, installation, configuration, maintenance, and troubleshooting techniques. An ability to run down and research information about software, hardware components, systems, and technologies on the Internet and elsewhere is also an essential job skill.

➤ A thorough understanding of key networking protocols, addressing, and name resolution, including Transmission Control Protocol/Internet Protocol (TCP/IP) and Internetwork Packet Exchange/Sequenced Packet Exchange (IPX/SPX). Also, some knowledge of Systems Network Architecture (SNA), Digital Equipment Corporation Network (DECnet), Xerox Network System (XNS), Open Systems Interconnection (OSI), and NetBIOS Enhanced User Interface (NetBEUI) is strongly recommended.

➤ A thorough understanding of Novell's naming conventions, directory services, and file and print services is absolutely essential.

➤ Familiarity with key NetWare-based TCP/IP-based services, including Hypertext Transfer Protocol (HTTP) Web servers, Dynamic Host Configuration Protocol (DHCP), and Domain Name System (DNS), plus familiarity with one or more of the following: BorderManager, NetWare MultiProtocol Router (MPR), ManageWise, and other supporting Novell products and partner offerings.

➤ Working knowledge of Windows NT is an excellent accessory to this collection of facts and skills, including familiarity with Windows NT Server, Windows NT Workstation, and Microsoft's implementation of key technologies, such as Internet Information Server (IIS), Internet Explorer, DHCP, Windows Internet Name Service (WINS), and Domain Name Service (DNS).

Fundamentally, this boils down to a bachelor's degree in computer science, plus three or more years of work experience in a technical position involving network design, installation, configuration, and maintenance. We believe that less than half of all CNE candidates meet these requirements and that, in fact, most meet less than half of these requirements—at least, when they begin the certification process. However, because all 160,000 people who already have been certified have survived this ordeal, you can survive it, too—especially if you heed what our Self-Assessment can tell you about what you already know and what you need to learn.

Put Yourself To The Test

The following series of questions and observations is designed to help you figure out how much work you must do to pursue Novell certification and what types of resources you may consult on your quest. Be absolutely honest in your answers, or you'll end up wasting money on exams you're not yet ready to take. There are no right or wrong answers, only steps along the path to certification. Only you can decide where you really belong in the broad spectrum of aspiring candidates.

Two things should be clear from the outset:

➤ Even a modest background in computer science will be helpful.

➤ Hands-on experience with Novell products and technologies is essential for certification success. If you don't already have it, you'll need to get some along the way; if you do already have it, you still need to get more along the way.

Educational Background

1. Have you ever taken any computer-related classes? [Yes or No]

    If Yes, proceed to Question 2; if No, proceed to Question 4.

2. Have you taken any classes on computer operating systems? [Yes or No]

    If Yes, you'll probably be able to handle Novell's architecture and system component discussions. If you're rusty, brush up on basic operating system concepts, especially virtual memory, multitasking regimes, program load and unload behaviors, and general computer security topics.

    If No, consider some basic reading in this area. We strongly recommend a good general operating systems book, such as *Operating System Concepts*, by Abraham Silberschatz and Peter Baer Galvin (Addison-Wesley, 1997, ISBN 0-201-59113-8). If this title doesn't appeal to you, check out reviews for similar titles at your favorite online bookstore.

3. Have you taken any networking concepts or technologies classes? [Yes or No]

    If Yes, you'll probably be able to handle Novell's networking terminology, concepts, and technologies (brace yourself for occasional departures from normal usage). If you're rusty, brush up on basic networking concepts and terminology, especially networking media, transmission types, the OSI reference model, networking protocols and services, and networking technologies, such as Ethernet, token ring, Fiber Distributed Data Interface (FDDI), and wide area network (WAN) links.

    If No, you might want to read several books in this topic area. The two best books that we know of are *Computer Networks, 3rd Edition*, by Andrew S. Tanenbaum (Prentice-Hall, 1996, ISBN 0-13-349945-6), and *Computer Networks and Internets*, by Douglas E. Comer (Prentice-Hall, 1997, ISBN 0-13-239070-1). We also strongly recommend Laura

Chappell's book, *Novell's Guide to LAN/WAN Analysis* (IDG/Novell Press, 1998, ISBN 0-7645-4508-6), for its outstanding coverage of NetWare-related protocols and network behavior. In addition, Sandy Stevens and J.D. Marymee's *Novell's Guide to BorderManager* (IDG/Novell Press, 1998, ISBN 0-7645-4540-X) is also worth a once-over for those who wish to be well-prepared for CNE topics and concepts.

Skip to the next section, "Hands-On Experience."

4. Have you done any reading on operating systems or networks? [Yes or No]

If Yes, review the requirements stated in the first paragraphs after Questions 2 and 3. If you meet those requirements, move on to the next section, "Hands-on Experience."

If No, consult the recommended reading for both topics. A strong background will help you prepare for the Novell exams better than just about anything else.

Hands-On Experience

The most important key to success on all the Novell tests is hands-on experience, especially with NetWare 4.x, intraNetWare, and NetWare 5, plus the many system services and other software components that cluster around NetWare—such as GroupWise, Novell Directory Services (NDS), and Netscape FastTrack Server—which appear on many of the Novell certification tests. If we leave you with only one realization after taking this Self-Assessment, it should be that there's no substitute for time spent installing, configuring, and using the various Novell and ancillary products upon which you'll be tested repeatedly and in depth.

5. Have you installed, configured, and worked with: NetWare 3.x? NetWare 4.x? NetWare 5? [Yes or No]

The more times you answer Yes, the better off you are. Please make sure you understand basic concepts as covered in Test 050-639 and advanced concepts as covered in Test 050-640.

You should also study the NDS interfaces, utilities, and services for Test 050-634 and plan to take Course 580: Service and Support, to prepare yourself for Test 050-635. To succeed on this last exam, you must know how to use the Micro House Support Source product, which costs more than $1,000 for a yearly subscription, but to which you'll have a week's exposure and after-hours access in Course 580.

> **TIP:** You can download objectives, practice exams, and other information about Novell exams from the company's education pages on the Web at **http://education.novell.com**. Use the "Test info" link to find specific test information, including objectives, related courses, and so forth.

If you haven't worked with NetWare, NDS, and whatever product or technology you choose for your elective subject, you must obtain one or two machines and a copy of NetWare 5. Then, you must learn the operating system and IPX, TCP/IP, and whatever other software components on which you'll be tested.

In fact, we recommend that you obtain two computers, each with a network board, and set up a two-node network on which to practice. With decent NetWare-capable computers selling for under $600 apiece these days, this shouldn't be too much of a financial hardship. You can download limited use and duration evaluation copies of most Novell products, including NetWare 5, from the company's Web page at www.novell.com/catalog/evals.html.

> **TIP:** For any and all of these Novell exams, check to see if Novell Press (an imprint of IDG Books Worldwide) offers related titles. Also, David James Clarke IV has recently completed NetWare 5 updates to his outstanding *CNE Study Guide* series. These books should be essential parts of your test preparation toolkit.

6. For any specific Novell product that is not itself an operating system (for example, GroupWise, BorderManager, and so forth), have you installed, configured, used, and upgraded this software? [Yes or No]

   If the answer is Yes, skip to the next section, "Testing Your Exam-Readiness." If it's No, you must get some experience. Read on for suggestions on how to do this.

   Experience is a must with any Novell product test, be it something as simple as Web Server Management or as challenging as NDS installation and configuration. Here again, you can look for downloadable evaluation copies of whatever software you're studying at www.novell.com/catalog/evals.html.

> **TIP** If you have the funds, or your employer will pay your way, consider checking out one or more of the many training options that Novell offers. This could be something as expensive as taking a class at a **Novell Authorized Education Center (NAEC)**, to cheaper options that include Novell's Self-Study Training programs, their video and computer based training options, and even classes that are now available online. Be sure to check out the many training options that Novell itself offers, and that it authorizes third parties to deliver, at **http://education.novell.com/general/trainopt.htm**.

Before you even think about taking any Novell test, make sure you've spent enough time with the related software to understand how it may be installed and configured, how to maintain such an installation, and how to troubleshoot that software when things go wrong. This will help you in the exam, as well as in real life.

Testing Your Exam-Readiness

Whether you attend a formal class on a specific topic to get ready for an exam or use written materials to study on your own, some preparation for the Novell certification exams is essential. At $95 a try, pass or fail, you want to do everything you can to pass on your first try. That's where studying comes in.

We have included a practice test in this book, so if you don't score that well on the first test, you need to study more and then locate and tackle a second practice test. If you still don't hit a score of at least 75 percent after two or more tests, keep at it until you get there.

For any given subject, consider taking a class if you've tackled self-study materials, taken the test, and failed anyway. The opportunity to interact with an instructor and fellow students can make all the difference in the world, if you can afford that privilege. For information about Novell courses, visit Novell Education at **http://education.novell.com** and follow the "Training options" link.

If you can't afford to take a class, visit the Novell Education page anyway, because it also includes pointers to a CD that includes free practice exams (it's called "The Guide" CD, and you can read more about it at **http://education.novell.com/theguide/**). Even if you can't afford to spend much at all, you should still invest in some low-cost practice exams from commercial vendors, because they can help you assess your readiness to pass a test better than any other tool. The following Web sites offer practice exams online for less than $100 apiece (some for significantly less than that):

- www.bfq.com Beachfront Quizzer
- www.certify.com CyberPass
- www.stsware.com Self Test Software
- www.syngress.com Syngress Software

7. Have you taken a practice exam on your chosen test subject? [Yes or No]

If Yes, and your score meets or beats the cut score for the related Novell test, you're probably ready to tackle the real thing. If your score isn't above that crucial threshold, keep at it until you break that barrier.

If No, obtain all the free and low-budget practice tests you can find (see the previous list) and get to work. Keep at it until you can break the passing threshold comfortably.

> **TIP**
> Taking a good-quality practice exam and beating Novell's minimum passing grade, known as the *cut score*, is the best way to assess your test readiness. When we're preparing, we shoot for 10 percent over the cut score—just to leave room for the "weirdness factor" that sometimes shows up on Novell exams.

Assessing Readiness For Exam 050-640

In addition to the general exam-readiness information in the previous section, there are several things you can do to prepare for the "NetWare 5 Advanced Administration" exam. As you're getting ready for Exam 050-640, visit the Novell Education forums online. Sign up at **http://education.novell.com/general/forumlogin.htm** (you'll need to agree to some terms and conditions before you can get in, but it's worth it). Once inside these forums, you'll find discussion areas for certification, training, and testing. These are great places to ask questions and get good answers or to simply to watch the questions that others ask (along with the answers, of course).

You should also cruise the Web looking for "braindumps" (recollections of test topics and experiences recorded by others) to help you anticipate topics you're likely to encounter on the test. The Novell certification forum at **http://www.saluki.com:8081/~2/** is a good place to start, as are the forums at www.theforums.com. Also, you can produce numerous additional entry points by visiting Yahoo! or Excite and entering "NetWare braindump" or "Novell braindump" as your search string.

> **TIP** When using any braindump, it's okay to pay attention to information about questions. However, you can't always be sure that a braindump's author will always be able to provide correct answers. Therefore, use the questions to guide your studies, but don't rely on the answers in a braindump to lead you to the truth. Double-check everything you find in any braindump.

Novell exam mavens also recommend checking the Novell Support Connection CDs for "meaningful technical support issues" that relate to your test's topics. Although we're not sure exactly what the quoted phrase means, we have noticed some overlap between technical support questions on particular products and troubleshooting questions on the tests for those products. For more information on these CDs, visit **http://support.novell.com/** and click on the "Support Connection CD" link on that page.

Onward, Through The Fog!

Once you've assessed your readiness, undertaken the right background studies, obtained the hands-on experience that will help you understand the products and technologies at work, and reviewed the many sources of information to help you prepare for a test, you'll be ready to take a round of practice tests. When your scores come back positive enough to get you through the exam, you're ready to go after the real thing. If you follow our assessment regime, you'll not only know what you need to study, you'll know when you're ready to make a test date at Sylvan or VUE. Good luck!

Novell Certification Exams

Terms you'll need to understand:
- √ Radio button
- √ Checkbox
- √ Exhibit
- √ Multiple-choice question formats
- √ Careful reading
- √ Process of elimination
- √ Adaptive tests
- √ Form (program) tests
- √ Simulations

Techniques you'll need to master:
- √ Assessing your exam-readiness
- √ Preparing to take a certification exam
- √ Making the best use of the testing software
- √ Budgeting your time
- √ Guessing (as a last resort)

Exam taking is not something that most people anticipate eagerly, no matter how well prepared they may be. In most cases, familiarity helps offset test anxiety. In plain English, this means you probably won't be as nervous when you take your fourth or fifth Novell certification exam as you'll be when you take your first one.

Whether it's your first exam or your tenth, understanding the details of exam taking (how much time to spend on questions, the environment you'll be in, and so on) and the exam software will help you concentrate on the material rather than on the setting. Likewise, mastering a few basic exam-taking skills should help you recognize—and perhaps even outfox—some of the tricks and snares you're bound to find in some of the exam questions.

This chapter, besides explaining the exam environment and software, describes some proven exam-taking strategies that you should be able to use to your advantage.

Assessing Exam-Readiness

Before you take any more Novell exams, we strongly recommend that you read through and take the Self-Assessment included with this book (it appears just before this chapter, in fact). This will help you compare your knowledge base to the requirements for obtaining a CNE, and it will also help you identify parts of your background or experience that may be in need of improvement, enhancement, or further learning. If you get the right set of basics under your belt, obtaining Novell certification will be that much easier.

Once you've gone through the Self-Assessment, you can remedy those topical areas where your background or experience may not measure up to an ideal certification candidate. What's more, you can also tackle subject matter for individual tests at the same time, so you can continue making progress while you're catching up in some areas.

Once you've worked through an *Exam Cram*, have read the supplementary materials, and have taken the practice test, you'll have a pretty clear idea of when you should be ready to take the real exam. We strongly recommend that you keep practicing until your scores top the 75 percent mark; you may want to give yourself some margin for error, though, because in a real exam situation, stress will play more of a role than when you practice. Once you hit that point, you should be ready to go. If you get through the practice exam in this book without attaining that score, you should keep taking practice tests and studying the materials until you get there. You'll find more information about other practice test vendors in the Self-Assessment, along with even more pointers on how to study and prepare. But now, on to the exam!

The Exam Situation

When you arrive at the testing center where you scheduled your exam, you'll need to sign in with an exam coordinator. He or she will ask you to show two forms of identification, one of which must be a photo ID. After you've signed in and your time slot arrives, you'll be asked to deposit any books, bags, cell phones, pagers, or other items you brought with you. Then, you'll be escorted into a closed room. Typically, the room will be furnished with anywhere from one to half a dozen computers, and each workstation will be separated from the others by dividers designed to keep you from seeing what's happening on someone else's computer.

You'll be furnished with a pen or pencil and a blank sheet of paper or, in some cases, an erasable plastic sheet and an erasable pen. You're allowed to write down anything you want on both sides of this sheet. Before the exam, you should memorize as much of the material that appears on The Cram Sheet (in the front of this book) as possible. You can then write that information on the blank sheet as soon as you're seated in front of the computer. You can refer to your rendition of The Cram Sheet anytime you like during the test, but you'll have to surrender the sheet when you leave the room.

Most test rooms feature a wall with a large picture window. This allows the exam coordinator to monitor the room, to prevent exam-takers from talking to one another, and to observe anything out of the ordinary that might go on. The exam coordinator will have preloaded the appropriate Novell certification test—for this book, that's Test 050-640—and you'll be permitted to start as soon as you're seated in front of the computer.

All Novell certification exams allow a certain maximum amount of time in which to complete your work (this time is indicated on the exam by an onscreen counter/clock, so you can check the time remaining whenever you like). Test 050-640, "NetWare 5 Advanced Administration," is what Novell calls a *form test* or a *program test*. This means it consists of a set of 73 questions. You may take up to 105 minutes to complete this exam. The cut score, or minimum passing score, for this test is 596 out of 800 (or 74.5 percent).

All Novell certification exams are computer generated and use a combination of questions that include several multiple-choice formats, interacting with illustrations (sometimes called *exhibits*), and operating simulations. In short, Novell provides plenty of ways to interact with the test materials. These tests not only check your mastery of facts and figures about NetWare 5, but they also require you to evaluate multiple sets of circumstances or requirements. Sometimes, you'll be asked to give more than one answer to a question (in these cases, though, Novell almost always tells you how many answers you'll need to choose). Sometimes, you'll be asked to select the best or most effective solution to a problem from a range of choices, all of which may be correct from a technical standpoint. Taking such a test is quite an adventure, and it involves real thinking. This book shows you what to expect and how to deal with the potential problems, puzzles, and predicaments.

Many Novell tests, but not the "NetWare 5 Advanced Administration" exam, employ more advanced testing capabilities than might immediately meet the eye. Although the questions that appear are still multiple choice and so forth, the logic that drives them is more complex than form or program tests (like this exam), which use a fixed sequence of questions. Most Novell tests, including "NetWare 5 Advanced Administration," that cover specific software products employ a sophisticated user interface, which Novell calls a *simulation*, to test your knowledge of the software and systems under consideration in a more or less "live" environment that behaves just like the original.

Eventually, most Novell tests will employ *adaptive testing*, a well-known technique used to establish a test-taker's level of knowledge and product competence. Adaptive exams look the same as form tests, but they interact dynamically with test-takers to discover the level of difficulty at which individual test-takers can answer questions correctly. Normally, when new tests are introduced in beta form (and for some time even after the beta is over), they are form tests. Eventually, most of these tests will be switched over to an adaptive format. That is, once Novell has run its question pool past enough test-takers to derive some statistical notion of how to grade the questions in terms of difficulty, it can then restructure the question pool to make a test adaptive.

On adaptive exams, test-takers with differing levels of knowledge or ability see different sets of questions. Individuals with high levels of knowledge or ability are presented with a smaller set of more difficult questions, whereas individuals with lower levels of knowledge are presented with a larger set of easier questions. Even if two individuals answer the same percentage of questions correctly, the test-taker with a higher knowledge or ability level will score higher because his or her questions are worth more.

Also, the lower-level test-taker will probably answer more questions than his or her more-knowledgeable colleague. This explains why adaptive tests use ranges of values to define the number of questions and the amount of time it takes to complete the test. Sooner or later, we expect this test, 050-640, to become adaptive as well.

Adaptive tests work by evaluating the test-taker's most recent answer. A correct answer leads to a more difficult question (and the test software's estimate of the test-taker's knowledge and ability level is raised). An incorrect answer leads to a less difficult question (and the test software's estimate of the test-taker's knowledge and ability level is lowered). This process continues until the test determines a test-taker's true ability level (presenting a minimum of 15 questions to all test-takers). A test concludes when the test-taker's level of accuracy meets a statistically acceptable value (in other words, when his or her performance demonstrates an acceptable level of knowledge and ability) or when the maximum number of items has been presented (in which case, the test-taker is almost certain to fail; no adaptive Novell test will present more than 25 questions to any test-taker).

Novell tests come in one form or the other—either they're form tests or they're adaptive. Therefore, you must take the test in whichever form it appears; you can't choose one form over another. If anything, it pays off even more to prepare thoroughly for an adaptive test than for a form test: The penalties for answering incorrectly are built into the test itself on an adaptive test, whereas the layout remains the same for a form test, no matter how many questions you answer incorrectly.

In the section that follows, you'll learn more about what Novell test questions look like and how they must be answered.

Exam Layout And Design

Some exam questions require you to select a single answer, whereas others ask you to select multiple correct answers. The following multiple-choice question requires you to select a single correct answer. Following the question is a brief summary of each potential answer and why it's either right or wrong.

Question 1

Which of the following protocols listed is required to be configured on both the NetWare 3.x server and the NetWare 5 server?

○ a. IP
○ b. TCP
○ c. IPX
○ d. ARP
○ e. NLSP

The correct answer is c. IP can be bound to the server's network board, but it's not required for the migration. Therefore, answer a is incorrect. TCP, the Transport Control Protocol, is not required for an across-the-wire migration.

Therefore, answer b is incorrect. ARP is a protocol in the IP suite and is not required for an across-the-wire migration. Therefore, answer d is incorrect. NLSP is a protocol in the IPX suite and is not required for migration. Therefore, answer e is incorrect.

This sample question format corresponds closely to the Novell certification test format—the only difference on the test is that questions are not followed by answers. In the real test, to select an answer, you position the cursor over the radio button next to the correct answer (in this case, answer c) and then click the mouse button to select the answer.

Let's examine a question that requires choosing multiple answers. This type of question provides checkboxes rather than radio buttons for marking all appropriate selections.

Question 2

> Migrating a NetWare 3.x server to NetWare 5 has several requirements. Which of the following would satisfy those requirements? [Choose the four best answers]
>
> ❑ a. An existing NetWare 5 network
>
> ❑ b. 92MB RAM on the NetWare 5 server
>
> ❑ c. An IPX connection between the NetWare 3.x server and the NetWare 5 server
>
> ❑ d. An IP connection between the NetWare 3.x server and the NetWare 5 server
>
> ❑ e. A Pentium Pro processor on the NetWare 5 server

The correct answers are a, b, c, and e. The NetWare 3.x server and the NetWare 5 server need to have a direct connection using the IPX protocol. Therefore, answer d is incorrect.

For this type of question, more than one answer is required. As far as the authors can tell (and Novell won't comment), such questions are scored as wrong unless all the required selections are chosen. In other words, a partially correct answer does not result in partial credit when the test is scored. For Question 2, you have to check the boxes next to items a, b, c, and e to obtain credit for a correct answer. Notice that picking the right answers also means knowing why the other answers are wrong.

Although these two basic types of questions can appear in many forms, they constitute the foundation on which most of Novell's certification test questions rest. More complex questions include *exhibits*, which are usually screenshots of some kind of network diagram or topology, or *simulations*, which mock up some NetWare administrative utility, installation program, or other system component. For some of these questions, you'll be asked to make a selection by clicking on a checkbox, entering data into a text entry box, or clicking on a radio button on a simulated screen. For others, you'll be expected to use the information displayed on a graphic to guide your answer to a question. Because software is involved, familiarity with important NetWare 5 administrative tools and utilities is the key to choosing the correct answer(s).

Other questions involving exhibits use charts or network diagrams to help document a workplace scenario that you'll be asked to troubleshoot or configure. Careful attention to such exhibits is the key to success. Be prepared to toggle frequently between the exhibit and the question as you work.

Test-Taking Strategy For Form And Adaptive Tests

When it comes to either kind of Novell test—be it a form test or an adaptive test—one principle applies: Get it right the first time. You cannot elect to skip a question and move on to the next one when taking either of these types of tests. In the form test, the testing software forces you to go on to the next question, with no opportunity to skip ahead or turn back. In the adaptive test, the testing software uses your answer to the current question to select whatever question it plans to present next. In addition, you can't return to a question once you've answered it on an adaptive test, because the test software gives you only one chance to answer each question.

On an adaptive test, testing continues until the program settles into a reasonably accurate estimate of what you know and can do, taking anywhere between 15 and 25 questions. On a form test, you have to complete an entire series of questions, which usually takes an hour or longer and involves many more questions than an adaptive test (73 questions for Test 050-640).

The good news about adaptive tests is that if you know your stuff, you'll probably finish in 30 minutes or less; in fact, Novell never schedules more than 60 minutes for any of its adaptive tests. The bad news is that you must *really* know your stuff to do your best on an adaptive test. That's because some questions are difficult enough that you're bound to miss one or two, at a minimum, even if you do know your stuff. Therefore, the more you know, the better you'll do on an adaptive test, even accounting for the occasionally brutal questions that appear on these exams.

Of course, it's also true on a form test that you must know your stuff to do your best. But for us, the most profound difference between a form test and an adaptive test is the opportunity to cover a broader range of topics and questions on the form test versus the randomness of the adaptive test. If the adaptive test engine happens to hit a hole in your knowledge base early on in the testing process, that can make it harder for you to pass, as the test engine probes your knowledge of this topic. On a form test, if some questions hit a hole, you can assume that other questions will appear that you'll be able to answer.

Either way, if you encounter a question on an adaptive test or a form test that you can't answer, you must guess an answer immediately. Because of the way the adaptive software works, you may have to suffer for your guess on the next question if you guess right, because you'll get a more difficult question next. On a form test, at least, a lucky guess won't cost you in terms of the difficulty of the next question (but that doesn't mean the next question won't be a real skull-buster, too).

Test-Taking Basics

The most important advice about taking any test is this: Read each question carefully. Some questions may be ambiguous, whereas others use technical terminology in incredibly precise ways. Your authors have taken numerous Novell exams—both practice tests and real tests—and in nearly every instance, we've missed at least one question because we didn't read it closely or carefully enough.

Here are some suggestions on how to deal with the tendency to jump to an answer too quickly:

- ▶ Make sure you read every word in the question. If you find yourself jumping ahead in the question impatiently, read the question again.

- ▶ As you read, try to restate the question in your own terms. If you can do this, you should be able to pick the correct answer(s) much more easily.

- ▶ Some questions may be long and complex, to the point where they fill up more than one screen's worth of information. You might find it worthwhile to take notes on such questions and to summarize the key points in the question so you can refer to them while reading the potential answers to save yourself the effort of ping-ponging up and down the question as you read.

- ▶ Some questions may remind you of key points about NetWare tools, terms, or technologies that you might want to record for reference later in the test. Even if you can't go back to earlier questions, you can indeed go back through your notes.

Above all, try to deal with each question by thinking through what you know about NetWare 5, the administrative utilities, and other aspects of the system—its characteristics and behaviors—plus all the facts and figures involved. By reviewing what you know (and what you've written down on your information sheet), you'll often recall or understand things sufficiently to determine the answers to the questions you'll encounter on the test.

Question-Handling Strategies

Based on exams we've taken, some interesting trends have become apparent. For those questions that take only a single answer, usually two or three of the answers will be obviously incorrect, and two of the answers will be plausible—of course, only one can be correct. Unless the answer leaps out at you (if it does, reread the question to look for a trick; sometimes those are the ones you're most likely to get wrong), begin the process of answering by eliminating those answers that are most obviously wrong.

Things to look for in obviously wrong answers include spurious menu choices or utility names, nonexistent software options, and terminology you've never seen. If you've done your homework for an exam, no valid information should be completely new to you. In that case, unfamiliar or bizarre terminology probably indicates a totally bogus answer. In fact, recognizing unlikely answers is probably the most significant way in which preparation pays off at test-taking time.

Numerous questions assume that the default behavior of some particular utility is in effect. If you know the defaults and understand what they mean, this knowledge will help you cut through many potentially tricky problems.

Mastering The Inner Game

In the final analysis, knowledge breeds confidence, and confidence breeds success. If you study the materials in this book carefully and review all the practice questions at the end of each chapter, you should become aware of those areas where additional learning and study are required.

Next, follow up by reading some or all of the materials recommended in the "Need To Know More?" section at the end of each chapter. The idea is to become familiar enough with the concepts and situations you find in the sample questions that you can reason your way through similar situations on a real test. If you know the material, you have every right to be confident that you can pass the test.

You should also visit (and print or download) the Test Objectives page for Course 570: NetWare 5 Advanced Administration" at **/http://education. novell.com/testinfo/objectives/570tobj.htm/**. Here, you'll find a list of 82 specific test objectives that will help guide your study of all the topics and technologies that Novell thinks are relevant to the 050-640 test. In fact, you can use this as a kind of road map to help guide your initial studying and to help you focus your efforts as you gear up to take your practice test(s)—and then, for the real thing when you're ready.

After you've worked your way through this book and the Test Objectives page, take the practice test in Chapter 26. This will provide a reality check and help you identify areas to study further. Make sure you follow up and review materials related to the questions you miss on any practice test before scheduling a real test. Only when you've covered all the ground and feel comfortable with the scope of the practice test should you take the real one.

> **TIP**
> If you take the practice test and don't score at least 75 percent correct, you'll want to practice further. Novell provides free practice tests on its "The Guide" CD. To obtain this CD, you must contact a local NetWare Authorized Education Center (NAEC) and request that one be sent to you. For more information on how to obtain this CD, you can use the Training Locator on the Novell certification pages at **http://education.novell.com/** to locate the NAEC(s) nearest you.

Armed with the information in this book and with the determination to augment your knowledge, you should be able to pass the "NetWare 5 Advanced Administration" test. However, you need to work at it; otherwise, you'll spend the exam fee more than once before you finally pass. If you prepare seriously, you should do well. Good luck!

Additional Resources

A good source of information about Novell certification tests comes from Novell itself. Because its products and technologies—and the tests that go with them—change frequently, the best place to go for test-related information is online.

If you haven't already visited the Novell Education site, do so right now. The Novell Education home page resides at **http://education.novell.com/** (see Figure 1.1).

> *Note: This page might not be there by the time you read this, or it may be replaced by something new and different, because things change on the Novell site. Should this happen, please read the sidebar titled "Coping With Change On The Web."*

Novell Certification Exams 11

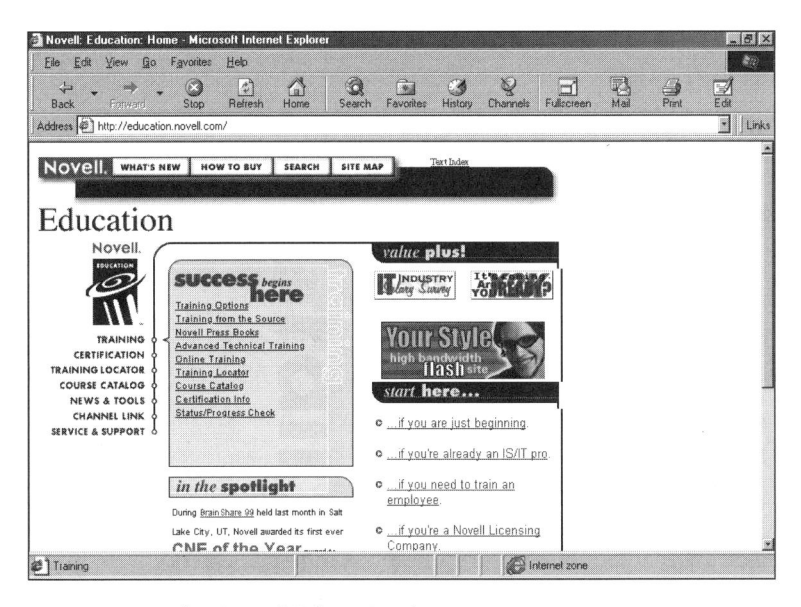

Figure 1.1 The Novell Education home page.

The menu options on the left side of the home page point to the most important sources of information in these pages. Here are some suggestions of what to check out:

➤ **Training** Use this link to locate an NAEC in your vicinity, to learn more about available training, or to request "The Guide" CD (which includes practice tests, among other materials).

➤ **Certification** This option is the ultimate source of information about the various Novell certifications. Use this menu entry to find a list of the courses and related tests, including test objectives, test data, testing FAQs (a list of frequently asked questions about Novell's testing policies, strategies, and requirements), and more.

➤ **News & Tools** Check this item to get news about new tests, updates to existing tests, retirement of obsolete tests, and for information about software and practice tests.

These are just the high points of what's available on the Novell Education pages. As you browse through them—and we strongly recommend that you do—you'll probably find other informational tidbits mentioned that are every bit as interesting and compelling.

The following vendors offer practice tests for Novell certification topics:

➤ www.certify.com is the Cyber Pass Web site. This company makes "CNEQuizr."

➤ www.stsware.com is the Self Test Software Web site. This company makes practice tests for most of the Novell curriculum.

➤ www.bfq.com is the Beach Front Quizzer Web site. This company makes practice tests for most of the Novell curriculum.

➤ www.syngress.com is the Syngress Software Web site. This company has a set of NetWare 5 practice exams in the works. Visit the Web site for more information.

You can find still more sources of practice exams on the Internet if you're willing to spend some time using your favorite search engines.

Here's the bottom line about testing readiness: If you don't score 75 percent or better on the practice test in this book, you'll probably be well served by buying one or more additional practice tests to help get you ready for the real thing. It may even be cheaper than taking the Novell test more than once, and it will certainly increase the pool of potential questions to use as practice.

Coping With Change On The Web

Sooner or later, all the information we've shared with you about the Novell Education pages and the other Web-based resources mentioned throughout the rest of this book will go stale or be replaced by newer information. In some cases, the URLs you find here might lead you to their replacements; in other cases, the URLs will go nowhere, leaving you with the dreaded "404 File Not Found" error message. When that happens, don't give up.

There's always a way to find what you want on the Web if you're willing to invest some time and energy. Most large or complex Web sites—and Novell's qualifies on both counts—offer a search engine. On all of Novell's Web pages, a Search button appears along the top edge of the page. As long as you can get to Novell's Web site (it should stay at www.novell.com for a long time), you can use this tool to help you find what you need.

The more focused you can make a search request, the more likely the results will include information you can use. For example, you can search for the string

```
training and certification
```

to produce a lot of data about the subject in general, but if you're looking for the objectives for Test 050-640, "NetWare 5 Advanced

Administration," you'll be more likely to get there quickly if you use a search string similar to the following:

```
050-640 AND objectives
```

Also, feel free to use general search tools—such as **www.search.com**, **www.altavista.com**, and **www.excite.com**—to look for related information. Although Novell offers great information about its certification tests online, plenty of third-party sources of information and assistance are available that need not follow Novell's party line. Therefore, if you can't find something where the book says it lives, start looking around. If worse comes to worst, you can always email us. We just might have a clue.

Upgrading To NetWare 5

Terms you'll need to understand:

- √ In-Place Upgrade
- √ NetWare 5 installation program
- √ INSTALL.BAT
- √ Pure IP
- √ Internetwork Packet Exchange (IPX)
- √ Storage device drivers and network board drivers

Techniques you'll need to master:

- √ Listing the types of servers that can be upgraded with the In-Place Upgrade
- √ Identifying some of the advantages and disadvantages of the In-Place Upgrade
- √ Understanding the hardware requirements necessary for the In-Place Upgrade
- √ Explaining the different protocol options available during an upgrade
- √ Listing several pre-upgrade and post-upgrade procedures
- √ Outlining the In-Place Upgrade steps

This chapter introduces you to one of the two common methods for upgrading a pre-NetWare 5 server to NetWare 5. The In-Place Upgrade, covered in this chapter, allows you to upgrade an existing NetWare 4.x server to NetWare 5 on the same hardware. This option is useful for networks that have had NetWare 4.11 installed recently and have hardware that satisfies NetWare 5's requirements.

Upgrade Options

There are two ways to upgrade NetWare 3.x and NetWare 4.x servers to NetWare 5: In-Place Upgrade and across-the-wire migration. This chapter concentrates on the In-Place Upgrade.

You can use the In-Place Upgrade to upgrade NetWare 3.x, NetWare 4.x, intraNetWare, and intraNetWare for Small Business servers. Non-NetWare servers cannot be upgraded to NetWare 5 with the In-Place Upgrade. In this chapter, we specifically cover upgrading NetWare 4.11 servers to NetWare 5.

The In-Place Upgrade involves installing NetWare 5 on a NetWare 4.11 server using the same hardware. When you use the In-Place Upgrade, NetWare 5 files are installed in the existing NetWare 4.11 directories on the SYS volume, new NetWare 5 directories are created on the SYS volume, existing NetWare 4.11 files that have the same name as NetWare 5 files are replaced, and any NetWare 4.11 files that do not have NetWare 5 versions are left untouched.

A newly installed NetWare 5 server usually has fewer files than a NetWare 5 server created from NetWare 4.11 with the In-Place Upgrade. NetWare 4.11 utilities, such as NETADMIN.EXE, are found on an upgraded server, but not on a new install of NetWare 5. The server files are different because the upgrade process preserves NetWare 4.11-only files. The type of upgrade used to create a NetWare 5 server should be documented to account for these differences.

In-Place Upgrade Advantages

The In-Place Upgrade has several advantages that are beneficial to certain organizations. If the NetWare 4.11 hardware meets the minimum NetWare 5 specifications, the In-Place Upgrade can be a useful option. If the NetWare 4.11 has block suballocation, volume compression, and optimal block sizes activated, the In-Place Upgrade retains these configurations.

In-Place Upgrade Disadvantages

There are several factors to consider before performing an In-Place Upgrade. Because the In-Place Upgrade does not delete any 4.11 files, the size of the directories on the 4.11 SYS volume may be larger than those of a NetWare 5 installation on a new server.

During the In-Place Upgrade, there's always the chance of a hardware problem. This can lead to data loss and a nonfunctional server. If this occurs, you'll need to rebuild your 4.11 server and restore all the data files.

> **TIP:** Always remember to back up all your files before performing an installation of any type.

The In-Place Upgrade option cannot be used to upgrade NetWare 2.x servers and non-NetWare servers to NetWare 5. A NetWare 2.x server must first be updated to NetWare 3.x before using the In-Place Upgrade.

If the 4.11 server is not configured with block suballocation, volume compression, and optimized block sizes, you won't be able to turn these on during the upgrade. To use these features with existing volumes, you need to back up all the data on each volume you wish to change. The next step is to delete the volumes and re-create them with these features enabled. Finally, all the data can be restored from the backups.

Existing NetWare 4.11 volumes cannot be converted to the new NetWare 5 Novell Storage Services (NSS) volumes. However, unused disk space or new drives can be used to create NSS volumes.

Requirements

To use the In-Place Upgrade, the existing NetWare 4.11 server must meet the minimum NetWare 5 hardware requirements. If the hardware is insufficient or if the size of the DOS partition or SYS volume is incorrect, the In-Place Upgrade might not work properly.

> **ALERT:** The minimum NetWare 5 hardware and space requirements are as follows:
> - Pentium processor on an IBM PC or PC-compatible architecture
> - 64MB of RAM
> - 30MB DOS partition
> - A network board
> - A minimum of 200MB of free space on the SYS volume

Note: *A network board is also called a Network Interface Card (NIC), network adapter, and network interface board. Novell uses the term network board most often. However, network board vendors usually call it a NIC.*

These requirements are the bare minimum. However, for a production-grade server, the memory requirements will be larger and more processing power may be necessary. In addition, the size of the DOS partition and the amount of free space on the SYS volume should be increased. In this situation, more is better.

Protocol Options

The In-Place Upgrade allows you to specify which protocol (or protocols) you wish to use on the new NetWare 5 server. During the In-Place Upgrade, NetWare 5 automatically loads the appropriate network board drivers and binds *Internetwork Packet Exchange (IPX)* with all detected frame types. If the frame type for IPX cannot be determined, the server binds IPX to the Ethernet_802.2 frame type. You can modify the IPX bindings parameters during the In-Place Upgrade, or you can do it later.

One of NetWare 5's new features is *pure IP*, which allows you to run a network without IPX. Using a single communication protocol is one way to help reduce network traffic. Pure IP also provides an easier way to share data with other IP networks, such as the Internet. A network that uses pure IP can still use applications that depend on IPX. NetWare 5 loads the Compatibility Mode Drivers (CMDs) on the server by default. The current Client 32 software automatically loads the CMDs on the workstations. Organizations don't have to replace their IPX-dependent applications. When an IPX-only application needs to send data out on the network, the CMD encapsulates the data in an IP packet and delivers the data to the destination using the IP protocol. The CMDs also handle packets generated from NetWare/IP sources. When you configure pure IP during the upgrade process, you must provide the server an IP address, subnet mask, and gateway address.

Both IP and IPX can be bound to the same network board(s) in the NetWare 5 server. Removing and configuring IPX and/or IP can always be done at a later time—it doesn't have to be performed during the In-Place Upgrade.

In-Place Upgrade Procedures

There are several tasks that should be completed before, during, and after you perform an In-Place Upgrade. In the following sections, we'll introduce you to these tasks and take you step by step through the In-Place Upgrade.

Pre-Upgrade Procedures

Before you perform the In-Place Upgrade, you should take certain precautions and verify information. Be sure to do or check the following:

➤ Document the hardware and software configurations of the NetWare 4.11 servers, including the network board specifics.

➤ Verify that the existing NetWare 4.11 hardware is compatible with NetWare 5. Novell provides hardware compatibility information on its Web site.

➤ NetWare 5 cannot use storage device drivers that use the .DSK extension. If the NetWare 4.11 server uses these drivers and there's not a compatible NetWare 5 driver, contact the device vendor to obtain a NetWare 5 version of the driver. NetWare 5 storage device drivers have a .HAM (which means host adapter module) extension and often come with a .CDM (which means custom device module) extension file as a pair.

➤ Verify that any third-party drivers, such as network board drivers (.LAN), disk drivers (.HAM), backup device drivers, redundant array of independent disks (RAID) drivers, and CD-ROM bay drivers, are compatible with NetWare 5.

➤ Perform two complete backups of each NetWare 4.11 server that will be upgraded, and then verify the backups. These backups should include the file system data and Novell Directory Services (NDS). In addition, make sure the backup software is certified for both NetWare 4.11 and NetWare 5.

➤ Users will not be able to access the server while the upgrade is in progress. Before beginning the In-Place Upgrade, inform the users that the server and its associated services will not be available. You can send a broadcast message to the users to save and close their files and to disconnect from any servers that will be upgraded.

➤ When upgrading multiple NetWare 4.11 servers that reside in the same NDS tree, upgrade the server that holds the master replica of the [Root] partition first. If the tree will contain a mixture of NetWare 4.11 and NetWare 5 servers, you'll need to update the 4.11 NDS NetWare Loadable Module (NLM) to the most recent version. Novell's Web site has several good technical information documents (TIDs) concerning mixed NetWare 4.11 and NetWare 5 trees.

In-Place Upgrade Steps

To begin the In-Place Upgrade, the NetWare 4.11 server must be brought down with the **DOWN** and **EXIT** commands. Insert the NetWare 5 Installation

CD-ROM and access the CD-ROM by changing to the appropriate drive letter. You begin the In-Place Upgrade by running the INSTALL.BAT file from the DOS prompt. INSTALL.BAT is located on the root of the NetWare 5 Installation CD-ROM. This is the same file used to begin a new install, except you choose the Upgrade From 3.1x or 4.1x option instead of the New Server option. The following is an outline of the In-Place Upgrade steps:

1. Run INSTALL.BAT, which is located at the root of the NetWare 5 Installation CD-ROM.

2. The license agreement screen appears. Accept the license agreement to continue.

3. From the Options menu, choose Modify. This is a very important step because if you do not choose Modify, you'll perform a new server installation and overwrite all your files.

4. From the menu, select Upgrade From 3.1x or 4.1x.

5. From the menu, specify the appropriate video and mouse configurations.

6. At this point, files are copied from the DOS partition to the NWSERVER directory.

7. The screen displays the storage device information. Verify or change the information as necessary and select Continue.

8. At this point, the SYS volume is mounted. The screen displays the network board information. Verify or change the information as necessary and then select Continue.

9. More files and existing NetWare 4.11 driver files are copied to SYS:SYSTEM\DRIVERS.OLD.

10. Java is loaded, and the graphical user interface (GUI) installation phase begins.

11. Using the mouse, choose the option to mount the volumes now.

12. In the next screen, configure the protocol information for IP or IPX (or both).

13. Verify the NDS information displayed on the next screen.

14. After you've verified the NDS information, you install the licenses. With the mouse, navigate to the location of the server base license file. This is usually located on the NetWare 5 Server + 5 Connections license floppy disk as a license envelope file (*.NLF).

15. Next, install additional products and services. (You can also add and remove additional products and services later.)

16. The last phase copies the remaining files to the SYS volume. Depending on the number of services selected, this may take some time.

17. Choose to reboot the server, and you're done.

Post-Upgrade Procedures

Most of the post-upgrade procedures concern issues that affect your clients. Most, if not all, of these items need to be performed before the users can use the new NetWare 5 server:

➤ If necessary, modify any container, profile, and user login scripts. You may need to specify the name of the server or servers in Client 32 settings, login scripts, and Application objects. If the server name is not specified in the **MAP** commands, NetWare 5 will use the value of the Message Server property of the User object.

➤ You can upgrade the existing NetWare 4.11 printing environment to Novell Distributed Print Services (NDPS), or it can remain as the queue-based structure in NetWare 4.11. NDPS and queue-based printing can coexist with each other in the same NDS tree.

➤ You may need to upgrade the client software so users can take full advantage of the new NetWare 5 services. Version 2.2 or higher is required for Windows 95/98, and version 4.5 or higher is necessary for Windows NT to access servers providing the new NetWare 5 services.

Practice Questions

Question 1

The NetWare 5 In-Place Upgrade can be used to update which of the following servers? [Choose the three best answers]

❑ a. NetWare 2.2 servers

❑ b. NetWare 4.1 servers

❑ c. Windows NT 3.51 servers

❑ d. NetWare 3.11 servers

❑ e. NetWare 4.11 servers

The correct answers are b, d, and e. NetWare 2.2 servers must first be upgraded to NetWare 3.x. Therefore, answer a is incorrect. Non-NetWare servers cannot be upgraded to NetWare 5 on the same hardware because of the differences in the operating systems and structures of the databases that contain user and resource information. Therefore, answer c is incorrect.

Question 2

The NetWare 5 In-Place Upgrade begins with the execution of which file located on the root of the NetWare 5 Installation CD-ROM?

○ a. INSTALL.CFG

○ b. SETUP.EXE

○ c. INSTALL.BAT

○ d. NWSETUP.COM

○ e. INSTALL.COM

The correct answer is c. INSTALL.CFG is a configuration file used by the Client 32 install process on non-Registry based workstations, such as Windows 3.x and DOS. Therefore, answer a is incorrect. SETUP.EXE is typically used to install user applications. Therefore, answer b is incorrect. NWSETUP.COM and INSTALL.COM are made-up files. Therefore, answers d and e are incorrect.

Question 3

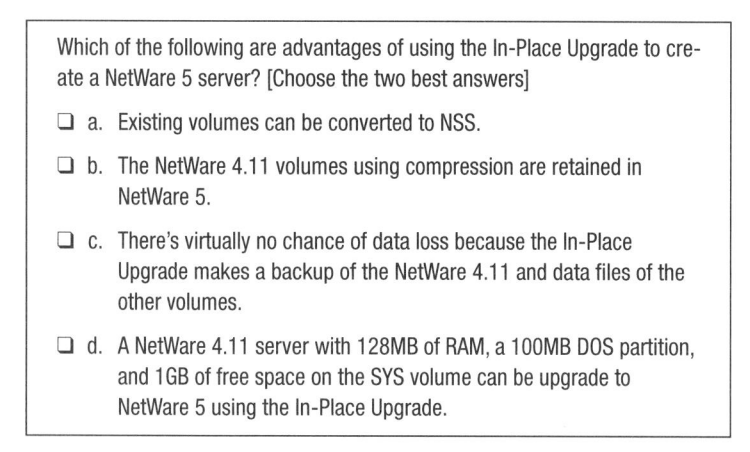

> Which of the following are advantages of using the In-Place Upgrade to create a NetWare 5 server? [Choose the two best answers]
>
> ❏ a. Existing volumes can be converted to NSS.
>
> ❏ b. The NetWare 4.11 volumes using compression are retained in NetWare 5.
>
> ❏ c. There's virtually no chance of data loss because the In-Place Upgrade makes a backup of the NetWare 4.11 and data files of the other volumes.
>
> ❏ d. A NetWare 4.11 server with 128MB of RAM, a 100MB DOS partition, and 1GB of free space on the SYS volume can be upgrade to NetWare 5 using the In-Place Upgrade.

The correct answers are b and d. NSS volumes can only be created using new or unused disk space. Therefore, answer a is incorrect. The In-Place Upgrade suffers from the potential of data loss when a hardware failure occurs during the upgrade. NetWare 5 does not copy all the NetWare 4.11 files, only the NetWare 4.11 drivers. Therefore, answer c is incorrect.

Question 4

> Updating a NetWare 4.11 server to NetWare 5 has several requirements. Which of the following would satisfy those requirements? [Choose the four best answers]
>
> ❏ a. 200MB SYS volumes
>
> ❏ b. 92MB RAM
>
> ❏ c. 200MB DOS partition
>
> ❏ d. 200MB RAM
>
> ❏ e. Pentium Pro processor

The correct answers are b, c, d, and e. At least 200MB of free disk space is needed on the SYS volume. Therefore, answer a is incorrect.

Question 5

When creating a NetWare 5 server by using the In-Place Upgrade on a NetWare 4.11 server, you need to specify protocol information. Which of the following protocols can be configured during the upgrade? [Choose the two best answers]

- ❑ a. IP
- ❑ b. TCP
- ❑ c. ARP
- ❑ d. IPX
- ❑ e. SPX

The correct answers are a and d. IP and IPX are used for routing and must be configured properly for servers to communicate with each other during the upgrade. TCP and ARP are other protocols in the IP suite. Therefore, answers b and c are incorrect. SPX is another protocol in the IPX suite. SPX is not configured during the upgrade because it's not used for routing, and it functions properly using the default parameters. Therefore, answer e is incorrect.

Question 6

Which of the following are disadvantages of using the In-Place Upgrade method to update a NetWare 4.11 server to NetWare 5? [Choose the two best answers]

- ❑ a. The existing volumes cannot be converted to NSS.
- ❑ b. Windows NT 3.51 servers cannot be upgraded using the In-Place Upgrade.
- ❑ c. NetWare 4.11 servers using volume compression and suballocation cannot be upgraded with the In-Place Upgrade.
- ❑ d. 250MB RAM is required for the In-Place Upgrade.
- ❑ e. The NetWare 4.11 server's hardware will satisfy the NetWare 5 requirements because it's already running as a NetWare server.

Upgrading To NetWare 5   25

The correct answers are a and e. Windows NT 3.51 is not a NetWare 4.11 server. Therefore, answer b is incorrect and the reason this is a trick question. NetWare 4.11 servers using volume compression and suballocation can use the In-Place Upgrade. Therefore, answer c is incorrect. The existing NetWare 4.11 server's hardware must meet the NetWare 5 requirements regardless of which operating system is running. Only 64MB of RAM is required for a NetWare 5 server. Therefore, answer d is incorrect.

Question 7

> Before performing an In-Place Upgrade, which of the following procedures need to be completed? [Choose the three best answers]
> - ❏ a. Document all NetWare 3.x servers, including the network boards
> - ❏ b. Verify that third-party drivers are compatible with NetWare 5
> - ❏ c. Upgrade the server that holds the read-only copy of the [Root] partition first
> - ❏ d. Replace DSK drivers with HAM drivers
> - ❏ e. Perform at least two complete backups of the NetWare 4.11 server

The correct answers are b, d, and e. Documentation needs to be performed on the NetWare 4.11 servers that will be upgraded. Therefore, answer a is incorrect. You upgrade the server that holds the master replica of the [Root] partition first. Therefore, answer c is incorrect.

26 Chapter 2

Question 8

> Here are the In-Place Upgrade steps in random order:
>
> 1. Accept the license.
> 2. Run INSTALL.BAT.
> 3. Java is loaded.
> 4. Select the video and mouse configuration.
> 5. Configure protocols.
> 6. Install additional products and services.
>
> Indicate the correct order of steps by choosing one of the following choices:
>
> ○ a. 1, 3, 5, 2, 4, 6
>
> ○ b. 2, 1, 3, 4, 5, 6
>
> ○ c. 2, 1, 4, 3, 5, 6
>
> ○ d. 1, 3, 4, 5, 6, 2

The correct answer is c. The nongraphical and license phases begin before Java is loaded, and the entire process begins with INSTALL.BAT. Therefore, answers a, b, and d are incorrect.

Question 9

> After completing the In-Place Upgrade, the network administrator may need to perform some tasks. Which of the following are post-upgrade duties? [Choose the three best answers]
>
> ❑ a. Modify any login scripts so the new name of the NetWare 5 user is placed in the **MAP** statements
>
> ❑ b. Upgrade the Windows 95 Client 32 software to at least version 2.2
>
> ❑ c. Upgrade the Windows NT Client 32 software to at least version 4.5
>
> ❑ d. Convert the NetWare 4.11 queue-based printing environment to NDPS because the queue-based printers will not function in NetWare 5
>
> ❑ e. Make sure the NetWare 5 server name is placed in all login script **MAP** statements so that the system does not have to rely on the Message Server property of the User object

Upgrading To NetWare 5

The correct answers are b, c, and e. Because answer e is correct, answer a is incorrect. NetWare 5 NDPS printers and queue-based printers can both coexist in the same tree. Therefore, answer d is incorrect.

Question 10

Which directory contains the NetWare 4.11 drivers after the upgrade?

○ a. C:\NWSERVER\\DRIVERS.OLD
○ b. SYS:\DRIVERS.OLD
○ c. SYS:\SYSTEM\DRIVERS.OLD
○ d. SYS:\DRIVERS.411
○ e. SYS:\SYSTEM\DRIVERS.411

The correct answer is c. The other locations do not exist by default. Therefore, answers a, b, d, and e are incorrect.

Need To Know More?

www.novell.com/whitepapers covers issues surrounding upgrading to NetWare 5. On this Web site, read the following two white papers: "Upgrading To NetWare 5" and "NetWare 5—Pure IP: Delivering NetWare Services On TCP/IP."

www.support.novell.com/servlet/Knowledgebase offers TIDs related to the topics covered in this chapter. At Novell's support Knowledgebase Web site, perform a search using the following TID numbers:

➤ **TID 2944576** IP Compatibility Mode

➤ **TID 2943750** Understanding NetWare 5 Licensing

➤ **TID 2944702** Installing NW5 Evaluation And Demo License

➤ **TID 2942633** NW5 Upgrade Hangs At License Screen

Migrating To NetWare 5

Terms you'll need to understand:

- √ Novell Upgrade Wizard
- √ Across-the-wire migration
- √ Upgrade Wizard project

Techniques you'll need to master:

- √ Listing the advantages and disadvantages of an across-the-wire migration
- √ Identifying the requirements for an across-the-wire migration
- √ Listing the steps for installing the Novell Upgrade Wizard
- √ Listing the steps for performing a migration from NetWare 3.x to NetWare 5
- √ Identifying the pre-upgrade procedures
- √ Listing the post-upgrade procedures
- √ Explaining the role of Internetwork Packet Exchange (IPX) in a migration from NetWare 3.x to NetWare 5

If you're a network administrator who's currently running NetWare 3.x, chances are you'll be upgrading to NetWare 5 very soon. If this is the case, your existing hardware might not be capable of supporting NetWare 5. In this situation, you'll need to install NetWare 5 on new servers and migrate the NetWare 3.x network to NetWare 5. This is done using the second method of upgrading to NetWare 5: across-the-wire migration. (The first method, the In-Place Upgrade, was covered in Chapter 2.) In this chapter, you'll learn how to perform an across-the-wire migration using the Novell Upgrade Wizard.

Migration Options

The upgrade utilities available for a migration are the Novell Upgrade Wizard, REXXWARE Migration Toolkit (RMT), and the Automatic Client Upgrade (ACU). RMT is provided by Simware Inc. and is available at no charge from www.simware.com/products/rmt. The RMT product provides customization and performance features for moving files and bindery information from NetWare 3.x servers to NetWare 5. The ACU provides a centralized solution for updating older client software to the current client software. This chapter covers the Novell Upgrade Wizard as a method of upgrading a NetWare 3.x network to NetWare 5.

The Novell Upgrade Wizard is run from a workstation and provides a graphical interface for migrating bindery data and files from NetWare 3.x to NetWare 5. This type of migration is called an *across-the-wire migration* because the NetWare 3.x source servers are left intact, and "copies" of the bindery and data files travel across the network and are "copied" to a NetWare 5 server. This method also allows you to migrate several NetWare 3.x servers onto a single NetWare 5 server.

> *Note: The across-the-wire migration is sometimes referred to as an across-the-wire upgrade or migrating across the wire. Regardless of what it's called, the process moves user accounts, data, printers, and rights to a new server across the network.*

Advantages

Across-the-wire migration offers several advantages over the In-Place Upgrade. Even if your existing NetWare 3.x hardware and available disk space are capable of running NetWare 5, an across-the-wire migration is a better solution. Here's a list of some of these advantages:

➤ There's considerably less danger of data loss. If a power failure or connection error occurs during the migration, the original NetWare 3.1x server is left intact because it's untouched during an across-the wire migration.

Migrating To NetWare 5   **31**

➤ Block suballocation, volume compression, optimal block sizes, and Novell Storage Services (NSS) volumes can all be used because you're migrating the data from a NetWare 3.x volume to a NetWare 5 volume.

➤ Any version of NetWare 3.x can be migrated. This includes NetWare 3.11, NetWare 3.12, and NetWare 3.2.

➤ You can migrate multiple NetWare 3.x servers into a single NetWare 5 server to consolidate them.

➤ The Novell Upgrade Wizard checks for conflicts and problems before the actual migration of information occurs.

➤ Because you're migrating to a NetWare 5 network, the pure IP or Internetwork Packet Exchange (IPX) protocol (or both) can be configured after the migration. Therefore, you can migrate from a NetWare 3.x IPX network to a pure IP NetWare 5 network.

➤ The Novell Upgrade Wizard is a graphical modeling tool that runs on a workstation—you do not need direct access to the server consoles.

➤ You have the option of moving or not moving the NetWare 3.x print configuration. NetWare 5 networks can contain a mixture of Novell Distributed Print Services (NDPS) and queue-based print elements.

➤ If the destination container and/or directory does not exist before the migration, you can create them with the Novell Upgrade Wizard.

Disadvantages

There are few disadvantages to an across-the-wire migration, and the benefits usually far outweigh the risks. Some disadvantages follow:

➤ If a power failure or some other event occurs during the bindery or data migration, you could have incomplete bindery information or file transfers.

➤ Only entire NetWare 3.x volumes can be migrated. However, you can migrate the volumes to NetWare 5 directories, which can help you sort out what's needed and what's not necessary.

Protocols

The NetWare 3.x server and NetWare 5 server need to be able to directly communicate with each other during the information transfer. If the NetWare 5 server is only running pure IP, you'll need to bind IPX to the NetWare 5 server before using the Novell Upgrade Wizard. When the migration is complete, you can remove IPX from the NetWare 5 server.

If the users have not been using a pure IP NetWare 5 network, changing the protocol may affect the clients. IP may need to be added and configured on the users' workstations for a pure IP network to be used.

> **ALERT:** Across-the-wire migration of NetWare 3.x to NetWare 5 uses a graphical user interface (GUI) utility: Novell Upgrade Wizard. This utility is run from a Windows workstation that has the Novell Client (Client 32) installed and configured to connect to the NetWare 5 and NetWare 3.x networks with IPX. The wizard "copies" the NetWare 3.x bindery and data files from the NetWare 3.x server to the NetWare 5 network using the network communication media and leaves the NetWare 3.x server intact.

Requirements

Before you can use the Novell Upgrade Wizard, you must already have a NetWare 5 network in place. This is necessary because you'll choose the container for the bindery information and a NetWare 5 server for the NetWare 3.x files.

The same NetWare 5 hardware requirements must be met before performing an across-the-wire migration. These requirements are as follows:

➤ Pentium processor on an IBM PC or PC-compatible architecture
➤ 64MB of RAM
➤ A network board

> *Note: A network board is also called a Network Interface Card (NIC), network adapter, network card, and network interface board. Novell uses the term network board most often. However, network board vendors usually call it a NIC.*

Although these are the minimum values to operate, they are not realistic values for a production-grade server (which would need more memory and perhaps more processing power). More is always better in this situation.

Upgrade Wizard

The Novell Upgrade Wizard handles migration configuration information through *projects*. Each project has a name and contains two areas in a project window. The left area, which is the source information, displays the NetWare 3.x Bindery and Volume objects. The right area displays the NetWare 5 Novell Directory Services (NDS) and destination volume information. To specify what you want to migrate, drag the 3.x Bindery object from the left area and drop it

Migrating To NetWare 5   **33**

on top of the destination container displayed in the right window area. Using the same procedure, drag the 3.x Volume objects on the left to either NetWare 5 volumes or directories on the right. One of the best features of these projects is that everything you do is offline—nothing is changed or moved until you choose the Migrate option from the menu or toolbar. If the destination container or directory does not exist, you can create these in the project window. In addition, the Novell Upgrade Wizard allows you to check for conflicts and problems before you begin the migration. Potential problems, such as object name conflicts and insufficient disk space, can be corrected and addressed before you begin the migration.

> **TIP**
> If you want to migrate the NetWare 3.x SYS volume, migrate the volume to a directory on the NetWare 5 server. The PUBLIC and SYSTEM directories' NetWare 3.x files will not migrate, but by using a destination directory rather than a NetWare 5 volume, you can more easily determine which NetWare 3.x SYS files you need to keep.

Across-the-wire migration securely moves the NetWare 3.x bindery users, groups, rights, and passwords to the destination container in the NetWare 5 tree. The selected NetWare 3.x volume data files and all associated trustee assignments are moved to the destination volume or directories on the NetWare 5 server.

> **TIP**
> Another nice feature of the Novell Upgrade Wizard is that you can apply a Template object's values to the migrated user accounts. You can set identical property values for these users, such as the company address, department, fax, phone numbers, volume space restrictions, and NDS group memberships. You can also create a Template object with the Novell Upgrade Wizard if one is not already present in the NetWare 5 tree.

Installing The Upgrade Wizard

The Novell Upgrade Wizard is not installed when NetWare 5 is installed. The application is located on the NetWare 5 Installation CD-ROM at \Products\ UPGRDWZD\UPGRDWZD.EXE and is approximately 11MB in size. The application can be copied to another location for installation. Here's an outline of the steps necessary to install the Novell Upgrade Wizard:

1. Make sure all shared network applications, such as NetWare Administrator, are closed.

2. Copy the UPGRDWZD.EXE file to a local drive. This is not necessary, but it speeds up the installation.

3. Run the UPGRDWZD.EXE application and accept the license and the default storage location on your workstation.

At this point, the files are copied to the location specified in Step 3, and several dynamic link libraries (DLLs) are copied to the NetWare 5 SYS:SYSTEM directory. When the installation is complete, the wizard can be launched from Start|Programs|Novell|Novell Upgrade Wizard.

Pre-Upgrade Procedures

Before you begin an across-the-wire migration, you have several tasks that should be completed. Some of these suggested procedures may take some time; they should be scheduled and performed prior to the upgrade. These pre-upgrade tasks include:

➤ Run BINDFIX on the NetWare 3.x binderies at least twice. This repairs any errors in the database and reclaims any space from deleted items.

➤ Backup the NetWare 5 NDS tree and destination volumes in case there's an incomplete migration due to events such as an extended power loss.

➤ When migrating multiple NetWare 3.x server binderies to the same context, determine what to do with User or Group objects with the same names. If the User objects of the same name in different binderies represent different users, rename the bindery user in the conflicting bindery so each user has a unique name. If the identical user names in different binderies all refer to the same user, determine what you want to happen when identical object names are encountered.

➤ If necessary, upgrade the users' Windows 95 Novell Client to version 2.2 or greater and for Windows NT to version 4.5 or greater. This can be done before the upgrade, but additional modification may still be necessary after the migration. Certain items, such as changing from a bindery to NDS connection and setting the workstation context, may need to be adjusted.

➤ To perform the migration, you must have sufficient rights in both the NetWare 3.x server and the NetWare 5 tree and servers. It's better to authenticate to both environments with full file system rights, as well as NDS and bindery rights.

➤ Make sure the NetWare 5 servers have IPX bound to their network boards. This is necessary in a pure IP NetWare 5 network because the NetWare 3.x IPX servers must make direct connections to the NetWare 5 servers. Entering "DISPLAY SERVERS" at the NetWare 3.x server console is one way to determine whether the NetWare 5 server is reachable with IPX. When you finish the migration, IPX can be removed from the NetWare 5 server if necessary.

➤ If the servers involved in the migration have been configured to filter Service Advertising Protocols (SAPs) or the servers are on either side of a router that's blocking SAPs, SAP filtering may need to be disabled.

➤ Some of the NetWare Loadable Modules (NLMs) on the NetWare 3.x servers may need to be updated. The first step is to unload the following NLMs (in the order indicated) on the NetWare 3.x servers:

➤ TSA312.NLM or TSA311.NLM

➤ SMDR.NLM

➤ SMDR31X.NLM

➤ SPXS.NLM

➤ TLI.NLM

➤ AFTER311.NLM

➤ CLIB.NLM

➤ A3112.NLM

➤ STREAMS.NLM

➤ MAC.NAM (this might not be loaded)

After these are unloaded, change the attributes of these files to read/write. You can use NetWare Administrator, FILER, or FLAG to accomplish this task. When you install the Novell Upgrade Wizard, updated versions of these NLMs are placed in the following directory, assuming the default location was specified during installation: C:\Program Files\Novell\Upgrade\Products\Nw3x.

➤ If you'll be migrating non-DOS files, such as Windows long file name (LFN) files or Macintosh files, the destination volume on the NetWare 5 server must be configured to support these additional name spaces.

TIP
To configure the NetWare 5 server to support the additional name spaces, use the following:
➤ LONG.NAM for Windows 95/98, Windows NT, and OS/2
➤ MAC.NAM for Macintosh files
➤ NFS.NAM for NFS (Unix) files

Chapter 3

➤ Enter "LOAD TSA312" at the NetWare 3.12 server consoles and "LOAD TSA311" at the NetWare 3.11 server consoles. This automatically loads all the updated NLMs.

➤ Determine which objects you'll be migrating—bindery and/or data files. After you migrate the bindery, you can migrate the files later; however, beware of delays in which the NetWare 3.x bindery may change (changes to the account property values, for example).

> **EXAM ALERT**
>
> The Novell Upgrade Wizard is *not* installed automatically when you install a NetWare 5 server or the Novell Client software. Updated NetWare 3.x NLMs are included in the wizard's installation program, and you'll need to place these in the SYS:SYSTEM directories on the NetWare 3.x servers.

Using The Wizard

When you open the Novell Upgrade Wizard for the first time, it presents you with a dialog box to create a new project. You assign the project a name and specify the location to store the project. The process of creating a project is outlined as follows:

1. From the Start menu, run the Novell Upgrade Wizard, accept the license agreement, and choose Create New Upgrade Project.

2. Assign a project name and specify the default location as C:\Program Files\Novell\Upgrade. Click on Next.

3. Verify or choose the NetWare 3.x source server and NetWare 5 destination tree. You can browse and authenticate at this point if necessary.

4. Click on Create to open the new project and close the Getting Started dialog box.

5. Figure 3.1 shows the Novell Upgrade Wizard project window. In this window, you drag the Bindery object on the left to the destination container on the right. Drag the NetWare 3.x Volume objects on the left to the NetWare 5 volumes or directories on the right.

6. Choose Verify Project from the Project menu. This allows you to check for any problems or conflicts before the actual migration of information.

7. The next screen presents you with the option to migrate the bindery print configuration information to NDS. If you do choose to migrate this information, you must select the NetWare 5 volume for the Print Queue objects.

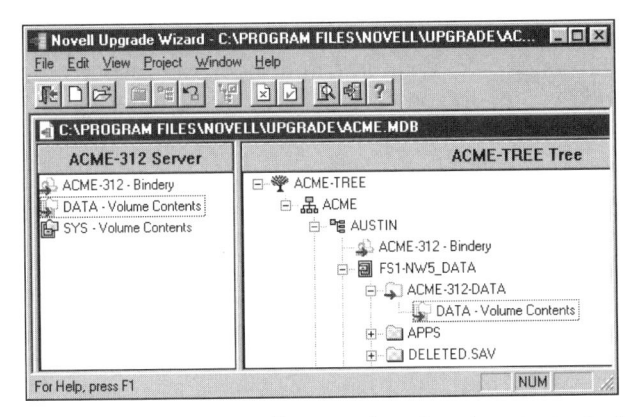

Figure 3.1 The Novell Upgrade Wizard project window.

8. On the next screen, you can select a Template object in the destination tree to apply to the migrated User objects.

9. In the next screen, you have the option of creating a Template object from the attributes of the migrated users.

10. At the Duplicate File Resolution screen, you have three choices:

    ➤ Don't copy the file
    ➤ Rename the file
    ➤ Copy the file if newer

    All renamed files are indicated in the resulting error log, but skipped files are not listed.

11. On the next screen, you must authenticate to both NetWare 3.x and NetWare 5.

12. At the next screen, you can choose to check for duplicate objects and sufficient disk space. After this screen, the verification process begins. Once you have the project defined and verified, you can begin the migration of information.

13. Choose Upgrade from the Project menu or click on the Upgrade button. The Novell Upgrade Wizard will go through the verification process again and any unresolved items will be displayed.

14. When there are no more errors, click on the Proceed button, and the migration begins. While the information is migrating, a progress window is displayed on the screen. You also have the option of canceling the migration from the same progress window.

> **Exam Alert:** Make sure you're comfortable with the Novell Upgrade Wizard window areas and features. You should be able to perform and describe the process to indicate where the NetWare 3.x bindery and data files will reside in the NetWare 5 NDS tree.

Post-Upgrade Procedures

The post-upgrade (also called *post-migration*) procedures are basically the same as described in Chapter 2 for the In-Place Upgrade. The following list provides a summary of these items:

- Modify any container, profile, and user login scripts that refer to the NetWare 3.x server name.

- If the NetWare 3.x printing environment has been upgraded to NDPS, you'll need to eliminate **CAPTURE** statements in login scripts that refer to the NetWare 3.x bindery print environment.

- You may need to upgrade the client software so users can take full advantage of the new NetWare 5 services.

Practice Questions

Question 1

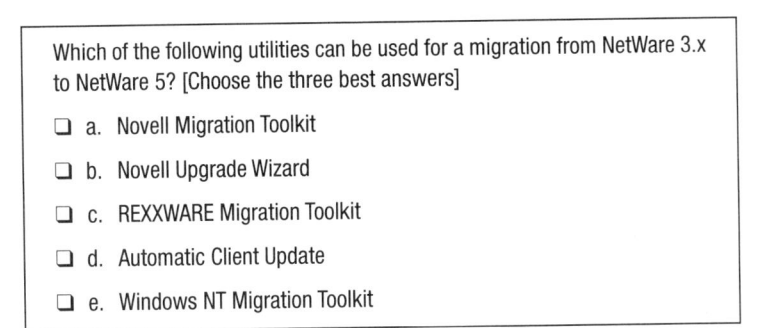

Which of the following utilities can be used for a migration from NetWare 3.x to NetWare 5? [Choose the three best answers]

- ❑ a. Novell Migration Toolkit
- ❑ b. Novell Upgrade Wizard
- ❑ c. REXXWARE Migration Toolkit
- ❑ d. Automatic Client Update
- ❑ e. Windows NT Migration Toolkit

The correct answers are b, c, and d. There's no such product as the Novell Migration Toolkit. Therefore, answer a is incorrect. The Windows NT Migration Toolkit is used to migrate from NetWare to Windows NT. Therefore, answer e is incorrect.

Question 2

The Novell Upgrade Wizard provides an interface to configure the NetWare 3.x to NetWare 5 migration. From which location does the Novell Upgrade Wizard run?

- ○ a. The NetWare 5 Java server screen
- ○ b. The NetWare 5 Remote Console screen
- ○ c. Windows NT workstation running Novell Client 4.5
- ○ d. A Windows 95 workstation running Client 32 1.10
- ○ e. WIZARD.BAT executed from a DOS prompt

The correct answer is c. The Novell Upgrade Wizard is an EXE file and cannot run at the server. Therefore, answers a and b are incorrect. The wizard can run from Windows 95, but it requires version 2.2 or greater of Client 32. Therefore, answer d is incorrect. WIZARD.BAT is a made-up file. Therefore, answer e is incorrect.

Chapter 3

Question 3

> Which of the following are advantages of using an across-the-wire migration? [Choose the four best answers]
>
> ❑ a. Migrated data can be placed on NSS volumes.
> ❑ b. There's virtually no chance of data loss because the original files and bindery remain on the NetWare 3.x servers.
> ❑ c. There's virtually no chance of data loss because an across-the-wire migration makes a backup of the NetWare 3.x bindery and data files.
> ❑ d. You can migrate a NetWare 3.11, NetWare 3.12, and a NetWare 3.2 server to one NetWare 5 server.
> ❑ e. The Novell Upgrade Wizard allows you to verify the project configuration before the migration.

Trick! question

The correct answers are a, b, d and e. The Novell Upgrade Wizard does not make backup copies of the NetWare 3.x bindery and data files because they're left intact on the NetWare 3.x server. You have to know that the data left on the NetWare 3.x server is not called a "backup." Therefore, answer c is incorrect.

Question 4

> Migrating a NetWare 3.x server to NetWare 5 has several requirements. Which of the following would satisfy those requirements? [Choose the four best answers]
>
> ❑ a. An existing NetWare 5 network
> ❑ b. 92MB RAM on the NetWare 5 server
> ❑ c. IPX connection between the NetWare 3.x server and the NetWare 5 server
> ❑ d. IP connection between the NetWare 3.x server and the NetWare 5 server
> ❑ e. Pentium Pro processor on the NetWare 5 server

The correct answers are a, b, c, and e. The NetWare 3.x server and the NetWare 5 server need to have a direct connection using the IPX protocol. Therefore, answer d is incorrect.

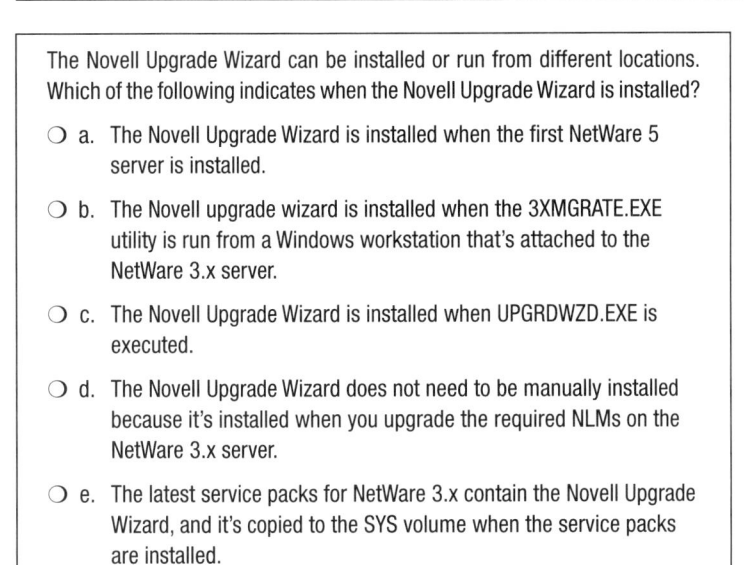

Migrating To NetWare 5   **41**

Question 5

> The Novell Upgrade Wizard can be installed or run from different locations. Which of the following indicates when the Novell Upgrade Wizard is installed?
>
> ○ a. The Novell Upgrade Wizard is installed when the first NetWare 5 server is installed.
>
> ○ b. The Novell upgrade wizard is installed when the 3XMGRATE.EXE utility is run from a Windows workstation that's attached to the NetWare 3.x server.
>
> ○ c. The Novell Upgrade Wizard is installed when UPGRDWZD.EXE is executed.
>
> ○ d. The Novell Upgrade Wizard does not need to be manually installed because it's installed when you upgrade the required NLMs on the NetWare 3.x server.
>
> ○ e. The latest service packs for NetWare 3.x contain the Novell Upgrade Wizard, and it's copied to the SYS volume when the service packs are installed.

The correct answer is c. The wizard is not installed when a NetWare 5 server is installed. The utility is located on the NetWare 5 Installation CD-ROM. Therefore, answer a is incorrect. There's no such utility named 3XMGRATE.EXE. Therefore, answer b is incorrect. Upgrading the NLMs on the server does not install the Novell Upgrade Wizard. Therefore, answer d is incorrect. The NetWare 3.x service packs do not contain the Novell Upgrade Wizard. Therefore, answer e is incorrect.

Question 6

> Before performing an across-the-wire migration, which of the following procedures must you complete? [Choose the best answers]
>
> ❑ a. Run BINDFIX on the NetWare 3.x bindery.
>
> ❑ b. Back up the NetWare 5 NDS tree and destination volumes.
>
> ❑ c. Make sure the NetWare 3.x server and NetWare 5 server have IPX bound to their network boards.
>
> ❑ d. Determine if SAPs are being filtered and disable the SAP filters.
>
> ❑ e. Update the NetWare 3.x server with the NLMs provided by the Novell Upgrade Wizard installation.

All of the options, a through e, are correct.

Question 7

Indicate the correct order of unloading the NLMs on a NetWare 3.12 server that needs to be updated prior to a migration.

1. TSA312
2. AFTER311
3. STREAMS
4. SMDR
5. SMDR31X
6. CLIB
7. SPXS
8. TLI
9. MAC
10. A3112

- ○ a. 1, 2, 3, 4, 5, 6, 7, 8, 9, 10
- ○ b. 1, 4, 5, 7, 8, 2, 6, 10, 3, 9
- ○ c. 1, 3, 5, 7, 9, 2, 4, 6, 8, 10
- ○ d. 10, 9, 8, 7, 6, 5, 4, 3, 2, 1
- ○ e. 1, 2, 4, 6, 8, 10, 3, 5, 7, 9

The correct answer is b. Therefore, answers a, c, d, and e are incorrect.

Question 8

Which of the following are migrated from a NetWare 3.x server to a NetWare 5 network. [Choose the best answers]

- ❑ a. NetWare 3.x file trustee information
- ❑ b. NetWare 3.x user accounts
- ❑ c. NetWare 3.x groups
- ❑ d. NetWare 3.x user account passwords
- ❑ e. NetWare 3.x user account restrictions

All of the options, a through e, are correct.

Question 9

> Which of the following protocols is required to be configured on both the NetWare 3.x server and the NetWare 5 server?
>
> ○ a. IP
> ○ b. TCP
> ○ c. IPX
> ○ d. ARP
> ○ e. NLSP

The correct answer is c. IP can be bound to the server's network board, but it isn't required for the migration. Therefore, answer a is incorrect. TCP is the Transport Control Protocol and is not required for an across-the-wire migration. Therefore, answer b is incorrect. ARP is a protocol in the IP suite and is not required for an across-the-wire migration. Therefore, answer d is incorrect. NLSP is a protocol in the IPX suite and is not required for migration. Therefore, answer e is incorrect.

Question 10

> Which of the following statements about the Novell Upgrade Wizard and across-the-wire migration is correct?
>
> ○ a. An across-the-wire migration is the only upgrade path for a NetWare 3.x server when you want the SYS volume to be a NSS volume.
> ○ b. The Novell Upgrade Wizard is a graphical tool that runs from a workstation. It can be used to upgrade NetWare 2.2 and NetWare 3.2 servers to NetWare 5.
> ○ c. The Novell Upgrade Wizard checks for conflicts and problems before the actual migration of information occurs.
> ○ d. You have the option of moving the NetWare 3.x print configuration to NetWare 5, but it must be converted to NDPS to exist in the NetWare 5 network.
> ○ e. The destination container and/or directories must exist before using the Novell Upgrade Wizard.

The correct answer is c. The SYS volume cannot be a NSS volume. Therefore, answer a is incorrect. The Novell Upgrade Wizard cannot be used to upgrade NetWare 2.2 servers. Therefore, answer b is incorrect. NetWare 5 networks can contain both NDPS and queue-based print configurations. Therefore, answer d is incorrect. The destination container and/or directories can be created with the Novell Upgrade Wizard. Therefore, answer e is incorrect.

Need To Know More?

www.novell.com/netware5/upgrade/ is a Novell Web site that contains useful information for upgrading to NetWare 5. Two articles at this location are relevant to the topics covered in this chapter: "Upgrading From NetWare 3.1x To NetWare 5" and "Novell Upgrade Wizard Step Guide."

www.simware.com/products/rmt/ offers information about the REXXWARE Migration Toolkit.

http://support.novell.com offers TIDs that contain information related to the topics covered in this chapter. At Novell's support Web site, go to the Knowledgebase and perform a search using the following TID numbers:

➤ TID 2943060 NW5 Upgrade Wizard Issues

➤ TID 2944655 Upgrade Wizard Fails To Migrate Trustees

➤ TID 2945381 Upgrade Wizard v2.3

➤ TID 2936905 Upgrade Wizard Trustee Assignments

➤ TID 29455004 NW5 889C Error Running Upgrade Wizard

Traditional NetWare Volumes

Terms you'll need to understand:
- √ Volume
- √ Spanning
- √ Disk blocks
- √ Disk block size
- √ Disk suballocation
- √ Block suballocation
- √ Suballocation Reserved Block (SRB)
- √ Volume compression

Techniques you'll need to master:
- √ Defining a NetWare volume
- √ Describing disk suballocation
- √ Defining volume compression
- √ Identifying the features of traditional NetWare volumes
- √ Creating and configuring traditional NetWare volumes

NetWare 5 servers are commonly used to hold large amounts of data. To make this data more manageable and to provide quicker access, NetWare storage space is logically divided into volumes. In NetWare 5, these volumes can either be created as traditional or Novell Storage Services (NSS) volumes. Traditional volumes are covered in this chapter and are essentially the same as NetWare 4.x volumes. NSS volumes are covered in Chapter 5.

Features Of Traditional NetWare Volumes

When a NetWare 5 server running on IBM-compatible architecture is powered on, the server runs DOS so the main program, SERVER.EXE, can be executed. To store DOS and the server's startup program and files, the startup hard drive must contain a DOS partition, which is usually created and configured before the NetWare 5 installation program is started. Utilities such as FDISK can be used to create this primary DOS partition and make it active. FORMAT is then used with the /S switch, which allows the server to execute the DOS startup files from the hard drive.

All or portions of the remaining non-DOS space on the hard drive (or drives) may be defined as NetWare partitions. NetWare partitions are created during the NetWare 5 server installation process or when additional storage is added. This NetWare partition is then further subdivided into logical units of space called *volumes*.

One physical disk can contain one volume or many volumes. You can also define a volume that uses space from multiple disks. This is called *spanning* and requires the proper amount of hardware fault tolerance in the event of a disk failure. The maximum number of hard drives per volume is 32.

Every NetWare 5 server must have at least one volume, and the name of that volume must be SYS. The SYS volume has to be a traditional volume created on a NetWare partition. The minimum size of the SYS volume when installing NetWare 5 is 500MB. However, the size of the SYS volume on a production-grade server needs to be much larger. The size depends on the services provided by the server and future growth considerations.

> Remember that every NetWare 5 server has at least one volume; this volume's name is SYS, it has to be at least 500MB in size, and it must be a traditional NetWare volume.

Traditional NetWare Volumes

The traditional NetWare volume file system uses a 32-bit interface, which limits the size of the files to a maximum of 4GB each and volumes no larger than 1TB each. Each server has a maximum of 64 traditional volumes and 16 million files per volume. Also, each name space added to a traditional volume reduces the maximum number of files by half. In NetWare 5, you can define up to four NetWare partitions per physical disk. This is a useful management option for very large hard drives. The maximum number of subdirectory levels on a traditional NetWare volume is 100, and the maximum number of open files is 100,000.

The traditional NetWare file system uses file allocation tables (FATs) to organize the storage space. When a traditional volume is placed online (mounted), the entire FAT is placed in RAM. It's from this FAT that the system generates the directory entry tables (DETs). Because the entire FAT of all mounted volumes is cached into memory, the amount of memory the server requires to support these volumes is roughly linear to the number of volumes on the server and the number of files per volume. The larger a volume gets, the more memory NetWare requires to mount the volume. For example, a 10GB volume might require 160MB of RAM, and a 100GB volume would require more—as much as 1GB of RAM. Very large traditional volumes may take several minutes to mount due to the caching of the FATs into memory.

Traditional volumes also support Novell's Transaction Tracking System (TTS). TTS keeps track of all completed transactions. In the event of a failure that causes incomplete transactions, TTS allows you to roll back the transactions to the last good transaction. An example of software that uses TTS is Novell Directory Services (NDS). NDS uses TTS to keep track of changes in the database. In addition, NetWare stores the NDS data in a hidden directory on the SYS volume. This is one of the reasons why the SYS volume on a NetWare 5 server has to be a traditional volume.

When a traditional NetWare 5 volume is created, two features and one value are typically enabled and set. These are block suballocation, volume compression, and optimal disk block sizes.

> **TIP** If a legacy application or data file does not work with block suballocation and/or volume compression, the file can have the DS (don't suballocate) or DC (don't compress) attribute enabled. You can use NetWare Administrator or the FILER or FLAG utility to accomplish this task.

Disk Blocks

Disk block size on a NetWare volume is similar to the term *cluster size*, which refers to the size of the minimum file allocation unit for local hard drives. NetWare allows a disk block size value of 4K, 8K, 16K, 32K or 64K. Using the largest block size results in faster disk operations, because more data can be transferred to and from the disk in a single request. Therefore, a 100K file stored on a 64K block size volume can be read in two disk requests, whereas under a 4K block size volume, the same file would take 25 disk requests. In addition, larger block sizes require less memory because the FATs are smaller and read-ahead operations work faster.

During the creation of a volume, the installation program displays a value for the block size that's dependent on the size of the volume. It's usually recommended that you stick with the default value, which has been selected to provide a balance between file access and disk thrashing. *Disk thrashing* is a term used to define excessive hard drive activity, where the disk's mechanical components are moving constantly to fulfill the disk read and write requests. Table 4.1 lists the recommended disk block sizes.

Block Suballocation

Imagine that a volume has been created that's defined with 64K blocks. This basically means that the storage space on the disk is divided into 64K chunks. When you create and save a new file, the file always begins on a new block whether suballocation is enabled or not.

Block suballocation is the ability to use partially used disk blocks to hold data. Suppose that block suballocation is not enabled and the volume is defined with 4K block sizes. If a user is saving a new 5K file, one block is used for a new file and 1K of the next block is used to hold the rest of the data. The next file is also a 5K file; therefore, one block is used for the new file and the next block is used to hold the rest of the file. After a period of time, the volume storage space is sprinkled with gaps of unused disk space. However, when block suballocation

Table 4.1 NetWare's recommended disk block sizes for traditional volumes.

Volume Size	Disk Block Size
0 to 31MB	4K or 8K
32 to 149MB	16K
150 to 499MB	32K
500MB and larger	64K

is enabled, these unused portions of blocks can be used to save data. Therefore, in the two 5K file examples with suballocation, three blocks are used rather than four blocks without suballocation. Suballocation can make a huge difference in disk space usage—particularly for very large hard drives.

> **EXAM ALERT:** Block suballocation is a feature that's currently available for traditional NetWare volumes only. NetWare 5 NSS volumes do not support block suballocation.

When suballocation is enabled on a volume, the server designates blocks for a specific range of file sizes or ending data fragments. *Data fragments* are the result of data that cannot completely fill a block. Each Suballocation Reserved Block (SRB) is specific to a narrow range of file sizes or ending data fragments based on multiples of 512 bytes. Once an SRB is full, another block is dynamically created and chained to suballocation use. Therefore, there are chains of blocks used specifically for suballocation. All files with fragments in the same range will have their ending data stored in the same SRB chain. As files are created, expanded, or contracted, data may be moved from one SRB to another. This can leave gaps in the SRBs; and because SRBs take up disk space, they're periodically cleaned up by compacting the entire chain and releasing unused blocks for primary storage.

The maximum number of files that can be stored on a volume depends on the number of directory entries and available blocks. Directory entries are used by subdirectories as well as files, and the DET itself is also a file. Because each file requires at least one disk block, the number of files that can be stored on a volume without suballocation is determined by the number of blocks. But with suballocation enabled, significantly more files can be created because each file doesn't necessarily use one complete block.

Suballocation thrashing is caused by low disk space on the volume. This will often cause an increase in server utilization, which can affect other services. Suballocation is a *low-priority thread*, which means that under normal conditions, it only runs when the processor is idle. This state of suballocation is termed *nonaggressive mode*. When less than 10 percent of disk space is available on the volume, suballocation goes into *aggressive mode*. Under these conditions, suballocation is bumped up to a regular priority mode and can take "control" of the server until enough disk space is freed up. This situation can also cause an increase in Receive Discarded, No Available Buffers (called *packet receive buffers* in pre-NetWare 5) and File Service Processes. When the Receive Discarded, No Available Buffers reach their maximum, the server will begin dropping connections and users won't be able to log in and run other services.

Suballocation can also cause disk thrashing when not enough free blocks are available. The lack of free blocks can also cause an increase in server utilization. Lack of free blocks is different than lack of disk space. When files are deleted, they are left in a "deleted" state, which means the file actually exists and is not visible to the user and does not show up in volume statistics as free space. Ideally, you should maintain a minimum of 1,000 free blocks per volume for each NetWare server that has suballocation enabled. In addition, you should use the Purge attribute on directories that hold temporary files and print files.

Volume Compression

Volume compression is the ability to store less frequently used files in a compressed state, thereby making more efficient use of the storage space. Volume compression comes with a number of parameters whose values are set to reduce the impact of the compression action. A newly created volume with compression enabled has these parameters set to the default values.

> Volume compression is a feature that's currently available only for traditional NetWare volumes. NetWare 5 NSS volumes do not support volume compression.

Compression of files does not occur immediately when the file is saved or closed. Rather, NetWare analyzes the files to determine how much space can be saved by compression. If the savings is at least 20 percent and the file has not been accessed for 14 days, the operating system will "mark" the file to be compressed. Then, beginning at midnight, the system begins compressing all marked files until either all marked files are compressed or the time is 6:00 A.M., whichever occurs first.

> The start and stop time values for file compression can be altered and should be adjusted outside the hours of the server's backup and other busy times.

Configuring Traditional NetWare Volumes

The utility for creating and configuring traditional NetWare volumes is NWCONFIG.NLM, which is run on the server. From the initial menu displayed, select Standard Disk Options and then choose NetWare Volume Options. The next screen displays any existing volumes, and you can select one of these and press Enter to view the settings. To create a new volume with any space in a NetWare partition, press the Insert key and then enter a name and size for the volume.

Advantages Of Traditional NetWare Volumes

The advantages traditional NetWare volumes have over NSS volumes are as follows:

- ➤ NetWare compression
- ➤ NetWare disk suballocation
- ➤ Volume space restrictions
- ➤ NetWare disk mirroring and duplexing
- ➤ NetWare auditing
- ➤ NetWare hot fix
- ➤ Directory size restrictions

> Volume compression, suballocation, volume space restrictions, disk mirroring, auditing, hot fix, and directory size restrictions cannot be enabled on NSS volumes.

Practice Questions

Question 1

Which of the following utilities can be used to enable the DS or DC attributes on a file stored on a traditional NetWare volume? [Choose the three best answers]

❑ a. ATTRIB

❑ b. FLAG

❑ c. NetWare Administrator

❑ d. SUBST

❑ e. FILER

The correct answers are b, c, and e. ATTRIB is a DOS utility and cannot be used to set or view NetWare attributes. Therefore, answer a is incorrect. SUBST is a DOS utility used to define a letter to a storage device or area. Therefore, answer d is incorrect.

Question 2

Which of the following statements defines block suballocation on a traditional NetWare volume?

○ a. Portions of new disk blocks are used to save the file's last segment of data.

○ b. A new file created and saved by a user always begins on a new disk block.

○ c. Files that have been compressed by NetWare cannot use block suballocation.

○ d. You can turn off block suballocation with NWCONFIG on a volume that has been created and is actively storing data.

○ e. Files that are stored on a volume using volume compression cannot be compressed.

The correct answer is b. "A new file created and saved by a user always begins on a new disk block" accurately defines block suballocation on a traditional NetWare volume. Portions of partially used disk blocks may be used to save the file's last segment of data. Therefore, answer a is incorrect. Block suballocation and volume compression can both be set on a traditional NetWare volume. Therefore, answers c and e are incorrect. Once a volume has been created and mounted, you cannot turn off block suballocation unless you delete and re-create the volume. Therefore, answer d is incorrect.

Question 3

Which of the following are advantages of the traditional NetWare file system? [Choose the four best answers]

- ❏ a. Disk suballocation can be enabled when the volume is created.
- ❏ b. Traditional volumes support NetWare auditing and hot fix.
- ❏ c. TTS can only be used on NSS volumes because of the number and size of the TTS log files.
- ❏ d. Volume compression can be enabled when the volume is created.
- ❏ e. Traditional NetWare volumes can use Novell's disk-mirroring system.

The correct answers are a, b, d, and e. TTS can only be enabled on traditional NetWare volumes. Therefore, answer c is incorrect.

Question 4

Creating the NetWare 5 SYS volume has several requirements. Which of the following would satisfy those requirements? [Choose the two best answers]

- ❏ a. The minimum size of the NetWare 5 SYS volume has to be at least 5,000MB.
- ❏ b. The amount of memory required to support the SYS volume is dependent on the size of the volume and any additional name spaces.
- ❏ c. The NetWare 5 SYS volume can either be a traditional NetWare volume or a NSS volume.
- ❏ d. The INSTALL.NLM utility is used to view the SYS volume configuration information.
- ❏ e. The minimum size of the NetWare 5 SYS volume has to be at least 500MB.

56   Chapter 4

The correct answers are b and e. Because answer e is correct, answer a is incorrect. The NetWare 5 SYS volume can only be a traditional NetWare volume. Therefore, answer c is incorrect. In NetWare 5, the server utility to view volume configuration information is NWCONFIG.NLM. INSTALL.NLM is the name of a similar utility in NetWare 4.x and NetWare 3.x. Therefore, answer d is incorrect.

Question 5

NetWare volume compression compresses files only when certain criteria are met. Assuming the default settings are used, which of the following are correct? [Choose the best answers]

- a. The server begins compressing files at midnight.
- b. If the server determines that at least 20 percent of disk space will be saved by compressing the file, the file will be marked for compression.
- c. The server will stop compressing files when all the marked files have been compressed or at 6:00 A.M., whichever comes first.
- d. If a file has not been accessed for a month and the amount of disk savings is at least 20 percent, the file will be compressed during the next compression cycle.
- e. Volume compression can be enabled on a volume that's configured with disk suballocation.

All the options, a through e, are correct.

Question 6

> When a traditional NetWare volume is created on a server, the utility displays a default block size. Under which condition(s) should you use these default values? [Choose the best answer(s)]
>
> ○ a. If the volume size is greater than 2TB, you should not use the default block size.
>
> ○ b. You should use the default block size for all sizes of traditional NetWare volumes.
>
> ○ c. The value of the block size should be adjusted to reflect the number of name spaces the volume will support.
>
> ○ d. If after a period of time the server's statistics reflect inefficient disk space usage, you should not use the default value and adjust accordingly.

The correct answer is b. Traditional NetWare volumes cannot be larger than 1TB. Therefore, answer a is incorrect. The size of the block has no dependency on name spaces. Therefore, answer c is incorrect. Once a volume is created, you cannot change the block size. Therefore, answer d is incorrect.

Chapter 4

Question 7

You're embarking on a consulting job to supervise a company's migration from NetWare 3.x to NetWare 5. The following list shows the results of the hardware and software inventory you perform once you're at the client's site:

➤ The NetWare 3.x servers all have 1GB SYS volumes with at least 650MB free space on each system.

➤ The NetWare 4.x server used for testing has disk suballocation and volume compression enabled.

➤ The client is using a third-party NLM for backing up the NetWare 3.x file systems.

➤ The NumCrunch accounting software developed by your client uses NetWare's TTS.

Which of the following choices offer the correct advice for your client? [Choose the best answers]

❑ a. The new NetWare 5 server SYS volume will have disk suballocation and volume compression enabled.

❑ b. The third-party NLM used to backup the NetWare 3.x file system must first be verified to support NetWare 5's NDS stored on the SYS volume.

❑ c. The client's NumCrunch software should be moved to another traditional NetWare volume on the NetWare 5 server to reduce usage of the SYS volume.

❑ d. The NetWare 4.x server's volumes can remain intact, and its tree can be merged with the new NetWare 5 tree you'll create.

❑ e. The default disk block size of the new 2GB NetWare 5 SYS volume will be 64K.

All the options, a through e, are correct answers, which you would not expect and is the reason this is a trick question.

Need To Know More?

http://developer.novell.com/research/appnotes/1994/june/03/04.htm is a 1994 AppNote that covers disk block suballocation.

http://support.novell.com offers TIDs that contain information related to the topics covered in this chapter. At Novell's support Web site, go to the Knowledgebase and search using the following TID numbers:

➤ TID 1005436 Suballocation And High Utilization

➤ TID 1202046 NetWare 3.x And 4.x Directory Entry Limits

➤ TID 2943794 Vrepair Will Not Function On A Traditional Vol

➤ TID 1000173 Adding Volume Segment In NetWare

➤ TID 2942254 NetWare 5 Advanced Volume Features

➤ TID 2944093 HCSS Not Supported On NW5

NSS Volumes

Terms you'll need to understand:
- Novell Storage Services (NSS)
- B-tree
- Provider
- NSS Media Manager Provider (MMPRV)
- NSS File Provider (NWPRV)
- Consumer
- Storage group

Techniques you'll need to master:
- Defining Novell Storage Services (NSS)
- Describing the components of NSS: providers, consumers, and storage groups
- Identifying the advantages and limitations of NSS volumes
- Creating NSS volumes, starting with the providers, to specifying the sizes and names of the NSS volumes

One of the key new features of NetWare 5 is *Novell Storage Services* (*NSS*). This new system for managing storage space eliminates many of the constraints of the traditional NetWare file system. NSS provides the ability to create very large volumes that contain many files and mount extremely fast without extra memory overhead. Furthermore, NSS works in conjunction with the traditional NetWare file system, giving you more flexibility on how you design your file storage needs.

In this chapter, you'll learn the structure of NSS, the advantages and limitations of NSS volumes, and the procedures for creating a NSS-managed storage space.

Features Of NSS Volumes

NSS uses a 64-bit interface to manage storage space, which permits much larger volumes than the 32-bit traditional NetWare file system. The maximum size of a NSS volume is 8 exabytes (8EB), and the maximum file size is 8 terabytes (8TB). NSS volumes can hold billions of files, and there's no limit to the number of NSS volumes on a NetWare 5 server. Novell engineers have tested NSS volumes with more than one billion files. NSS volumes theoretically support 2^{64} files per volume.

> *Note:* *NSS volumes allow the storage of very large files. The maximum size of a file on a NSS volume is 8TB. The maximum file size on a traditional NetWare file system volume is 4GB.*

No special or new hardware or additional memory is needed to support NSS volumes. It's an optional NetWare 5 file system, and it works with traditional NetWare file system volumes. The goal of NSS is to provide a method of managing storage space that will suit your server's storage needs into the next decade.

How NSS Organizes Storage Space

NSS permits full utilization of the NetWare 5 server's disk space and is designed to eventually support every type of storage space. NSS was structured to make use of the server's storage space regardless of the location or type of the physical storage device. This includes space that's used or unused, traditional file system partitions or volumes, and unpartitioned storage space.

One of the major advantages of NSS is the ability to support very large volumes that contain many files. A reason for this is that NSS does not use the file allocation tables (FATs) that traditional volumes use to indicate where files are located in the volume space. Instead, NSS uses a very efficient organizational

NSS Volumes 63

structure called *B-trees*, or *balanced trees*. By using B-trees, NSS can retrieve file blocks that are not in the server's memory within four processor cycles.

When you install a server, a minimum of two partitions exist: a DOS partition to launch the server and a NetWare partition to hold the SYS volume. With the initial release of NSS for NetWare 5, the SYS volume must be a traditional NetWare file system volume. Any other volume you create can be a NSS volume or a traditional NetWare volume.

NSS organizes unused space into storage groups and volumes. Depending on how many physical storage devices the server has, you may have several storage groups and NSS volumes in your configuration. Before you can create storage groups, the system must determine what free space is available. The NSS provider identifies free space and the NSS consumer registers the found free space to NSS. Once these deposits of free space are registered, you create storage groups and organize the space into NSS volumes.

> NSS is an optional file system compatible with the traditional NetWare file system. The maximum size of a NSS volume is 8EB, and the maximum file size is 8TB. NSS uses B-trees to locate data instead of FAT. The initial release of NetWare 5 and NSS specifies that the SYS volume cannot be a NSS volume.

Provider

The role of a NSS provider is to scan all the storage devices and locate free space. There are two providers supplied with NetWare 5—the NSS Media Manager Provider (MMPRV) and the NSS File Provider (NWPRV)—and each represents a particular type of storage area.

The MMPRV provider scans for free space on IBM-formatted partitions. An IBM-formatted partition is space that's neither a NetWare partition nor a DOS partition. It's space on a hard drive that's low-level formatted but not high-level formatted. When you purchase a drive from a vendor, it's usually low-level formatted. This preparation of the hard drive is referred to as *IBM formatted*. If the vendor has used utilities such as FDISK and FORMAT to create DOS partitions that occupy the entire disk space, you need to remove these partitions. This is necessary if you want to use the MMPRV provider to find free drive space. To remove the DOS and extended-DOS partitions, you can use FDISK or any other compatible partition-removal application. Of course, if the hard disk is the server's startup drive that will contain the SYS volume, the drive will still need a primary DOS partition and a NetWare partition.

The second provider supplied with NetWare 5 is NWPRV; it's not loaded automatically when NSS is loaded. However, you can load it by entering

"NWPRV.NSS" at the server console. This provider searches for free space on traditional NetWare file system volumes.

Once these areas of free space, called *storage deposits*, are identified, the spaces you want to use with NSS need to be registered with a consumer.

Consumer

The *consumer* is a component of NSS that registers the free space to be managed by NSS so other storage file systems cannot claim the same space. The NSS consumers also handle the logical input and output data paths so NSS knows where the data resides.

NSS consists of three types of consumers:

- **DOS consumer** The DOS consumer's role is to recognize primary DOS partitions, and make them available for mounting as NSS volumes. Free space from DOS partitions doesn't get registered with NSS by the DOS consumer.

- **CD-ROM consumer** The CD-ROM consumer recognizes CD-ROMs and marks them as read-only so their free space doesn't appear as available to a NSS volume.

- **ZLSS consumer** The ZLSS consumer is the one most often used; it communicates with available free disk space.

Not all objects can be registered to NSS because their free space is not available to the user for data storage. Examples of this are CD-ROMs. NSS will manage CD-ROMs but will not list their free space as a storage deposit because it's read-only space.

The NSS consumer service is the default consumer, which means this free space is now part of a NSS partition. Once the free space is registered by a consumer, you can decide how much space you want for storage groups and NSS volumes.

Storage Group

With the amount of free space discovered by the providers and registered by the consumers, you can group these storage deposits into storage groups. You can either choose to create one storage group from all the free space found or to create several storage groups.

Once you have your storage groups defined, you create your NSS volumes. You specify the names and sizes of the NSS volumes in a process similar to how you

NSS Volumes

create traditional NetWare file system volumes. Once the NSS volumes are created, you mount and unmount them using the same commands and procedures as with traditional NetWare volumes. The presentation of the NSS volumes to the client is the same as traditional volumes; there's no indication of any differences.

> **EXAM ALERT**
>
> NSS uses providers to scan the storage space for free areas. Two providers are supplied with NetWare 5: MMPRV and NWPRV. MMPRV scans IBM-formatted partitions, and NWPRV scans traditional NetWare file system volumes.

Support For CD-ROMs And Server DOS Partitions

One of the nice features of NSS is the enhanced support for CD-ROMs. Without NSS support, you have to load CDROM.NLM, insert the CD-ROM, mount the CD-ROM, and then wait for the index to be built or read from the CD-ROM before it's available for use. In NetWare 5, after NSS is loaded, all you need to do is load the CD9660.NSS module and insert the CD-ROM. The CD9660.NSS module automatically checks the CD-ROM drives and automatically mounts any CD-ROMs physically located in the bays. When you eject a CD-ROM, it's unmounted automatically.

Another very nice feature of NSS is the ability to mount the server's DOS partition as a volume so you can easily access the server's files and directories. In previous versions of NetWare, this was often an inconvenient task because you had to bring the server down to access the DOS partition. You could also access the DOS partition without bringing the server down using NetBasic, which allows you to perform some DOS-based tasks.

In NetWare 5, with NSS loaded, you can enter "DOSFAT.NSS" at the server console to mount the server's primary DOS partition as a volume titled DOSFAT_C, which is visible from a client workstation. Now you can easily copy, move, or perform various available tasks from a client workstation just as you would with any other NetWare volume. When you're done with the volume, you can unmount it like any other NetWare volume.

> **TIP**
>
> The ability to mount NetWare 5 server primary DOS partitions as volumes is very handy for administrative tasks. However, it's recommended that you don't leave the DOS partition mounted other than for administrative tasks to reduce unauthorized access.

ALERT: In NetWare 5, CD-ROMs are mounted automatically when CD9660.NSS is loaded. You can also mount the server's DOS primary partition by entering "DOSFAT.NSS" at the server console.

Advantages Of NSS Volumes

NSS-managed storage space offers several advantages compared to the traditional NetWare file system. Some of these advantages were discussed in the previous section. The following list describes some additional advantages:

- On a NetWare 5 server, you can mount an unlimited number of NSS volumes. The workstation software limits the number of volumes visible to the client at his or her workstation. The current maximum number of volumes visible to the user is 253. A NetWare 5 server can mount a maximum of 64 traditional NetWare file system volumes.

- NSS allows an unlimited number of directory levels. However, the number of levels visible by a client is based on the client's software limitations. A traditional NetWare file system volume allows only a maximum of 100 directory levels.

- NSS allows extremely fast volume mount times regardless of the NSS volume size. In most cases, mounting and rebuilding a NSS volume takes less than a minute. Novell has demonstrated the ability to mount a NSS volume with 400 million files in 3 seconds. The reason for these fast volume mounts is because NSS uses B-trees instead of FATs to keep track of file locations.

- NSS volumes have very fast recovery times when there's a corruption due to events such as a server crash. When a traditional file system volume crashes, the recovery process may take several minutes or longer because the system must scan the entire volume for corruption. In the traditional NetWare file system, creating, modifying, and deleting file operations are recorded in memory. When the server is not busy, these operations are then written to the hard drive. This procedure of holding changes in memory could result in problems if the user has made changes to the volume and the server crashes before the changes are written to the disk.

  The VREPAIR utility is used to restore traditional NetWare file system volumes. The utility scans the entire volume, and it may have to re-create the FATs from scratch in an attempt to match the copies of the FATs stored on the volume. If the volume is large, this may take a long time, ranging from minutes to hours.

NSS Volumes

On a damaged NSS volume, the system quickly "replays" data that has not been changed, and the volume is back online in less than a minute. Every change on a NSS volume is associated with a *transaction*. A transaction includes all the steps to complete a single change. Depending on the type of change, this may actually be several steps, and the entire process to accomplish the task is one transaction. Each transaction on an NSS volume is recorded in a journal, which is stored on the volume. The size of the journal files tends to be small because they're not dependent on the size of the volume, but rather the volume's modification rate. When all the steps that make up a journal entry are completed, the system removes the successful transaction from the journal. If the server crashes at any step that makes up a particular file action, the journal entries indicate which of the steps were successful before the crash. When the NSS volume is brought back online, the system "undoes" the completed steps in the partial transaction and puts the system back before the unsuccessful file action was attempted. The utility that performs these actions is NSS.NLM, using the /REBUILDVOLUME and /VERIFYVOLUME switches.

If there are no problems with a NSS volume and you unmount the volume, the journal files will have no transaction entries. Therefore, when you remount the volume, it's extremely fast because there are no journal entries to "play back." Novell states that it takes approximately one-tenth of one second to remount an undamaged NSS volume, regardless of size.

➤ The size of the NSS volume has no effect on the server's memory requirements. This is in contrast to the traditional NetWare file system, where the amount of memory to support traditional volumes rises as the size of the volume increases. According to Novell, a server with only 32MB of memory can mount any size NSS volume.

➤ NSS allows a much larger number of files to be open at any point in time. NSS allows 1 million files to be open simultaneously. This is in contrast to the traditional file system volumes, which only permit 100,000 open files per server.

➤ NSS is not tied to a NetWare partition as the traditional NetWare volumes are. NSS "pools" and uses all available space on all storage devices and is not limited by the physical storage on a particular device.

➤ NSS supports an unlimited number of extended attributes and data streams. A traditional NetWare volume has a limit of 16 attributes and 10 data streams.

Chapter 5

➤ NSS supports Unicode, which allows much more flexibility in international organizations. The traditional NetWare file system supports ASCII double-byte characters, which are more restrictive for internationalization issues.

ALERT

Here's a list of the major advantages of NSS:

➤ Volume sizes up to 8EB
➤ Files sizes up to 8TB
➤ Unlimited number of NSS volumes per server
➤ Unlimited number of files per volume
➤ Very fast volume mounts
➤ Very fast volume recovery time
➤ No extra memory overhead requirements
➤ Enhanced CD-ROM support

Limitations Of NSS

The first release of NetWare 5 includes the first release of NSS. The items in the following list are the NSS limitations applicable to the first release of NetWare 5 and NSS. Some of them may disappear as NSS continues to evolve:

➤ The following features are not supported on NSS volumes, but they are available on traditional NetWare file system volumes:

➤ **Transaction Tracking System (TTS)** Applications that use NetWare TTS have the ability to "roll back" incomplete transactions when a failure occurs. An example of a system that uses TTS is Novell Directory Services (NDS). NSS volumes do not support TTS-based applications or systems.

➤ **Disk striping** When a system has several disk drives, you can spread the data across the multiple devices in segments called *stripes*. This often helps to improve read and write speed. NSS volumes do not support disk striping.

➤ **Disk mirroring** Mirroring of data allows you to maintain a complete copy of your volumes on another storage device. In the event of a failure of the primary drive, the mirrored drive provides access to the data. NSS does not support disk mirroring, which is a low-level form of hardware fault tolerance.

NSS Volumes

- **Hierarchical Storage Management (HSM) and Real Time Data Migration (RTDM)** These systems are used by some third-party vendors as methods of accessing and managing data. If the vendor's software is using HSM or RTDM, you'll need to check for an update of the product that does not rely on HSM or RTDM.

- Traditional NetWare volumes have the ability to compress less frequently accessed data to maximize usage of the storage space. NSS volumes do not support NetWare volume compression.

- The NetWare 5 SYS volume must be a traditional NetWare file system volume and cannot be a NSS volume. One reason is related to NDS, which stores data on the SYS volume and uses TTS to maintain database integrity.

> **EXAM ALERT**
>
> Major limitations of NSS are as follows:
> - No support for TTS
> - Volumes cannot use disk striping or disk mirroring
> - No support for HSM or RTDM
> - Volume compression is not available

Creating A NSS Volume

In the initial release of NSS, you'll probably create your storage groups and volumes from unused and unpartitioned physical hard disk space. However, if you upgrade a server using the In-Place Upgrade (covered in Chapter 2), all the physical hard disk space may already be allocated to the DOS partition and NetWare partitions. In this situation, you have some options to consider:

- The NSS product includes an In-Place Upgrade utility that's designed to convert existing traditional NetWare file system volumes, except the SYS volume, to NSS. The utility, IPCU.NLM, is run on the server.

- If you have space on a hard disk that's not part of a DOS or NetWare partition, this space can be registered to NSS.

- Unused, existing traditional NetWare file system volume space can be assigned to NSS to manage.

- You can delete the server's existing traditional NetWare volumes and repartition the NetWare partition for the SYS volume and leave the remaining space open for NSS. Of course, if you want to retain the data on the traditional volumes, you must back up the data before repartitioning.

Chapter 5

▶ If none of these options are appealing, you can install a new hard drive or drives and dedicate this space to NSS.

To create a NSS volume, perform the following steps:

1. At the server console, enter "NWCONFIG". This loads the utility to perform all the steps to create a NSS volume.

2. Select NSS Disk Options. This automatically loads NSS.NLM if it's not already loaded.

3. From the options displayed, select Storage. The next series of screens allows you to scan for available disk space and to register the space with a consumer.

4. From the Available NSS Storage Options menu displayed, select Update Provider Information.

5. The next screen displays the available providers from which you can choose. If you do not see the NWPRV entry for scanning NetWare partitions, exit the screen and switch to the server console. At the server console, enter "NWPRV.NSS" and then return to the NWCONFIG screen. Select Update Provider Information again, and this time you'll see NWPRV listed in addition to MMPRV.

6. To scan for free space on unpartitioned areas, select the MMPRV provider and press Enter. The resulting screen indicates whether the scan was successful.

7. Select Assign Ownership from the available options. This screen displays a list of free space objects that NSS can own and manage. Select the space you want NSS to own and press Enter.

8. Choose the Return To Previous Menu option to return to the NSS Disk Options menu.

9. Select NSS Volume Options from the items displayed. You'll have to authenticate to NDS with NDS Supervisor rights.

10. From the Available NSS Volume Options menu, choose Create. This allows you to create storage groups and NSS volumes.

11. At the Select Create Options menu presented, select Storage Group. Specify the default size of the storage group or modify the size. Press Esc to return to the Select Create Options menu.

12. Choose NSS Volume from the items displayed and enter the size and name of the volume at the appropriate prompts.

13. Exit the NWCONFIG utility, and your NSS volume is ready to use.

NSS Volumes

NSS.NLM has many options, and the best way to see what's available is to enter "NSS –HELP" at the server console screen when NSS is loaded. NSS has a MENU option that allows you to do some of the previous steps without loading the NWCONFIG utility.

> **EXAM ALERT**
>
> Make sure you're comfortable with the process of creating a NSS volume from scratch—that is, from provider scan, to consumer registration, to storage group specification and volume creation.

Practice Questions

Question 1

Which NetWare 5 utility is used to create NSS volumes?
- ○ a. INSTALL
- ○ b. NDS Manager
- ○ c. NetWare Administrator
- ○ d. NSSCONFIG
- ○ e. NWCONFIG

The correct answer is e. NWCONFIG is the utility used to create NSS volumes. INSTALL is a NetWare 3.x and 4.x utility. Therefore, answer a is incorrect. NDS Manager is a Windows-based utility that's used to manage NDS partitions and replicas. Therefore, answer b is incorrect. NetWare Administrator can be used to view NSS volume information, but it cannot be used to create new NSS volumes. Therefore, answer c is incorrect. NSSCONFIG does not exist. Therefore, answer d is incorrect.

Question 2

Which of the following statements defines an NSS provider?
- ○ a. NSS providers are separate NLMs that are installed to register free space with NSS storage areas.
- ○ b. NSS providers scan the server's hard disk space to locate unused space.
- ○ c. NSS providers allow the SYS volume to use NSS because the providers support TTS.
- ○ d. NSS providers are added to the workstation connection software so the administrator can manage NSS volumes.
- ○ e. NSS providers scan the server's memory, determine which file blocks are in RAM, and register this information with NSS.

The correct answer is b. NSS providers scan the server's hard disk space to locate unused space. NSS providers are separate NLMs, but they are not used to register the space—registration of free space is done by the consumers. Therefore, answer a is incorrect. The SYS volume cannot be a NSS volume, and the providers have nothing to do with TTS. Therefore, answer c is incorrect. NSS providers are NLMs running on the server. Therefore, answer d is incorrect. Providers do not perform any actions on the server's memory. Therefore, answer e is incorrect.

Question 3

Which of the following are advantages of NSS volumes? [Choose the best answers]

- a. NSS volumes can be as large as 8EB.
- b. Files of up to 8TB can be stored on a NSS volume.
- c. You can have any number of NSS volumes you want on a NetWare 5 server.
- d. A NSS volume mounts faster that a traditional NetWare file system volume.
- e. The size of a traditional NetWare volume may require more memory. The NetWare 5 server can mount any size NSS volume without any need for additional memory.

All of the options, a through e, are correct answers.

Question 4

Which of the following statements define NSS storage groups? [Choose the two best answers]

- a. Storage groups are created from the storage deposits discovered by the NSS providers and registered by the NSS consumers.
- b. Storage groups represent the space already occupied by the DOS partition and NetWare partitions so the space cannot be used by NSS.
- c. Storage groups represent specific types of physical devices such as CD-ROMs and hard drives.
- d. Storage groups allow you to mount the server's DOS partition as a NetWare volume.
- e. Once storage groups are defined, you can create NSS volumes.

74 Chapter 5

The correct answers are a and e. Storage groups are created from the storage deposits discovered by the NSS providers and registered by the NSS consumers; and once storage groups are defined, you can create NSS volumes. Storage groups represent free space, not occupied space. Therefore, answer b is incorrect. One of the advantages of NSS is the elimination of the volume's linkage to specific physical devices. Therefore, answer c is incorrect. Storage groups have no involvement in the server's DOS partition. Therefore, answer d is incorrect.

Question 5

Which of the following statements defines a NSS consumer?

- ○ a. NSS consumers represent the entries on a file or directory ACL and specify the privileges the user, or consumer, has at that location.
- ○ b. NSS consumers group the storage deposits the NSS providers have discovered into storage groups.
- ○ c. NSS consumers scan the server's hard disk space to locate unused space.
- ○ d. NSS consumers register the free space found by the NSS providers so other systems cannot claim the same space.
- ○ e. NSS consumers allow you to define the sizes and names of the NSS volumes.

The correct answer is d. NSS consumers register the free space found by the NSS providers so other systems cannot claim the same space. Consumers are not involved in file system security. Therefore, answer a is incorrect. The NSS consumers are not involved in the creation of storage groups. Therefore, answer b is incorrect. NSS providers scan the hard disks for free space. Therefore, answer c is incorrect. NSS consumers are not involved in the definition of the NSS volume names or sizes. Therefore, answer e is incorrect.

NSS Volumes 75

Question 6

> Which of the following are limitations of NSS? [Choose the three best answers]
>
> ☐ a. NSS volumes support disk mirroring, but not disk striping.
> ☐ b. NSS volumes cannot take advantage of NetWare 5 volume compression.
> ☐ c. NSS volumes can take advantage of NetWare 5 volume compression.
> ☐ d. An application that uses TTS to maintain information integrity cannot be stored on a NSS volume.
> ☐ e. The NetWare 5 SYS volume must be a traditional NetWare file system volume.

The correct answers are b, d, and e. NSS volumes do not support either disk striping or disk mirroring. Therefore, answer a is incorrect. Because answer b is correct, answer c is incorrect.

Question 7

> You have just installed a new NetWare 5 server and need to mount a CD-ROM on the server. Which of the following are possible correct actions to take to mount the CD-ROM on the server? [Choose the two best answers]
>
> ☐ a. Insert the CD-ROM in the CD-ROM bay.
> ☐ b. Enter "CDROM.NLM" at the server's command prompt.
> ☐ c. Enter "CD9660.NSS" at the server's command prompt.
> ☐ d. Enter the **MOUNT ALL** command at the server's console to mount the CD-ROM.
> ☐ e. To ensure that the CD-ROM's index is new, enter "CDROM PURGE" at the server's command prompt.

The correct answers are a and c. You could insert the CD-ROM in the CD-ROM bay or enter "CD9660.NSS" at the server's command prompt. The CDROM.NLM is the utility used in NetWare 3.x and NetWare 4.x servers to enable CD-ROM support. Therefore, answer b is incorrect. In NetWare 5 with NSS, CD-ROMs are automatically mounted. Therefore, answer d is incorrect. With NSS, the CD-ROM's index files are not used. Therefore, answer e is incorrect.

Chapter 5

Question 8

One of the features of NSS allows you to mount the server's primary DOS partition as a volume. Which of the following is the correct procedure to mount the DOS partition?

- ○ a. Enter "DOSFAT_C.NSS" at the server's command prompt.
- ○ b. In the NWCONFIG utility, use the NSS Options menu to scan the server's hard drives and to create a DOSFAT partition.
- ○ c. Enter "DOSFAT.NSS" at the server's command prompt.
- ○ d. If the server had been upgraded to NetWare 5 using the In-Place Upgrade, the server's DOS partition cannot be mounted as a volume.
- ○ e. Enter "ENABLE DOS" and then enter "MOUNT DOSFAT_C" at the server's command prompt to make the volume visible.

The correct answer is c. Enter "DOSFAT.NSS" at the server's command prompt to mount the DOS partition. The name of a server's DOS partition when it's mounted as a NSS volume is DOSFAT_C. Therefore, answer a is incorrect. The NWCONFIG utility is not involved in mounting the server's DOS partition. Therefore, answer b is incorrect. The procedure used to create the NetWare 5 server has no reflection on the ability to mount the server's DOS partition. Therefore, answer d is incorrect. There is no command titled ENABLE DOS that permits the mounting of the server's DOS partition. Therefore, answer e is incorrect.

Question 9

The following is a list of the steps necessary to create a NSS volume. Which of the following choices presents the correct order of these steps?

1. Select Update Provider Information from the Available NSS Storage Options menu.
2. Choose Create from the Available NSS Volume Options menu to create the NSS volume.
3. From the Available NSS Volume Options menu, choose Create to create the storage group.
4. Enter "NWCONFIG" at the server console.
5. Select Assign Ownership from the Available NSS Storage Options menu.

○ a. 4, 5, 1, 3, 2.
○ b. 4, 1, 3, 2, 5.
○ c. 4, 3, 2, 1, 5.
○ d. 4, 5, 3, 2, 1.
○ e. 4, 1, 5, 3, 2.

The correct answer is e. First, you enter "NWCONFIG" at the server console. Second, you select Update Provider Information from the Available NSS Storage Options menu. Third, you select Assign Ownership from the Available NSS Storage Options menu. Fourth, from the Available NSS Volume Options menu, choose Create to create the storage group. And, finally, you choose Create from the Available NSS Volume Options menu to create the NSS volume.

Question 10

You have won the bid to advise a large government agency on its Y2K project. Part of the project involves upgrading the agency's NetWare 3.2 server to NetWare 5. Because the hardware was purchased recently and is Y2K compliant, the agency will be using the In-Place Upgrade to move the NetWare 3.2 server to NetWare 5. The following is a list of the hardware and partition information you have collected on the NetWare 3.2 server along with other information:

➤ The NetWare 3.2 server has a 1GB SYS volume with 700MB of free space.

➤ The NetWare 3.2 server has two internal hard drives. The first drive contains the SYS volume and a DATA volume. The second hard drive has not been used and was part of the system when purchased from the vendor.

➤ The tracking software used by the agency is predicted to create millions of files. Some of these files will hold data for entire states and will grow to be several terabytes in the next few years.

➤ The accounting software the agency is running uses TTS to maintain the integrity of the application's data files.

Which of the following choices offers good advice for your client? [Choose the two best answers]

❏ a. Because the existing SYS volume is large enough and the DATA volume is a traditional NetWare volume, place the accounting software on the DATA volume.

❏ b. The existing SYS volume is large enough, but the DATA volume, a traditional NetWare volume, cannot be used to house the accounting software unless you use IPCU.NLM to convert DATA to a NSS volume.

❏ c. Remove any existing partitions on the second unused drive and dedicate this space to NSS to hold the tracking software.

❏ d. Advise the agency to purchase several more hard drives of the same size as the second unused hard drive. Then, after these are installed, create this new space as NSS volumes and enable disk striping to decrease read and write access time.

❏ e. Because the agency will be using the In-Place Upgrade to move from NetWare 3.2 to NetWare 5, it will be able to use volume compression on any new NSS volumes that are created.

The correct answers are a and c. You should tell your client that because the existing SYS volume is large enough and the DATA volume is a traditional NetWare volume, it should place the accounting software on the DATA volume. Also, it should remove any existing partitions on the second, unused drive and dedicate this space to NSS to hold the tracking software. Because the accounting software is using TTS, it cannot reside on a NSS volume. Therefore, answer b is incorrect. NSS volumes cannot take advantage of disk striping. Therefore, answer d is incorrect. One of the limitations of NSS volumes is the inability to support volume compression. Therefore, answer e is incorrect. This is labeled as a trick question not to confuse you, but to incorporate a lot of the advantages and limitations of NSS in one question.

Need To Know More?

www.novell.com/whitepapers contains several Novell white papers related to NetWare 5—one of which is dedicated to Novell Storage Services.

www.novell.com/products/nss/ is an area of Novell's Web site that is dedicated entirely to NSS.

www.novell.com/products/nss/whtpaper.html is another version of the NSS white paper; it contains some graphics to illustrate the NSS concepts.

www.novell.com/products/nss/prodinfo.html takes you to the document "Novell Storage Services (NSS) Product Information/README," which is a good source of information on NSS.

http://support.novell.com offers TIDs that contain information related to the topics covered in this chapter. At Novell's support Web site, go to the Knowledgebase and search using the following TID numbers:

➤ TID 2942686 What Is Novell Storage Services (NSS)

➤ TID 2942059 Create NSS Vol On Traditional NetWare Volume

➤ TID 2942350 NSS Administration Utility

➤ TID 2942349 NSS Command Line Options

➤ TID 2942352 How To Mount DOS Partition As A Volume

➤ TID 2943794 Vrepair Will Not Function On A Traditional Volume

➤ TID 2942838 Cannot Do Space Restrictions On NSS Volume

File System Design

Terms you'll need to understand:

- √ Volume
- √ Directory
- √ SYS volume
- √ System-created directory
- √ Application directory
- √ Home directory
- √ Shared data directory
- √ Profile directory

Techniques you'll need to master:

- √ Planning and setting up custom NetWare volumes
- √ Listing the system-created directories and their contents
- √ Listing the directories suggested for customizing the file system
- √ Identifying strengths and weaknesses in different directory designs
- √ Planning and creating a custom directory structure based on a given scenario

In this chapter, we look at designing and setting up a customized network file system based on the features of Novell's traditional NetWare file system. Novell Storage Services (NSS), an optional file system available with NetWare 5, was discussed in Chapter 5. Included in this chapter is an overview of the built-in features of the NetWare file system, suggestions for customizing the directory structure, and an analysis of the advantages and disadvantages of several styles of directory design.

Features Of The Traditional NetWare File System

A properly designed network file system allows controlled user access to shared storage media. As a result, users can run shared copies of applications, rapidly access shared data, and store personal files on the shared media without compromising performance or privacy. In addition, users gain the following benefits:

➤ Increased personal storage space due to the larger capacity typical of network storage devices.

➤ The convenience of having personal data archived during system backups.

➤ The additional security features offered by the network operating system (NOS).

NetWare File System Components

The NetWare file system uses logically defined volumes as the highest level in the file system. The volumes are divided into logical storage units called *directories*. The directories, in turn, may contain files and additional subdirectories.

Some of the directories in the NetWare file system are created automatically by the NOS. The other directories should be administratively planned and created to leverage the features of the system-created directory structure. Knowledgeable planning accomplishes this in a way that best meets the needs and capacities of the network.

Planning the directory structure should be done with the following goals in mind:

➤ It should be easy to use.

➤ It should be easy to manage administratively.

➤ It should be easy to secure.

The goals are met, in part, if the directory structure is kept simple and intuitive. This allows users and administrators to navigate the file system without difficulty. To enhance the intuitiveness and navigability of the system, you should create short, meaningful volume and directory names that suggest content or who's likely to have access.

In the following sections, you're introduced to several critical design issues. Suggestions are provided for methods to address the issues. Also included are general guidelines for you to follow when taking into account the variables posed by differences in organizational structures.

Because volumes form the basic unit of storage in the NetWare file system, the first step to setting up the file system is creating volumes. The following section introduces you to the concepts and guidelines you need to be familiar with as you begin this process.

Creating System And Custom Volumes

Due to certain limitations of NSS, the System volume (or *SYS volume*) must use the traditional NetWare file system. You can create custom volumes that use the traditional NetWare file system during installation at the time the SYS volume is defined and created. You can create additional volumes, as needed, at any time—as long as free space is available on a NetWare partition.

System Volumes

A SYS volume is required on every NetWare server and is the only volume required in the traditional NetWare file system. It contains system files and utilities and includes the Novell Directory Services (NDS) database. The following guidelines should be used with the SYS volume:

➤ Reserve the SYS volume for NetWare files and create additional volumes to store application and data files. This makes the SYS volume less volatile and reduces the chance of it running out of disk space.

➤ Make the volume large enough to accommodate the NDS database and periodic system updates and enhancements. The NDS database is located in a hidden directory at the root of the SYS volume. Free space, on a volume sized to accommodate only the visible NetWare files, can become critically low as the network grows and new objects are added to the Directory database. Although space can be added to the SYS volume, the process may require considerably more effort than planning the initial size with future growth in mind.

Custom Volumes

The creation of additional volumes is the first step to customizing the network file system. Use the following guidelines when planning new volumes:

- ▶ If your network includes multiple client operating systems that use different file types, and the users do not share files, consider creating separate volumes to store each operating system's files. Accommodating multiple name spaces on each volume, when it's not required, results in unnecessary overhead.

- ▶ If the users accessing the network from clients with different file systems share files, ensure that all appropriate name spaces are enabled on the volumes where the shared files are stored.

- ▶ Enable long name space capability on all volumes accessed from workstations requiring long file names.

- ▶ Create one volume per physical disk if fault tolerance is more important than performance. If one drive fails, the data in other volumes is unaffected.

- ▶ To improve performance, you can span a volume across multiple disks. With more input/output (I/O) channels available, read and write access time is improved; however, failure of one disk in the volume set makes the data on the other disks unavailable. To ensure fault tolerance, each hard disk in the set should be duplexed.

- ▶ Give volumes descriptive names that are meaningful. DATA, APPS, QUEUES, and PAYROLL are examples of possible names that give an indication of a volume's content.

Once the volumes are planned and created, the directory structure is created. Remember that the features of the system-created directory structure should be leveraged to your benefit. In the following section, you'll identify the system-created directories and become familiar with their contents.

System-Created Directories

During installation, the operating system creates several files and directories on the SYS volume. Most are created as the SYS volume is mounted for the first time; others are created as products and options are installed. The directories are created to contain system files used to maintain normal server operations. The names and locations of the system-created directories are critical to their functionality. Modifying them in any way could result in severe operational

File System Design **85**

problems with NetWare. Unless you happen to have an inordinate amount of time on your hands for disaster recovery, don't delete, rename, or move any of these directories. Figure 6.1 shows a typical set of system-created directories located on the SYS volume after a NetWare 5 installation.

You need to be familiar with the contents of the following system-created directories:

➤ **LOGIN** This is the only NetWare network directory accessible prior to a successful login. The LOGIN directory contains the programs necessary for you to log into the network, along with additional utilities that aid you in locating and attaching to other available servers.

➤ **PUBLIC** This directory contains the network programs, files, and utilities that network users can execute. All logged-in users have default access to the PUBLIC directory. Examples of programs include NWADMIN32 and NWBACKUP32.

➤ **SYSTEM** This directory contains the NetWare Loadable Modules (NLMs) and many of the configuration files necessary for server startup. It also contains supervisory tools used to configure and manage the server. By default, no user receives explicit rights to this directory.

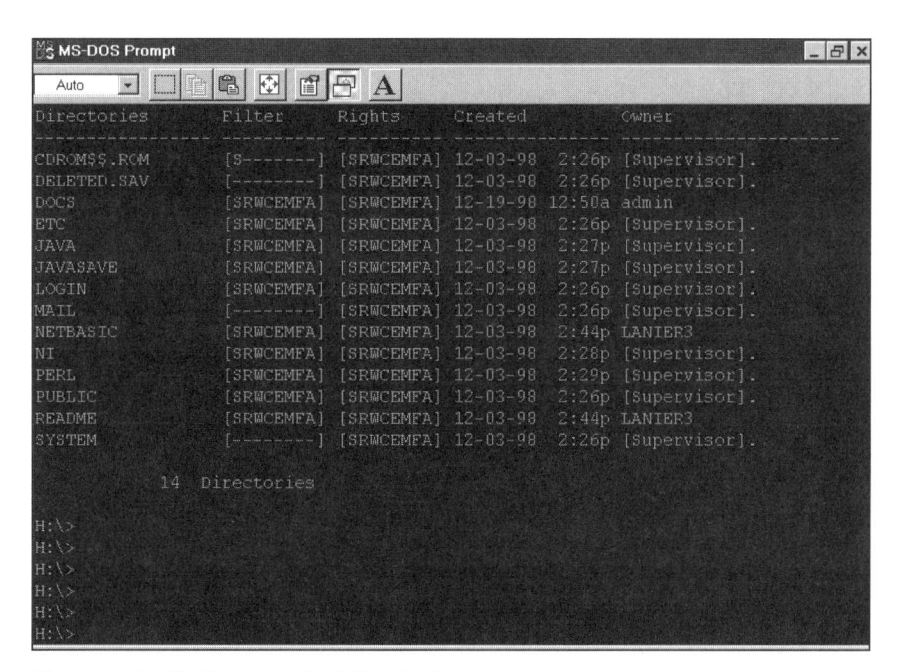

Figure 6.1 System-created directories.

TIP: The original Admin account is the only account allowed access to the SYSTEM directory without an administrative trustee (security) assignment being made. The access rights of the system-created Admin account are the result of a default trustee assignment for the original Admin account of Supervisor to the NDS file server object. The assignment gives all rights to the file system and is necessary for setting up and customizing the file system.

ALERT: Do not confuse the SYSTEM directory with the SYS volume. They are two different entities.

- **DELETED.SAV** Files that are deleted from the NetWare file system are tagged as deleted and hidden. They remain in the directory they were deleted from until they are either purged from the system administratively or removed by the system to make room for newer deleted files as the volume becomes full. If the original directory is deleted, the deleted files that were in that directory are moved to the DELETED.SAV directory located at the root of each volume. The files are stored there and are available for salvage until they are purged from the system.

- **ETC** The ETC directory contains sample files that assist in configuring TCP/IP protocols on the server.

- **MAIL** This directory may or may not contain files. An upgrade from a bindery-based NetWare version will retain the MAIL subdirectories of existing users along with user login scripts and print job configurations. The upgraded user accounts are assigned ownership of their original MAIL subdirectories. If users are created after the upgrade, they will not have associated subdirectories under the MAIL directory. A new installation of NetWare 5 results in an empty MAIL directory.

- **CDROM$$.ROM** Contains the index for a traditionally mounted CD-ROM.

TIP: When a CD-ROM is mounted as a volume, the operating system builds an index of the files and directories on the CD. The file includes a file allocation table (FAT) and directory entry table (DET). The index file is placed in the CDROM$$.ROM directory. Indexing improves CD access and allows NetWare to treat the mounted CD as a NetWare volume without actually writing the required information on the CD.

➤ **JAVA** Contains the files that provide Java support.

➤ **JAVASAVE** Contains the Java-related files.

➤ **NDPS** Contains the Novell Distributed Print Services (NDPS) files.

➤ **NETBASIC** Contains the support files for NetBasic.

➤ **NI** Contains NetWare installation files.

➤ **PERL** Contains the files related to Perl script.

Custom Directories

You should add additional directories to the system-created directories to customize the directory structure for your network environment. As with volume names, Novell recommends using short, descriptive directory names to help users identify the contents and functions of the directories. Novell also recommends using the four directory types, shown in the following list, to organize the files in your directory:

➤ Home directories

➤ Z.E.N.works profile directories

➤ Application directories

➤ Shared data directories

Note: The Z.E.N.works profile directories are dependent on the installation of Z.E.N.works, which is covered in Exam Cram for NetWare 5 Administration CNE/CNA, *also published by The Coriolis Group.*

We'll look at what you need to know about these directory types in the following sections.

Home Directories

Each user should be provided with a home directory on the network to which he or she has exclusive access with full rights to store and manage files. For uniformity and ease of creating login scripts, you should make the home directory name the same as the user login name. The task of creating and managing the home directories can be simplified by making them all subdirectories under a single parent directory (such as USERS, for example).

The home directory, from the user perspective, is functionally equivalent to a private local drive with some nice "extras" provided by the operating system.

The following examples are representative of the extras offered by the network home directory:

➤ Users can leverage the security features of the NetWare file system to allow and restrict access to files and subdirectories within their home directories with a degree of granularity not currently available at the local level.

➤ Storing files in a network home directory allows user files to be archived during the regular system backup. This simplifies the task from the perspective of both the user and the administrator, and it provides an additional level of fault tolerance for the user.

➤ Users have a much more powerful tool available for recovering files that are deleted from their home directories than is available when files are deleted from their local drives. The NetWare Salvage utility provides total recovery capability for deleted files (even multiple files with the same name), within the constraints of the disk storage capacity. The utility can be used to recover any files that have not been purged from the system.

Application Directories

The contents of application directories are restricted to program files (EXE, COM, and BAT files) and any associated files necessary to run the applications. Files created by a user when running these applications are considered data files and stored elsewhere. The data files are commonly stored in the user's home directory or in an administratively created data directory.

> **TIP** Do not confuse data files with application or program files. Think of data files as being user-generated or owned by someone (other than the application developer).

Because running applications requires a different operating set of file system rights than creating and manipulating data files, segregating the program and data files eases the task of establishing security over the applications.

As with home directories, a parent directory for all application subdirectories (such as APPS, for example) simplifies application management and access.

Shared Data Directories

Shared data directories should be created to allow groups of users to share information. Shared data directories provide the easiest method to allow, as well as restrict, access to shared information on a multiple user or group basis.

Possible Directory Structures

The organization of a paper-based filing system using a filing cabinet with drawers, hanging folders, file folders, and documents often reflects the type of information kept in the system. However, it may reflect almost anything, including the personality of the person who set it up. The same holds true for an electronic filing system. Although there are few absolute rights and wrongs associated with setting up the network directory structure, a general evaluation of the known strengths and weaknesses of some possible structures provides a solid base form which to work.

One-Volume Directory Structures

One-volume directory structures are most appropriate for small organizations that require minimal administrative support. The following advantages are realized with this structure:

- A limited number of users and applications requires less depth in the directory structure, thus resulting in shorter path names.
- With a single volume, file storage is limited only to the size of the hard disk.
- Navigation and management of the file system is simplified for users and administrators.

The primary disadvantage of a one-volume system is associated with not reserving the SYS volume for NetWare files.

Multiple-Volume Directory Structures

Multiple-volume directory structures are appropriate for larger organizations that have proper administrative support. The following advantages become available with a multiple-volume approach:

- Different administrators can manage each volume.
- The SYS volume can contain only NetWare files, thus making it less volatile.

Chapter 6

➤ Applications and data can be located on different volumes. In addition to the previously mentioned reasons for segregating programs and data, this can improve efficiency when archiving because only data needs to be backed up regularly.

➤ Sensitive programs and data that are accessed infrequently can be placed on a volume that's mounted only when access is required. While offline, the data is not susceptible to unauthorized access.

The primary disadvantage of this approach involves the additional planning and management tasks associated with multiple volumes.

> **EXAM ALERT**
>
> When evaluating a directory structure, you need to check the following:
>
> ➤ Are the system-created directories present on the SYS volume?
>
> ➤ Are the following suggested directories present?
>
> > ➤ User home directories
> >
> > ➤ Z.E.N.works profile directories
> >
> > ➤ Application directories
> >
> > ➤ Shared data area
>
> ➤ Are user directories in one location under a parent directory?
>
> ➤ If using a multiple-volume approach, is the SYS volume reserved for NetWare files?

Practice Questions

Question 1

> Which of the following directory names are associated with system-created directories? [Choose the three best answers]
>
> ❏ a. SYS
> ❏ b. ETC
> ❏ c. Public
> ❏ d. NI
> ❏ e. APPS

The correct answers to this question are b, c, and d. The ETC, Public, and NI directories are created by the system during the installation of NetWare 5. The name SYS is associated with the SYS volume, not a system-created directory. Therefore, answer a is incorrect. APPS is normally associated with a custom volume or directory and is not created by the system. Therefore, answer e is incorrect.

Question 2

> Which of the following cannot be mounted as an NSS volume?
>
> ○ a. The SYS volume
> ○ b. The DOS partition on the C drive
> ○ c. A custom volume named DATA
> ○ d. A custom volume named APPS
> ○ e. An installation CD-ROM for a new scanner

Trick question

The correct answer to this question is a. The SYS volume must be mounted as a traditional NetWare volume due to certain limitations of NSS. Because answer a is correct, answers b, c, d, and e are incorrect. This is a trick question because answer b requires specific knowledge of NSS to be eliminated. Without the information presented in this chapter that specifically states the traditional file system requirement of the SYS volume, answer b would appear to be the most likely choice. Based solely on the information provided, the only way to eliminate answers b, c, d, and e is to know that answer a is correct.

Question 3

A user has accidentally deleted several important files from the DOCS subdirectory in his network home directory. The user is not certain when the files were deleted but thinks that it may have happened more than a month ago. Which recovery options, if any, are available to the user? [Choose the two best answers]

❑ a. Use the Salvage utility to retrieve the files from the DELETED.SAV directory.

❑ b. Recover the deleted files from the most recent system backup.

❑ c. Find and recover the deleted files from the most recent system backup that was run before the files were deleted.

❑ d. Use the Salvage utility to recover the files from the DOCS subdirectory.

❑ e. The files are automatically purged from the system upon deletion; recovery is not an option.

The correct answers to this question are c and d. A system backup done both prior to the deletion and after the creation of the files would contain the files, and deleted files may be recovered from the directory they were deleted from by using the Salvage utility. Answer a is incorrect because the deleted files would only be in the DELETED.SAV directory if the DOCS subdirectory had been deleted. Answer b is incorrect because a recent backup would not contain files that were deleted over a month ago. Answer e is incorrect because deleted files are automatically saved on the system after they are deleted.

Question 4

Which of the following is not an advantage associated with multiple-volume directory structures?

○ a. File storage is limited to the size of the hard disk only.

○ b. The SYS volume can contain only NetWare files, thus making it less volatile.

○ c. Distributed management of the file system is made easier.

○ d. Applications and data can be located on different volumes.

The correct answer to this question a. In a multiple-volume directory structure, file storage in a volume is limited to the size of the volume and the amount of space not occupied by other volumes. File storage limited to the size of the hard disk only is an advantage of single-volume directory structures. Answers b, c, and d are incorrect because they are all advantages of multiple-volume directory structures.

Question 5

Which of the actions listed is appropriate when creating multiple volumes if fault tolerance is more important than performance?

- ○ a. Create multiple volumes with the same name to ensure that data is always duplicated as it's written to the disk.
- ○ b. Span the volumes across multiple hard disks to prevent losing all data from the volume if one disk in the system fails.
- ○ c. Create each volume on a separate hard disk so that the failure of one disk only affects the volume on that disk.
- ○ d. Back up all data daily to ensure restoration of critical data in the event a hard drive fails.

The correct answer to this question is c. In order to be mounted, an entire volume must be intact. If each volume resides on a separate disk, then the failure of one disk would not prevent other volumes from being mounted. Therefore, answer c is correct and answer b is incorrect. Answer a is incorrect because volume names must be unique within a file system. Answer d is incorrect because it does not address the issue of creating multiple volumes.

Question 6

What would you expect to find in the MAIL directory located at the root of the SYS volume after performing a new install of NetWare 5?

- ○ a. Subdirectories for user email accounts.
- ○ b. Individual user subdirectories for login scripts and personal print job configurations.
- ○ c. Universal mailbox directories for GroupWise accounts.
- ○ d. Nothing.
- ○ e. The MAIL directory is only created when upgrading from a previous version of NetWare.

The correct answer to this question is d. The MAIL directory will not be empty only following an upgrade. Existing subdirectories and their contents are retained during the upgrade process. Therefore, answer d is correct and answers a, b, and c are incorrect. Answer e is incorrect because the MAIL directory is created during a new installation of NetWare 5.

Question 7

> Which of the following files might you find in an application directory? [Choose the three best answers]
>
> ❑ a. WP.EXE
>
> ❑ b. RESUME.DOC created using MSWORKS
>
> ❑ c. START.BAT
>
> ❑ d. EDIT.COM

The correct answers to this question are a, c, and d. Application directories should only contain executable files (COM, EXE, and BAT files, for example) and files necessary for programs to run. Answer b is incorrect because files created via an application are considered data files and would be stored in a data directory.

File System Design   **95**

Need To Know More?

Clarke, David James IV. *CNE Study Guide intraNetWare/NetWare 4.11*. Novell Press: San Jose, CA, 1997. ISBN: 0-7645-4512-12. Chapter 10 provides information pertinent to this chapter.

http://support.novell.com/servlet/Knowledgebase yields numerous helpful documents to lead you through setting up your NetWare file system. Search for "traditional file system."

Queue-Based Printing

Terms you'll need to understand:

√ Print queue

√ Auto load and manual load printer

√ Print server

√ PSERVER.NLM

√ NPRINTER.EXE, NPTWIN95.EXE, and NPRINTER.NLM

√ Print server operator

√ Print server user

Techniques you'll need to master:

√ Describing the print process and path from user to network printer

√ Configuring the queue-based print objects

√ Managing the queue-based printing environment

√ Specifying users and operators of print queues and print servers

The number one reason for using a network is most likely so users can share resources. These resources consist of software and hardware elements, and one of the most common hardware resources to share is printers. Novell has provided the ability to share printers with several versions of NetWare for quite some time. NetWare 5 continues that tradition and provides two environments for managing network printing: Novell Distributed Print Services (NDPS) and queue-based printing.

NDPS is included with NetWare 5 and allows you to set up a "plug and print" configuration. The second method is referred to as *queue-based printing* and is very similar to NetWare 3.x and NetWare 4.x network printing. This mechanism allows you to easily "mix" the NetWare 5 queue-based printing world with NetWare 3.x and NetWare 4.x networks. In this chapter, you'll learn about queue-based printing—what it is, how to configure it, and how to manage it.

> *Note: NDPS is not an advanced administration topic and is, therefore, not covered in this book. For more information on NDPS, see the NetWare 5 online documentation at www.novell.com/documentation or Exam Cram for NetWare 5 Administration CNE/CNA.*

Queue-Based Printing Process

Before we begin discussing network printing, let's review the process that happens when a Windows 95 user prints to a printer attached directly to his or her computer and no network is installed. When the user chooses Print from the File menu, the application and operating system (OS) create a print file that's stored locally (spooled). The operating system then sends this print file, which is stored on the user's local hard disk, to the physical printer attached to the machine.

Portions of the print file contain information and instructions that are specific to a particular print language and/or printer. To get the correct commands to the proper printer, Windows 95 installs software called a *print driver* for the manufacturer and model of the printer specified in the setup. The print file constructed by the application contains a header, body, and tail. The header contains information about the type of printer; this is derived from the information contained in the print driver. If the incorrect print driver is used to compose the header and the resultant print file is sent to a printer that does not understand the commands, the output is usually unreadable. Therefore, it's very important that the correct print driver is selected for the type of printer used.

The process for printing to a network printer is very similar to the process for printing to a local printer, except some of the storage locations are on a server and the software that handles delivery of the print file to the printer is handled

Queue-Based Printing 99

by server software. With NetWare-controlled printing, you can basically think of the network as a very long printer cable.

The NetWare queue-based printing environment has three main objects: the print queue, the printer, and the print server that you create in Novell Directory Services (NDS). Each of the NDS print objects represents a hardware resource or a software component. None of these items is configured automatically, and you cannot print to a NetWare-controlled printer until you configure and initialize these components.

Print Queue

The NetWare 5 *print queue* is the storage location of the print file generated by the user. The queue is a directory located on a server, and it contains no special directory properties. When you create the queue, you specify the volume on which you want this queue to reside. The system then creates a directory on that volume titled QUEUES and a subdirectory below that for your queue. The name of this subdirectory is a hexadecimal value with a .QDR extension. You don't usually have to concern yourself with this directory at the file level because NetWare Administrator handles the interface between the name of the queue and the associated QDR directory.

> **ALERT**
> Novell tends to refer to the print files generated by the user's application as *print jobs*. You'll see this term used in NetWare Administrator and NetWare-related literature.

> **TIP**
> Depending on the applications in use, the size of these print files may be very large. Also, there may be "bursts" of network printing as with tax seasons, quarterly and annual reports, and inventory. You should take into account the worst possible scenario to determine the required disk space necessary to support storage of the print files. It's highly recommended that the print queues are *not* placed on the SYS volume. Serious problems may result if the SYS volume runs out of disk space.

Printer

The Printer objects created in NDS represent the physical printers on the network. The printers may be physically attached to various points on the network. Network-aware printers are connected directly to the network and are often configured for a specific protocol or protocols. Depending on the configuration and manufacturer, these printers may have a network address and a network name. In addition, the vendor may also provide utilities for managing and configuring the printer.

Another attachment point for a printer is on a user's workstation. This configuration works well only in very small environments where extensive amounts of printing are not performed.

The third network connection point for a printer is the server. In this scenario, the printer is attached directly to a server, and the server does not have to be running the print service's software. This configuration is probably realistic for administrative purposes, such as when the information printed shouldn't be accessible to the general user.

Print Server

That last of the three print objects is the *print server*. In NetWare 5, the print server is a NetWare 5 server running an application to provide network printing. The application is a NetWare Loadable Module (NLM) and can be loaded and unloaded at your discretion. Once this software is loaded, the print server software (PSERVER.NLM) controls the communication between the print files stored in the queue to the printer specified in the setup.

Once the printing environment is configured and tested to make sure everything is set up correctly, you can place the command to launch the print server software in the server's AUTOEXEC.NCF file. This enables you to load the print server automatically when the server is launched.

Configuring Print Objects

The primary tool for configuring the print objects is NetWare Administrator. As with other objects, you'll need to decide in which container (or containers) your print objects will reside. Depending on the size of the network, you may have many print objects to create and configure. The location, name, and properties of these print objects should be decided on during the NetWare 5 network design process. You do have the ability to move the objects in the NDS database later, but whenever possible, you should try to plan for current and future network needs.

The NDS print objects have several properties, some of which are critical. These properties, sometimes referred to as *required properties*, must have values in order for the object to be created and function properly. Also, some property values are filled in automatically for you as you create these objects. These values must also remain for the printing environment to function properly.

Queue-Based Printing   **101**

> **TIP**
> It's easy to move objects around the database with NetWare Administrator. However, changing an object's context may have an impact on users that may require a great deal of your time to correct. For example, if login scripts refer to print objects, the scripts will all need to be edited to reflect the new location. Anything done on a per-workstation basis—such as using the Windows Add Printer Wizard to point the user's workstation to the proper printer—may need to be adjusted on each workstation involved. If you think this type of situation may arise, it might be a good time to investigate Z.E.N.works to help reduce these types of time-consuming tasks.

Creating A NDS Print Queue

You use NetWare Administrator to create and manage your print queues. The following steps outline the process you use to create a print queue:

1. Select the container in which you want the print queue to reside.

2. Choose Create from the Object menu, right-click on the container and choose Create, click on the toolbar button for creating a new object, or press Insert.

3. Select Print Queue from the New Object dialog box.

4. Enter the name of the queue. NDS is not case sensitive, but part of your design may use mixed case as a mechanism to make the name more readable to users (for example, Research-Q versus researchq).

5. Use the browse button to select the volume on which you want the resultant queue directory to reside.

6. When you've entered both of these properties, the Create button is enabled. Click on Create to create the print queue. Figure 7.1 shows the Create Print Queue dialog box.

When the NDS queue object is created, the system creates the corresponding physical subdirectory containing the .QDR extension under the QUEUES directory on the volume you specified in Step 5.

Creating A NDS Printer (Non-NDPS)

The Printer object you create in NDS represents the physical printer located on the network. Novell uses two terms to identify the location of the printer in respect to the print server. This is necessary so the print server software running on a

102   Chapter 7

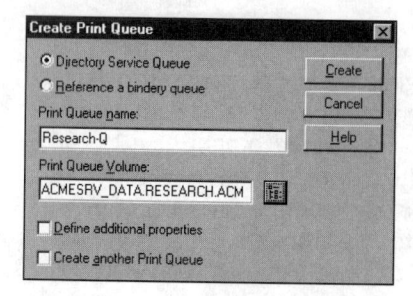

Figure 7.1 The NDS Create Print Queue dialog box.

server knows where to "look" for the printer; this enables the print server to communicate with the printer. You'll also need to have this information available when you create the Printer object because this is one of the required properties. As an example, we'll take you through the steps of creating a NDS Printer object that's attached to the parallel (or LPT1) port of a workstation.

If the printer is attached to the server running the print server software, it's referred to as an *auto load printer*. A printer attached to anything else is referred to as a *manual load printer*. This includes printers attached to workstations and those connected directly to the network. The word *load* in both of these terms refers to additional software that needs to be loaded—either automatically or manually. We'll discuss the additional software and its configuration later in this chapter.

The following steps outline the process for creating a non-NDPS printer:

1. Select the container in which you want the printer to reside.
2. Choose Create from the Object menu, right-click on the container and choose Create, click on the toolbar button to create a new object, or press Insert.
3. Select Printer (Non NDPS) from the New Object dialog box.
4. Enter the name of the printer, check the Define Additional Properties checkbox, and click on Create.
5. Select the Configuration button displayed on the left of the dialog box presented.
6. At the top of the dialog box that appears, select the printer type from the available options (see Figure 7.2). Select Parallel because the printer in this example is attached to the LPT1 port of a workstation.
7. To specify the hardware settings of the printer, click on the Communication button.

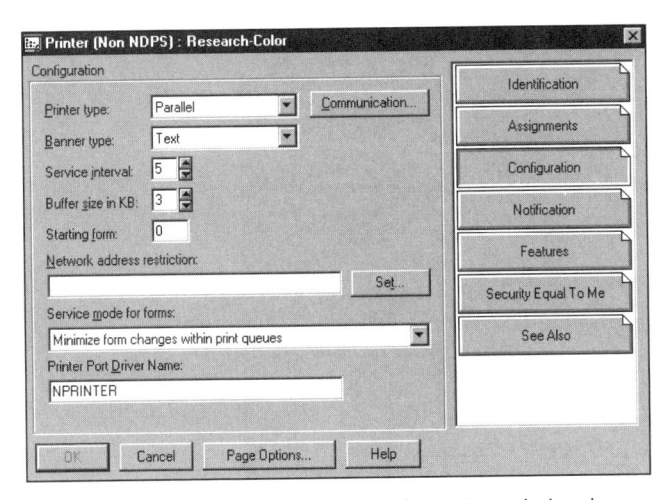

Figure 7.2 The NDS Printer Configuration dialog box.

8. In the Parallel Communication dialog box, select the port to which the printer is physically attached (see Figure 7.3).

9. Indicate whether you want to use interrupts; if you do, specify the correct interrupt value. If you select Polled, the computer that the printer is attached to uses the computer's timer interrupt to determine signals destined for the printer. This option is useful in situations where the interrupt is unknown or may vary (as is the case with plug-and-play configurations).

10. At the bottom of the dialog box, specify the printer connection type. If the printer is attached to the server running the print service's software, select Auto Load (Local To Print Server). If the printer is attached anywhere else on the network, choose the other option—Manual Load (Remote From Print Server). Click on OK.

11. In the Printer dialog box, click on the Assignments button to view the Printer Assignments dialog box (see Figure 7.4). This allows you to

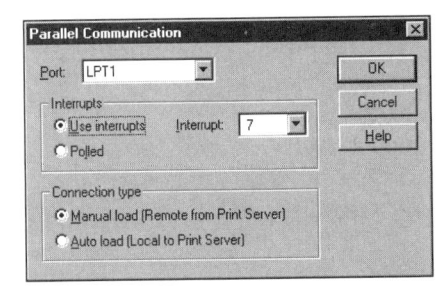

Figure 7.3 The Printer Parallel Communication dialog box.

Chapter 7

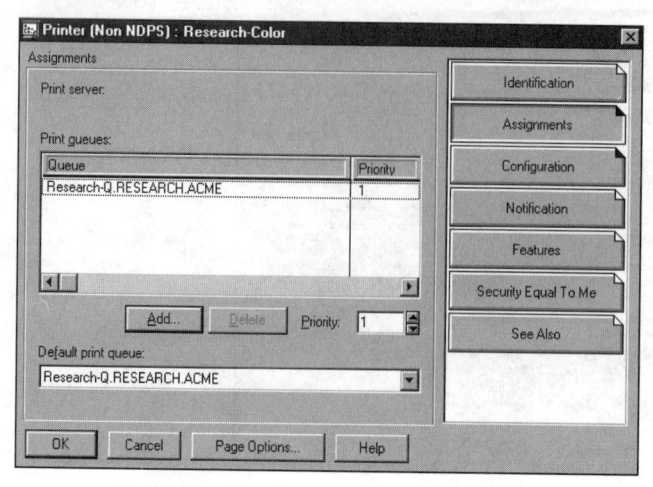

Figure 7.4 The Printer Assignments dialog box.

indicate which print queue's print files will go to the printer you're creating.

12. Click on the Add button and navigate to the printer you want assigned to this queue. Click on OK.

> **EXAM ALERT**
> The step in which you assign the print queue to the printer is very important. If this step is omitted, the user's printout will not go to the printer. The print files will "sit" in the queue until a printer is assigned to a queue. Remember to "connect your Ps to your Qs."

As you can see from the Assignments screen, you can attach several queues to a printer. If this is done, make sure the workstations using the different queues are all using the same print driver.

> **TIP**
> In the Assignments screen, there's also the option to indicate a priority value for the queue attached to the printer. This value ranges from 1 (the default) to 10—where 1 is the highest and 10 is the lowest. If you want to assign print priority to users, create a queue for each priority you want to support. Then, when you add these queues to the printer, you can specify a priority value for each of the queues. NetWare uses these priority values to indicate the processing order of the queues; the queues with a value of 1 are serviced first.

Queue-Based Printing **105**

Creating A NDS Print Server (Non-NDPS)

The last object to create and configure for queue-based printing is the Print Server object. This NDS object represents the print server software that will run on a NetWare 5 server.

The following steps outline the process for creating a non-NDPS print server:

1. Select the container in which you want the print server to reside.

2. Choose Create from the Object menu, right-click on the container and choose Create, click on the toolbar button for creating a new object, or press Insert.

3. Select Print Server (Non NDPS) from the New Object dialog box.

4. Enter the name of the print server, check the Define Additional Properties checkbox, and click on Create.

5. In the Print Server Identification screen, click on the Assignments button to specify which printer or printers the print server will be servicing.

6. Click on the Add button and navigate to the printer you want to place on the Assignments list. Click on OK.

> **TIP**
> As with the print queues, it's very important that you assign the printer or printers to the print server. If this step is omitted, the user's print files will accumulate in the print queue because there's no print server specified to service the queue attached to the printer.

> **ALERT**
> The Print Server details window contains a Print Layout (Non NDPS) button that presents a graphic of all the connected objects and their statuses. This is useful for checking to make sure all components are assigned properly as well as for troubleshooting. In Figure 7.5, notice there's an exclamation point next to the Print Server object. This indicates that something about that object is not configured properly or that there may be a problem. Also, note that a Status button is enabled when an object is selected. In this example, the problem is simple. All the objects have been created and assigned properly, but the print server software is not running on the server.

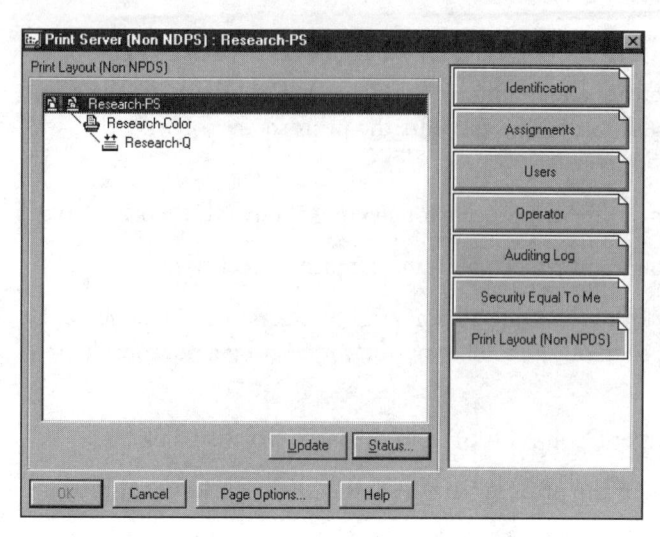

Figure 7.5 The Print Server Print Layout dialog box.

Print Services Quick Setup (Non-NDPS)

A quick setup option is available for you to use, but the initial configuration of the objects is not as flexible as the methods described previously. To access the quick setup option, select Print Services Quick Setup (Non-NDPS) from the Tools menu in NetWare Administrator. In the Print Services Quick Setup dialog box (shown in Figure 7.6), you can either accept the default names of the print server, printer, and print queue or modify these values. You must specify the queue volume before you can create the object.

You have some restrictions when using the quick setup method, and these should be considered before using this option. Some of these limitations are as follows:

➤ All three print objects reside in the same container.

Figure 7.6 The Print Services Quick Setup (Non-NDPS) dialog box.

Queue-Based Printing 107

➤ The quick setup method cannot be used to modify or edit existing print objects.

➤ You cannot modify other property values not presented in the dialog box during the creation process. However, you can edit them after the object is created.

Now that we've discussed the queue-based print objects and their creation process, the next step is to load the print server software on your NetWare 5 server.

Starting Queue-Based Print Services

In NetWare 5, the queue-based print server software is run on a NetWare 5 server. The software can be loaded manually or the appropriate command can be placed in the server's AUTOEXEC.NCF file so that when the server is brought up, the print server software loads automatically.

The print server software is an NLM called PSERVER.NLM. To load the print server software, you enter "PSERVER" followed by the name of the NDS Print Server object at the server's console prompt. Here's an example:

PSERVER .RESEARCH-PS.RESEARCH.ACME

You can use either the distinguished name (DN) or relative distinguished name (RDN) of the print server; also, the case is not significant.

> **EXAM ALERT**
>
> In NetWare 5, the use of **LOAD** before the name of the NLM you're launching is optional. For example, the following command will perform the same action as the previous line of code:
>
> LOAD PSERVER .RESEARCH-PS.RESEARCH.ACME
>
> You may see **LOAD** used in Novell literature, especially if the NLM is the same on NetWare 4.x and/or NetWare 3.x, where the use of **LOAD** is required.

When the print server software is loaded and running, all the information about the configuration is stored in the server's memory. If you make changes to the print objects' configurations when the print server is running, these may not take effect. To enable these new changes, you need to unload and reload the print server. This causes a brief disruption in print services; therefore, this should be performed at times that result in the least inconvenience.

> **TIP:** It's usually a good practice to use the DN of objects instead of the RDN, because you're not dependent on the context of the server where you're loading the print services.
>
> If you do not know or are not sure of the distinguished name of the print server, you can enter "PSERVER" without a name at the server's console. This allows you to navigate to the container of the Print Server object, and then you can select the object.
>
> You can only load one instance of PSERVER per server. This should not be a limitation in most cases because one print server can service up to 254 printers.

You can unload the print server software several different ways. One procedure is at the server console in the NetWare Print Server screen. Select Print Server Information and then press Enter on the Current Status field. Two options are available: Unload and Unload After Active Print Jobs. The first option unloads the print server immediately, and the second choice unloads it when the files currently being printed are completed. In both cases, inactive or waiting print files remain in the queues.

Configuring Network Printers

In a NetWare-controlled printing environment, the printer may be connected to the print server, to a workstation, or directly to the network. As stated earlier, the term *auto load* is used to define printers attached directly to the print server, and the term *manual load* is used for printers attached elsewhere. If you have a printer attached to the print server that has been defined as an auto load printer, when you load PSERVER, the server automatically loads additional software. This additional software is NPRINTER.NLM, and it will load for each printer assigned to that print server as auto load.

For a printer attached elsewhere, there's no automatic loading of software. In the previous configuration example, the printer is specified as manual load because it's attached to a workstation. For the print server to "find" this printer and communicate with it, you need to manually load software on the workstation. This software is generically called NPRINTER, and there are specific versions for DOS/Windows 3.x, Windows 95/98, and Windows NT. These are all found in the SYS:\PUBLIC directory—either at the root or in a subdirectory.

NPTWIN95.EXE is the application you run on a Windows 95/98 machine that has the network printer attached to it. This is a graphical utility and can be run automatically using the Windows Startup folder, NetWare login scripts, or

Z.E.N.works. When the utility is run, you select the NDS printer defined for the workstation's printer. Once this is accomplished, users on the network can use the printer.

To manually load software on DOS and Windows 3.x workstations, you use the NPRINTER.EXE application. This may be placed in a workstation's AUTOEXEC.BAT file after the Novell Client software is run and the user has logged onto the network. For Windows 3.x, make sure NPRINTER is loaded before launching Windows.

There's a version of NPRINTER for Windows NT, but it's not shipped with the initial release of NetWare 5 because the Windows NT product was not available at that time. You can download the software and supporting documentation from Novell's Web site (www.novell.com) at no cost.

If you have a printer attached to another server that's *not* running the print server software (PSERVER) and you want this printer to be serviced by a print server, you need to load NPRINTER.NLM manually on the server that has the printer attached. The syntax for this is:

```
NPRINTER PrintServerName PrinterName
```

In the previous example, if the printer was *not* attached to the print server, you would enter the following at the server's console:

```
NPRINTER .RESEARCH-PS.RESEARCH.ACME .RESEARCH-COLOR.RESEARCH.ACME
```

Again, case is not important when entering the command. This can also be placed in the server's AUTOEXEC.NCF file so the software is loaded when the server is launched.

Managing Print Services

When you create the various print objects discussed in the previous sections, you'll notice two buttons titled Users and Operator in some of the dialog boxes. In this section, you'll learn about the print object operators and their management capabilities.

An operator of a print object can manipulate and modify the object, whereas a user cannot. This operator role is designed for network administrators or individuals who are responsible for network printing. When the print queue and print server are created, the default operator of these objects is the user who created the objects. An operator can add other operators, and administrators with NDS supervisory rights can manipulate the operator lists.

Managing The Print Queue

The print queue operator controls the flow of print jobs entering and leaving the queue. There are three operator flags, and they're all turned on by default. These are viewed and configured in the Identification screen when you select the print queue's details.

> **TIP:** You can obtain details on the various objects presented in NetWare Administrator by right-clicking on and selecting Details from the pop-up menu. You can also double-click on leaf objects. With the object selected, you can select Details from the Object menu or press Enter for leaf objects.

Here are the three operator flags:

➤ **Allow users to submit print jobs** If this flag is turned off, users will not be able to print from the applications to the queue. A situation in which you may have to turn off this flag is when the volume holding the print queue is running low on disk space.

➤ **Allow service by current print servers** When this flag is inactive, the print files generated by the users will be submitted to the queue, but will remain in the queue until this flag is activated.

➤ **Allow new print servers to attach** In this option, if you're creating additional Print Server objects that will be servicing this queue, when you load the other print servers, they will begin to service the queue immediately. If this is disabled, new print servers cannot service the queue. This will have no affect on the active print server that's servicing the queue.

Print queue operators can also manipulate the print jobs in the queue. In the Print Queue details window, you can select the Job List button to display any print files in the queue. Each print job has a sequence number that can be modified by double-clicking on the job or by selecting the print job and clicking on the Job Details button. In the resultant dialog box, you simply enter in the new sequence number for the job in the Service Sequence field.

The following list describes several other options available in the Job Details dialog box:

➤ **User Hold and Operator Hold** The print queue operator can select either one of these. If you choose User Hold, either an operator or the owner of the print job can release the print job. If you choose Operator, only a print queue operator can release the job.

➤ **Print Banner** This checkbox allows you to turn the print banner on or off. If the banner is turned on, the Name and Banner Name fields become enabled. The banner page is printed before the print file and is sometimes used to help separate printed documents for sorting purposes.

➤ **Form Feed** This checkbox allows you to turn form feed on or off. *Form feed* ejects an empty page at the end of the printed document.

➤ **Defer Printing** When this checkbox is enabled, you can specify a time and date for the file to be printed. This is a useful feature if you want to print a very large file after business hours. This option can also be set by the owner of the print file.

The operator can also remove a print file from the queue by selecting the print file and pressing Delete or clicking on the Delete button. More than one file can be removed at a time by selecting multiple entries with the aid of the Ctrl or Shift key.

Managing The Printer

The printer does not have an operator list, but there are several items that can be configured. NDS security is used to control who has the rights to modify the printer's properties.

You can view the status of the printer through either NetWare Administrator or at the server console by running PSERVER. Both interfaces give similar management options. In NetWare Administrator, open the Details window for the printer and select the Printer Status button. On the next screen displayed, you have several options:

➤ **Service Mode** This specifies how the print server servicing this printer handles forms. Forms are defined paper dimensions tied to a particular print job.

➤ **Mount Form** This button allows you to specify a predefined form to mount on the printer.

➤ **Eject Page** This option, which is similar to a Form Feed, tells the printer to eject the page being printed, or if the printer is paused, a blank piece of paper will be ejected.

➤ **Pause** This option allows you to pause and restart the printer.

➤ **Abort Job and Mark Top Of Form** These options are self-explanatory. They can be performed from the print server's Printer Status screen on the server.

Another useful item to configure on the printer is the handling of messages. The printer's details screen contains a Notification button that allows you to specify who will receive messages generated by the printer, such as the Out Of Paper message. By default, the owner of the print file currently being serviced will receive the message. If certain people are responsible for handling printer error messages, you may want to disable the Notify Print Job Owner checkbox and then add the appropriate NDS object to the notification list. You can also specify the time interval for the first and repeated printer messages.

Managing The Print Server

In contrast to the print queue and printer, the print server has a few management tasks. These include unloading the print server, specifying operators and users, and viewing the status.

On the print server's Identification page is the advertising name of the print server. This is the name that the print server will use to communicate on the network. By default, it's the same name as the NDS object's, but you can change the name if you like. The Unload button deactivates the print server and unloads PSERVER on the server. Also, the Auditing Log button allows you to enable auditing of the print server, which generates a log of all print jobs handled by the print server.

Configuring Usage Rights For The User

For users to print to queue-based printers, they must be defined as users of the print queue or queues and associated print servers. Default user assignments are specified when the objects are created; depending on your network design, these defaults may be quite sufficient. The objects' operators, as well as network administrators with NDS supervisory rights, can manipulate the user lists.

The default print queue user is the container in which the print queue was created and the User object that created the Print Queue object. The default print server user is the container in which the Print Server object was created.

Queue-Based Printing   **113**

Practice Questions

Question 1

> Which NetWare 5 utility is used to create queue-based print objects?
>
> ○ a. PCONSOLE
>
> ○ b. NDS Manager
>
> ○ c. NetWare Administrator
>
> ○ d. PRINTCFG
>
> ○ e. PSERVER

The correct answer is c. NetWare Administrator is used to create queue-based print objects. PCONSOLE is a text-based utility that existed in NetWare 3.x and NetWare 4.x. It's not available in NetWare 5. Therefore, answer a is incorrect. NDS Manager is used to manage NDS partitions and replicas. Therefore, answer b is incorrect. PRINTCFG is a made-up name and does not exist. Therefore, answer d is incorrect. PSERVER is the NLM you load at the server console to activate print services after the objects are created. Therefore, answer e is incorrect.

Question 2

> Which of the following statements defines a NetWare 5 print queue?
>
> ○ a. A NetWare 5 print queue is a directory created on the user's workstation that holds the print files before printing.
>
> ○ b. A NetWare 5 print queue is a directory created on the server that holds the print files before printing.
>
> ○ c. A NetWare 5 print queue is a mapped drive letter created on the user's workstation that points to the queue on the server.
>
> ○ d. A NetWare 5 print queue is a specialized volume created to hold the print files so there's no risk of running out of space on the SYS volume.
>
> ○ e. A NetWare 5 print queue is defined as a bindery-based object, so it's compatible with NetWare 4.x.

Trick question

114 Chapter 7

The correct answer is b. A NetWare 5 print queue is a directory created on the server that holds the print files before printing. Because answer b is correct, answer a is incorrect. The print queue has no interaction with any mapped drive letters. Therefore, answer c is incorrect. The print queue is not a volume, but rather a directory that's stored on the volume you specified in the creation process. Therefore, answer d is incorrect. The NetWare 5 print queue can be a bindery-based queue, but not for NetWare 4.x compatibility reasons. This may be necessary for compatibility with legacy third-party print servers. Therefore, answer e is incorrect. Because answer e was partially correct, we labeled this a trick question.

Question 3

Which of the following define the roles of the queue-based NetWare 5 print server? [Choose the two best answers]

- a. The NetWare 5 print server is responsible for directing the print files from the user's workstation to the printer.
- b. The NetWare 5 print server manages the network traffic and performs load balancing so that the server running PSERVER is optimized for printing.
- c. The NetWare 5 print server is an NLM running on a NetWare 5 server.
- d. The NetWare 5 print server verifies and modifies the print file header as necessary to make sure the printer can understand the print commands.
- e. The NetWare 5 print server is responsible for managing the flow of print jobs from the queue to the printer.

The correct answers are c and e. The NetWare 5 print server is an NLM running on a NetWare 5 server, and it's responsible for managing the flow of print jobs from the queue to the printer. Because answer e is correct, answer a is incorrect. The print server does not monitor network traffic or perform load balancing—these actions are performed by other NLMs or other workstation-based products. Therefore, answer b is incorrect. The print server does not modify the print file header to adjust for incorrect print drivers selected at the workstation. The composition of the print file header that contains printer language information and printer information is performed at the workstation when the user selects Print. Therefore, answer d is incorrect.

Queue-Based Printing **115**

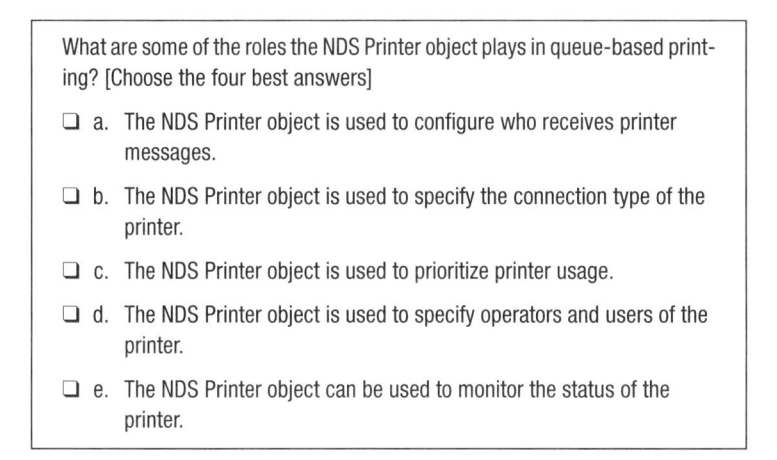

Question 4

> What are some of the roles the NDS Printer object plays in queue-based printing? [Choose the four best answers]
>
> ❑ a. The NDS Printer object is used to configure who receives printer messages.
>
> ❑ b. The NDS Printer object is used to specify the connection type of the printer.
>
> ❑ c. The NDS Printer object is used to prioritize printer usage.
>
> ❑ d. The NDS Printer object is used to specify operators and users of the printer.
>
> ❑ e. The NDS Printer object can be used to monitor the status of the printer.

The correct answers are a, b, c, and e. The NDS Printer object does not have operator or user lists. Users of the printer are specified in the print queue assigned to the printer. Therefore, answer d is incorrect.

Question 5

> Which of the following statements define the two available connection types for a printer? [Choose the two best answers]
>
> ❑ a. An auto load printer is a printer attached directly to the workstation.
>
> ❑ b. An auto load printer is a printer attached directly to the server running PSERVER.
>
> ❑ c. NPTWIN95.EXE is the name of the file for a Windows 95-associated manual load printer.
>
> ❑ d. NPTWIN95.EXE is the name of the file for a Windows 95-associated auto load printer.
>
> ❑ e. NPRINTER.NLM is the name of the file loaded on a server with a network printer attached.

The correct answers are b, c, and e. Because answer b is correct, answer a is incorrect. Because answer c is correct, answer d is incorrect.

Question 6

The following is a list of steps necessary to set up a NetWare 5 queue-based printing environment. Which of the following choices presents the correct order of these steps?

1. Create the print server and assign the printers.
2. Create the print queue.
3. Specify the volume on which the print queue will reside.
4. Assign the print queue to the printer.
5. Create the Printer object.
6. Load the print server software at the server console.

○ a. 2, 3, 5, 4, 1, 6.
○ b. 2, 5, 4, 1, 3, 6
○ c. 5, 1, 3, 2, 4, 6
○ d. 6, 2, 3, 5, 4, 1
○ e. 2, 5, 3, 4, 1, 6

The correct answer is a. First, you create the print queue. Second, you specify the volume on which the print queue will reside. Third, create the Printer object. Fourth, you assign the print queue to the printer. Fifth, you create the print server and assign the printers. Finally, you load the print server software at the server console.

Question 7

> You have just set up all the proper NDS queue-based printing objects and are ready to load the print server software on the server. The name of the print server is Office-PS, and it's located in the Austin Organizational Unit. Above the Austin container lies the Organization object ACME. Which of the following is the proper way of loading this print server on the Advertising server located in the Austin container?
>
> ○ a. **PSERVER .OFFICE-PS.SALES.ACME**
>
> ○ b. **PSERVER OFFICE-PS**
>
> ○ c. **PSERVER .OFFICE-PS.ACME.AUSTIN**
>
> ○ d. **PSERVER .OFFICE-PS.AUSTIN.ACME**
>
> ○ e. **LOAD PSERVER .OFFICE-PS.AUSTIN.ACME.ROOT**

The correct answer is d. The first answer uses a distinguished name, but does not specify the correct context for the print server. Therefore, answers a and c are incorrect. The second choice would work if the server was located in the same container as the print objects, the Austin container, but it's not. Therefore, answer b is incorrect. The last choice uses **LOAD**, which is correct except that the name of the print server is incorrect. **ROOT** is not part of a distinguished name. Therefore, answer e is incorrect. This question is a bit tricky because you need to be comfortable with distinguished object names and whether or not they're print objects.

Need To Know More?

http://developer.novell.com/research/appnotes/1998/septembe/05/05.htm offers a few pages from an AppNotes article dealing with NDPS and queue-based printing.

http://support.novell.com offers the following TIDs that contain information related to the topics covered in this chapter. At Novell's support Web site, go to the Knowledgebase and perform a search using the following TID numbers:

➤ TID 2939025 NWAdmin32: Missing Tabs In Print Queue Object

➤ TID 2943419 How To Set NDPS Printer To Service A Queue

➤ TID 2928524 Troubleshooting Nprinter95 Summary

➤ TID 2943200 Print Job Notify Off, Still Being Notified

➤ TID 2931460 Nprinter For Windows NT Available

➤ TID 2934151 NprinterNT—Questions And Answers

➤ TID 2945303 Error Writing To LPT1 On NT With NW5 Client

➤ TID 2943863 Print Problems After 3.12 To 5.0 Upgrade

➤ TID 2944870 Novell Client v3.02 For Win95

Backing Up And Restoring Files And NDS

Terms you'll need to understand:

√ Storage Management Services (SMS)
√ Host server
√ Target
√ Target Service Agent (TSA), TSA500, TSANDS, TSAPROXY
√ NetWare Backup/Restore
√ SBCON
√ NWBACK32.EXE
√ Parent
√ Child

Techniques you'll need to master:

√ Explaining backup strategies
√ Performing a backup and restoration of a NetWare 5 server
√ Performing a backup and restoration of a workstation

Many factors and conditions can cause or lead to the failure of hardware and software. One of these factors is time. The hardware that's hosting your servers is not designed to run forever. Therefore, as time goes by, components in your network will begin to fail. The question is not *if* they will fail, but *when* they will fail. There are also other events beyond your control that can lead to data loss, for example, fires, floods, and earthquakes. To reduce the side effects of these types of failures, practices need to be in place to ensure that a current, reliable copy of the network data is available on mobile media.

In this chapter, we'll discuss the backup system that's delivered with NetWare 5. Novell has included backup software with previous versions of NetWare, but for NetWare 5, it has greatly enhanced the flexibility and interface. You'll learn the various backup and restore strategies, and we'll outline the steps and components of NetWare 5's backup and restore product.

> **TIP** Many network administrators use third-party applications for their backup and restore strategies. Most of these programs use some of the same components and strategies covered in this chapter.

Strategies For Information Backup And Restore

The primary reason for backing up network and/or workstation data is to provide a mechanism for restoring data when a failure occurs so your business can keep running. A backup system provides a way of placing a copy of your valuable data onto portable storage media. In the event of a failure, you can use this backup to restore the environment to a functional state that existed before the failure occurred.

Part of your backup strategy should also include the placement of the backup media at a separate physical location. This practice helps reduce the impact of a multisystem failure or a catastrophe, such as a fire or a flood. In these types of failures, several systems are often involved, and the buildings and other support services might not be available or usable for an extended period of time. In these situations, you can restore the data at the organization's temporary offices so the company can continue conducting business.

Another very important part of your backup strategy is the reliability of the data backup. You should periodically test the integrity of your backups to make

Backing Up And Restoring Files And NDS   **121**

sure what you want backed up is indeed present on the storage media. You can verify the backup with a test restore to determine whether the restored information is reliable and accurate. Remember, the backup is only good if the data can be restored.

> *Note: Some networks have specific guidelines for data backup and restoration. For example, in some government agencies, the data backup and storage procedures are defined and controlled by local or state laws.*

Novell refers to the NetWare 5 backup and restore process and architecture as *SMS*, or *Storage Management Services*. This suite of products includes components that run on the server and workstation. Before we can begin a discussion of these products, we need to clarify the terminology used in SMS.

Many networks typically use digital tape drives that are designed for the sole purpose of data backup and restoration. These can range from the simple, single-tape system to very high-end systems that hold many tapes with automated hardware to switch and change tapes as needed. Novell uses the term *host server* to define the server to which the tape or backup hardware is attached and that is also running the backup software. You can think of this as the server that is "hosting" the backup device and "hosting" the backup software.

The backup software running on the server must be able to communicate and interact with the backup hardware. To do this, you'll need to load the backup device's driver software before loading the backup software. Typically, during the server install process, this software is not loaded automatically. NetWare 5 includes a generic driver called NWTAPE.CDM that can be used to support digital tape devices. If the vendor of the hardware device provides a driver for NetWare, you should check to make sure the driver is compatible with NetWare 5.

NetWare 5's backup and restore process uses the term *target* to refer to the device whose data is being backed up. The types of target information that can be backed up with NetWare 5 are as follows:

➤ You can back up files (data and/or applications) stored on a NetWare server. You can use SMS to backup NetWare 3.x, NetWare 4.x, and NetWare 5 files. On a NetWare 5 server, these files can be on a traditional NetWare volume or on a Novell Storage Services (NSS) volume.

➤ You can use SMS to back up the server's DOS partition. This partition contains important server files that are used in the server startup process.

➤ You can back up Novell Directory Services (NDS) using NetWare 5's backup and restore system.

Chapter 8

➤ You can use SMS to backup the data created by GroupWise. (GroupWise is an email, scheduling, and workgroup product developed by Novell that uses NDS to store information.)

➤ You can back up a Windows 95/98 or Windows NT workstation with SMS.

For the backup software to communicate with the target, the target needs to be running a piece of software or service referred to as a *Target Service Agent (TSA)*. TSAs run on either a server or workstation, depending on which system is being backed up. If you want to back up a NetWare 5 server's files, you load TSA500.NLM on the NetWare 5 server. To back up NDS, you load a different TSA software component called TSANDS.NLM. When you've completed your backup or restore session, these TSA components can be unloaded or remain active on the target.

> **EXAM ALERT**
> You need to be able to list the types of data SMS can back up as well as name and identify the TSAs (TSA500 for NetWare 5 server files, TSANDS for NDS, TSAPROXY service for recognizing imported workstations, and TSADOSP for backing up a server's DOS partition).

The last major component in the NetWare 5 backup and restore system is the software that actually places data on or moves data from the backup storage device to the target. This is referred to as the *backup engine*, and it consists of several NetWare Loadable Modules (NLMs) that together provide the ability to backup and restore data (see Table 8.1). Some of these NLMs are automatically loaded by other NLMs.

Note: SBCON is the NetWare 5 version of SBackup. The term SBackup isn't used much anymore, but it may still appear occasionally.

Table 8.1 NetWare 5 Backup/Restore NLMs.

NLM	Name
SMDR.NLM	NetWare Storage Management Data Requester
QMAN.NLM	NetWare Storage Management QManager
SMSDI.NLM	Storage Device Interface
SBSC.NLM	NetWare SBackup Communication Module
SBCON.NLM	NetWare Storage Management Console
SME.NLM	Storage Management Engine

A major design consideration of a network's backup and restore procedure is how often the data is backed up and what data is backed up. Different types of backups are provided with NetWare 5, and which one you choose is dependent on your network's activity and recovery activities.

Types Of Backups

There are three different types of backups, and they each vary in the amount of data backed up at each session. Each type also presents different variations on the procedures to restore data. Most networks have a backup policy that backs up data once every 24 hours; backups should occur during times of little or no network activity. Furthermore, backup strategies are typically on a weekly cycle and include rotation of storage media to ensure retention of backed-up data for several weeks. Whichever strategy you implement, you need to take into account the time necessary to manage the backups and restorations.

The backup engine determines what's backed up to the storage system using the status of the file's archive attribute. When you create a new file and save the file to a NetWare volume, the archive attribute on the file is enabled. This means that the file has changed and needs to backed up. The archive attribute is also enabled or set when you edit an existing file and save the changes. You can view the attributes of a file with NetWare Administrator or with Windows Explorer. You can also use the text utility FILER to view the state of this attribute.

The first of the three types of backups is a *full backup*. In this setup, all the data on the target device is backed up once every 24 hours. Once the data has been backed up, the software removes the archive attribute on the files. If a system failure occurs on the third day, for example, all you need to do is to use the last full backup to restore the data. This is one of the advantages of a full backup, and if a lot of your data changes on a daily basis, this may be a good strategy. The downside of a full backup is that you need to have sufficient storage for each 24-hour session, and the time required to perform the backup may be lengthy.

The second type of backup is called *incremental*. An incremental backup always begins the weekly cycle with a full backup. So, for example, early on Monday morning while the server and network are "quiet," a full backup of all available targets is performed. On day two, the system checks to determine whether any files have changed since the last backup and then these are backed up. On day three, the only data that's backed up is the data that has changed from day two to day three. On day four, the data that's backed up is the changed information between day three to day four. This strategy is called incremental because each day you do not backup all the files, but only small "increments."

This system also uses the status of the archive attribute to determine what will be backed up. Files that have the archive attribute enabled are backed up. When the file has been backed up, the software turns off the archive attribute. An advantage of the incremental backup is the time to do each session is relatively short. The disadvantage of this procedure is in the event of a failure requiring a full restore, you would have to restore the full backup first and then each incremental backup in the proper order.

The last of the three methods is called *differential*. In this strategy, the backup cycle also begins with a full backup. On the second day, any files with the archive attribute enabled are backed up. One day three, the differential method will back up all files that have changed since the last full backup. When the system backs up the data, the archive attribute on the files is not altered. This is necessary so that all the files that have changed since the full backup are included in the next backup session. In the event of a restoration, you only need to restore the last full backup and the last differential. In this strategy, the amount of storage space required and the time needed to perform the backup will take a little longer each day.

The strategy you use depends on your network and users. If a lot of data is changing, a full backup may be a good choice. If you decide to use an incremental or differential backup procedure, do not change the strategy in the middle of a backup cycle. Assume you have started the backup cycle on Monday with a full backup for an incremental strategy. Later in that same week you determine that a differential backup process would better suit your network's needs. Do not change the backup type in midcycle. Instead, change the type at the start of the next weekly cycle or start a new cycle at this point. Changing backup strategies in midstream may lead to network failure and/or the corruption of the server's volume or the volumes' data.

> You need to be comfortable in defining the three types of backups and their differences. Notice in the full backup and incremental backup strategies that the archive attribute is removed after the files are backed up.

Rights Needed To Back Up Information

To back up the requested data, the user who is initiating the procedure must have sufficient rights. If you are planning to back up NDS, the minimum that's necessary is the Browse right on the NDS objects and the Read right on all the objects' properties. The minimum file system rights needed to back up files and directories on the servers are Read and File Scan. To restore either NDS information or files, you need to have the Create right in addition to the rights already mentioned.

Note: Most third-party backup products create additional objects and/or different User objects in the tree. These products often assume that the account you're using to perform backups and restores has full rights to the NDS tree and to the server's file system.

The NetWare 5 backup and restore product also allows you to back up data across different NetWare servers, which can include NetWare 3.x, NetWare 4.x, and NetWare 5 servers. Whenever you select a target for backup or restore, you're prompted to authenticate to gain access to the target. Therefore, the user who's performing the backup or restore will need to have the proper account names and passwords. If the targets include workstations, you may need to authenticate to those systems as well.

SMS Components And Guidelines

The NetWare backup and restore service consists of components that execute on the server and the workstation. The client component, NWBACK32.EXE, allows you to configure the backup device, specify what to back up or restore, and specify the locations to which to back up or restore. This utility runs under Windows 95/98 and Windows NT and provides a graphical interface for configuring the backup or restore session. NWBACK32.EXE is located in the SYS:\PUBLIC directory.

The second component is the server piece, and it consists of several NLMs that together are referred to as *NetWare Backup/Restore*. These NLMs process the jobs submitted by the client component, NWBACK32.EXE. The server components are also responsible for establishing and maintaining communications with the targets.

Before we can cover the guidelines and processes for performing a backup or restore, you need to be familiar with the requirements. One of the requirements of the NetWare 5 backup product is that the physical backup storage device must be connected to the same server running the backup software.

Targets are devices that contain the data you want to back up or the location where you want to place the restored information. These can include NetWare servers and workstations. One of the nice features of the backup product is the ability to specify individual directories, files, or NDS objects to back up or restore. When you specify a directory that contains files, this directory is referred to as a *parent*. If you specify a file to back up that has no subordinates, that file is referred to as a *child*. You'll see these terms displayed if you watch the progress of the backup or restore session on the server.

You need to follow several guidelines to ensure a successful backup or restore session. These include the following:

- The NetWare Backup/Restore server components must be loaded on the server to which the backup hardware is attached.

- To allow for completion of the backup or restore session during your desired time frame, make sure the backup media has enough storage capacity. For example, if you're using a digital tape device and the tape cannot hold all the data, the system will wait until another blank tape is inserted before continuing. If the system then resumes the backup and the time is now during the network's busy hours, performance will be affected, which appears to the user as a slow and sluggish network.

- The NetWare Backup/Restore NLMs will generate log and temporary files that can be several megabytes in size. If you're supporting name spaces such as the long name space for Windows 95/98 files, the temporary files may become quite large. Make sure you have enough storage capacity on the volume that stores these log and temporary files.

- To protect the integrity of the network's data on the backup storage media, you should limit access to the media and to the server hosting the backup software and hardware.

- You should try to schedule the network backup during a time of day with little activity. This will shorten the time it takes to perform the backup. Performing this activity during quiet times will also help reduce the likelihood of dismounting a volume or unloading a needed driver, which could result in data loss or cause the server to *abend* (abnormal end).

- When you've completed the backup or restore, you may want to unload the related NLMs on the server to free up memory and resources. Some of the NLMs you loaded earlier automatically load other NLMs. To remove all the related NLMs, you should follow an order similar to this:

    1. Exit the NetWare Backup/Restore application on the server or **UNLOAD SBCON**.

    2. **UNLOAD QMAN**.

    3. **UNLOAD SMSDI**.

    4. **UNLOAD TSA500** and/or **UNLOAD TSANDS** (TSA500 is the TSA for NetWare 5 files, and TSANDS is the TSA for NDS). There are other TSAs that may be loaded: TSAPROXY (service for

Backing Up And Restoring Files And NDS   **127**

recognizing imported workstations) and TSADOSP (the TSA for backing up a server's DOS partition).

5. UNLOAD SMDR.
6. UNLOAD SME.
7. UNLOAD <backup device driver>.

> **TIP** Instead of typing in these commands one by one, you can create a server batch file (.NCF) that contains these commands. Then, all you need to do is to execute the batch file at the server console to unload these NLMs.

Backing Up A NetWare 5 Server

In this section, we'll describe the process of backing up a NetWare 5 server's files and NDS. There are several files that need to be loaded on the server and some tasks performed on the workstation for the backup to proceed. In this example, we outline the steps for performing a backup of data to a digital tape drive:

1. On the server that has the tape drive attached, load the tape driver software. This may consist of more than one NLM, and NWTAPE.NLM may be included.

2. Load the TSAs. To back up the server's files, enter **TSA500** at the server console; to back up NDS, enter **TSANDS**; and to back up the server's DOS partition, enter **TSADOSP**.

3. Load the NetWare Backup/Restore NLMs:

   ▶ **SMDR** This is the SMS communication module that provides access to local or remote SMS services. Version 5 of SMDR is protocol independent and can run on either IP or IPX. When you load this for the first time, you're prompted for the context and name of the SMS NDS objects. You also need to specify an account and password that has administrative rights. The SMDR configuration creates two objects in the context you specified. Their default names are SMS SMDR Group, which is an NDS Group object, and <servername> SMS RPC, which is an SMS remote procedure call (RPC) object. At this time, a configuration file, SMDR.CFG, is created and is stored in the SYS:ETC\SMS directory.

128 Chapter 8

➤ **QMAN** NetWare 5 Backup/Restore uses a print queue to hold the backup jobs. When you run the backup/restore server components for the first time, you're prompted to create this object. You can either accept the displayed context and name of the object or enter the values you want. You also need to enter an account and password that has administrative rights. Creating these objects creates a configuration file called SBACKUP.CFG, which is located in the SYS:ETC\SMS directory.

Note: Even though this Queue object appears as a NDS, non-NDPS Print Queue object, it's not the same as a print queue used for printing.

➤ **SBCON** You can configure and run a backup or restore session at the server console with SBCON and Figure 8.1 appears. However, in this chapter, we cover the graphical workstation component.

Note: Once these NDS objects exist, you won't be prompted to create them again. If you chose to install SMS when installing NetWare 5 or later as an added product, these objects are already present and were created at the time of the product installation.

4. On the workstation that's authenticated to the network, run NWBACK32.EXE. This application is located in SYS:\PUBLIC. You may need to specify the tree and administrative account name and password.

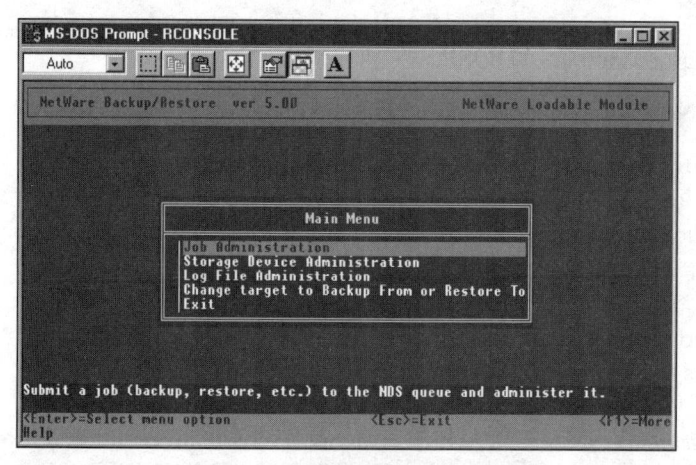

Figure 8.1 The NetWare Backup/Restore server component—SBCON.

Backing Up And Restoring Files And NDS 129

5. A Quick Access dialog box is displayed when the application opens. This allows you to choose the operation you want to perform: Backup, Restore, Verify, Create Session, Job Administration, Device Administration, Reports, or Exit.

6. The NWBACK32 application presents the backup environment in two panes. The left pane presents the target information, and the right pane displays the backup destination (see Figure 8.2).

7. In the left pane, five different target types are displayed: NDS, NetWare Servers, Workstations, NetWare Server's DOS Partition, and GroupWise Database. Click on the expand/collapse (+ and -) buttons to the left of the target types and sublevels until the target you want to back up is displayed. You can expand the file system volumes and select individual directories or several directories. Make sure that the items you want to back up have an X in the square to the left of the item.

8. The right pane allows you to choose in which queue and server's storage device the data is to be placed. Using the expand/collapse buttons, expand down to the queue and sublevels to select the storage device.

9. After you have the What To Backup and Where To Backup panes configured, right-click on the backup device in the right pane. Choose Submit The Job from the menu displayed.

10. The next screen displayed allows you to specify the type of backup. These include Full, Differential, and Incremental. Choose the type you want.

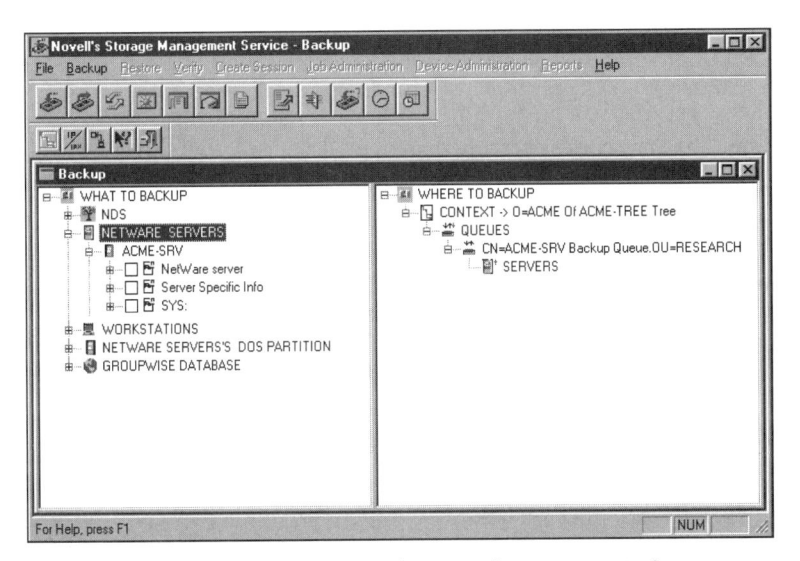

Figure 8.2 The NWBACK32 Backup configuration window.

11. On the next screen displayed, you specify the date and time the backup will run. You can also specify a rerun interval and the number of reruns.

12. The Session Description is optional data, but the information you enter here will help document what is being backed up.

13. When the last screen is completed, click on Finish to submit the job. If the data will not fit on the backup media, you'll need to insert additional tapes when prompted by the application.

> **TIP** It's highly recommended that you test and practice your backup configurations. This testing includes restoring data from the backups and verifying the data's integrity. Your backups are only good if the data can be restored!

> **ALERT** Make sure you're comfortable with the NWBACK32 interface and know how to set up a backup session.

Backing Up A Windows Workstation

The process of backing up a workstation is very similar to the procedure for backing up the server. You have the options of backing up the entire workstation or selected directories. To back up a workstation, follow these steps:

1. On the server that has the tape drive attached, load the tape driver software. This may consist of more than one NLM, and NWTAPE.NLM may be included.

2. Load TSAPROXY on the server.

3. Run the TSA on the workstation. For Windows 95/98, it's Target Service Agent For Windows 95, and for Windows NT, it's Novell Target Service Agent For Windows NT.

4. Load the NetWare Backup/Restore NLMs. If these have been loaded and configured before, you'll not receive any prompts. If these have not been run before, you'll need to configure the components (SMDR, QMAN, and SBCON), as discussed in the "Backing Up A NetWare 5 Server" section earlier.

5. On the workstation that's authenticated to the network, run NWBACK32.EXE. This application is located in SYS:\PUBLIC. You may need to specify the tree and administrative account name and password. A Quick Access dialog box is displayed when the application opens. This allows you to choose the operation you want to perform.

6. The NWBACK32 application presents the backup environment in two panes. The left pane presents the target information, and the right pane displays the backup destination.

7. In the left pane, five different target types are displayed: NDS, NetWare Servers, Workstations, NetWare Server's DOS Partition, and GroupWise Database. Click on the expand/collapse buttons to the left of the target types and sublevels until the target you want to back up is displayed. You can expand the workstation's drives and select individual directories or several directories. Make sure that the directories you want to back up have an X in the square to the left of the directory.

8. The right pane allows you to choose in which queue and server's storage device the data is to be placed. Using the expand/collapse buttons, expand down to the queue and sublevels to select the storage device.

9. After you have the What To Backup and Where To Backup panes configured, right-click on the backup device in the right pane. Choose Submit The Job from the menu displayed.

10. The next screen displayed allows you to specify the type of backup. These include Full, Differential, and Incremental. Choose the type you want.

11. On the next screen displayed, you can specify the date and time the backup runs. You can also specify a rerun interval and the number of reruns.

12. The Session Description is optional data, but the information you enter here will help document what is being backed up.

13. When the last screen is completed, click on Finish to submit the job. If the data will not fit on the backup media, you'll need to insert additional tapes when prompted by the application.

Restoring Data

Restoring data using the NetWare 5 SMS system is very similar to the backup procedure. As with the backup, you can specify what you're restoring and where to place the restored information. If the data recovery requires NDS and

NetWare 5 files to be restored, the NDS data must be restored before the file system. This is necessary in order for trustee, ownership, and NetWare attribute information to be properly recovered.

The process for restoring data using the NetWare 5 SMS product is outlined in the following steps:

1. On the server that has the tape drive attached, load the tape driver software. This may include more than one NLM and may be specific for your hardware.

2. Load the TSAs. To restore the server's files, enter **TSA500** at the server console. To restore NDS, enter **TSANDS**. To restore data to a workstation, load **TSAPROXY** at the server console and run the TSA on the workstation. For Windows 95/98, it's Target Service Agent For Windows 95, and for Windows NT, it's Novell Target Service Agent For Windows NT.

3. Load the NetWare Backup/Restore NLMs. If these have been loaded and configured before, you will not receive any prompts. If these have not been run before, you'll need to configure the components (SMDR, QMAN, and SBCON), as discussed in the "Backing Up A NetWare 5 Server" section earlier in this chapter.

4. On the workstation that's authenticated to the network, run NWBACK32.EXE. This application is located in SYS:\PUBLIC. You may need to specify the tree and administrative account name and password. A Quick Access dialog box is displayed when the application opens. This allows you to choose the operation you want to perform.

5. The NWBACK32 application presents the restore environment in two panes. The left pane displays the backup queue and storage device, and the right pane presents the destination information.

6. In the right pane, five different destination or target types are displayed: NDS, NetWare Servers, Workstations, NetWare Server's DOS Partition, and GroupWise Database. Click on the expand/collapse buttons to the left of the target destination types and sublevels until the target you want to restore to is displayed. You can expand the file system volumes or drives and select individual directories or several directories. Make sure that the directories you want to restore have an X in the square to the left of the directory.

7. The left pane allows you to choose in which queue and server's storage device the data is located. Using the expand/collapse buttons, expand down to the queue and sublevels to select the storage device.

Backing Up And Restoring Files And NDS   **133**

8. After you have the What To Restore and Where To Restore panes configured, right-click on the selected storage device in the left pane. Choose Submit The Job from the menu displayed.

9. The next screen displayed allows you to specify the type of restore. These include Full, Differential, and Incremental. Choose the type you want.

10. On the next screen displayed, you can specify the date and time the restore runs. You can also specify a rerun interval and the number of reruns.

11. The Session Description is optional data, but the information displayed here will help describe what is being restored.

12. When the last screen is completed, click on Finish to submit the job. If the data does not fit on the backup media, you'll need to insert additional tapes when prompted by the application.

Practice Questions

Question 1

> Which NetWare 5 workstation utility is used to configure a backup or restore session?
>
> ○ a. SBACKUP
>
> ○ b. NWBACK32
>
> ○ c. NetWare Administrator
>
> ○ d. SBCON
>
> ○ e. NetWare Backup/Restore

The correct answer is b. SBACKUP is the name of the backup and restore NLM that runs on a NetWare 3.x or NetWare 4.x server. Therefore, answer a is incorrect. You can view the SMS objects in NetWare Administrator, but you cannot configure a backup session. Therefore, answer c is incorrect. You can configure a backup or restore session with SBCON, but SBCON runs on the server, not the workstation. Therefore, answer d is incorrect. NetWare Backup/Restore is another name for SBCON. Therefore, answer e is incorrect.

Question 2

> Which of the following items can be backed up with the NetWare 5 backup and restore product? [Choose the four best answers]
>
> ❑ a. NetWare 3.x file system
>
> ❑ b. GroupWise information
>
> ❑ c. NetWare 5 file system except for NSS volumes
>
> ❑ d. NetWare server's DOS partition
>
> ❑ e. Windows NT workstation

The correct answers are a, b, d, and e. NetWare 5 NSS volumes can be backed up with NetWare 5 backup and restore product. Therefore, answer c is incorrect.

Question 3

The NetWare 5 backup and restore product is referred to as SMS. What does SMS stand for?

○ a. System Management Services

○ b. Storage Management Services

○ c. Storage Mobile Systems

○ d. Standard Management Service

○ e. Standard Mobile System

The correct answer is b. The remaining choices consist of nonexistent services or systems on NetWare 5. Therefore, answers a, c, d, and e are incorrect.

Question 4

What are the roles of the host server in NetWare 5's SMS product? [Choose the two best answers]

❑ a. The host server stores the backup data onto its large NSS volumes.

❑ b. The host server has the physical backup device attached to it.

❑ c. The host server runs NWBACK32.NLM for configuring and submitting backup jobs.

❑ d. The host server cannot run any TSAs, and the TSAs are run on external targets.

❑ e. The host server runs the backup NLMs, such as SBCON and QMAN.

The correct answers are b and e. The backup data is not placed onto an NSS volume, but rather on some type of mobile media. Therefore, answer a is incorrect. The NBACKUP32.EXE application runs on the workstation and there is no NWBACK32.NLM. Therefore, answer c is incorrect. The host server can run TSAs, so there is the ability to back up the host server's files and/or DOS partition. Therefore, answer d is incorrect.

Question 5

The various components for performing a backup in the SMS product must be able to communicate with the server where the files are located. These components are referred to as what? [Choose the two best answers]

- ❏ a. Target Service Agents
- ❏ b. Terminal System Agents
- ❏ c. TSAs
- ❏ d. TSA.NLM
- ❏ e. TSA.COM

The correct answers are a and c. The remaining choices—Terminal System Agents, TSA.NLM, and TSA.COM—are terms and files that do not exist in NetWare 5. Therefore, answers b, d, and e are incorrect.

Question 6

In the following items, match the appropriate file to the type of target data.

_____ NetWare 5 server files

_____ NetWare 5 DOS partition

_____ NetWare 5 NDS

_____ Windows 95/98 workstation

- a. TSANDS
- b. TSA500
- c. TSADOSP
- d. TSAPROXY

The correct answers from top to bottom are b, c, a, d.

Question 7

> To back up data, the account used to initiate the backup needs to have certain rights. These are: [Choose the three best answers]
>
> ❏ a. Browse and Read on all NDS objects
> ❏ b. Read on all NDS objects' properties
> ❏ c. Browse on all NDS objects
> ❏ d. Read and File Scan on all files and directories
> ❏ e. Read and Browse on all NDS objects; Read, File Scan, and Create on all files and directories

The correct answers are b, c, and d. Read is *not* a NDS object right; it's a NDS property right. Therefore, answer a is incorrect. The same applies to answer e, plus you do not need the Create right to perform a backup. You need the Create NDS object and File System right to restore data. Therefore, answer e is incorrect.

Question 8

> Below is a list of the steps necessary to perform a NetWare 5 file system restore.
>
> 1. **LOAD TSA500**
> 2. **LOAD <backup device driver>**
> 3. **LOAD SBCON**
> 4. **LOAD QMAN**
> 5. **LOAD SMDR**
>
> Which of the following choices presents the correct order of these steps?
>
> ○ a. 1, 2, 5, 4, 3
> ○ b. 2, 1, 3, 5, 4
> ○ c. 1, 2, 3, 5, 4
> ○ d. 2, 1, 5, 4, 3
> ○ e. 2, 1, 5, 3, 4

The correct answer is d.

Chapter 8

Question 9

A large company's network administrator has contacted you for assistance with the company's migration from NetWare 3.x to NetWare 5. The network administrator wants to make sure that data is not lost or damaged during the migration and has proposed some actions. Your job is to review these items and determine which ones would be in the best interest of the client. [Choose the two best answers]

Trick! question

- ❑ a. The NetWare 3.2 servers all have 2GB SYS volumes and each have at least 1GB free. The NetWare 3.2 servers' hardware has been upgraded over the last seven years. More memory has been added, and to increase disk space, the administrators have added more drives to the existing drives in the server. Because the amount of free disk space is sufficient, the company would like to upgrade these NetWare 3.2 servers using the In-Place-Upgrade.

- ❑ b. The existing NetWare 4.11 tree contains several servers that have critical data. These servers will all be upgraded using an across-the-wire migration to new hardware. Immediately after the migration, the administrator plans on placing the 10-bay auto-change tape device on a workstation in the server room. At this location, the backup can be monitored, and the storage media will not be accessible to unauthorized personnel.

- ❑ c. After the migration, the network administrator would like to change the existing backup strategy from an incremental backup to a differential backup. This will reduce the time it takes to do a full restore.

- ❑ d. The network administrator is concerned that the existing backup hardware will not function under NetWare 5. The name of the current driver is TAPEDRV.DSK, and the network administrator would like to replace the driver and use another one.

The correct answers are c and d. Answer a would not be a good choice because of the age of the hardware. The purpose of a backup and restore scheme is to help in recovery when hardware fails. However, because answer b mentions new hardware, it would be better to migrate the NetWare 3.2 servers "across-the-wire." Furthermore, the age of any existing backup devices and drivers on the NetWare 3.2 servers may not be compatible with NetWare 5. Therefore, answer a is incorrect. Answer b would be fine except the 10-bay backup device needs to be attached to the NetWare 5 server running the backup software. Placing the media and a monitoring station in an area to reduce unauthorized access is a good strategy. Therefore, answer b is incorrect for the first reason given. This question is tricky because you need to know what an In-Place Upgrade is and that NetWare 5 does not support DSK drivers.

Need To Know More?

NetWare 5 includes a readme file titled SMS_RDME.TXT. This file can be found on either the root of the NetWare 5 Operating System installation CD-ROM or in the SYS:README directory on a NetWare 5 server. This file goes into some detail on the server components, FAQs, and limitations.

http://support.novell.com contains TIDs related to the topics covered in this chapter. At Novell's support Web site, go to the Knowledgebase and perform a search using the following TID numbers:

➤ **TID 2946745** How To Configure SMS On NetWare 5/ NWSB 4.2?

➤ **TID 2944976** NW5 SMDR Group Context Is Invalid

➤ **TID 2945644** Unable To Backup With SBCON

➤ **TID 2945847** TSA4X And TSA5X Backing Up Compressed Files

➤ **TID 2945504** NW5 889C Error Running Upgrade Wizard

➤ **TID 2943556** NW5 Tape Drive Supported By SBCON/ SBACKUP

➤ **TID 2941993** NW5 Release Notes Known Utilities Limitations

NetWare Operating System And Configuration Basics

9

Terms you'll need to understand:

- √ NetWare kernel
- √ Server console
- √ NetWare Loadable Modules (NLMs)
- √ Load balancing
- √ Memory protection
- √ Multiprocessor support
- √ Preemption
- √ Scheduling
- √ Virtual memory

Techniques you'll need to master:

- √ Identifying the modular components of the NetWare 5 operating system
- √ Describing the features of the NetWare 5 operating system
- √ Identifying and explaining the function of the server configuration files
- √ Editing the appropriate server configuration files to customize the server
- √ Navigating the server console and executing console commands
- √ Loading and unloading NLMs
- √ Automating execution of console commands with script files

A NetWare 5 server is a combination of hardware and software that provides network services to clients. The NetWare 5 hardware component is typically a Pentium-class Intel or Intel-compatible computer. The software component is the NetWare 5 operating system. In this chapter, you'll learn more about the function of a NetWare server and its components and become familiar with the server console interface. In addition, you'll learn basic server management and maintenance skills such as loading and unloading NetWare Loadable Modules (NLMs), executing console commands, and maintaining server configuration files.

NetWare Operating System Overview

The NetWare operating system runs in server RAM and regulates communication between itself, clients on the network, and shared network resources. You load the operating system into server RAM by running a DOS executable file named SERVER.EXE. This file has two components—the main operating system file, SERVER.NLM, and a loader utility, LOADER.EXE, that loads the SERVER.NLM into RAM. The operating system itself is modular in design, with components falling into one of the following general categories:

➤ Kernel

➤ NetWare Loadable Modules (NLMs)

➤ Server console

The NetWare Kernel

The kernel represents the core of the operating system. This component is loaded into RAM when the SERVER.EXE file is executed. The network kernel provides the following features:

➤ **Multiprocessor support** The NetWare multiprocessor kernel (MPK) automatically detects and supports up to 32 processors in a server.

➤ **Memory protection** Protected mode memory is currently provided for Java applications. Protected mode memory isolates corrupt applications from the operating system so the server won't crash when the file becomes corrupt.

➤ **Virtual memory** Virtual memory reduces the total amount of RAM required on a NetWare server by moving the least recently used data from memory to a swap file on the hard disk. This frees up memory to load and run other programs. When data in the swap file is needed

NetWare Operating System And Configuration Basics   143

again, it's moved back into memory and swapped for other data that's moved to the hard disk. This memory management scheme allows execution of programs that are larger than the size of the physical memory in a server. It's particularly useful when you're running memory-intensive Java applications.

➤ **Load balancing** The MPK automatically detects and intelligently distributes the processing load across all detected processors.

➤ **Scheduling** The kernel allows administrative configuration of the processing time allocated to each application.

➤ **Preemption** Preemption allows the operating system to take control of the processor at any time. This technique enables administrative scheduling of the processing time for applications.

Additional operating system functionality is provided by modules—called NetWare Loadable Modules (NLMs)—that can be selectively plugged into the operating system as needed. NLMs are explained in the following section.

NetWare Loadable Modules (NLMs)

NLMs are programs that are selectively loaded and unloaded to provide additional services, management utilities, or enhancements to the operating system. Typically, NLMs can be loaded and unloaded without affecting the general operation of a server. The following distinct advantages are provided by the modular design of the operating system:

➤ Only the NLMs that are necessary to fulfill the client needs in a particular environment need to be loaded. This eliminates unnecessary resource consumption by unneeded modules.

➤ NLMs can be loaded and unloaded without restarting the server.

➤ Additional enhancements, services, and utilities for the NetWare operating system can be written by third-party developers.

You can recognize most NLMs by their .NLM file name extension. However, you need to know that other file name extensions are used with NLMs, and you also need to know the types of NLMs to associate with the commonly encountered extensions. The following list associates common NLM file name extensions with one of four general NLM categories. It also includes the key information and functional characteristics you need to associate with each category.

➤ **Disk drivers** These have file name extensions of .HAM and .CDM. The disk drivers control communications between the operating system and attached storage devices. The NetWare 5 disk driver modules are written to NetWare Peripheral Architecture (NPA) specifications and represent the only type of storage device drivers supported by NetWare 5. The HAM drivers (called *host adapter modules*) and the CDM drivers (called *custom device modules*) are defined by the NPA specification and control the host bus adapter and the storage devices attached to the host bus adapter, respectively.

➤ **LAN drivers** These have the file name extension .LAN (for local area network). These drivers control communications between the operating system and the network boards.

➤ **Name space modules** These have the file name extension .NAM. The name space modules provide support for storage of non-DOS file name formats. NetWare ships with the MAC.NAM (for Macintosh), LONG.NAM (for OS/2, Windows 95/98, and Windows NT long name space), and NFS.NAM (for Network File System) name space support modules.

> NetWare 5 automatically loads the long name space support module when the SYS volume is mounted. In addition, any new volume that's created will automatically have DOS and long name support added to the volume. Other name space support must be added to volumes manually.

➤ **NLM utilities** These have the file name extension .NLM. These NLMs are typically management utilities and server applications representing services that are not built into the core operating system, but are selectively available by simply loading the modules into server RAM.

> The following list contains examples of the network services provided by NetWare 5 NLMs that you need to be aware of:
> ➤ Authentication
> ➤ Novell Directory Services (NDS)
> ➤ Network printing
> ➤ File services
> ➤ Storage Management Services (SMS)
> ➤ Security
> ➤ Java Virtual Machine (JVM)
> ➤ Routing
> ➤ Remote server console

- Server monitoring
- Network management

Network management utilities do not ship with NetWare 5. These and many other utilities and enhancement NLMs are available from Novell and third-party vendors.

NLMs can be loaded and unloaded manually at the file server console and automatically through the use of server configuration and script files. In the following section, you learn about the server console and become familiar with the types of tasks you typically perform there; then, in the subsequent section, you learn about server configuration and script files.

The Server Console

The server console provides an interface for controlling and managing the NetWare server. From the console command prompt, you can load and unload NLMs and execute console commands. In addition, you can modify the server configuration, edit configuration files, view network traffic, bring down and restart the server, and view and manage server connections.

Loading And Unloading NLMs

NLMs are NetWare-specific programs that run only on a NetWare server. You load an NLM at the server console by typing its name and pressing Enter. Here's the syntax for loading an NLM at the server console:

```
[path] NLMname [parameters]
```

Here, [path] indicates the location of the file, *NLMname* is the name of the NLM being loaded, and [*parameters*] is the desired setting or value for an associated variable. The path is only required if the NLM is not in the SYS:SYSTEM directory (the default location searched by the system for NLMs when a path is not specified).

The **LOAD** console command can also be used to load an NLM, as follows:

```
LOAD [path] NLMname [parameters]
```

You terminate NLMs by unloading them. If the NLM has a user interface, choosing the menu option to exit the interface will, in most cases, unload that NLM. You can also use the **UNLOAD** console command with the following syntax, to terminate an NLM:

```
UNLOAD NLMname
```

Console Commands

Console commands represent a different category of NetWare server utilities. Unlike NLMs, console commands are integrated into the core operating system. They are command-line utilities that can only be executed at the server console. They are analogous to DOS internal commands, such as COPY, DEL, DIR, MD, and PATH, that are encoded into the DOS command interpreter, COMMAND.COM. NLMs, on the other hand, are analogous to DOS utilities, such as XCOPY.COM, FDISK.COM, and FORMAT.COM, that exist as individual program files.

You execute console commands by typing the name of the command at the console prompt and pressing Enter. A list of available console commands can be displayed by executing the **HELP** console command. You can obtain detailed help for specific commands by executing the **HELP** command and including the name of the command about which you want information. The syntax for displaying detailed help on the **BIND** command is shown in the following example:

```
HELP BIND
```

The detailed help screen provides you with parameters and options for the specific command and includes examples of usage.

The **SET** console command can be used to view and change server configuration parameters. (The default server parameters are set to maximize performance for most situations and should not be changed without sufficient reason.) You can view the settable configuration parameter categories by executing the **SET** command with no parameters at the server console. Selecting one of the numbered categories from the list that's displayed lets you view detailed information about each of the settable parameters in that category, including the current settings, default settings, range for settings, and usage examples, among other things.

Many of the configuration parameters can be changed while the server is running. The following command, executed at the console prompt (or from within the appropriate configuration file), would be used to change a configuration setting:

```
SET parameter = value
```

Changing a **SET** parameter at the console prompt results in a temporary configuration change that lasts until the parameter is reset or until the server is brought down. To make the change permanent, you should place the **SET**

NetWare Operating System And Configuration Basics   147

command in the appropriate configuration file. In fact, some SET parameters can only be configured during system startup because they specify values that cannot be altered while the server is running—for example, the minimum number of buffers allocated.

Navigating The Console

The following hot key sequences are supported to make navigation of the console easier:

➤ **Ctrl+Esc** Brings up the Current Screens menu. This menu provides a numbered list of all the NLM screens currently running on the server. Typing the number associated with the NLM screen and pressing Enter takes you to that screen.

> **TIP** The order of the screens in the numbered list on the Current Screens menu represents the order in which the NLMs were loaded. Note that the console screen is always listed first.

➤ **Alt+Esc** Toggles through the NLM screens that are currently running on the server.

➤ **Ctrl+Alt+Esc** Brings up the Hung Console screen. This screen gives you a way to safely bring down the server in the event that you're unable to execute any commands at the server console. From this screen, you have the option to either bring the server down or cancel a volume mount.

Server Configuration Files

Server configuration files are text files that contain a sequence of configuration commands recognized by the NetWare operating system. These NetWare configuration files have the file name extension .NCF and are used to automate processes that would normally require manual input each time the process is repeated. They are particularly useful for automating the configuration of a server during the startup process. When used in conjunction with a DOS AUTOEXEC.BAT file, the entire process of starting and configuring the server can be automated.

You start a NetWare server by booting DOS and then running the DOS executable file SERVER.EXE. You can automate this step by placing the instructions to execute SERVER.EXE in the AUTOEXE.BAT file. Upon execution, SERVER.EXE—in addition to loading SERVER.NLM into file server RAM—looks for two configuration files: STARTUP.NCF and AUTOEXEC.NCF. If found, these files are executed in that order, and the command parameters they specify are incorporated into the server startup configuration.

> You need to know the startup files used to automate the server initialization process and the proper sequence for their execution. The startup files, listed in the order of their execution, are shown in the following list:
> - AUTOEXEC.BAT
> - SERVER.EXE
> - STARTUP.NCF
> - AUTOEXEC.NCF

Both STARTUP.NCF and AUTOEXEC.NCF are special files that warrant additional attention.

STARTUP.NCF

The STARTUP.NCF file is generated by the operating system during installation and stored in the server boot directory on the DOS partition. The default server boot directory is C:\NWSERVER. The file contains the configuration commands and parameters required by the server during the boot process. The commands in a typical STARTUP.NCF file will load disk drivers and name space NLMs as well as configure **SET** parameters that cannot be altered while the server is running.

STARTUP.NCF, like all NCF files, is a text file that can be edited with any text editor. It can also be edited from the server console with the EDIT.NLM utility or the NWCONFIG.NLM utility.

During server startup, two STARTUP.NCF-associated command-line options are available for use with SERVER.EXE:

- **SERVER -S** *\path\filename* Allows you to specify an alternate STARTUP.NCF file, where *path* is the path to the alternate file location and *filename* is the name of the alternate startup file. A practical use of an alternate STARTUP.NCF file would be when a server needs to be booted with a special configuration for maintenance purposes.

- **SERVER -NS** Allows you to boot the server without executing the STARTUP.NCF file. This may need to be done for maintenance reasons, but can also be done for troubleshooting purposes.

NetWare Operating System And Configuration Basics   **149**

> **TIP:** Booting the server without executing the STARTUP.NCF file will prevent automatic execution of the AUTOEXEC.NCF file because it's located, by default, on the SYS volume. The SYS volume can only be mounted if the disk drivers for the storage device it's on have been loaded—a task usually accomplished by commands in STARTUP.NCF.

AUTOEXEC.NCF

The AUTOEXEC.NCF file is generated by the operating system during installation and is stored in the SYS:SYSTEM directory. It can be edited with the NWCONFIG.NLM utility, the EDIT.NLM utility, or any text editor.

The commands in the AUTOEXEC.NCF file complete the server boot process and customize the server configuration. Information in the file includes:

- Time zone
- Server name
- Internal network number
- Load commands for NLMs that do not have to be started from the STARTUP.NCF file
- Console commands, including **SET** parameters, that do not have to be executed from the STARTUP.NCF file
- Comment lines, used as documentation, that are ignored by the server

For maintenance or troubleshooting purposes, the following SERVER.EXE command-line option can be used to avoid automatic execution of AUTOEXEC.NCF:

```
SERVER -NA
```

Server Script Files

Server script files can be used to automate tasks, such as executing a series of console commands or loading and unloading a group of NLMs. Server script files are text files that contain a sequence of commands that perform the desired task or series of tasks. They can be created with any text editor and must be saved with a .NCF extension to be recognized by the operating system as a NetWare batch file. To make these files available without specifying a path during execution, you should store them in the SYS:SYSTEM directory.

You need to be aware of the following issues when using the EDIT.NLM utility:

➤ When editing an existing file, you must include the path for any file that's not in the SYS:SYSTEM directory.

➤ When creating a file, you must enter a file name extension if you want one; no default extension is created by EDIT.NLM.

➤ You can use the EDIT.NLM utility to edit text files on the DOS partition.

Other products installed on the server, including third-party products, may create NCF files that are used to automate the tasks performed by the products. One such product is the NetWare GUI, which is discussed in detail in Chapter 10. For this to be activated, several different NLMs need to be loaded in the proper sequence. The STARTX.NCF file included with NetWare 5 can be executed to automatically load the NLMs.

Practice Questions

Question 1

> Which of the following are features of the NetWare kernel? [Choose the three best answers]
> - a. Scheduling unattended startup of applications
> - b. Preemptive processing
> - c. NLMs
> - d. Protected mode memory support for Java applications
> - e. Virtual memory

The correct answers are b, d, and e. The scheduling feature supported by the kernel is for processor time allocated to different tasks. Therefore, answer a is incorrect. The kernel and NLMs represent two different modular components of the NetWare operating system. Therefore, answer c is incorrect.

Question 2

> What's the proper sequence for execution of the server startup files?
> - a. AUTOEXEC.BAT, SERVER.EXE, STARTUP.BAT, AUTOEXEC.NCF
> - b. CONFIG.SYS, AUTOEXEC.BAT, STARTUP.NCF, AUTOEXEC.NCF
> - c. AUTOEXEC.BAT, SERVER.EXE, STARTUP.NCF, AUTOEXEC.NCF
> - d. CONFIG.SYS, AUTOEXEC.BAT, SERVER.EXE, STARTUP.NCF, AUTOEXEC.NCF
> - e. AUTOEXEC.BAT, STARTUP.NCF, AUTOEXEC.NCF

The correct answer is c. Answers a and d are incorrect because STARTUP.BAT and CONFIG.SYS are not server startup files. Answer b includes the CONFIG.SYS file and excludes the SERVER.EXE file and is therefore incorrect. SERVER.EXE is one of the server startup files and because answer e does not list this file, it's incorrect.

Question 3

Which of the following commands, typed at the server console, would boot the server without executing the AUTOEXEC.NCF file? [Choose the best answer(s)]

○ a. **STARTUP -NS**

○ b. **SERVER -NA**

○ c. **AUTOEXEC -NA**

○ d. **SERVER -NS**

○ e. None of the above

Trick question

The correct answer is e. This is a trick question because the command-line option for booting the server without executing the AUTOEXEC.NCF file is associated with the SERVER.EXE file, a DOS executable that can only be run from DOS. Therefore, answers a, b, c, and d are incorrect.

Question 4

Which of the following disk driver types are supported by NetWare 5? [Choose the two best answers]

❏ a. LAN

❏ b. HAM

❏ c. CDM

❏ d. DSK

❏ e. NAM

The correct answers are b and c. Answers a and e are incorrect because they're not disk driver types. Answer d is incorrect because DSK disk driver types are not supported by NetWare 5.

NetWare Operating System And Configuration Basics   153

Question 5

> Help is available from the file server console. Which of the following commands, when entered at the console command line, will display help information? [Choose the two best answers]
>
> ❏ a. **HELP /?**
> ❏ b. **LOAD HELP**
> ❏ c. **HELP**
> ❏ d. **HELP LOAD**

The correct answers are c and d. **HELP**, when entered at the command line, displays a list of available console commands. **HELP LOAD**, when entered at the command line, provides detailed help on the **LOAD** console command. Answer a is incorrect because the **HELP** console command does not have a /? option. Answer b is incorrect because the **LOAD** console command is used to load NLMs from the console command line, and HELP is not an NLM.

Question 6

> Which of the following statements about console commands is not true?
>
> ○ a. Console commands are command-line utilities that can only be executed at the server console.
> ○ b. Console commands are part of the NetWare core operating system.
> ○ c. Console commands can be executed from within NCF files.
> ○ d. Console command-line parameters can be displayed by typing **HELP** at the console command prompt and pressing Enter.

Trick question

The correct answer is d. Typing **HELP** at the console command prompt displays a list of available console commands, not console command-line parameters. Therefore, statement d is not true of console commands and is the correct answer. The statements in the other answers are all true of console commands. Therefore, answers a, b, and c are incorrect. This is a trick question because answers a and c appear mutually exclusive, which points to one of these as the most likely answer. In fact, console commands can *only* be executed at the server console. Even when run from within an NCF file, the commands are still executed at the server console.

Need To Know More?

http://support.novell.com/servlet/Knowledgebase provides you with a search engine that leads you to numerous articles on the various subjects covered in this chapter. Search for "NetWare Kernel," "Console Commands," and "Configuration Files" to obtain a information on these subjects.

www.novell.com/documentation is the Web site where you can access the same documentation that ships with the various NetWare products. Click on NetWare 5 and search for "NetWare Kernel," "Console Commands," and "Configuration Files" to obtain information on these subjects.

The NetWare GUI And Java

Terms you'll need to understand:

- √ Graphical user interface (GUI)
- √ NetWare GUI
- √ Java Abstract Windowing Toolkit (AWT)
- √ Java application
- √ Java class
- √ Java applet

Techniques you'll need to master:

- √ Recommending hardware component modifications to properly support the NetWare GUI
- √ Explaining the difference between Java classes and Java applets
- √ Loading Java applications
- √ Configuring the NetWare GUI
- √ Installing additional NetWare products from the NetWare GUI
- √ Customizing the NetWare GUI

Previous versions of NetWare required users to interact with NetWare Loadable Modules (NLMs) on the NetWare server through a text-based interface. NetWare 5 introduces a graphical user interface (GUI) that supports user interaction with a mouse and graphical display. The GUI interface is a product of NetWare 5 support for applications written in the Java programming language.

In this chapter, you learn how to load and configure GUI support on a NetWare 5 server, launch Java programs and applets from the NetWare GUI, and configure and customize the NetWare GUI. The following overview of NetWare 5 Java support lays the groundwork for your mastery of the NetWare GUI.

NetWare 5 Java Support

NetWare 5 provides Java-based GUI support for NLMs and Java applications that require a GUI. Most Java applications that require a GUI are developed using the Java Abstract Windowing Toolkit (AWT). NetWare 5 supports Java Foundation Class applications developed using AWT.

Hardware Requirements

Running GUI-based Java applications on your NetWare server may require changes in your server hardware and necessitate adding RAM if your server is currently operating with a minimal resource configuration. To run Java applications that use a GUI, your server must meet the following minimum requirements:

➤ **Memory** 48MB of RAM is the minimum requirement for GUI support; however, 64MB or more is recommended.

➤ **Mouse** Microsoft serial and PS/2 mice are supported by the NetWare GUI. The mouse type is selected and configured during NetWare 5 installation. The GUI can also be configured, during installation, to work with the numeric keypad if the server does not have a mouse.

➤ **Video** Extended Industry Standard Architecture (EISA), Industry Standard Architecture (ISA), and Peripheral Component Interconnect (PCI) video cards are all supported by the NetWare GUI. A PCI video card that conforms to the Video Emulation Standard Association (VESA) specifications 1.2 or higher is recommended.

During NetWare 5 installation, the operating system automatically detects and loads the proper video driver to support your video card. The driver is loaded with one of the two following *default* settings:

➤ 640-by-480 resolution with 16 colors, if the video card does not meet the VESA 1.2 or higher specification

➤ 640-by-480 resolution with 256 colors, if the video card conforms to the VESA 1.2 or higher specification

> Video resolutions higher than 640 by 480 are supported by the VESA video driver, but they cannot be selected during installation. If your video card and monitor support higher video resolutions, you can configure them manually by selecting Novell|Tools|Properties in the NetWare GUI. When you select the resolution you want from the list of available resolutions, you should use the Test option to ensure that the resolution mode is supported by your hardware. After verifying that the test pattern for the mode you have selected is properly displayed, you must restart the GUI to activate the change.

A NetWare configuration file (NCF), VESA_RSP.NCF, is available for you to use to redetect the drivers for your mouse or video card if either is changed. The file is located in the SYS:\JAVA\NWGFX\ directory. Because this location is added to the server search path when the AUTOEXEC.NCF file executes, you can redetect your mouse and video drivers at the server console by entering the following (without having to include the path):

VESA _RSP

Note: When the VESA_RSP.NCF file is executed, the detected video driver is configured with the default resolution setting. If you were using a higher resolution setting prior to redetecting your drivers, you'll have to reconfigure the driver from the NetWare GUI to restore settings.

Java Classes And Java Applets

Java support for NetWare 5 is provided through the JAVA.NLM file. This program is a part of the JavaSoft Java Virtual Machine (JVM) interpreter for Java classes. With the JAVA.NLM loaded, NetWare can execute Java classes and Java applets. You can load the Java Virtual Machine by entering the following at the console prompt:

JAVA

Java classes are full-blown applications that are written in Java. Java applets are programs written in Java that run within a Java-compatible browser. In the following two sections, you'll learn how to run both types of Java applications.

Java Classes

You can use the following syntax to run Java applications from the console prompt:

```
Java [-options] path_to_Java_class
```

Runtime options are also available with many Java applications. You can view the available options while the application is running by entering the following at the console prompt:

```
JAVA -help
```

> **EXAM ALERT**
>
> It's important to remember the following information about the names of Java classes:
> - The names are case sensitive.
> - The names require the long name space support.

Java Applets

Java applets that have been defined as part of a Hypertext Markup Language (HTML) document can be run as an application on the server with an applet viewer called APPLET. The applet viewer is provided as a server console command by JAVA.NLM. Use the **APPLET** command to run a Java applet by entering the following at the console prompt:

```
APPLET HTTP://URL
```

or

```
APPLET path_to_local_filename_of_HTML_document
```

When executing the **APPLET** command, include the URL or file name of an HTML document to specify the HTML document to be opened by the applet viewer in order to read and execute the Java applet code. Within the HTML document, the applet is defined between the **<APPLET>** and **</APPLET>** HTML tags.

When the **APPLET** command runs, the only HTML code executed within the specified HTML document is the code defined as the applet; the other HTML code in the document is not recognized. The applet viewer, in essence, pulls the applet code from the document and executes it as an independent program while ignoring the rest of the document. Opening an HTML document like this results in a different appearance than opening the same document

The NetWare GUI And Java   **159**

with a Java-enabled browser. The browser views the entire document, whereas the applet viewer displays the applet only.

In the following section, you'll learn about the NetWare GUI. In particular, you'll learn how to load and unload Java GUI support, use the NetWare GUI, and add Java programs and applets to the NetWare GUI menu.

NetWare GUI Support

The NetWare GUI runs on top of an implementation of X-Windows and displays Java programs that conform to the Java AWT standard. Access to the underlying X-Server layer, for users and application developers, is obtained through the Java AWT only.

> **EXAM ALERT:** Because GUI applications must conform to the Java AWT standard, reliance on the underlying X-Windows layer is removed. This means that if Novell changes the GUI implementation in NetWare to something other than X-Windows, existing applications will still run without having to be rewritten.

Java GUI support can be dynamically loaded and unloaded. In other words, GUI support can be added and removed without affecting normal server operations. (No annoying messages such as, "For the changes you have made to take effect, your computer must be restarted. Would you like to restart your computer now?")

The STARTX.NCF file is used to load GUI support on the NetWare server. This NCF file loads JAVA.NLM, mouse and video drivers, and the NetWare GUI. You can launch the STARTUP.NCF file in either of the following two ways:

➤ Enter **STARTX.NCF** at the console prompt.

➤ Load a Java class or applet that requires GUI support. This action causes the STARTX.NCF file to be launched automatically.

> **EXAM ALERT:** STARTX.NCF is run automatically from the AUTOEXEC.NCF when the server initializes. To prevent the GUI from loading automatically, you should comment out the line in the AUTOEXEC.NCF that launches STARTX.NCF.

The GUI is designed to allow you to run Java programs and applets on your NetWare server. The preconfigured menu includes Java utilities you can use to manage your network and configure the NetWare GUI. In addition, you can configure the GUI menu so you can launch your own Java programs and applets.

Note: The NetWare GUI is neither the front end to a high-performance graphical workstation nor a full-featured desktop environment. It fulfills a marketing need, but it's currently engineered as a low-priority process running on the server.

Using The NetWare GUI

You need to know how to use the NetWare GUI to install additional NetWare products and services, change the GUI configuration, and add programs and applets to the GUI menu. The following sections supply the pertinent information and step-by-step instructions necessary for you to perform these tasks.

Installing Additional NetWare Products And Services

You can rerun the NetWare installation program from the NetWare GUI if you want to install additional products and services not included in the initial installation. Complete the following steps to install additional products and services from the GUI:

1. Click on the Novell button in the lower-left corner of the server screen.

2. Click on Install. A list of currently installed NetWare products appears.

3. If you want to add new products, click on New Product and supply the path to the product source files. Click on OK to display the Additional Products And Services dialog box.

4. In that dialog box, select the products you want installed by highlighting them. Click on Next.

5. If prompted, supply the additional configuration information that's required. The products you're about to install are then displayed in a Summary window.

6. If you wish, you may customize the installation of any of the products by clicking on the Customize button.

7. Click on Finish to start the file copy. Reboot the server when prompted at the completion of the file copy.

Changing The Video Resolution

You can change the video resolution with the Display Properties configuration tool provided in the NetWare GUI. Use the following steps to set a different video resolution:

1. From the GUI, select Novell|Tools|Display Properties.
2. Select the desired resolution from the list provided.
3. Select Test.
4. Click on OK when asked if you want to test the resolution mode.
5. Click on OK when asked if the test pattern was displayed properly.
6. Click on OK to acknowledge instructions to restart the GUI for changes to be activated.

Changing The GUI Background

You can change the NetWare GUI background to one of the alternate backgrounds supplied with the product or even add your own background graphics (they must be in the XPixMap, or XPM, format, which is a popular image format) to use in the GUI. The background graphics files you add need to be placed in the SYS:JAVA\NWGFX\PIXMAPS directory.

Use the following steps to change the current NetWare GUI background:

1. Select Novell|Tools|Backgrounds.
2. From the list provided, choose the background you want.
3. Optionally, click on Test to display the selected background.
4. Either click on OK to set the background and exit the utility, or click on Cancel to exit the utility without changing the background color.

Changing The Keyboard Configuration

The Keyboard Property utility allows you to specify the keyboard type for keyboards that support international character sets. Use the following steps to change to a different keyboard type:

1. Select Novell|Tools|Keyboard Properties.
2. Select the keyboard type you want from the list provided.
3. Click on Apply.

Adding Java Programs And Applets To The NetWare GUI Menu

If you want to customize the NetWare GUI menu with items that launch your own Java programs or applets, do the following:

1. Use a text editor to open the file SYS:JAVA\NWGFX\FVWM2\FVWM2RC5XX.

2. Locate the MENUS section and then find the subsection that defines the menu where you want to add the item.

3. Use the following syntax to add the new Java program or applet to the menu:

   ```
   + "menu_item" Exec command
   ```

   In this syntax, *menu_item* is the text displayed on the menu select button and *command* is the command or utility you want to execute.

4. Restart the NetWare GUI to force the changes to take effect.

Practice Questions

Question 1

> Which of the following items should be considered if you decide to add support for the NetWare GUI to your server? [Choose the three best answers]
>
> ❏ a. Type of mouse attached
>
> ❏ b. RAM requirements
>
> ❏ c. Size of the server monitor
>
> ❏ d. Video card and driver
>
> ❏ e. Length of the backbone connection to the nearest neighbor running the NetWare GUI

The correct answers are a, b, and d. The GUI requires a Microsoft-format PS/2 or serial mouse, additional RAM above the minimum required for NetWare 5 installation, and a video card and driver that supports at least 640-by-480 resolution with 16 colors. The size of the monitor is immaterial as long as it supports the minimum resolution and colors. Therefore, answer c is incorrect. The length of the backbone has nothing to do with hardware support for the NetWare GUI. Therefore, answer e is incorrect.

Question 2

> Which of the following files, when executed, could result in the NetWare GUI being loaded? [Choose the best answers]
>
> ❏ a. AUTOEXEC.BAT
>
> ❏ b. STARTX.NCF
>
> ❏ c. AUTOEXEC.NCF
>
> ❏ d. SERVER.EXE
>
> ❏ e. None of the above

Trick question

The correct answers are a, b, c, and d. STARTX.NCF starts Java, loads the mouse and video drivers, and then starts the GUI. STARTX.NCF is run from the AUTOEXEC.NCF file, by default. Any file that results in the AUTOEXEC.NCF being executed (such as AUTOEXEC.BAT and

SERVER.EXE) can launch STARTX.NCF and start the GUI. Answer e is incorrect because the others answers are correct.

Question 3

> Which of the following disk driver types are not supported by the NetWare GUI? [Choose the four best answers]
>
> ❑ a. SCSI
> ❑ b. PCI VESA (version 1.2 and higher)
> ❑ c. ISA
> ❑ d. PCI VESA (version 1.2 and lower)
> ❑ e. EISA

The correct answers are b, c, d, and e. All of these video cards are supported. Answer a is incorrect because SCSI is not a video card type.

Question 4

> Help is available from the file server console for JAVA.NLM. Which of the following, when entered at the console command line, will display help information for JAVA.NLM?
>
> ○ a. **HELP /?**
> ○ b. **HELP JAVA**
> ○ c. **JAVA -help**
> ○ d. **HELP JAVA.NLM**

The correct answer is c. Typing **JAVA -help** displays information about available runtime options for currently running Java applications. **HELP** is a console command that provides help on console commands (not NLMs). Therefore, answers a, b, and d are incorrect.

Need To Know More?

http://support.novell.com/servlet/Knowledgebase provides you with a search engine that will lead you to numerous articles on the subjects covered in this chapter. Search for "Java support," "Java applets," and "NetWare GUI."

www.novell.com/documentation is the Web site where you can access the same documentation that ships with the various NetWare products. Click on NetWare 5 and search for "Java support," "Java applets," and "NetWare GUI."

ConsoleOne, Remote Access, And Server Security

Terms you'll need to understand:

√ Console screen

√ ConsoleOne shortcut

√ Asynchronous connection

√ Synchronous connection

√ Password encryption

Techniques you'll need to master:

√ Explaining the features of ConsoleOne

√ Performing administrative and management functions with ConsoleOne

√ Customizing the ConsoleOne interface

√ Setting up your server for remote management

√ Accessing a NetWare 5 server console with remote access utilities

√ Securing a NetWare 5 server console against unauthorized access

In this chapter, you become familiar with the ConsoleOne interface, learn about its currently available features, and learn how to use it to perform basic management tasks. In addition, you learn about the utilities (including ConsoleOne) that can be used to access the console screen of a remote server, and you learn how to secure your server against unauthorized access.

> It's essential that you take the time to become adept at using each of the utilities introduced in this chapter. In particular, you need to know how to access all the options available on pull-down and pop-up menus when using the Java utilities. Be aware (or beware) that which options show up (even if grayed out) on a given pull-down or pop-up menu depend on the active browser and view selections.

ConsoleOne

ConsoleOne is the fundamental component of Novell's new generation of Java-based utilities for network management. It provides the framework and programming interfaces to accept the snap-in components that contain the actual management features available in the utility.

The ConsoleOne framework is intentionally extensible to allow full support for both Novell and third-party snap-ins. The management capability of ConsoleOne is defined by the snap-ins that are employed. This means that, as a full complement of management snap-ins becomes available, ConsoleOne will provide a standard pull-featured, customizable management console that's accessible from any networked machine capable of supporting a Java Virtual Machine (JVM).

ConsoleOne alone doesn't provide any management functions. The management capabilities currently available with ConsoleOne are provided through the default snap-in components that Novell supplies with NetWare 5.

> Remember that the set of management options you learn about in this section apply to the current default snap-in. The set of options will certainly change over time, but the basics of the interface should remain static. Once you become familiar with and learn how to use the tool, additional or upgraded snap-ins will only require that you learn the new capabilities and functions provided. You won't be required to learn how to use a new tool to take advantage of the new capabilities.

ConsoleOne, Remote Access, And Server Security   **169**

The default snap-in components provide ConsoleOne with the functionality necessary for you to learn to use its built-in features. In the following section, you learn the basics of using ConsoleOne.

Starting ConsoleOne

ConsoleOne can run on both NetWare servers and clients. It gives you the ability to perform basic server and Novell Directory Services (NDS) administrative tasks with the same utility from either a server or a workstation. To start ConsoleOne from a server, perform one of the following actions:

➤ At the server console prompt, execute the C1START.NCF file.

➤ Include the command to execute the C1START.NCF file in another NetWare configuration file (NCF).

➤ From the NetWare graphical user interface (GUI), pull up the Start menu and select the ConsoleOne button.

When the C1START.NCF file executes, it loads Java support and starts the NetWare GUI before executing ConsoleOne. If Java and GUI support are already running when C1START.NCF executes, error messages to that effect are displayed and the console screen is switched to the GUI where ConsoleOne is executed.

To start ConsoleOne from a workstation, you must execute CONSOLE1.EXE from a network drive that has the SYS volume mapped as its root. The default location of CONSOLE1.EXE on a NetWare 5 server is the SYS:Public\mgmt subdirectory.

> **TIP:** If you have difficulty starting ConsoleOne from a workstation, make sure your workstation meets the minimum hardware requirements. Also, make sure you're not trying to launch the utility by browsing to the executable from the Network Neighborhood. ConsoleOne can only be started from a mapped network drive that has the SYS volume as its root.

The ConsoleOne User Interface

The ConsoleOne user interface consists of a set of basic components that allows you to access the tasks and management features made available through the active snap-in modules. The user interface elements, shown in Figure 11.1, that are provided by the ConsoleOne GUI include the following:

Chapter 11

- **Main menu** The main menu provides the standard set of drop-down submenus: File, Edit, View, Tools, and Help. The submenus and submenu selections that are available in the main menu depend on the active object browser window and view window selections.

- **Toolbar** The toolbar provides a user-configurable set of buttons to offer quick access to frequently used features. The toolbar contents available depend on the active selection in the object browser and the view windows.

- **Status bar** The status bar displays context-sensitive statistics for the active selections in the object browser and view windows.

- **Browser** The browser provides a hierarchical display of the objects you can view and manage from the file server console or workstation. The left pane of the browser, called the *object browser*, allows you to browse the available objects. The hierarchical display in the object browser window is navigated by expanding and collapsing the container objects. Double-clicking on the object or clicking on the dot that's to the left of the object expands or collapses the object. The right pane of the browser, called the *view*, displays the contents of the active object in the object browser window.

> **EXAM ALERT**
> Most applets launched from ConsoleOne are displayed in the view window.

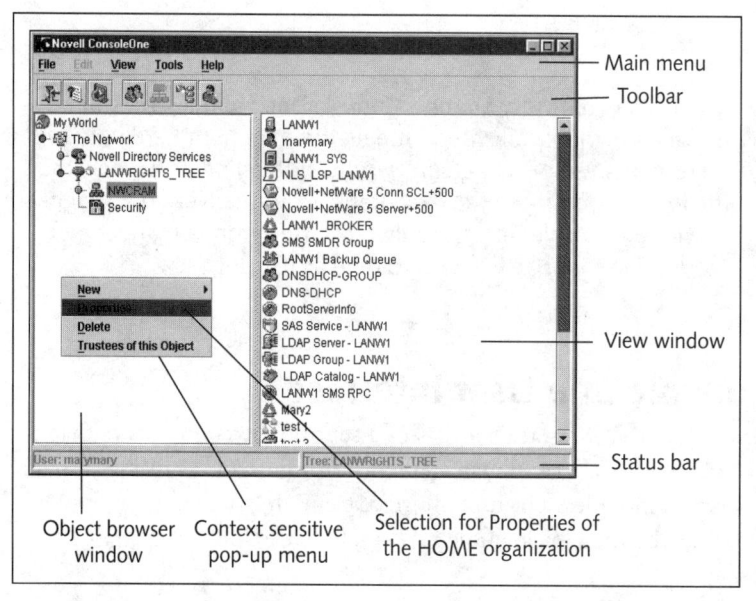

Figure 11.1 Elements of the ConsoleOne user interface.

ConsoleOne, Remote Access, And Server Security   171

➤ **Context menus** The context menus provide access to the tasks, features, and functions specific to the types of objects that appear in the object browser and view windows.

The My World object located in the object browser window (left pane) contains all the object types that can be browsed using ConsoleOne. When you're using ConsoleOne at the file server, the default object types under the My World object are as follows:

➤ My Server

➤ The Network

➤ Shortcuts

> **EXAM ALERT:** From a workstation, only the object called *The Network* and its functions are available.

These three object types provide access to the management features available with the default snap-in modules. You'll learn how the management tasks are organized under these objects and how to use these features in the following sections.

My Server: Managing The File Server With ConsoleOne

The My Server object contains the following three objects through which most of the server management functions are accessed:

➤ Volumes

➤ Configuration Files

➤ Tools

The Volumes Object

Use the Volumes object to browse the file system on the local server and perform the following basic file-system management tasks with the files and directories:

➤ Edit (text files)

➤ Delete

➤ Rename

- Create a new folder
- Cut
- Copy
- Paste

The Configuration Files Object

Use the Configuration Files object to view and select server configuration files to edit. When you double-click on one of the files to edit, it's automatically opened in the Java-based text editor that's included in ConsoleOne. (This text editor can be used to edit any text file located on any of the file server's volumes.)

Follow these steps to edit a server configuration file:

1. Expand the My Server object by clicking on the dot to its left.
2. Click Configuration Files in the object browser window, which displays the file list in the view window.
3. Double-click on the desired configuration file in the view window, which launches the text editor and opens the file.
4. Modify the file as necessary and then select File|Save from the menu bar to save the changes.
5. Select File|Exit from the menu bar to quit the editor and return to the ConsoleOne main menu.

Follow these steps to edit other text files that are not contained in the Configuration Files object:

1. Expand the My Server object, then the Volumes object by clicking on the dots to left of them.
2. Select the desired Server or Volume object and expand it by clicking on the dot to its left.
3. Browse to and click on the folder containing the text file to be edited.
4. In the view window, click the text file to be edited.
5. From the main menu bar, select File|Edit to launch the text editor and open the file.
6. Modify the file as necessary and then select File|Save from the menu bar to save the changes.
7. Select File|Exit from the menu bar to quit the editor and return to the ConsoleOne main menu.

ALERT: You need to be aware that nearly all the tasks discussed here can be accomplished in more than one way. For example, when you use the Configuration Files object to select a configuration file to edit, right-clicking on the file invokes a pop-up menu. From the pop-up menu, you can select Edit to launch the text editor and open the file. Note that Edit is the only option present on the pop-up menu when it's invoked from within the Configuration Files object.

Right-clicking on the same configuration file from within the Volumes object invokes the file system management pop-up menu. This menu includes all the file system management options, including the option to edit the file. Selecting Edit will, of course, launch the text editor and open the file. In addition, once the text editor is open, you can use the main menu bar's File|Open selection to locate and open any other text file in the local file server's file system.

You should spend some time experimenting with the utility to familiarize yourself with the alternatives that are available for accomplishing all the standard tasks.

The Tools Object

Use the Tools object to access the Console Manager and RConsoleJ utilities. These utilities allow you to gain access to your server console screens (except Java GUI console screens) and remotely manage your servers.

The RCONSOLE agent, RCONAG6.NLM, must be running on servers that will be accessed by either Console Manager or RConsoleJ. The RCONSOLE agent is required to set the password, the Transmission Control Protocol (TCP) port, and the Sequenced Packet Exchange (SPX) port used to gain access to the server.

RCONAG6.NLM can be loaded at a console prompt by typing "RCONAG6" and pressing Enter. You are then prompted for the RCONSOLE password, the TCP port, and the SPX port.

The command to load RCONAG6.NLM can also be included in an NCF file using the following syntax:

```
LOAD RCONAG6 <password> 2034 16800
```

Replace *password* with the password that you'll use for remote access. The numbers 2034 and 16800 are the default TCP and SPX listening ports, respectively.

This command is automatically added to the AUTOEXEC.NCF file during server installation, but it's disabled by default. The disabled command is shown

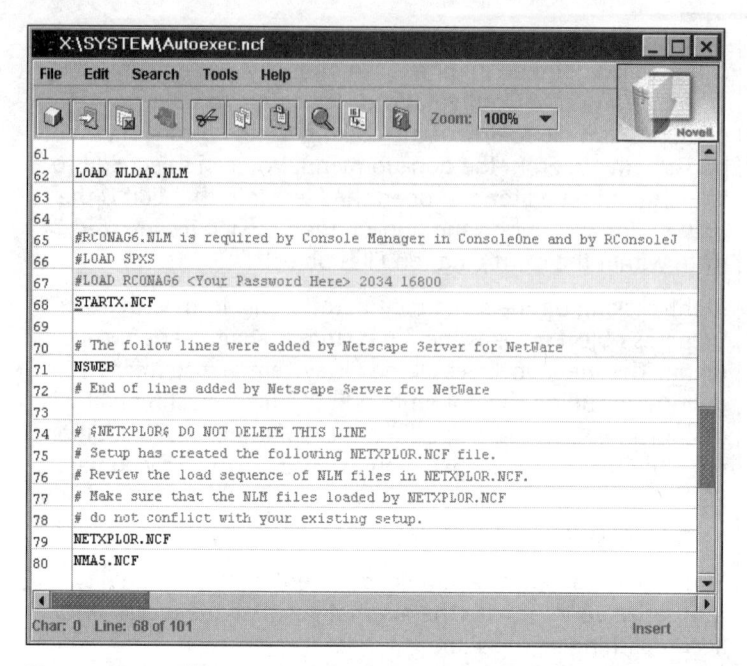

Figure 11.2 The command to start the RCONSOLE agent is automatically added to the AUTOEXEC.NCF file and disabled during server installation.

in Figure 11.2 on line 67 of the text editor. The command can be enabled by removing the pound sign (#) from the beginning of the line.

Console Manager

You use Console Manager to display the server console screens currently running on your *local* server. Console Manager is accessed from ConsoleOne. To access Console Manager expand My Server and Tools; click on Console Manager; change connection information if necessary and supply the password; then, click on Connect.

> **TIP** It may be necessary to resize the screen or use the scrollbar at the bottom of the window to be able to view the Connect button.

The Java GUI display shows the running screens as named tiles in the view window (see Figure 11.3). You can display an individual console screen in its own window by clicking on the appropriate tile. Multiple console screens can be displayed concurrently (see Figure 11.4).

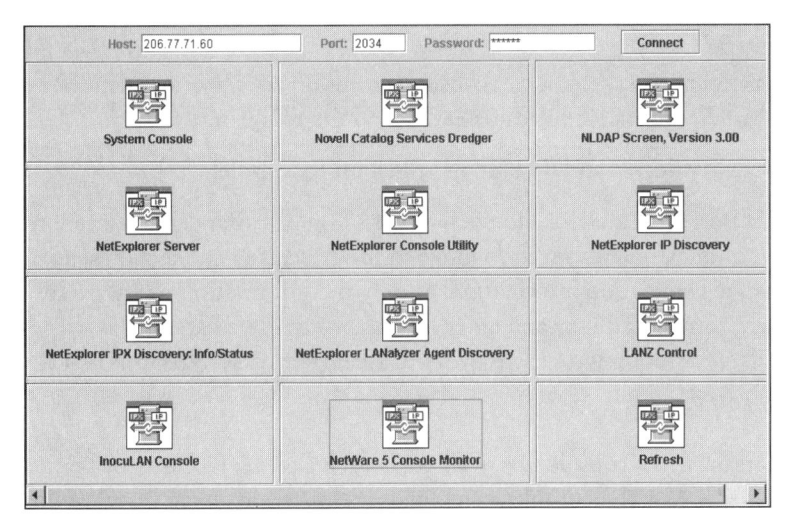

ConsoleOne, Remote Access, And Server Security 175

Figure 11.3 Java GUI display of Console Manager in the ConsoleOne view window.

Figure 11.4 Multiple console screens visible in their own individual windows.

The screens that are visible when Console Manager starts are the ones (minus the Java GUI screen) currently running on the server. If additional screens are loaded, click on the Refresh tile in the view window of the Console Manager to add them to the display.

RConsoleJ

Use RConsoleJ to access the server console screens on *remote* servers with IP or IPX. To start RConsoleJ from ConsoleOne, do the following:

1. Expand My Server and then Tools. Click on RConsoleJ.

2. Supply the server address and the password from the Standard connection screen or click on Advanced to move to the Advanced connection screen to change connection information. Supply the information necessary to connect through a proxy and enter the password. (The password is the one that was set up with the RCONSOLE agent, RCONAG6.NLM.)

3. Click on Connect.

Navigation through a console screen when using RConsoleJ is not seen on the remote server unless the console screen being remotely accessed matches the console screen that's displayed on the server. You can use the Activate button on the RConsoleJ menu bar to switch the remote screen display to match the RConsoleJ screen selection or you can put a check in the Sync checkbox to synchronize the remote display with the RConsoleJ screen selection (see Figure 11.5).

The Network: Managing NDS With ConsoleOne

The Network object in ConsoleOne provides access to NDS management from the server console. All the NDS trees in your network are displayed under The Network object when it's expanded. Authenticating to any of the trees displayed

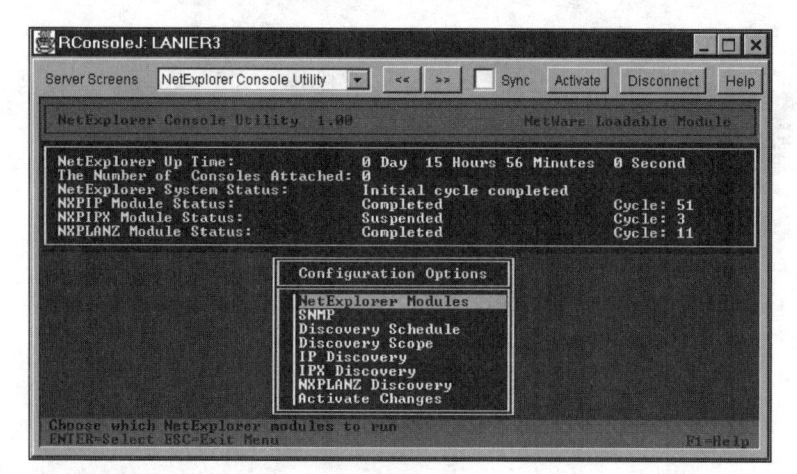

Figure 11.5 The RConsoleJ console.

ConsoleOne, Remote Access, And Server Security

allows you to browse, create, and manage the NDS objects for that tree (within the constraints of your authentication rights).

A login window is provided for authentication if you attempt to expand a tree object to which you're not currently authenticated.

> **TIP:** ConsoleOne does not currently support logging out from individual trees during your ConsoleOne session. In addition, within a ConsoleOne session, you may have only one authentication active for each NDS tree. Reauthenticating to a tree as a different user logs you out of that tree first and then authenticates the new account through login. When you exit a ConsoleOne session, you're automatically logged out of all trees to which you were authenticated within that session. You may, however, run multiple concurrent sessions of ConsoleOne with different accounts authenticated to the same tree from different ConsoleOne sessions. Also, running ConsoleOne from a client, you can switch out of ConsoleOne to log in and log out of NDS trees using the client utilities. You can then switch back to ConsoleOne and select View|Refresh from the menu bar to make changes visible.

Creating NDS Objects

Four types of NDS objects may be created using ConsoleOne:

- Organizations
- Organizational Units
- Groups
- Users

To create an NDS object, select the container object where the new object will be created and then perform one of the following actions:

- Select File|New from the menu bar and click on the object type that you want to create.
- Right-click on the container object and select New and click on the object type that you want to create.
- Select the Create *object type* button from the toolbar for the object type you want to create. For example, if you want to create a user, you would select the Create User button.

Managing NDS Objects

ConsoleOne gives you the ability to manage the four NDS objects types that you create and that already exist in NDS from the server console. Use the following procedure to manage NDS objects with ConsoleOne:

1. In the object browser window, find the NDS container that contains the object you want to manage and click on the container. The contents of that container appear in the view window.

2. Select the object you want to administer. Right-click on it and choose Properties, which displays the NDS object's Properties window (see Figure 11.6).

    The details are displayed one property category at a time by selecting the desired property tab at the top of the NDS Properties window. If a property has more than one page of details, when you click on the property tab, a drop-down selection menu allows you to choose the page you want displayed.

3. Make any necessary changes to the NDS properties of the object and click on Apply to save changes and keep the NDS Properties window open. Click on OK to save changes and exit.

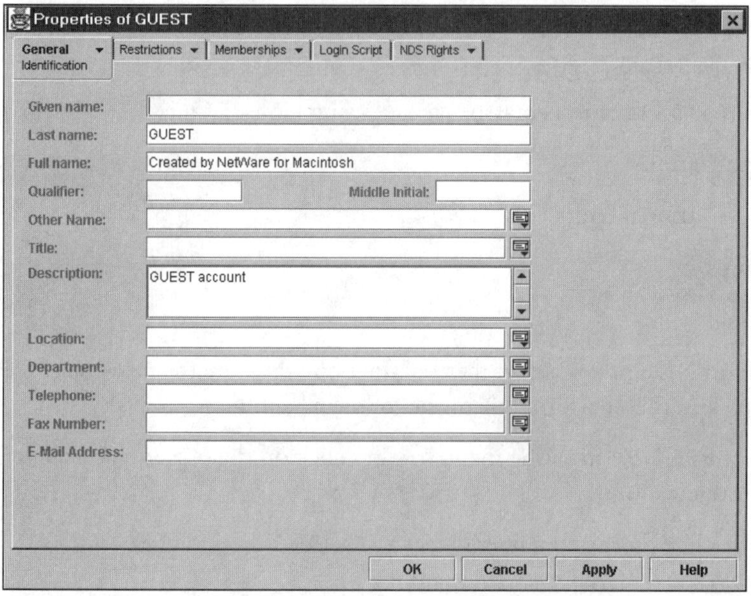

Figure 11.6 NDS Properties window in ConsoleOne.

> **TIP:** When you click on Apply or OK, all changes (on all pages of all properties) are saved immediately. When you click on Cancel, changes that have been made to any properties on any page are canceled.

Shortcuts: Adapting The ConsoleOne Interface To Your Needs

As mentioned previously, ConsoleOne is extensible. Both developers and network administrators can customize the ConsoleOne interface. Developers use snap-in components to customize the interface, and in addition, they can use these snap-in components to add functionality to ConsoleOne. Network administrators customize the interface by adding shortcuts to Java applets, files, and folders, which makes these objects easier to access. The shortcut is a text file that specifies the name and location of a Java applet, file, or folder to be added to the ConsoleOne interface. The shortcut text file is saved with the name that you want to appear as the name of the shortcut in ConsoleOne.

Shortcuts to configuration files let you open specific configuration files that reside on your local server without having to start a text editor first to open the file. The shortcuts appear in ConsoleOne as an icon under the My Server|Configuration Files object.

To add a configuration file to list of files under the Configuration Files object, you should do the following:

1. Open a text editor, such as Notepad. Create a local text file that contains only the path and file name of the configuration file you want added to the menu (for example, SYS:etc\hosts).

2. Name the text file whatever you want the configuration file icon to be called in ConsoleOne (for example, Hosts) and save the text file in the SYS:Public\mgmt\console1\ConfigFiles folder.

    Note: If you use a file name extension, the extension will display as part of the shortcut name in ConsoleOne.

3. Click on Refresh in the View menu to see the new configuration file shortcut in ConsoleOne.

Shortcuts to folders are ConsoleOne icons that provide access to specific folders in the local file system without you having to browse to them. The default shortcuts to commonly accessed folders appear in ConsoleOne as icons under the Shortcuts|Folders object.

To add a folder to the list of folders under the Folders object, you should do the following:

1. Use a text editor to create a local text file that contains only the *path* of the directory you want added to the menu. For example, to add the ETC directory, the path would be SYS:ETC.

2. Name the text file whatever you want the folder icon to be called in ConsoleOne (for example, SYS_ETC), and save the text file to the SYS:Public\mgmt\Console1\ShortCuts\Folders folder.

3. Click on Refresh in the View menu to see the new folder shortcut in ConsoleOne.

Shortcuts to applets are ConsoleOne icons that let you run specific Java applets without having to create a Hypertext Markup Language (HTML) page that loads the applet in a Web browser. The shortcut text file you create contains applet configuration information. The shortcut icon will appear in ConsoleOne in one of two places, depending on where you save the shortcut text file. If the file is saved to SYS:Public\mgmt\Console1\ShortCuts\tools, the shortcut appears in My Server|Tools. If it's saved to SYS:Public\mgmt\Console1\ShortCuts\Applets, the shortcut appears in My Server|Applets.

Remote Access

In this section, you'll learn about the two utilities, RConsoleJ and Remote Console, you can use to gain access to your server console from a workstation. These are standalone utilities that can, for convenience, be accessed from the Tools menu of Network Administrator.

RConsoleJ

The RConsoleJ utility is the same whether it's accessed from the server console or from a workstation over an IP connection. You use RConsoleJ on a workstation to gain access to the file server's console over an IP connection. The RCONSOLE agent, RCONAG6.NLM, must be running on the NetWare 5 server that you want to access. Remember that the RCONSOLE agent sets the password, TCP port, and SPX port that will be used to gain access to the remote server.

> *Note: RConsoleJ also can be used to gain access to a console in a NetWare server running only the IPX protocol using Remote Console proxy agents.*

Perform one of the following actions to run RConsoleJ from a workstation:

▶ From NetWare Administrator, select Tools|Pure IP Remote Console.

▶ Execute RCONJ.EXE, located in the SYS:Public directory, from a drive mapped to the root of the SYS volume.

▶ Execute RCONJ.BAT, located in the SYS:Public\mgmt directory, from a drive mapped to the root of the SYS volume.

Remote Console

Use Remote Console (RCONSOLE.EXE) to access your NetWare server console over SPX and asynchronous connections. This utility can be used on NetWare servers running NetWare 3.x and higher.

To use RCONSOLE, the server must be running the appropriate Remote Console NetWare Loadable Modules (NLMs) to support the remote connection type.

To enable your server to establish a Remote Console connection over a LAN, the following NLMs must be loaded at the server:

▶ **RSPX.NLM** This NLM provides connection-oriented, acknowledged communication support and advertises the server's remote access availability.

▶ **REMOTE.NLM** This NLM manages information exchange between the server and the remote workstations.

Note: REMOTE.NLM is loaded when you load the RSPX.NLM.

An asynchronous connection requires that both the workstation and server have modems. In addition, the following NLMs must be loaded on the server:

▶ **REMOTE.NLM** This NLM provides the same function as it does for a connection over a LAN.

▶ **RS232.NLM and AIO.NLM** These NLMs enable the server's communications port. In addition they transmit information, such as keystroke and screen information, to and from REMOTE.NLM.

Once the server has Remote Console access set up, RCONSOLE.EXE can be executed from a DOS prompt at the workstation or by selecting Remote Console from the Tools menu in NetWare Administrator. The default location of RCONSOLE.EXE on the network is the SYS:Public directory. If you're establishing an asynchronous connection, RCONSOLE.EXE must reside in the local file system.

182 Chapter 11

When RCONSOLE executes, you're presented with the Connection Type menu, which allows you to select either a LAN or asynchronous connection for the session (see Figure 11.7).

To connect from a workstation on the network, all you have to do is select LAN, select the server to which you want to connect from the list of available servers, and enter the Remote Console password.

To connect from a workstation over a modem, select Asynchronous, select Connect To Remote Location from the Asynchronous Options menu, and enter the Remote Console password.

Once the remote session is established, you're presented with the current server console screen. You can perform any tasks from this screen that you can at the server itself. There are even some functions that are not available from the actual server console, but are available in the remote session—such as scanning server directories, shelling to a DOS prompt, and moving files to the server.

This additional functionality is provided through the Available Options pop-up menu (see Figure 11.8) that you can access by holding down the Alt key and pressing the F2 function key.

You can also perform the additional tasks with the following hot-key combinations:

➤ **Alt+F1** Allows you to access the Available Options menu

➤ **Alt+F2** Allows you to quit the Remote Console session

➤ **Alt+F3** Allows you to toggle forward through server console screens

➤ **Alt+F4** Allows you to toggle backward through server console screens

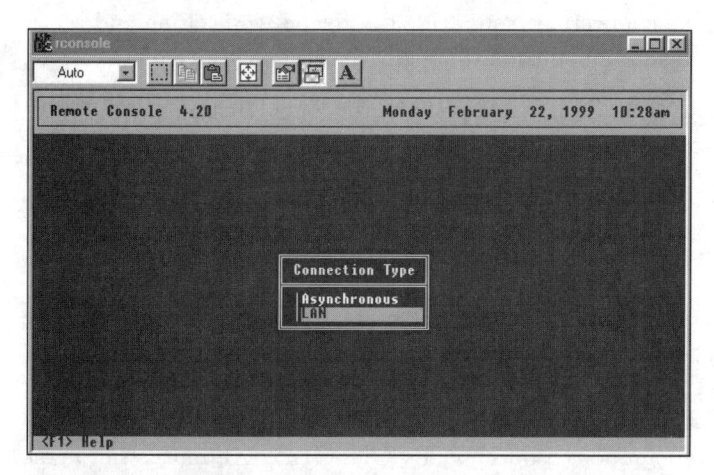

Figure 11.7 Remote Console's Connection Type screen.

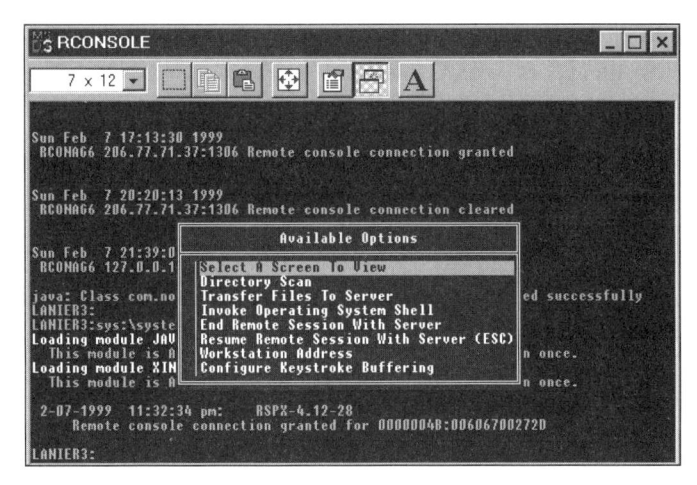

ConsoleOne, Remote Access, And Server Security   **183**

Figure 11.8 RCONSOLE's Available Options menu.

➤ **Alt+F5** Displays the workstation's network and node address

➤ **Esc** Allows you to resume the remote session with the server

Server Security

In this section, you'll learn some measures that can be taken to protect your NetWare server. Consideration here is devoted to the physical security of your server. Additional aspects of security (file-system security, NDS security, and so on) are covered in Chapters 15 and 16.

To physically protect your server, you should do the following:

➤ Lock the server in a room or secure area that has restricted access.

➤ Make sure all remote-access agents have passwords so they can't be loaded if the user doesn't have the password.

➤ Use the **SECURE CONSOLE** command to prevent anyone from changing the time and date on the server and to prevent anyone from loading NLMs from outside the SYS:System directory.

➤ Use the keyboard-locking feature in SCRSAVER.NLM to prevent unauthorized access to the server keyboard.

Note: Type "SCRSAVER HELP" at the server console to see the parameters supported with SCRSAVER.NLM.

Both RCONAG6.NLM and REMOTE.NLM require passwords to be loaded. If the commands to load these agents are included in the AUTOEXEC.NCF file or any other NCF file, the password must be entered on the line with the command. Both of the agents support password encryption, which prevents the password from being read out of an NCF file.

To have RCONAG6.NLM generate an encrypted password, you type "RCONAG6 ENCRYPT" at the server console prompt. Next, you're asked to provide a password. After you provide a password, you're asked to provide TCP and SPX ports, respectively. When RCONAG6.NLM displays the command to use the encrypted password, select Yes if you want to place the command into the SYS:System\LDRCONAG.NCF file. Finally, you use the encrypted password by typing the following at the server console:

```
RCONAG6 -E <encrypted password> TCPport SPXport
```

> *Note:* *All the supported parameters can be viewed by typing "RCONAG6 /?".*

To have REMOTE.NLM generate an encrypted password, you type "REMOTE ENCRYPT" at the server console. (Note that ENCRYPT *must* be typed in capital letters.) Next, you provide a password. When REMOTE.NLM displays the command to use the encrypted password, select Yes if you want to place the command into the SYS:System\LDREMOTE.NCF file. Use the encrypted password by typing the following at the server console:

```
REMOTE -E <encrypted password>
```

All the supported parameters for REMOTE.NLM can be viewed by typing "REMOTE /?".

ConsoleOne, Remote Access, And Server Security   185

Practice Questions

Question 1

What default utilities are contained in the My Server|Tools object? [Choose the two best answers]

- ❏ a. Remote Console
- ❏ b. RConsoleJ
- ❏ c. The Configuration Files object
- ❏ d. Console Manager
- ❏ e. RCONJ.EXE

The correct answers are b and d. RConsoleJ and Console Manager are console-access utilities that can be accessed through the My Server|Tools object in ConsoleOne. Remote Console and RCONJ.EXE are both executed from a workstation outside of ConsoleOne. Therefore, answers a and e are incorrect. The Configuration Files object is contained in the My Server object. Therefore, answer c is incorrect.

Question 2

Which of the following must be loaded on a NetWare 5 server to set it up for Remote Console access via a LAN connection? [Choose the two best answers]

- ❏ a. REMOTE.NLM
- ❏ b. RCONAG6.NLM
- ❏ c. AIO.NLM
- ❏ d. RSPX.NLM

The correct answers are a and d. REMOTE.NLM and RSPX.NLM must be running on the server accessed with Remote Console over a LAN connection. RCONAG6.NLM is the remote agent that supports remote sessions with RConsoleJ and Console Manager. Therefore, answer b is incorrect. AIO.NLM is used to support asynchronous connections. Therefore, answer c is incorrect.

Question 3

What's the purpose of the pound sign (#) in the following line found in the AUTOEXEC.NCF file?

`#LOAD RCONAG6 tofu 2034 16800`

- ○ a. It forces the remote agent to load in the login script.
- ○ b. It's used to encrypt the password *tofu* when the AUTOEXEC.NCF file executes.
- ○ c. It deactivates the command to load RCONAG6.
- ○ d. It's used to add documentation to the AUTOEXEC.NCF file.

Trick! question

The correct answer is c. The system ignores anything to the right of the pound sign when processing the commands in the AUTOEXEC.NCF file. Answers a and b are incorrect, because answer c is correct. This is a trick question because answer d is a true statement but is not the correct answer. The purpose of the pound sign is to keep the command from being executed, not to provide documentation.

Question 4

How can network administrators customize the ConsoleOne user interface? [Choose the three best answers]

- ❏ a. Create shortcuts to Java applets
- ❏ b. Develop snap-in components to add functionality to the interface
- ❏ c. Add configuration files to the list of files under the Configuration Files object
- ❏ d. Create a shortcut to a directory on a server that's accessed frequently

The correct answers are a, c, and d. Network administrators can create shortcuts to text files, Java applets, and directories and add them to the ConsoleOne interface. Snap-in components are created by developers to customize the ConsoleOne interface. Therefore, answer b is incorrect.

Question 5

> Which of the following tasks is not currently supported in ConsoleOne?
>
> ○ a. Browsing multiple directory trees
> ○ b. Deleting all files from a directory on the local server
> ○ c. Creating a user account
> ○ d. Deleting a Printer object
> ○ e. Creating a Printer object

Trick! question

The correct answer is e. The only objects that can be created using ConsoleOne are Organizations, Organizational Units, Users, and Groups. Creating Printer objects is not currently supported. You can browse multiple directory trees and create user accounts in ConsoleOne. Therefore, answers a and c are incorrect. This is a trick question because you must know that creating Printer objects is not supported in ConsoleOne to eliminate answers b and d as the unsupported task, because it's never stated that deleting all files from a directory on the local server and deleting a Printer object is supported.

Question 6

> Which hot-key combination can be used to display the network and node address of the workstation you're using to access a server console using Remote Console?
>
> ○ a. Alt+F1
> ○ b. Alt+F2
> ○ c. Alt+F3
> ○ d. Alt+F4
> ○ e. Alt+F5

The correct answer is e. Pressing the Alt+F5 hot-key combination displays the network and node address of the workstation you're using to access a server console using Remote Console. The other hot-key combinations have different functions. Therefore, answers a, b, c, and d are incorrect.

Question 7

Which Java utility lets you establish an IP remote connection with a NetWare 5 server from a workstation? [Choose the two best answers]

❑ a. Remote Console

❑ b. RConsoleJ

❑ c. Telnet

❑ d. Console Manager

❑ e. RCONSOLE.EXE

Trick! question

The correct answers are b and d. RConsoleJ and Console Manager are both Java-based utilities that can be used to remotely access a NetWare 5 server console through an IP connection. A Remote Console session is started by executing RCONSOLE.EXE, which is not Java based and does not use IP connections. Therefore, answers a and e are incorrect. This is a trick question because Telnet is a utility that can be used for remote access to the server console using an IP connection. It is not, however, a Java-based utility. Therefore, answer c is incorrect.

Question 8

Which management features are integrated into the ConsoleOne shell (or framework)?

○ a. Basic file management

○ b. NDS property rights management

○ c. Remote server management

○ d. All of the above

○ e. None of the above

The correct answer is e. ConsoleOne, alone, provides no management functions. The management capabilities currently available with ConsoleOne are provided through the default snap-in components that Novell supplies with NetWare 5. Therefore, answers a, b, c, and d are incorrect.

Need To Know More?

www.novell.com/products/consoleone/whitepaper.html contains a very good technical overview of ConsoleOne.

www.novell.com/documentation/idx_console1.html contains the complete documentation for ConsoleOne. It also includes a troubleshooting Q&A section.

Server Management

Terms you'll need to understand:

√ MONITOR.NLM
√ General Information screen
√ Long Term Cache Hits value
√ Memory utilization
√ Processor utilization
√ Write cache
√ Read cache

Techniques you'll need to master:

√ Describing the information presented in MONITOR's General Information screen
√ Modifying the server's **SET** parameters

One of the network administrator's most critical tasks is evaluating and monitoring server performance. There may be times when you need to find out how hard the server is working to determine whether there's a problem. When one process uses all the server's processing power, other services running on the server begin to degrade. The administrator needs a tool to determine which resources the server is actually using to know whether there's a problem. NetWare 5 provides such a tool in the form of a NetWare Loadable Module (NLM)—MONITOR.NLM. This utility has been around for several versions of NetWare and has some new features in NetWare 5.

The MONITOR utility contains a great deal of information and can be used to change numerous settings. An entire book could be devoted to this topic. In this chapter, we highlight only a few of the areas that help in monitoring server performance.

MONITOR.NLM

You use MONITOR to monitor server performance and to change the various SET parameters. To load the utility, enter "MONITOR" at the server console. You can unload it either by using the utility's Exit command or by typing "UNLOAD MONITOR" at the server console. The utility has a text-based interface that's often referred to as *C worthy* or *blue screen*. Navigation through MONITOR is entirely keyboard based; you can access Help at any time by pressing the F1 key. Help information is context sensitive. To get help information about MONITOR in general, press the F1 key twice. To close a Help screen, press Esc until you return to the area you want. In general, the arrow keys are used to highlight items, and the Enter key is used to make the selection. The Esc key is used to back out of a location and return to the previous screen. You can Tab to collapse and expand a window. Also, in some screens, you can use the Page Down and Page Up keys to scroll through the information.

With each release of NetWare, the MONITOR utility has expanded, offering more information and permitting the editing of various aspects of the server's information. In contrast to earlier versions, the NetWare 5 MONITOR utility does not contain a screensaver. In NetWare 5, the screensaver is a separate NLM, SCRSAVER.NLM, and has more options and parameters than earlier versions.

> *Note:* Type "SCRSAVER HELP" at the server console for more information about the screensaver.

In earlier versions of MONITOR, the **SET** parameters were changed with a utility called SERVMAN.NLM. Starting with the release of NetWare 4.11,

Server Management 193

MONITOR contains Server Parameters as an Additional Options item. This item allows you to view, modify, and get help for the various **SET** parameters.

When you first run MONITOR, you see the General Information screen shown in Figure 12.1. This window has a lot of information about the general status of the server. By monitoring some of the values over time, you can determine trends and performance. At the very top of the screen, you can see the MONITOR version number, the server and tree names, and the version number of NetWare the server is running and the code compilation date. The options available on the General Information screen include the following:

► **Utilization** This is a dynamic value that's the average of the server's total processing capacity used in the last interval. An interval is one second.

► **Server Up Time** The number displayed here indicates how long the server has been running since the last server launch. The value is displayed as *DD:HH:MM:SS*, where *D*=day, *H*=hour, *M*=minute, and *S*=second.

► **Online Processors** This value indicates the number of active and enabled processors.

► **Original Cache Buffers** This number indicates the number of buffers available for caching immediately after the server was launched before any NLMs were loaded. A cache buffer is a 4,096-byte memory page. Multiplying the number of buffers by 4,096 should be roughly equivalent to the amount of RAM in the server.

► **Total Cache Buffers** This option displays how many buffers are presently accessible for file caching. Multiplying this value by 4,096 indicates the amount of memory available for caching files.

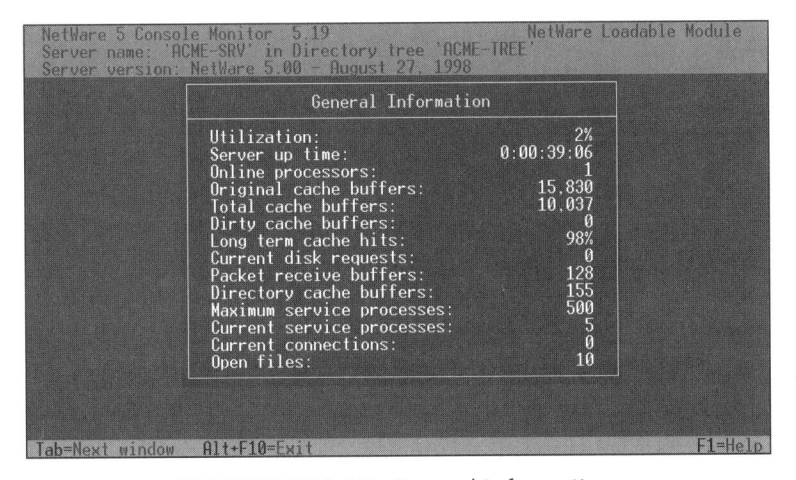

Figure 12.1 MONITOR.NLM's General Information screen.

▶ **Dirty Cache Buffers** This number indicates the number of cache buffers that contain data not written to storage. If this value is more than 50 percent of the total cache buffers, more RAM is needed. If the number of current disk requests is also high, this probably indicates a system bottleneck.

▶ **Long Term Cache Hits** This value indicates the cumulative percentage of requests for data that are in cache. The higher the value, the fewer the hits on the disk system required to deliver the requested information to the client. If this value falls below 90 percent, you need to install more memory.

▶ **Current Disk Requests** This option indicates how many disk requests are in the service queue.

▶ **Packet Receive Buffers** This value displays the number of buffers used to hold client requests until they can be processed.

▶ **Directory Cache Buffers** The most frequently requested directory entries are cached in these buffers.

▶ **Maximum Service Processes** This number indicates the maximum number of threads or task handlers that can be allocated. Threads are used to service client NetWare Core Protocol (NCP) requests.

▶ **Current Service Processes** This value is the number of currently allocated threads.

▶ **Current Connections** This value is the number of connections (licensed and unlicensed) on the server. In NetWare 5, licensing information is stored in Novell Directory Services (NDS), and a license connection for a user on any server in the tree allows the user to connect to as many servers in the tree as necessary.

▶ **Open Files** This is the number of files currently being accessed by clients and the server. Some files, such as NDS, are always open.

> You should be able to identify and understand the entries on MONITOR's General Information screen.

Understanding Cache Utilization

The NetWare operating system allocates the memory remaining after the operating system and NLMs are loaded and running. These memory areas are called *caches*, and they store frequently used information. Delivering the information

Server Management   195

to the user from memory is a lot faster than reading the information from a disk or CD-ROM. The more RAM the server has, the more cache space that's available. Adding more RAM can improve server performance even when the server has no obvious problems.

On some of the information screens in MONITOR or in related literature (such as the online documentation), you'll come across the term *cache hit*. A cache hit simply refers to when the server finds the requested information in RAM rather than accessing the hard disk. The area in MONITOR under Disk Cache Utilization has an entry called Long Term Cache Hits, a value that indicates the percentage of times requested data was found in RAM (see Figure 12.2)—the higher the value, the better. A higher value indicates that data requests are being satisfied the majority the time from memory instead of from the disk. If the value falls below 90 percent, additional RAM is needed. Other things may also be related to low memory (for example, SWAP file usage).

> **TIP**
> Don't look at the value of Long Term Cache Hits right after a server restart. Because the server has just started, there have been no requests to pull anything from disk to RAM. Let the server run for a while to allow users to access the system before you look at this value.

> **EXAM ALERT**
> You should add more RAM when the Long Term Cache Hits value is lower than 90 percent.

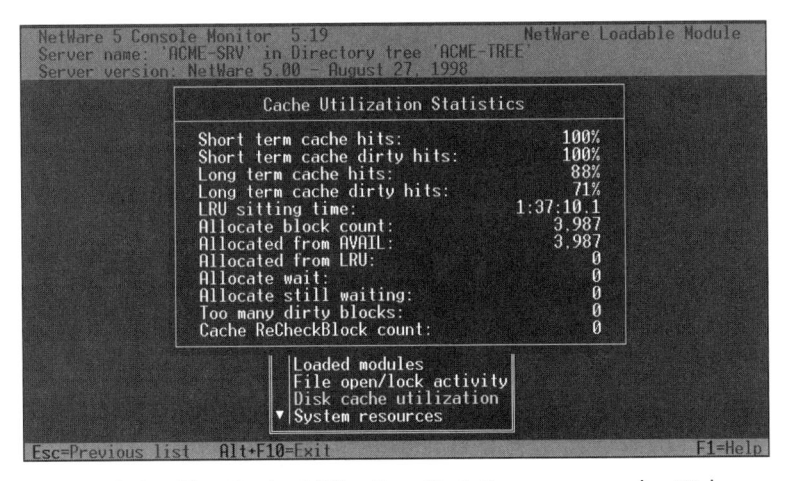

```
NetWare 5 Console Monitor 5.19                    NetWare Loadable Module
Server name: 'ACME-SRV' in Directory tree 'ACME-TREE'
Server version: NetWare 5.00 - August 27, 1998
              ┌─────────Cache Utilization Statistics─────────┐
              │ Short term cache hits:              100%     │
              │ Short term cache dirty hits:        100%     │
              │ Long term cache hits:                88%     │
              │ Long term cache dirty hits:          71%     │
              │ LRU sitting time:               1:37:10.1    │
              │ Allocate block count:               3,987    │
              │ Allocated from AVAIL:               3,987    │
              │ Allocated from LRU:                     0    │
              │ Allocate wait:                          0    │
              │ Allocate still waiting:                 0    │
              │ Too many dirty blocks:                  0    │
              │ Cache ReCheckBlock count:               0    │
              └──────┬───────────────────────────────────────┘
                     │ Loaded modules                │
                     │ File open/lock activity       │
                     │ Disk cache utilization        │
                     │▼ System resources             │
Esc=Previous list    Alt+F10=Exit                         F1=Help
```

Figure 12.2 The Cache Utilization Statistics screen under Disk Cache Utilization.

There are times when altering some parameters will improve server performance. For example, if the server performs a particular task frequently, you may want to tweak the parameters to help performance. Two examples of this are setting a write cache and setting a read cache.

A write cache is for situations in which users are writing to disk in small increments (for example, working with a database). If the NetWare 5 server is operating as an application server hosting a database, the information in the database can be scattered across many files. If a lot of changes are made to this database, there may be a large number of disk writes. You configure a write cache by modifying some of the **SET** parameters. As with any situation in which the **SET** parameters are changed, the effect of the changes should be monitored to make sure the modifications are not creating other problems. Details of setting the write cache and read cache are covered in Chapter 14.

You can change the value of a **SET** parameter either with MONITOR or by issuing the **SET** commands with parameters at the server console. Both interfaces have short descriptions of the parameters, including current values and minimum and maximum values, where appropriate. The majority of the **SET** parameters can be changed directly at the server console, thus putting the new value into effect immediately. However, if you want to make the change permanent—that is, set when the server is rebooted—you can place the appropriate command in the AUTOEXEC.NCF file. The values of some **SET** parameters can be changed only in STARUP.NCF, and these require a server reboot to reload the new environment. The following **SET** parameters can be changed only through the STARTUP.NCF file:

➤ Minimum Packet Receive Buffers

➤ Maximum Physical Receive Packet Size

➤ Reserved Buffers Below 16 Meg

➤ Auto Clear Interrupt Statistics

➤ Auto Start Processors

➤ Auto TTS Backout Flag

Understanding Memory Utilization

As mentioned earlier, servers use memory to cache users' files to improve file delivery times. When a NLM is no longer needed and is unloaded, the memory it was using is returned to the available memory.

So, how can you tell how much memory the NLM using? In addition to the NLM's memory footprint, you must take into account any prerequisite and/or dependent NLMs that are also loaded. Some NLMs will allocate more memory when running. The NLM's file size and the file sizes of any other prerequisite NLMs provide a rough estimate of the amount of memory they're using.

You can view the amount of cache buffers available by choosing System Resources in the Available Topics area in the General Information MONITOR screen. The percentage displayed to the right of Cache Buffer Memory In Bytes indicates the percentage of available memory. When you're testing a new NLM, you should monitor the cache buffers before loading, after loading, and after unloading the NLM. This information helps indicate any NLMs that are not releasing memory when they're unloaded.

Understanding Processor Utilization

The processor is another important element that affects server performance. The Utilization entry on MONITOR's General Information screen indicates the percentage of available processing power. If the server has more than one processor, you'll see an entry for each of the processors. If this value is close to or at 100 percent, the server's processor is well below the horsepower necessary. However, even when the server's processor is sufficient, there may be periods when utilization is very high. For example, when the server is compressing files, utilization will increase. If nothing else is going on during this time, you may see 100 percent utilization. This type of activity is normal, but if you see utilization at 100 percent over a period of time, something is probably awry. If user connections are being dropped or performance is dropping, a problem probably exists.

> Make sure you understand that Utilization values of 100 percent for short bursts is normal; however, Utilization values of 100 percent over an extended time period may not be normal.

Practice Questions

Question 1

> Which of the following can be used to change or view server **SET** parameters in NetWare 5? [Choose the two best answers]
>
> ❏ a. SERVMAN.NLM
> ❏ b. **SET**
> ❏ c. INSTALL.NLM
> ❏ d. MONITOR.NLM
> ❏ e. NWSET.NLM

The correct answers are b and d. SERVMAN.NLM is the name of the utility used to view and change SET parameters in pre-NetWare 5 versions. Therefore, answer a is incorrect. INSTALL.NLM exists in NetWare 5 as NWCONFIG.NLM, which can be used to change the AUTOEXEC.NCF and STARTUP.NCF files. Therefore, answer c is incorrect. NWSET.NLM is a made-up utility. Therefore, answer e is incorrect.

Question 2

> Which item on the MONITOR screen shown in Figure 12.3 needs your attention, and why?
>
> ○ a. Long Term Cache Dirty!Y...ts is too high.
> ○ b. Long Term Cache Hits is too low, and Long Term Cache Dirty Hits is too high.
> ○ c. Long Term Cache Hits is too high.
> ○ d. Long Term Cache Hits is too high, and Long Term Cache Dirty Hits is too low.
> ○ e. Long Term Cache Hits is too low.

The correct answer is e. Because e is correct, answers c and d are incorrect. We did not discuss Long Term Cache Dirty Hits in this chapter, but this value is cumulative, and if there are no problems or shortages, this number will increase over time. Therefore, answers a and b are incorrect.

Server Management

```
NetWare 5 Console Monitor  5.19                    NetWare Loadable Module
Server name: 'ACME-SRV' in Directory tree 'ACME-TREE'
Server version: NetWare 5.00 - August 27, 1998
              ┌─────Cache Utilization Statistics─────┐
              │ Short term cache hits:          100% │
              │ Short term cache dirty hits:    100% │
              │ Long term cache hits:            88% │
              │ Long term cache dirty hits:      71% │
              │ LRU sitting time:          1:37:10.1 │
              │ Allocate block count:         3,987  │
              │ Allocated from AVAIL:         3,987  │
              │ Allocated from LRU:               0  │
              │ Allocate wait:                    0  │
              │ Allocate still waiting:           0  │
              │ Too many dirty blocks:            0  │
              │ Cache ReCheckBlock count:         0  │
              └──────────────────────────────────────┘
                      │ Loaded modules         │
                      │ File open/lock activity│
                      │ Disk cache utilization │
                      │▼System resources       │
Esc=Previous list   Alt+F10=Exit                          F1=Help
```

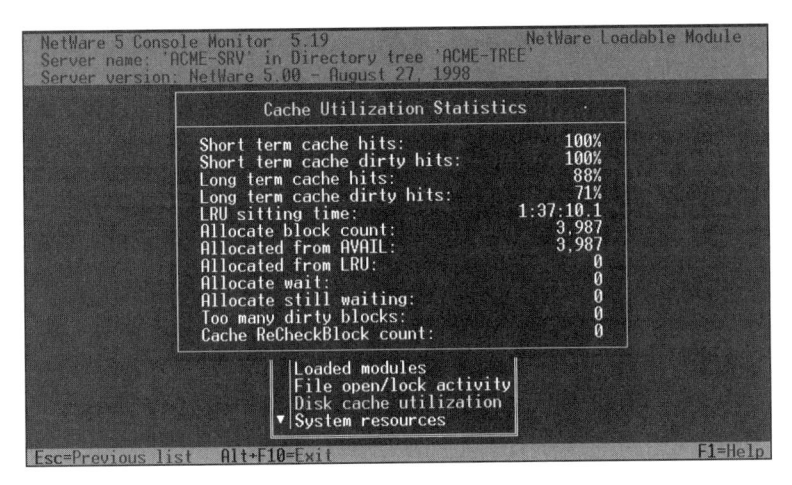

Figure 12.3

Question 3

Which of the following is true of the Long Term Cache Hits value?

- ○ a. It's the cumulative percentage of requests for data that's in cache.
- ○ b. It's the total number of requests for data that's in cache.
- ○ c. It's the number of cache buffers currently available for file caching.
- ○ d. It's the number of cache buffers that contain data that has not been written to disk.
- ○ e. It's the number of cache buffers available immediately after the server is started and before any NLMs are loaded.

The correct answer is a. Because answer a is correct, answer b is incorrect. The Total Cache Buffers value is the number of currently available cache buffers. Therefore, answer c is incorrect. The Dirty Cache Buffers value is the number of cache buffers containing data not written to disk. Therefore, answer d is incorrect. The Original Cache Buffers value is the number of available cache buffers immediately after starting the server and before loading NLMs. Therefore, answer e is incorrect.

Question 4

What is the Total Cache Buffers value?

- ○ a. The number of cache buffers that contain data that has not been written to disk.
- ○ b. The number of cache buffers available immediately after the server is started and before any NLMs are loaded.
- ○ c. The number of cache buffers currently available for file caching.
- ○ d. The number of buffers used to cache the most frequently requested directory entries.
- ○ e. The cumulative percentage of requests for data that's in cache.

The correct answer is c. Answer a is incorrect because it describes the Dirty Cache Buffers value. Answer b is incorrect because it describes the Original Cache Buffers value. Answer d is incorrect because it describes the Directory Cache Buffers value. Answer e is incorrect because it describes the Long Term Cache Hits value.

Question 5

What is the Dirty Cache Buffers value?

- ○ a. The number of buffers used to cache the most frequently requested directory entries.
- ○ b. The cumulative percentage of requests for data that's in cache.
- ○ c. The number of cache buffers available immediately after the server is started and before any NLMs are loaded.
- ○ d. The number of cache buffers currently available for file caching.
- ○ e. The number of cache buffers that contain data that has not been written to disk.

The correct answer is e. Answer a is incorrect because it describes the Directory Cache Buffers value. Answer b is incorrect because it describes the Long Term Cache Hits value. Answer c is incorrect because it describes the Original Cache Buffers value. Answer d is incorrect because it describes the Total Cache Buffers value.

Question 6

You've received an urgent page from the company's Chief Information Officer who is working late and is complaining that printing to the high-speed color printer is very slow. She has also indicated that access to the Internet is very slow. You arrive at the server room at 12:20 A.M. and notice that utilization on the BorderManager server used to cache Internet requests is running about 5 percent. The NDPS server handling the color printer reports an average of 10 percent utilization. The ACME-DATA server storing the user's files reports a continuous 100 percent utilization with nine active connections and six open files. LANalyzer reports the Cisco router acting as the Internet gateway has been reset 15 times since 12:00 A.M. Based on this information, what is your conclusion?

Trick! question

○ a. The ACME-DATA server is experiencing a disk input/output bottleneck and a better disk system is needed.

○ b. The ACME-DATA server is performing disk compression.

○ c. The ACME-DATA server is processing too many bad packets from the Cisco router.

○ d. The NDPS server's activities are causing excess traffic on the wire.

○ e. The user should not be printing and accessing Internet at the same time.

The correct answer is b. This question is tricky because you need to remember that the default start hour for compression is 12:00 A.M. There's no indication of a disk system bottleneck with only nine connections and six open files. Therefore, answer a is incorrect. The ACME-DATA server is probably not the only server processing bad packets if that were a reason. The Cisco router having been reset 15 times in 20 minutes explains the slow Internet access. Therefore, answer c is incorrect. NDPS activities do not cause excess traffic, especially if the server is only reporting utilization of 10 percent. Therefore, answer d is incorrect. The last answer goes against what a network is designed to do. Therefore, answer e is incorrect.

Need To Know More?

www.novell.com/documentation/lg/nw5/docui/index.html is the NetWare 5 online documentation. Search for MONITOR and SET for more information on the material covered in this chapter.

http://support.novell.com offers technical information documents (TIDs) that contain information related to the topic of this chapter. Go to the Knowledgebase and search using the following TID numbers:

➤ **TID 2944533** Identifying And Resolving Server Bottlenecks

➤ **TID 2941993** NW5 Release Notes Known Utilities Limitations

➤ **TID 2943356** Performance, Tuning And Optimization—Part 1

Managing Server Memory

Terms you'll need to understand:
- √ Protected memory
- √ Virtual memory
- √ Memory allocation
- √ Memory pools
- √ Garbage collection
- √ Memory model

Techniques you'll need to master:
- √ Describing the NetWare 5 memory architecture components
- √ Configuring and optimizing virtual memory
- √ Describing the virtual memory process
- √ Understanding the concept of memory pools
- √ Enabling an application to utilize protected memory
- √ Modifying server settings to optimize the available memory
- √ Monitoring server settings to diagnose memory problems

One of the most important server resources is memory. NetWare 5 uses a memory model that makes efficient use of available memory and overcomes the problem of fragmentation, which plagued earlier operating systems. NetWare 5 also maximizes the available memory by using virtual memory, and it provides memory protection for unstable applications or applications in testing. In this chapter, we explore the NetWare 5 server's memory model and look at how you can optimize the available memory on your server.

NetWare 5 Memory Architecture Key Components

To optimize the memory on a NetWare 5 server, you need to understand how memory is categorized and managed by the operating system. The following are the key components that make up the NetWare 5 memory architecture:

- 4K pages
- Memory pools
- The Free Application Programming Interface (API)
- Garbage collection

4K Pages

When you execute SERVER.EXE from DOS to start a NetWare 5 server, the operating system takes the available memory and divides it into pages. A *page* is defined as a 4K block of RAM. If an application or the server operating system requests memory, it receives the appropriate number of 4K pages to fulfill the request. If the memory weren't broken into pages, the operating system would have to look for a contiguous block of memory whenever you load an application. If there's no contiguous memory block, the application won't load.

In contrast, by dividing the memory into pages, the operating system no longer has to look for a contiguous block of space to assign to an application. Instead, the operating system will assign the appropriate number of 4KB pages from any location in memory.

Memory Pools

After the memory has been divided into pages, NetWare 5 allocates the available memory to a main *memory pool*. In NetWare 5, each process is given its own memory allocation pool as the process is started. Once a process has been assigned a memory pool, the process continues to draw from and return memory to the pool until the process ends.

Managing Server Memory 205

If a process requires more memory than is available in its pool, memory is borrowed from the cache buffers pool. Allocating each process its own memory pool allows NetWare to track and retrieve memory easily once a process is complete.

Free API

When a process is terminated, such as when a NetWare Loadable Module (NLM) is unloaded, the memory that process was using needs to be returned to the main memory pool. There's an API that runs when a process terminates and marks memory as free—it's appropriately named *Free*. The memory is then collected and returned to the main memory pool.

Garbage Collection

The *garbage collection* routine is run to retrieve the memory that has been marked as free by the Free API and return it to the cache buffers memory pool. Here are a couple of ways garbage collection can be triggered:

➤ When virtual memory is being used heavily

➤ Automatically every 1 to 60 minutes, depending on the value of the SET parameter (Set Garbage Collection Interval)

Note: The components that have just been described are transparent to the application. When third-party vendors are developing applications that run on NetWare 5, they don't have to worry about how to relinquish the memory their applications use.

Virtual Memory Basics

When the amount of free memory on the server begins to get very low, the operating system begins to use virtual memory. The use of a file on the hard drive to store inactive code that's occupying physical memory is referred to as *virtual memory*. When a program such as MONITOR.NLM is loaded, it uses only the portion of code that's required for the screen you're on and the code required to run the application. There can be a large portion of an application in memory that's never accessed.

> **ALERT**
> If your server is running very low on memory, disk thrashing may occur. To avoid this, add more RAM, because virtual memory can't make up for the lack of server memory. *Disk thrashing* is a term used to define excessive hard drive activity, where the disk's mechanical components are moving constantly to fulfill the disk read and write requests.

The NetWare 5 virtual memory system moves this inactive code to the swap file to free up physical memory for other processes. When the code is accessed from within the program, the operating system retrieves it from the swap file and places it in physical memory again. This process occurs for most modules that run on the server, with the exception of operating system NLMs and modules written to run in the operating system address space.

> The **SWAP** command is used to view and set virtual memory parameters.

Configuring And Optimizing Virtual Memory

When you configure the virtual memory system, note the defaults NetWare 5 implements. The virtual memory system is initially configured with a single swap file located on the SYS volume. This swap file is re-created every time the server is started. To optimize the configuration, use the following processes:

➤ To create a swap file on a volume other than SYS, use this console command:

```
SWAP ADD volume_name
```

➤ To remove the swap file from the SYS volume, use this console command:

```
SWAP DEL SYS
```

To confirm that the changes have taken effect, type "Swap" at the server console.

The optional parameters **Min**, **Max**, and **Min Free** can be used in conjunction with the **SWAP ADD** command. The **Min** and **Max** options specify the minimum and maximum sizes of the swap file. The **Min Free** option specifies the minimum free space that must be available on the volume. Here's an example of the syntax:

```
Swap Add volume_name Min=2 Max=100 Min Free=5
```

If the parameters aren't specified, the defaults are used. The defaults are the same as shown in the previous code, except that the **Max** setting defaults to the available free space on the volume.

You can use the **SWAP** command to modify the **Min**, **Max**, and **Min Free** parameter values after a swap file is initialized. Here's the syntax to change the value of a parameter:

```
SWAP volume_name parameter = value
```

You can have several swap files on different volumes, with only one swap file per volume allowed. When a volume is dismounted, the swap file is deactivated and is reactivated when the volume is mounted again.

> **TIP** Planning your swap files is a very important part of administration. The swap file(s) should be placed on your fastest drives with the most available disk space.

Protected Memory Basics

There are two areas of memory into which an NLM can be loaded on a NetWare 5 server: the operating system address space and a protected address space. Applications loaded in protected memory are monitored by the operating system for abnormal behavior and are not allowed to access resources outside the assigned address space. It's generally recommended that you test NLMs or run NLMs that have been known to cause problems in a protected address space. This protects the operating system and other processes that are running. To load an NLM into protected memory, use the following command:

```
LOAD PROTECTED NLM_Name
```

Once the NLM is loaded into protected memory, SYSCALLS.NLM and the memory protection subsystem prevent the NLM from directly accessing anything outside the assigned address space. If the NLM requires access outside its own address space, SYSCALLS.NLM and the memory protection subsystem act as interfaces for the communication.

When an NLM is loaded, it's not unusual for it to rely on other modules to function. If you load an NLM into a protected address space, the modules on which it relies will be loaded in the same space. If the NLM or one of the required modules must run in the operating system address space, the address space is terminated and the NLM fails to load. To see an example, try loading IPXCON.NLM in a protected address space with the following command:

```
Load Protected IPXCON.NLM
```

The following steps take you through loading NETBASIC.NLM in a protected address space and verifying that the modules it requires are loaded in the same address space:

1. At the server console, type "Load Protected NetBasic".

2. Once NetBasic is loaded, type "Protection" to see a list of address spaces and the modules loaded in them. Write down the name of the address space name in which NetBasic is running.

After an NLM is loaded in a protected address space, the address space can remain intact even if the NLM that initialized it is unloaded. The following commands can be used to remove an NLM from an address space and either leave the address space intact or terminate it:

▶ **Unload Address Space** = *Address_Space_Name Module_Name* This command unloads the specified module but leaves the address space and other NLMs in that address space intact.

▶ **Unload Address Space** = *Address_Space_Name* This command unloads all modules from the address space and closes the address space.

▶ **Unload Kill Address Space** = *Address_Space_Name* This command terminates the address space without unloading the modules.

You can always use the **PROTECTION** command at the console prompt to verify your actions when managing protected address spaces or to get the name of an address space already in use.

Optimizing Available Memory

The NetWare 5 operating system is generally said to be self-tuning and optimizing. This means that once you install NetWare 5, it dynamically increases most of its settings for optimal performance. Although Novell has published procedures for tuning a server's memory, these procedures apply only to optimizing systems using the traditional NetWare file system.

Monitoring Memory Usage

Available memory is one of the greatest contributors to your server's performance. You need to make sure there's enough memory to sustain current performance levels and to accommodate future demand. The following procedure walks you through viewing a memory counter that serves as an indicator that more RAM is required on the server:

1. Load the MONITOR utility at the server console by typing "Monitor".

2. Once MONITOR has loaded, select Disk Cache Utilization from the main screen.

3. The parameter to watch is Long Term Cache Hits. If this falls to 90 percent or less, you need to add more RAM.

> **ALERT** If the Long Term Cache Hits percentage is getting close to 90 percent, you may want to practice preventive maintenance and add RAM to the server before it becomes a problem.

Practice Questions

Question 1

Which of the following are benefits of protected address spaces? [Choose the two best answers]

- a. The operating system is protected from the failure of an application running in a protected address space.
- b. Inactive code is placed in a swap file to free up physical memory resources.
- c. Modules are not allowed access to resources outside their own address spaces.
- d. As soon as the modules within an address space are unloaded, the address space is terminated by the operating system.

The correct answers are a and c. Answer b is incorrect because it describes the virtual memory process. Answer d is incorrect because you must issue the **UNLOAD** console command and specify the address space name to terminate an address space.

Question 2

Which of the following is a **SET** parameter that can be used to tweak garbage collection?

- a. **Set Garbage Collection Immediate = On**
- b. **Set Garbage Collection Time Interval =**
- c. **Set Garbage Collection Interval =**
- d. **Set Garbage Collection Immediate = On**
- e. None of the above

The correct answer is c. **Set Garbage Collection Immediate = On** was available only on NetWare 4.x servers. Therefore, answer a is incorrect. **Set Garbage Collection Time Interval =** and **Set Garbage Collection Immediate = On** do not exist. Therefore, answers b and d are incorrect. Answer e is incorrect because answer c is correct.

Question 3

> Which of the following is true of the Free API?
>
> ○ a. It deallocates memory.
> ○ b. It returns memory to the main memory pool.
> ○ c. It runs at scheduled intervals.
> ○ d. It flags memory for deallocation.
> ○ e. None of the above.

The correct answer is d. The garbage collection process, not the Free API, deallocates memory and returns it to the main memory pool. Therefore, answers a and b are incorrect. Also, the garbage collection process, not the Free API, runs at scheduled intervals. Therefore, answer c is incorrect. Answer e is incorrect because answer d is correct.

Question 4

> Which of the following parameters change the functional characteristics of a swap file? [Choose the three best answers]
>
> ❑ a. **ADD**
> ❑ b. **MIN**
> ❑ c. **DEL**
> ❑ d. **MAX**
> ❑ e. **MIN_Free**

The correct answers are b, d, and e. This is a trick question because the answers are all parameters that can be specified. The question asks only for the parameters that modify the characteristics of a swap file. The **ADD** and **DEL** parameters don't change the functional characteristics of an existing swap file. Therefore, answers a and c are incorrect.

Question 5

Which of the following statements are true of the memory model in NetWare 5? [Choose the two best answers]

- ❏ a. The memory model is implemented in a way that's transparent to applications.
- ❏ b. There are four memory pools initially, as well as additional pools for each NLM that runs on the server.
- ❏ c. There's a main memory pool, and additional memory pools are created as applications are run on the server.
- ❏ d. It promotes fragmentation as a method of optimizing memory.

The correct answers are a and c. Answer b is incorrect because answer c is correct. The NetWare 5 memory model minimizes fragmentation. Therefore, answer d is incorrect.

Question 6

Which of the following statements about protected memory is false?

- ○ a. The operating system uses protected memory by default.
- ○ b. Applications that fail while running in protected memory do not cause an operating system failure.
- ○ c. The communication between applications running in protected memory is isolated to the protected address space.
- ○ d. The modules required by an application running in protected memory are loaded in the same address space as the application.

The correct answer is a. Answers b, c, and d are all characteristics of protected memory and are therefore incorrect.

Managing Server Memory   **213**

Need To Know More?

http://support.novell.com/servlet/Knowledgebase provides you with a search engine that leads you to numerous articles on the NetWare 5 memory architecture. You may want to review the available NetWare 4 documents, as well. The NetWare 4 and NetWare 5 memory architecture core components are the same.

www.novell.com/documentation is the Web site where you can access the documentation that ships with the various NetWare products. Click on NetWare 5 and search for "Memory" to obtain a plethora of information.

Other Optimization Options

14

Terms you'll need to understand:

- √ File cache buffers
- √ Directory cache buffers
- √ Disk subsystems
- √ Packet Burst
- √ Large Internet Packet (LIP) protocol
- √ Packet receive buffers
- √ Maximum Physical Receive Packet Size
- √ Reserved buffers
- √ Cache hit
- √ Service processes

Techniques you'll need to master:

- √ Describing the hardware issues that exist on a NetWare 5 server
- √ Optimizing disk usage
- √ Modifying **SET** parameters to improve server performance
- √ Identifying the benefits of the Packet Burst protocol
- √ Understanding and managing Large Internet Packet (LIP) support

The NetWare 5 operating system is, for the most part, self-tuning. What this really means is that the operating system will configure its own internal parameters to their optimal settings through the course of everyday operation. Several settings that contribute to the performance of the server operate within minimum and maximum values. When the server first starts, it begins with the minimum values, and as usage demand requires, the operating system increases the settings until their optimal or maximum values are reached.

In this chapter, you'll learn the settings that can be modified to further optimize a server's response time when dealing with user requests. We'll also explore the benefits of the Packet Burst protocol and Large Internet Packet (LIP) support. You'll also learn how to determine the appropriate values for various SET parameters.

Hardware Issues

When a NetWare 5 server is installed, the setup program attempts to detect the existing hardware in the server. When a device is detected, the setup program tries to locate the appropriate drivers and load them with parameters specified during the setup process. The following sections discuss problems that may occur with server hardware or the drivers that act as an interface between the server and its hardware.

Older Network Boards

The drivers for some older Industry Standard Architecture (ISA) and Micro Channel Architecture (MCA) network boards can't access memory above 16MB. These older drivers require that the server have enough memory below 16MB for them to load. To overcome this problem, Novell has included a SET parameter that allows you to reserve memory buffers below 16MB so these older device drivers can load. If you have a large number of ISA network boards in your server, you may have to increase the following setting to a higher number:

```
SET Reserved Buffers Below 16 MEG = 200
```

The buffers that the command refers to are cache buffers, and each one is 4K in size. Therefore, if you increase the setting from its default of 200 to 400, you're taking approximately 800K more memory from below 16MB and reserving it for older devices that can't access memory above 16MB.

There have been considerable improvements in network board technology since the release of ISA cards. If you're encountering a situation in which you need to use the previous SET command, you should consider purchasing a newer Peripheral Component Interconnect (PCI) card to replace the old card.

Failure To Recognize Memory

The NetWare 5 operating system automatically registers the memory above 16MB on newer machines. Unfortunately, on some older machines, the operating system will only recognize the memory below 16MB. To configure the operating system to recognize the memory above 16MB on these older machines, you must use the **Register Memory** command at the console prompt or in a NetWare configuration file (NCF). Here's the command:

```
Register Memory 1000000 800000
```

The value 1000000 in the previous command is the starting address in memory that you want additional memory added to. The value 800000 represents the amount of memory above the 16MB that exists in the server. For example, if the server only recognizes 16MB of memory and you know that the server has 48MB, you would type the following:

```
Register Memory 1000000 2000000
```

In this command, the starting address is 1000000 in hexadecimal notation, which is approximately 16000000 (or 16MB), because the server already recognized 16MB of memory. The value 2000000 is hex for 32000000 (or 32MB), and it specifies the amount of memory to add. In other words, the preceding command adds 32MB to the 16MB of memory that has already been recognized.

Once you've figured out the appropriate **Register Memory** command syntax, the command should be placed in the STARTUP or AUTOEXEC.NCF file so the memory will be registered every time the server is rebooted. It's also recommended that you upgrade your system board to a newer board so the server can automatically register the memory.

Optimizing Disk Usage

The file and directory cache settings on a NetWare 5 server are optimized for a balance between responding to read and write requests from clients. If users in your environment are performing considerably more writes than reads (or more reads than writes), there may be a performance gain realized from modifying the default file and directory cache settings. In some situations, you may even want to implement spanning as a method of improving the input/output (I/O) performance of your disk subsystem. Before we talk about modifying file and directory cache settings or spanning, let's explore the different disk subsystems available and their benefits.

Disk Subsystems

There are several technologies on the market from which you can choose when selecting a disk subsystem. Here are a few of the technologies that exist today:

➤ Integrated Drive Electronics (IDE)

➤ Enhanced Integrated Drive Electronics (EIDE)

➤ Ultra IDE

➤ Small Computer System Interface (SCSI), SCSI-2, and Fast Wide SCSI

These technologies are covered in the following sections.

Integrated Drive Electronics (IDE)

One of the more common disk interfaces is IDE. The IDE standard defines a drive and controller combination that allows for transfer rates of approximately 4 or 5MB per second, depending on the manufacturer. The IDE interface is quickly being outgrown due to limitations in drive size—a maximum of two drives on one channel and a limit of one active controller per channel.

> *Note:* *You'll also see IDE expanded as Intelligent Drive Electronics, but Integrated Drive Electronics is seen more frequently.*

Enhanced Integrated Drive Electronics (EIDE)

The EIDE standard is the successor to IDE; it overcomes a couple of the limitations associated with IDE. Systems that implement the EIDE standard can have two controllers: a primary and a secondary controller. Each controller can have two drives attached, which brings the total number of drives that can exist in an EIDE system to four.

> Although the EIDE standard improved on the IDE standard by allowing more controllers and devices, the speed limitations that applied to IDE and the limit of one request at a time per controller channel still exist.

Ultra IDE

Ultra IDE is an emerging standard that defines a method of increasing throughput to 33MB per second across an improved EIDE interface. The standard is widely implemented as a home PC standard. It's not used for servers often because it's limited to two controllers and two drives per controller.

SCSI

The most common disk subsystem used in servers today is SCSI. There are several generations of SCSI interfaces with speed improvements, as well as enhancements to the number of devices supported by a single controller. A SCSI drive and controller combination can achieve speeds of approximately 5 to 10MB per second. The newer standards that were built on SCSI, such as SCSI-2 and Fast Wide SCSI, have increased the transfer speeds to as much as 40MB per second with the proper drive and controller combination.

In addition to the speed benefits offered, the SCSI standards include support for multiple commands concurrently on a single channel, command queuing, and fault tolerance solutions, such as Redundant Array of Inexpensive Disks (RAID) Level 5.

> **TIP** The disk controller and drive combination chosen for a server deserves careful research. There are always new standards in the works, and old standards are constantly being improved.

Understanding File Caching

As users read and write files to a NetWare 5 server, the server places the files temporarily into *file cache buffers*. When the request to read a file is received, the server first checks to see whether that file is in cache, because it was accessed previously. If the file is not in cache, the server will retrieve the file from the file system, place it in memory (cache), and send the file to the user who issued the request. The server will respond quicker to user requests that are serviced from cache; therefore, the more files that are cached, the better the performance of the server.

The NetWare 5 MONITOR.NLM utility allows you to view the percentage of time the server finds the files users request in memory. Specifically, you can use the Long Term Cache Hits value, which reports the percentage of time user requests are satisfied from RAM instead of the disk. To view the Long Term Cache Hits value, perform the following at the server console:

1. Load the MONITOR utility by typing "Monitor" at the console prompt and pressing Enter.

2. Select Disk Cache Utilization from MONITOR's main menu.

3. The third statistic down is the Long Term Cache Hits percentage.

EXAM ALERT

If the value of this counter is 92 percent, the server is finding the files users are requesting in RAM 92 percent of the time, and the rest of the requests are being fulfilled from the hard drive. When the Long Term Cache Hits value falls to 90 percent or below, you should add more RAM to the server.

Tuning The File And Directory Cache Settings

As mentioned earlier in the chapter, the file and directory cache settings on the server are optimized for a balance between read and write performance. There are, however, some situations in which you may want to change the default settings of parameters related to file and directory caching. Before we get into the specific parameters that need to be changed in a write- or read-intensive environment, perform the following steps on your server so you can look at the parameters as they're discussed:

1. Load MONITOR at the server console by typing "Monitor" and pressing Enter.
2. Select Server Parameters from the main menu.

The settings used to optimize the server for read or write performance are accessible from this MONITOR screen.

To optimize the server for write performance, you need to modify four parameters. The first two can be found under the Directory Caching submenu off the Server Parameters screen mentioned previously. The last two are located under the File Caching submenu, which is also a submenu accessed through the Server Parameters screen. Now let's look at each setting that should be changed for a write-intensive environment. Follow these steps:

1. Select the Directory Caching submenu from the Server Parameters screen and press Enter.
2. Set the value for Dirty Directory Cache Delay Time to two seconds.
3. Set the number for Maximum Concurrent Directory Cache Writes to 185.
4. Press Esc to return to the Server Parameters screen.
5. Select File Caching.
6. Set the Dirty Disk Cache Delay Time to seven seconds.
7. Set the number for Maximum Concurrent Disk Cache Writes to 750.

If the demands being placed on the server are more read intensive, there are three settings you can change to optimize the server's cache. The following steps walk you through modifying the cache settings to optimize reads:

Other Optimization Options **221**

1. From the Server Parameters screen, select Directory Caching and press Enter.
2. Set the Maximum Concurrent Directory Cache Writes to 40.
3. Change Directory Cache Buffer NonReferenced Delay to 60 seconds.
4. Press Esc to return to the Server Parameters screen.
5. Select File Caching and press Enter.
6. Change the Maximum Concurrent Disk Cache Writes to 150.

Typing "Set" at the server console, followed by the parameter and value, will also change the file cache settings. For more information on **SET** parameter syntax, search the NetWare 5 online documentation using the keywords "SET parameter".

> **EXAM ALERT**
> Use caution when modifying the cache for read or write performance. If you optimize the server to perform writes more efficiently, the read performance will degrade. The reverse is also true. Therefore, make sure that the demands being placed on the server for disk reads or writes have been carefully analyzed before you change the cache-related settings.

Spanning Volumes To Improve Performance

On a NetWare 5 server, it's possible to have a single volume spread across areas of free space from multiple devices. When a volume is composed of multiple physical devices, the performance of the server when responding to read requests will improve.

If a volume encompasses a single drive, all read and write operations will be confined to that drive. On the other hand, if a volume is made up of multiple drives, the user requests to read files will be handled by the drive where the files are located. Files can be read from multiple drives within the volume, which makes the server's response to read requests quicker.

> **EXAM ALERT**
> Although spanning can make the server respond quicker to read requests, it's important to be aware that the performance gain previously mentioned will only be realized if the files that are accessed are located on different devices within a spanned volume. Another consideration is fault tolerance, because if a single drive fails, the entire volume will be unrecoverable. If you decide to span a volume, make sure there's a backup strategy implemented. Also, you should consider implementing mirroring or duplexing on the server.

SET Parameters

You can use various SET parameters to improve the performance or the overall resource utilization of a NetWare 5 server. The following subsection discusses some additional SET parameters that can be optimized for your network environment.

Packet Receive Buffers

When a user attempts to read or write to the server, the request is sent to the server in the form of a data packet. After the request reaches the server, it's placed in a packet receive buffer until the server has time to process it. As the server responds to each request stored in the packet receive buffers, the buffers are emptied and made available to receive the next user requests. If a packet receive buffer is not available and the server receives a user request, the server will allocate a new buffer until the maximum number of packet receive buffers has been reached. The following commands change the minimum and maximum values that the server allocates for packet receive buffers:

```
Set Minimum Packet Receive Buffers = 128

Set Maximum Packet Receive Buffers = 500
```

> *Note:* Both values shown in the previous commands are the default values for those settings.

When the server is first started, it allocates the appropriate number of packet receive buffers based on the Minimum Packet Receive Buffers value. New packet receive buffers are added when the number of user requests is greater than the number of currently available packet receive buffers. The server will be able to continue allocating packet receive buffers until the value of the Maximum Packet Receive Buffers parameter has been reached.

> Here are a couple ways to tell whether you need to change the Minimum Packet Receive Buffers value:
>
> ➤ If the server is slow to respond to user requests when it's first started
>
> ➤ If you notice a jump in the number of packet receive buffers currently allocated on the general information screen of the MONITOR utility
>
> It's important that you monitor the server parameters during the first few days after a reboot to determine whether you need to modify the Minimum Packet Receive Buffers parameter value.

The Maximum Packet Receive Buffers setting should be increased if the current number of packet receive buffers is reaching its maximum or if your server is fairly busy. Novell recommends that the Maximum Packet Receive Buffers setting be set between 700 and 1000 on busy servers.

Maximum Physical Receive Packet Size

The Maximum Physical Receive Packet Size setting on the server is used to specify the maximum size of a packet that the server will use in network communication. This setting should be configured based on the network topology implemented in your environment. If you have an Ethernet network, Maximum Physical Receive Packet Size should be set to 1514, and if you have a token ring network, it should be set to 4202. To change the Maximum Physical Receive Packet Size setting, use the following command in STARTUP.NCF:

```
SET Maximum Physical Receive Packet Size = 4224
```

Note: *The value shown in the preceding command is the default value for this setting.*

In the **SET** parameter, the value 4224 should be changed to match the maximum packet size allocated by your topology. Leaving the Maximum Physical Receive Packet Size setting at its default is not recommended, because this wastes a portion of the memory set aside in each packet receive buffer.

Let's assume that a server has currently allocated 200 packet receive buffers, and the value for the Maximum Physical Receive Packet Size is at its default of 4224. In this situation, the 200 packet receive buffers take up approximately 845K of server memory. If the network topology used in this scenario is Ethernet, there's 542K of wasted space.

The wasted space is the difference between the amount of memory allocated to packet receive buffers and the space actually used by each user request. Each user request is restricted to the maximum size of the topology in use. In the case of Ethernet, this maximum is 1,514 bytes. If you place a 1,514-byte data packet in a 4,224-byte packet receive buffer, a large portion of the packet receive buffer is not being used.

> Remember that this wasted space can be prevented by configuring the Maximum Physical Receive Packet Size to match the maximum packet size for your topology. Ethernet and token ring are the most common topologies in use today. Their maximum packet sizes are 1514 and 4202, respectively.

Service Processes

The service processes counter specifies the number task handlers for processing incoming requests placed by users that are currently on hold. Just as with other parameters we've explored, the service processes that are allocated by the server start at a minimum value and increase to a maximum. Here are the commands for configuring the minimum and maximum number of service processes on the server:

```
Set Maximum Service Processes = 560

Set Minimum Service Processes = 60
```

The maximum number of service processes should only be increased when the current number of service processes allocated has reached the maximum.

Packet Burst

When older clients communicated with a NetWare server, every packet that was sent required an acknowledgment that it had been received. Novell has since come out with a protocol that reduces the overhead required for a client to send files to a server, as well as the overhead required to receive them.

The Packet Burst protocol was developed by Novell to optimize communications between clients and servers. It defines a set of rules that allows for multiple data packets to be sent across the network with only a single acknowledgment. In fact, the Packet Burst protocol allows up to 64K of data to be sent in a single network transmission.

How It Works

When newer Novell clients attach to a NetWare 5 server, the server and clients negotiate two very important parameters: the burst gap time and the burst window size. Basically, the server and clients are negotiating how many packets can be sent at once and in what time frame that burst of packets must be sent.

The *burst gap time* specifies the amount of time the client or server has to send up to 64K of data, and the *burst window size* specifies the maximum number of packets to be sent within the burst gap time. The values for these settings may change at any time based on the client's analysis of the network capacity and the number of buffers available on the client.

To improve efficiency, if a packet that's part of a burst gets dropped due to congestion on the network or a collision, only that packet will be retransmitted. This is true of any packets that are dropped during communication. They will each be retransmitted individually instead of the entire burst being sent again.

> **EXAM ALERT:** Novell has stated that the implementation of Packet Burst as a core protocol supported by the operating system will improve performance anywhere from 10 to 300 percent.

Large Internet Packets (LIP)

The boundaries of networks today have grown to new horizons. Cable and telephone companies are using routers as a means to bring the Internet to the doorsteps of people across the world; businesses are using routers to connect their offices to remote sites and increase productivity.

The routing component of a NetWare 5 server is compatible with both new and old routers. To provide this compatibility, Novell designed the operating system to automatically reduce its own packet size to 512 bytes any time another router is detected on the network. The server also negotiates with clients that attach to configure their packet sizes to 512 bytes. Reducing the packet size used on the network allows the NetWare 5 router to communicate with older routers that were restricted to 512 bytes as a maximum packet size.

To allow for packets that are larger than 512 bytes to be used in the event a newer router is in place, Large Internet Packet (LIP) support can be enabled. Enabling LIP on the server tells the server to ignore the fact that other routers have been detected and to use the Maximum Physical Receive Packet Size value when sending packets or negotiating packet sizes with clients. The following server console command can be used to enable or disable LIP support on a NetWare 5 server:

SET Allow LIP = On

Note: On is the default for this setting.

The previous command can be placed in the STARTUP.NCF file. Be sure to specify either **On** or **Off** as the parameter.

> **EXAM ALERT:** Network performance is reduced if the clients and servers don't support LIP (as well as Packet Burst).

Practice Questions

Question 1

There are a number of disk subsystems to choose from on the market today. Which of the following offers the best performance?

- ○ a. EIDE
- ○ b. IDE
- ○ c. ST-506
- ○ d. SCSI
- ○ e. SCSI-2

The correct answer is e. The EIDE and IDE standards are not as fast as the SCSI and SCSI-2 standards. Therefore, answers a and b are incorrect. The ST-506 drive was a predecessor to SCSI and will probably only be found in a museum. Therefore, answer c is incorrect. The SCSI standard is older than the SCSI-2 standard and, as a result, is not as fast. Therefore, answer d is incorrect.

Question 2

What are the four parameters you must change to optimize the server for write performance? [Choose the four best answers]

- ❑ a. Maximum Concurrent Directory Cache Writes
- ❑ b. Dirty Directory Cache Delay Time
- ❑ c. Maximum Concurrent Disk Cache Writes
- ❑ d. Directory Cache Buffer NonReferenced Delay
- ❑ e. Dirty Disk Cache Delay Time

The correct answers are a, b, c, and e. The Directory Cache Buffer NonReferenced Delay setting is only modified to improve read performance. Therefore, answer d is incorrect.

Question 3

> A couple of hardware issues can arise before and after the server installation. This is especially true if the equipment being used is older or the technology implemented is out of date. Which of the following techniques are used to resolve hardware issues that occur as a result of using older hardware on the server? [Choose the two best answers]
>
> ❑ a. The **Register Memory** console command's **SET** parameter is used to register memory above 16MB when the system board in the server is unable to automatically detect it.
>
> ❑ b. The **Set Reserved Buffers** command can be used to reserve memory above 16MB so older device drivers will be guaranteed memory in which to load.
>
> ❑ c. The **Register Memory** console command is used to register memory above 16MB when the system board in the server is unable to automatically detect it.
>
> ❑ d. The **Reserved Buffers Below 16MB** command can be used to reserve memory above 16MB so older device drivers will be guaranteed memory in which to load.
>
> ❑ e. The **SET** command for changing the number of reserved buffers below 16MB can be used to reserve memory below 16MB so older device drivers will be guaranteed memory in which to load.

The correct answers are c and e. There is no parameter that can be used to register memory. Therefore, answer a is incorrect. There is no **Set Reserved Buffers** command or **Reserved Buffers Below 16MB** command. Therefore, answers b and d are incorrect. This is a trick question because if you don't read it carefully, you could easily choose the wrong answer.

Question 4

Which of the following items optimizes communication between a client and server by reducing the number of acknowledgments required and allowing up to 64K of data to be sent to or from the server in a single burst of packets?

○ a. LIP
○ b. Packet receive buffers
○ c. Reserved buffers
○ d. Packet Burst
○ e. SPX

The correct answer is d. LIP only helps if there are routers in your environment other than the Novell server. Therefore, answer a is incorrect. Packet receive buffers and reserved buffers have nothing to do with the number of acknowledgments sent. Therefore, answers b and c are incorrect. The SPX protocol is connection oriented and requires that acknowledgments be sent for every packet received. Therefore, answer e is incorrect.

Question 5

What are the three parameters you must change to optimize the server for read performance? [Choose the three best answers]

❏ a. Maximum Concurrent Directory Cache Writes
❏ b. Dirty Directory Cache Delay Time
❏ c. Maximum Concurrent Disk Cache Writes
❏ d. Directory Cache Buffer NonReferenced Delay
❏ e. Dirty Disk Cache Delay Time

The correct answers are a, c, and d. Answers b and e are parameters that can be modified to improve the performance of writes and are therefore incorrect.

Question 6

Which of the following is a consideration that would discourage the spanning of volumes across multiple disks?

- a. Performance will be degraded because the system has to work harder to manage the various devices that make up the volume.
- b. If a single drive fails, the entire volume will become unrecoverable.
- c. Spanned volumes can't be mirrored or duplexed for fault tolerance.
- d. When a volume is spanned across multiple drives, the server will use more memory and performance will suffer.
- e. The server's CPU utilization will be higher when a volume is spanned, which can potentially create a bottleneck on the server.

The correct answer is b. Performance is improved by spanning a volume. Therefore, answers a and d are incorrect. A spanned volume can be mirrored and duplexed. Therefore, answer c is incorrect. Spanning would never cause the CPU utilization to become a bottleneck. Therefore, answer e is incorrect.

Question 7

Users have complained that logging onto the server seems extremely slow after scheduled maintenance is performed. Which of the following **SET** parameter values most likely needs to be increased?

- a. Maximum Packet Receive Buffers
- b. Maximum Service Processes
- c. Minimum Service Processes
- d. Minimum Packet Receive Buffers
- e. Allow LIP

The correct answer is d. The Maximum Packet Receive Buffers setting should only be increased on busy servers or when the number of currently allocated cache buffers is reaching the current maximum value. Therefore, answer a is incorrect. The service processes values should only be changed if the server is incrementing the number of allocated service processes to the point where the maximum is reached. Therefore, answers b and c are incorrect. LIP is only a factor in routed networks. Therefore, answer e is incorrect.

Question 8

A NetWare 5 server will lower its Maximum Physical Receive Packet Size value any time a router is detected on the network. Which setting or console command tells the server not to lower its Maximum Physical Receive Packet Size value?

- ○ a. **Set Maximum Physical Receive Packet Size = 4224**
- ○ b. **Set Allow Packet Burst = On**
- ○ c. **Set Enable LIP = On**
- ○ d. **Set Allow LIP = On**
- ○ e. **Set Enable Large Internet Packets = True**

The correct answer is d. When LIP is enabled, the Maximum Physical Receive Packet Size value is the maximum size that a packet used in communication will be. Therefore, answer a is incorrect. Packet Burst can only be used if the clients and the server support the Packet Burst protocol, and it can't be disabled on the server with a **SET** parameter. Therefore, answer b is incorrect. Answers c and e are incorrect because these **SET** parameters don't exist.

Need To Know More?

http://support.novell.com/servlet/Knowledgebase contains a wide range of technical documents that discuss the optimization of NetWare 4.x and 5 servers. On the Web site, choose the NetWare product category in Step 1, Technical Information (TIDs) is selected by default in Step 2, type "server optimization" in the box provided in Step 3, and click on Search Now.

www.novell.com/documentation/lg/nw5/usserver/sos_enu/data/hx0rwd73.html contains the optimization options for a NetWare 5 server.

NDS Security Review

Terms you'll need to understand:

- √ NDS object rights
- √ NDS property rights
- √ Trustees
- √ Inherited rights
- √ Effective rights
- √ Inherited Rights Filter (IRF)
- √ Access control list (ACL)

Techniques you'll need to master:

- √ Defining the six NDS object rights
- √ Defining the six NDS property rights
- √ Describing and applying rights using NDS trustees
- √ Determining an object's effective rights
- √ Understanding the concept of inherited rights
- √ Comparing the differences and similarities between NDS and file system security

Chapter 15

One of NetWare 5's most powerful features is *Novell Directory Services (NDS)*. NDS is a global, distributed, and hierarchical database of all your network resources; it provides a very secure and flexible mechanism for controlling resource access. You have the ability to decide which resources your users can see, use, and/or manage.

The bulk of NetWare 5 NDS security is addressed in the *Exam Cram for NetWare 5 Administration CNE/CNA*; here we'll review some basic NDS security concepts.

Object And Property Rights

Users cannot use or modify the database until the necessary rights are assigned to them, and they do not have any NDS rights until those rights are assigned. Rights are granted in NDS for two categories: *object rights* and *property rights*. Each NDS object has properties, and these properties may or may not have values. Think of an NDS object as a box—object rights allow you to perform actions outside of the box, but not on the contents inside the box. The contents of the box are an NDS object's properties. Modifying the color or shape of the box requires object rights, whereas modifying, adding, or changing the contents requires property rights.

Here are the NetWare 5 NDS object rights:

- **Browse (B)** This object right allows the user to see the object, but not the object's properties. This right does not allow the user to obtain any other information about the object other than its name and its type, based on the icon.

- **Rename (R)** A user with this right can change the name of the object, but cannot change any of the object's properties.

- **Create (C)** This allows the user to create objects in the container and in [Root]. This right applies only to containers and [Root], because a user cannot create anything below or in a leaf object.

- **Delete (D)** With this right, the user can delete the object or objects.

- **Supervisor (S)** When a user has this object right, all the other object rights (B, R, C, D) are implied.

- **Inheritable (I)** This right is applicable only to containers and the [Root]. When this is enabled, any other assigned object rights can be passed down to objects in and below the container. Rights that are passed down to subordinate objects are referred to as *inherited*.

Here are the NetWare 5 NDS property rights:

- **Compare (C)** The Compare property right is useful for queries with a true or false result. The Compare right allows a user to perform such a query without seeing the values.

- **Read (R)** The Read property right allows the user to see the value of the property, but not to modify or change the value. The Read right implies the Compare right.

- **Add Self (A)** This right allows the object to add or remove itself from the value of a property. For example, a User object has the Add Self right to the Membership property of a Group. That user can add or remove him- or herself from the membership list, but cannot modify any other entries.

- **Write (W)** This right allows the user to change, add to, and/or delete the property value. The Write right implies the Add Self right.

- **Supervisor (S)** This right implies all the other property rights: C, R, A, and W.

- **Inheritable (I)** When this right is enabled, the other assigned property rights can flow down to subordinate objects. This right is applicable only to container objects and [Root].

> **EXAM ALERT:** You need to know what actions each of the object and property rights allows.

Trustees

In NDS, both object rights and property rights are assigned through *trustees*—objects with the rights to access certain network resources (see Figure 15.1). An NDS object can be a trustee of another NDS object with specific rights assigned. For example, suppose you have a situation in which a user needs to see the value of a container's address property. This can be accomplished by making the user a trustee of the container object and enabling the Read right. A second user who needs to be able to modify this entry can also be a trustee of the container object, but with different rights. This user would need to have the Write right. You can also assign rights using other objects, such as Group objects. If 10 people need to read the address property value, you can assign the Read right to an NDS Group object of which all 10 users are members.

Figure 15.1 The Trustees Of dialog box displaying the ACL contents.

When you assign an NDS object as a trustee of another NDS object, you're modifying the Object Trustees property, also called the *access control list (ACL)*. Suppose a user has been assigned certain rights to a container object. The container's ACL contains an entry for the user and indicates which explicit or granted rights the user has to that container. All NDS objects have an Object Trustees property, which may or may not contain entries.

> *Note: The Object Trustees property is also called the ACL, and you'll sometimes see it referred to as the Object Trustees (ACL) property, namely in the Selected Properties option of the Property Rights.*

It would be impractical to expect an administrator to edit each object in the NDS tree, modify the ACLs, and list who has which rights and where. Therefore, rights assigned at a particular location in the tree will flow down to all subordinate objects. Rights received this way are called inherited and can only flow down, not up or sideways. This feature means the design of your database can greatly facilitate your security needs where inheritance can do the majority of the work. Rights assigned at the Organization object can flow all the way down to the last leaf in the tree. If you have specific NDS rights needed by all users, this is a possible solution.

Because rights can flow down to all subordinate objects, a user is equivalent, in terms of security, to any parent objects. For example, the User object John is in the RESEARCH Organizational Unit object that's below the ACME Organization object. If ACME is assigned trustee rights to a Directory Map object, John inherits those rights; they flow from the ACME object, to the RESEARCH object, to the John object. This inheritance also includes the [Root] object. If the [Root] is assigned the rights, those rights flow down to all objects in the tree.

> **TIP:** Whenever possible, use container objects as trustees. If all User objects in the container have a particular need, use the container object rather than creating a separate Group object. Containers used in this sense are sometimes referred to as *natural groups*.

Property rights are further subdivided into two types: All Properties and Selected Properties. Imagine that you have a user who is responsible for changing specific information about a container, such as the address, state, phone number, and so on. You can make this user a trustee of the container and assign the Write right for All Properties. This allows the user to change all the information properties as well as all the other properties of that object.

A better way to produce the same result is to assign the Read right to All Properties and use the Selected Properties to scroll through and select each property you want the user to change. Assign Read and Write to just those properties. In this setup, the user can read all the property values, but he or she can edit only those property values that you have assigned the Write right through Selected Properties. Both All Properties and Selected Properties rights can be inheritable. When you assign rights through All Properties, the Inheritable right is enabled by default. When you assign rights using Selected Properties, the Inheritable right is not enabled by default.

One of the NDS security guidelines suggests assigning property rights through Selected Properties rather than through All Properties. This especially applies to the Write right. Remember that every NDS object has an Object Trustees property that contains a list of trustees and the assigned rights for that object. If you assign the Write right through All Properties, the user can modify the Object Trustees property. Then the user can change rights and add any other user or group to the list. This includes the ability to assign more rights than the user had originally (for example, the Supervisor right).

> **TIP:** When you enable the Selected Properties button, you can scroll through the list of properties. You may notice that to the left of the property name is a small triangular arrow. The properties in the list with this arrow are the properties that apply to the object whose trustees list is displayed. The other displayed properties are those that can be passed down (inherited) to subordinate objects; these do not apply to the object you're viewing.
>
> As you add more products that use NDS as a central repository of data, there will be more properties listed. As you'll see in the following section, you do not need to worry about the majority of these properties.

238 Chapter 15

> **EXAM ALERT:** Make sure you know how to add a trustee to an object and how to specify object rights as well as both All Properties and Selected Properties rights.

Effective Rights

A user can receive NDS rights through several object type assignments. If the User object is a trustee of another object, the user receives the rights assigned to the object. When the user is a member of a group or groups that are listed in another NDS object's ACL list, the user receives those rights through the group membership(s). In other words, if a user belongs to a group, and the group has been granted rights to an object in the NDS, the user's effective rights to the NDS object will include the rights assigned to the group. The previous statement also applies to an Organizational Role object, in that if a user is an occupant of an Organizational Role object, the user's effective rights will include the rights the role has been assigned to other objects. The user also receives rights whenever [Public] is a member of any object's ACL list.

The combination of a user's rights, obtained through explicit assignment at a particular object in the tree, inheritance, or through one of the objects previously listed, is referred to as *effective rights*. In each object's Trustee dialog box is an Effective Rights button that allows you to determine which rights an object has to the object's ACL list you're viewing. The Effective Rights button does *not* indicate where the rights came from, only what the rights are on that object (see Figure 15.2). You may have to do some detective work to determine the origin of the rights.

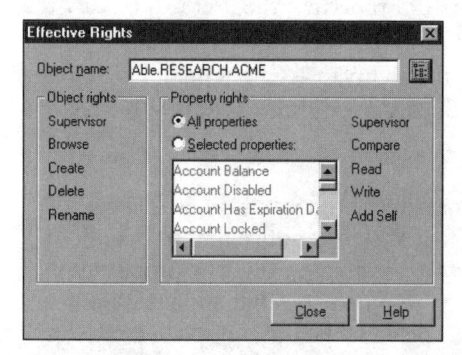

Figure 15.2 An example of the Effective Rights dialog box.

> **TIP:** A user can also receive rights if he or she is equivalent, in terms of security, to another user. This is *not* recommended. For example, suppose you need a user to have the same rights as the enterprise or a container administrator. In the user's Security Equal To property, you add the administrator's account, thus giving the user the same rights. Later, when the administrator is on an extended vacation rounding up cattle in an unknown rural area, the user's Security Equal To property value is "mysteriously" cleared so the user is not equal to any other account. The next morning the user arrives at work following an urgent page to unlock the president's account and discovers that all rights have disappeared. When you need to have another user with the same rights, make that user (or a group of which the user is a member) a trustee of the necessary objects and assign the needed rights.

Make sure you know how to "calculate" an object's effective rights based on a scenario that does not include any graphics or access to utilities. (Calculating an object's rights is covered in the *Exam Cram for NetWare 5 Administration CNE/CNA*. It's not an Advanced Administration topic. Also, search for "calculating effective rights" in NetWare Administrator help.)

Changing And Blocking Inherited Rights

There may be situations in which you want to change rights that flow down the NDS tree. NDS provides two methods to block or change rights as they flow down the hierarchy. The first of these is through the use of a trustee assignment; the second is via an *Inherited Rights Filter* (*IRF*).

Suppose a user is a trustee of the RESEARCH container and has been assigned the Browse, Create, Delete, Rename, and Inheritable rights—all the rights the user needs to administer this particular branch of the tree. However, below the RESEARCH container is another container, PATENTS. In this scenario, the user would have the same rights at the PATENTS container as at the RESEARCH container. However, you do not want the user to have all the rights in the PATENTS container. You can block these inherited rights at the PATENTS container by placing the user on the ACL list of PATENTS and assigning different rights, such as Browse. A new trustee assignment for an object lower down the directory tree will block any rights flowing from above from the same object. In this example, the user will have Browse, Create, Delete, Rename, and Inheritable rights at the RESEARCH container and all leaf objects in the RESEARCH container. The user has the Browse right on the

PATENTS container and all objects below. You can use this mechanism to block or modify the rights for all object and property rights, including the Supervisor right.

Placing a User object on the ACL list of an object lower in the tree will "override" only those rights flowing from above where the exact object is a trustee. For example, suppose a user, John, is a member of the ADMINSTAFF group. We have two containers—RESEARCH, and below that, PATENTS. ADMINSTAFF is a trustee of RESEARCH with Browse and Rename object rights. John is a trustee of PATENTS with the Write right. At the RESEARCH container, John's effective rights are Browse and Rename, because of his ADMINSTAFF group membership. At the PATENTS container, John's effective rights are Browse, Rename, and Write. The user trustee assignment on PATENTS (the container below RESEARCH) does not override any inherited rights because the rights flowing down into PATENTS are coming from a Group object trustee assignment.

The second mechanism for blocking or modifying rights is through the use of an IRF. An IRF is part of an NDS object's Object Trustees property, and it affects all inherited rights flowing into the object. For example, suppose a User object, Toby, is in the ACME container, and the Toby object has an IRF that allows Toby to inherit all rights, except for Browse. If all users in the ACME container have the Browse right on the ACME container, that right will flow down to all objects in the container. The users can see all objects in the ACME container *except* Toby. Because the object Toby has an IRF that blocks the Browse right, the users in the ACME container cannot see the object.

You can view or set an object's IRF with NetWare Administrator. Figure 15.3 shows a sample IRF window. When you open the Trustee dialog box for an object, you'll see an Inherited Rights Filter button in the lower-left corner. Selecting this brings up the Inherited Rights Filter dialog box. A checkmark next to the corresponding right indicates that the right can flow through. Notice

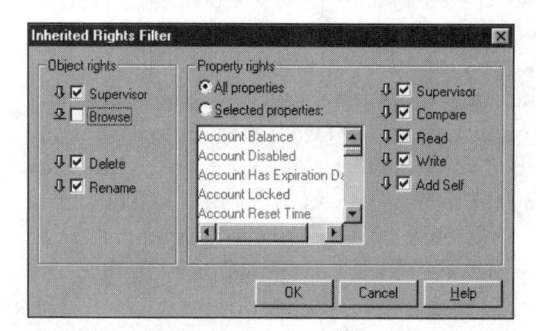

Figure 15.3 An example of the Inherited Rights Filter dialog box.

the arrow to the left of the checkbox—there's a line below the arrow to indicate when the right is blocked and cannot flow through.

Every NDS object has an IRF, and the default is that no rights are blocked; therefore, whatever rights can flow into the object, will. Another feature of IRFs is that they never *add* rights; they only take away rights or leave them untouched. An IRF is a filter, not a mechanism for assigning rights.

> **TIP** Generally, it's rare to have to block the Supervisor right with an IRF. Because an IRF will affect all users' rights that can flow down to that object, an IRF that blocks the Supervisor right may be too restrictive and lead to problems. If you don't want users to see an object, all you need to do is block the Browse right. Any user with Supervisor rights will still be able to access and manage the object.

It's extremely rare to use a completely restrictive IRF that blocks all rights. If this is necessary, there must be at least one trustee of the object that has Supervisor rights before the Supervisor right can be blocked with an IRF. This example and related security implementations are covered in more detail in the Chapter 16.

> **EXAM ALERT** Remember that IRFs are properties of objects and do not change depending on the user who is accessing the object. IRFs never add rights.

Supervisor Object Right To A Server Object

NetWare 5 file system security and NDS security are two separate security systems—they are managed and function separately. File system rights do not flow into NDS, nor do they create any NDS rights. A user does not receive any rights just because he or she has Supervisor file system rights to a server's volumes. The same applies to NDS; rights in NDS do not flow into the file system—*except in one case*. The one exception applies to the NDS Server object. If a user has the Supervisor object right to the Server object, that user receives all rights to that server's file system. Because the Supervisor file system right cannot be revoked in the file system security, the only way to prevent this user from receiving file system rights from NDS is to remove the user's Supervisor object right to the Server object. One way to do this is to place the user on the server's ACL list without assigning the Supervisor object right or the Write right to the Object Trustees property. You can also place an IRF on the Server object to block the Supervisor object right and the Write right to the Object Trustees property; however, this may adversely affect other administrative users and other operations.

> **EXAM ALERT:** When presented with a situation in which a user has too many rights in the file system, you need to know how to use NetWare Administrator to check the user's rights to the Server object.

Object Trustees Property

Every NDS object has an Object Trustees property (remember that this is also called the ACL) that contains a list of that object's trustees and assigned rights. This multivalued property also includes the IRF for that object. Every object has this property, although the contents of this property may or may not be empty.

Users with no rights to the Object Trustees property are not able to view the object's trustee list or IRF. This means that a user cannot determine who has rights on the object and cannot obtain any security information. A user who has the Read right on this property can see the trustees and the IRF, but cannot make changes. A user who has the Write right to the Object Trustees property can view the list of trustees and check their effective rights. However, the user cannot determine which rights are assigned to the trustees (the checkmarks are grayed out). In addition, the user cannot check any other object's effective rights to the NDS object whose trustee list is displayed. However, the user can change his or her assigned rights to anything, including Supervisor. Once this is done, the user can view and modify any value in the trustee list and IRF. This means the user can modify existing trustee rights, add or delete trustees, and view any object's effective rights.

Users with the Write right to a Server object's Object Trustees property can modify and view the server's trustee list and IRF. In addition, they receive all rights to that server's file system.

These situations we've just covered emphasize why you should *not* assign the Write right to All Properties. If an administrator grants a user the Write right using All Properties on a container and that right is inheritable, the user can modify any subordinates' ACLs and receive full file system rights to any server below the container.

> **EXAM ALERT:** Be very comfortable with the impact of a configuration in which a user has the Write right to an object's ACL list.

Comparison Of NDS And File System Security

You've probably noticed that there are a number of similarities and differences between the file system security and NDS security. These are outlined in the following list:

➤ **Trustees** Both the file system and NDS assign rights through trustees. An NDS object can be a trustee of a directory on the server and assigned the necessary file system rights. That same object can also be a trustee of an NDS object and is granted the necessary object and/or property rights.

➤ **Rights** The ability to perform a particular action on a file or an NDS object is enabled through the assignment of a right or rights. In the file system, the following rights apply to both files and directories:

  ➤ Supervisor

  ➤ Read

  ➤ Write

  ➤ Create

  ➤ Erase

  ➤ Modify

  ➤ File Scan

  ➤ Access Control

➤ **Inheritance** Both NDS and the file system use inheritance to allow rights at one level to flow down to all subordinate objects. The rights a user has on a directory in the file system will flow down to all files and subdirectories. In NDS, the rights a user has on a container will flow down to all leaf objects and subordinate containers.

➤ **IRF** The IRF allows you to block inherited rights as they flow into a file, directory, or object. Both NDS and the file system use filters to specify which rights can be inherited. An IRF never adds rights; it only takes away rights or leaves them unaltered.

➤ **Effective rights** Both security systems use the term *effective rights* to indicate which rights an object (for example, a User object) has to a specific file, directory, or NDS object. Because a user can receive rights through a variety of objects (Group Memberships, Organizational Roles, containers, [Root], and [Public]), the combination of these rights at a particular point is called effective rights.

To do anything in either the file system or NDS, the user must be granted rights some place in the respective system.

A few things are significantly different between the two systems. Rights do not flow from the file system into NDS, and vice versa, except in the case where a user has the Supervisor object right to a Server object. That user receives all file system rights to that server.

Supervisor rights in the file system cannot be revoked with either an IRF or a trustee assignment at a subordinate level. To eliminate a user's Supervisor right in the file system, you must remove the Supervisor right from the location it was granted. In NDS, the Supervisor object and property right can be blocked with an IRF or a trustee assignment lower in the tree hierarchy that uses the same object.

Practice Questions

Question 1

> Which of the following answers lists all container object rights?
>
> ○ a. Browse, Rename, Create, Delete, Supervisor, Inheritable
>
> ○ b. Browse, Read, Write, Delete, Supervisor, Inheritable
>
> ○ c. Browse, Rename, Create, Delete, Supervisor
>
> ○ d. Browse, Read, Write, Delete Supervisor
>
> ○ e. Browse, Read, Create, Delete, Supervisor, Inheritable

The correct answer is a. Read and Write are property rights. Therefore, answers b, d, and e are incorrect. Inheritable is a right applicable only to containers. Therefore, answer c is incorrect because Inheritable is missing.

Question 2

> A user needs to be able to modify the name of an object and to see the object. Which set of rights allows the user to perform the specified tasks?
>
> ○ a. Read, Modify
>
> ○ b. File Scan, Modify
>
> ○ c. Browse, Modify
>
> ○ d. Browse, Rename
>
> ○ e. Read, Rename

The correct answer is d. Read, Modify, and File Scan are file system rights. Therefore, answers a, b, c, and e are incorrect.

Chapter 15

Question 3

Which of the following answers lists all the property rights applicable to a leaf object?

- ○ a. Compare, Read, Add Self, Write, Supervisor, Inheritable
- ○ b. Compare, Read, Add Self, Modify, Supervisor, Inheritable
- ○ c. Compare, Read, Add Self, Write, Supervisor
- ○ d. Compare, Read, Add Self, Modify, Supervisor
- ○ e. Browse, Rename, Create, Delete, Supervisor

The correct answer is c. Modify is a file system right. Therefore, answers b and d are incorrect. Inheritable is a property right applicable only to containers and [Root]. Therefore, answer a is incorrect. Browse, Rename, Create, Delete, and Supervisor are NDS object rights. Therefore, answer e is incorrect.

Question 4

Rights are granted in NDS through _____.

- ○ a. ownership
- ○ b. trustees
- ○ c. attributes
- ○ d. IRFs
- ○ e. inheritance

The correct answer is b. Ownership of an object is not a term applicable to NDS security. Therefore, answer a is incorrect. Attributes are properties of a file or directory. Therefore, answer c is incorrect. IRFs are used to block inherited rights; they never grant or assign rights. Therefore, answer d is incorrect. Inheritance is a mechanism for receiving rights, but these are not granted. Therefore, answer e is incorrect.

Question 5

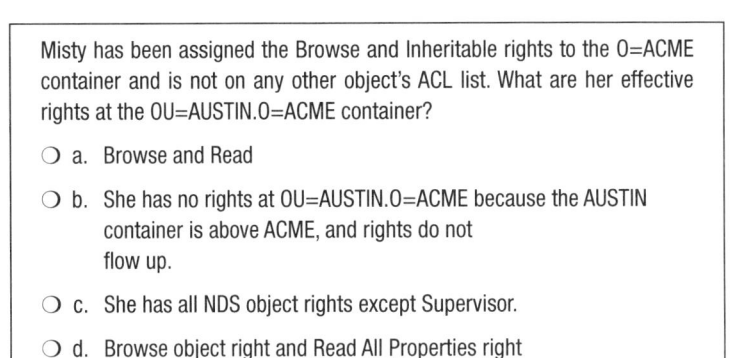

> Misty has been assigned the Browse and Inheritable rights to the O=ACME container and is not on any other object's ACL list. What are her effective rights at the OU=AUSTIN.O=ACME container?
>
> ○ a. Browse and Read
>
> ○ b. She has no rights at OU=AUSTIN.O=ACME because the AUSTIN container is above ACME, and rights do not flow up.
>
> ○ c. She has all NDS object rights except Supervisor.
>
> ○ d. Browse object right and Read All Properties right
>
> ○ e. Browse

The correct answer is e. Read is a property right. Therefore, answer a is incorrect. Answer b is incorrect because the AUSTIN container is below the ACME container. Assigning or inheriting the Browse object right does not imply any other object or property rights. Therefore, answers c and d are incorrect.

Question 6

> Sonny has been assigned the Browse and Inheritable rights to the OU=TEXAS.O=ACME container. He is also a trustee of O=ACME with the Create, Delete, Rename, and Inheritable rights. What are Sonny's effective rights at OU=TEXAS.O=ACME?
>
> ○ a. Browse
>
> ○ b. Browse, Create, Delete, and Rename
>
> ○ c. Create, Delete, and Rename
>
> ○ d. Browse, Delete, Rename, and Read All Properties
>
> ○ e. Supervisor

The correct answer is a. A trustee assignment for Sonny at a subordinate object to O=ACME overwrites his inherited rights flowing down from O=ACME. Therefore, answers b and c are incorrect. Object rights do not imply any property rights. Therefore, answer d is incorrect. The Supervisor right was never indicated in the scenario. Therefore, answer e is incorrect.

Question 7

All NDS objects have IRFs that allow you to modify rights flowing into an object. What does IRF refer to?

- ○ a. Inherited Rights Mask
- ○ b. Inherited Rights Flowing
- ○ c. Irrevocable Rights Filter
- ○ d. Inherited Rights Function
- ○ e. Inherited Rights Filter

The correct answer is e. Inherited Rights Mask is used in the NetWare 3.x file system to filter inherited rights. Therefore, answer a is incorrect. The remaining terms are fictional. Therefore, answers b, c, and d are incorrect.

Question 8

Lee is a trustee of OU=AUSTIN.O=ACME with the Supervisor and Inheritable rights assigned. She is also a trustee of O=ACME with the Browse right. What are Lee's effective rights to the SYS:\PUBLIC directory on the CN=PROD-SVR.OU=AUSTIN.O=ACME server?

- ○ a. Read and File Scan
- ○ b. Read, Write, Create, Erase, Modify, File Scan, and Access Control
- ○ c. Browse and Read
- ○ d. Supervisor, Read, Write, Create, Erase, Modify, File Scan, and Access Control
- ○ e. Lee has no rights in the file system unless they are explicitly granted in the file system.

The correct answer is d. In the scenario presented, Lee receives the Supervisor object right to the Server object through inheritance. This gives her all file system rights on that server. Therefore, answers a, b, and e are incorrect. Browse is an NDS object right. Therefore, answer c is incorrect.

Question 9

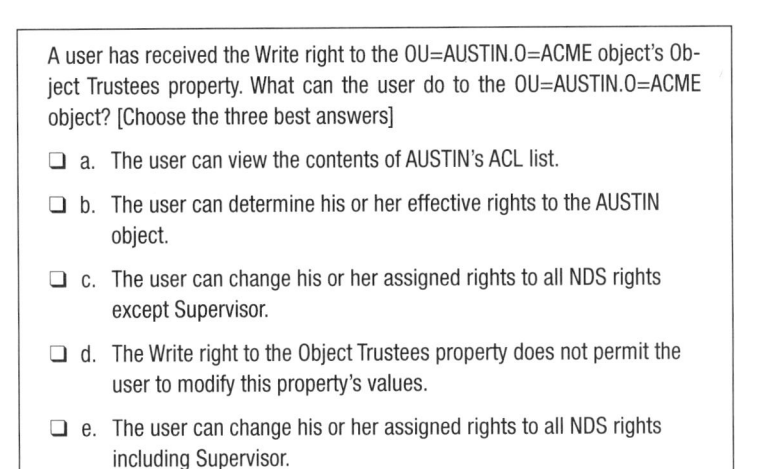

A user has received the Write right to the OU=AUSTIN.O=ACME object's Object Trustees property. What can the user do to the OU=AUSTIN.O=ACME object? [Choose the three best answers]

- ❑ a. The user can view the contents of AUSTIN's ACL list.
- ❑ b. The user can determine his or her effective rights to the AUSTIN object.
- ❑ c. The user can change his or her assigned rights to all NDS rights except Supervisor.
- ❑ d. The Write right to the Object Trustees property does not permit the user to modify this property's values.
- ❑ e. The user can change his or her assigned rights to all NDS rights including Supervisor.

The correct answers are a, b, and e. Because answer e is correct, answer c is incorrect. The Write right to the Object Trustees property gives the user the power to change the entries on the ACL rights assigned and the IRF. Therefore, answer d is incorrect.

Question 10

The administrator of the ACME-TREE has made several trustee assignments and is attempting to document users' effective rights. You've been brought in to assist the administrator who presents you with the following list (also refer to Figure 15.4):

➤ The RESEARCH container has an IRF that blocks the Browse right.

➤ Sunny is a trustee of the RESEARCH container with Supervisor and Inheritable rights.

➤ Lee is a trustee of the ACME container with Browse and Inheritable rights.

➤ Toby is a trustee of the ACME container with Browse and Inheritable rights.

➤ Toby is a trustee of the RESEARCH container with Browse, Create, Delete, Rename, and Inheritable rights.

Which of the following choices contains the correct information?

○ a. Sunny and Lee cannot see the RESEARCH container because of the IRF blocking the Browse right. Toby can see the RESEARCH container because he is a leaf object in the ACME container.

○ b. Toby, Lee, and Sunny cannot see the RESEARCH container because of the IRF on the RESEARCH container.

○ c. Lee cannot see the RESEARCH container because of the IRF on the RESEARCH container. Sunny can see the RESEARCH container because she is a trustee of RESEARCH with the Supervisor right. Toby can see the RESEARCH container because he is a trustee of RESEARCH with the Browse right.

○ d. Lee cannot see the RESEARCH container because of the IRF on the RESEARCH container. Sunny cannot see the RESEARCH container because her trustee assignment at RESEARCH does not include the Browse right. Toby can see the RESEARCH container because he is a trustee of RESEARCH with the Browse right.

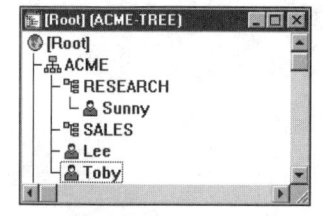

Figure 15.4

The correct answer is c. When an object is granted the Supervisor object right, all object and all property rights are implied. Therefore, answers b and d are incorrect. A leaf object on a parent container has no precedence over assigned rights. Therefore, answer a is incorrect. If you're familiar with how IRFs and trustee assignments work, this question is not tricky, just "busy."

Need To Know More?

Shilmover, Barry, and Doug Bamlett. *Exam Cram for NetWare 5 Administration CNE/CNA*. Coriolis Group: Scottsdale, AZ, 1999. ISBN: 1-57610-350-1. The book offers in-depth coverage of NetWare 5 NDS security. Also, the book addresses how to calculate an object's rights.

The Help available with NetWare Administrator is a good starting point for basic NDS security concepts and terms.

The online documentation shipped with NetWare 5 also covers NDS security.

www.novell.com/documentation/idx_nds.html is the main page for Novell's Web-based documentation for NDS. The subsections "NDS Concepts And Planning" and "NDS Object Administration" cover NDS security and implementation.

www.novell.com/products/nds is the Novell Web site for NDS that covers a range of NDS-related topics.

www.novell.com/products/wpnds.html points to Novell's "NDS White Paper," which covers topics such as the advantages of NDS and NDS's background.

http://developer.novell.com/research/appnotes.htm is Novell's Web site that offers most of the articles published in *AppNotes*, Novell's technical journal, during the past nine years. Several NDS-related articles have been published over the last few years. This site is searchable across all posted articles.

http://developer.novell.com/research/devnotes.htm is Novell's Web site for software developers. One of the resources is the journal *Developer Notes*, which often runs NDS-related articles not strictly related to programming and code design. This site is searchable across all posted articles.

NDS Security Implementations

Terms you'll need to understand:

- ✓ Enterprise administrator
- ✓ Container administrator
- ✓ Password manager
- ✓ Exclusive container administrator

Techniques you'll need to master:

- ✓ Defining the default NDS rights for a new tree
- ✓ Identifying the default NDS rights for a new server
- ✓ Outlining the default NDS rights for a new container
- ✓ Defining the default NDS rights for a new user
- ✓ Configuring access to network resources
- ✓ Outlining NDS security guidelines
- ✓ Specifying NDS security implementations
- ✓ Defining enterprise administrator tasks
- ✓ Identifying print-related administrative tasks
- ✓ Creating an exclusive and nonexclusive container administrator

NetWare 5 gives the administrator a great deal of control over resource access through the combination of Novell Directory Services (NDS) object and property rights and the features of inheritance, the Inherited Rights Filter (IRF), and trustees. Since NetWare 4's release, several NDS security guidelines have evolved from large and small NDS network implementations. In this chapter, we cover some of the common methods for administering and applying NDS security.

NDS Default Rights

Before we can begin the discussion of NDS security guidelines, we need to address the default NDS rights. Some of these defaults are set up when an object is created and can be changed to fit your needs.

> **EXAM ALERT**
> Make sure you know the NDS default security configurations and are able to display them in NetWare Administrator.

New Tree

[Root], [Public], and Admin are created automatically when you install a new server in a new tree. [Public] is made a trustee of [Root] and is assigned the Browse and Inheritable object rights. This allows users to see the NDS object in the tree. The Admin user is made a trustee of [Root] and receives the Supervisor and Inheritable rights, which allow the Admin user to have all rights to the entire tree.

> **TIP**
> When creating a new tree, you specify the name of the tree and the location of the server in the tree. At that time, you also specify the location of the Admin object in the tree and the password. In NetWare 4, the default location of the Admin object was in the Organization object. With NetWare 5, the default location is the container of the server you're installing. If you want to change the location of the Admin object, you need to enter the distinguished name of the container where you want the Admin object to reside.

New Container

When you create a new container, some default NDS security rights are enabled. The container is made a trustee of itself, and the Read right to the container's login script is set though Selected Properties. This allows the users in the container to run the container's login script during login. The Read right is also enabled for the container trustee through Selected Properties for the Print Job Configuration (Non NDPS) property. This allows the container's users to use the Non NDPS print job configuration for their printing needs. Because users in the container are security-equivalent to their parent container, they can run the container's login script and use the print job configuration for non-NDPS printers.

New Server

When you install a NetWare 5 server, the server is made a trustee of its Server object and assigned the Supervisor object right. This is necessary to allow the server to modify its own properties when necessary. For example, the Server object Net Address property stores all the protocols and associated network addresses that the server supports. If these are changed, the server needs to be able to reflect the changes by modifying its Net Address property. Remember that the Supervisor object right enables all object and property rights.

The [Public] object is also made a trustee of the Server object with only the Read right enabled for the Messaging Server property. This allows the client software to discover a server running a messaging service for products such as email and for network broadcast messages. This right is configured through Selected Properties; therefore, none of the other server properties can be read.

New User

When you create a User object, several trustee assignments are configured. The User object is automatically made a trustee of itself with the Read right to its properties through an All Properties assignment. In addition, the User object is granted the Read and Write rights to the Login Script and the Print Job Configuration (Non NDPS) properties. The Read and Write rights are enabled through Selected Properties. These rights allow users to change and modify their login script and print job configurations.

> **TIP** You can use a Template object to turn off the Write right to the login script and/or print job configuration properties when you create the User object. Create a Template object and go to the New Object's DS Rights page. Notice there is already a trustee assignment for <New User> with the Browse object and Read and Compare All Properties rights enabled. Choose the Selected Properties button and set Read for the Login Script and/or Print Job (Non NDPS) properties. When you create a new user with this Template object, the new user will not be able to modify his or her login script or print job configuration. You can also use this Template object to change existing user accounts' NDS rights to their User objects.

The [Root] object is also added as a trustee of a new User object. The Read right is granted for the Network Address and Group Membership properties through Selected Properties. This allows the environment to read the network addresses the client has used in the past when logging in. The system uses the Group Membership property entries to decide which groups the user is a member of in order to determine resource access.

The special [Public] object is also a trustee of the new User object with the Read right to the Default Server property. This is assigned through Selected Properties and allows the environment to read the user's default server setting.

> **TIP**
> To determine which property rights are set through Selected Properties, choose the Selected Properties button. As you scroll down the list, a checkmark appears to the left of any property that has been configured.

Configuring Access To Network Resources

Novell has developed a number of NDS guidelines for database security. These guidelines produce the best results when the NDS tree follows good design principles. One of the most important suggestions for NDS user security is to start with the NDS defaults. These give the user sufficient rights to access network resources without compromising security.

There are some additional considerations when dealing with resources in a heterogeneous environment. In such situations, a user may need access to resources that are not in his or her container. The user will not be able to access the resource because there are no default NDS rights created for resources outside the user's container. Two common resources to which users need access are Directory Map objects and Profile objects.

Directory Map objects are used to create an NDS object that refers to a NetWare file system directory. Directory Map objects can be used in login scripts with the **MAP** command and are available by browsing the workstation's desktop. A user must be able to read the Path property to use a Directory Map object. The Path property stores the name of the volume and the file system location of the directory. To ensure the user can use the Directory Map object, make sure he or she has the Read right to the Path property. If you enable the Read right through Selected Properties, the user cannot read any of the other Directory Map object values.

NDS Security Implementations   **257**

Users often use a Profile object to run a particular login script. Users need to have the Read right to the Login Script property to use the Profile object. The Read right allows a user to read and run the login script. If you assign the Read right through Selected Properties, no other information about the object will be available to users.

> Make sure you're able to configure the appropriate NDS rights with NetWare Administrator so a user can use a Directory Map and/or Profile object.

NDS Security Guidelines

A number of important NDS security guidelines should be enabled on a NetWare 5 network. These guidelines are detailed in the following list:

- Start with the default NDS security settings. For the majority of your users, the security defaults are all that's needed. The defaults enable the users to access resources in their parent containers without the ability to modify, delete, or add information.

- If you need to assign the Write right for a user, enable this through Selected Properties rather than through All Properties. Every object has an access control list (ACL), and this information is stored in the object's Object Trustees property, also called the Object Trustees (ACL) property. Once users have the Write right on the Object Trustees property, they can enable any rights for themselves, including Supervisor. They can also modify any other part of the object's ACL and IRF values.

  Note: The Object Trustees property is covered in detail in Chapter 15.

  A user with the Write right to the server's Object Trustees list has full file system rights on all volumes on that server. This is very important to remember in reference to the Server object.

- Assigning the Supervisor object right implies all object rights and the All Properties rights, including Supervisor.

- One way to modify or block inherited rights is to place an IRF on the object. However, be careful with IRFs that block the Supervisor right. If you need to remove a user's Supervisor right to an object, it's a better strategy to make the user a trustee of the object without assigning the Supervisor right. An IRF that blocks the Supervisor right may affect other administrative users who need the Supervisor right. If you need to prevent a user from seeing an object, you can use an IRF that removes only the Browse right. Administrative users will still be able to view and manage the object, even though other users cannot see the object.

▶ Remember to set the Inheritable right when assigning trustees to container objects if you want those rights to flow down to subordinate objects. If you want the trustee's rights to apply only to the container, turn off the Inheritable right. The Inheritable right can be set for Object, All Properties, and Selected Properties rights.

> **EXAM ALERT:** Be sure you can explain the result of the Write right to an object's Object Trustees property, especially with respect to a Server object.

Suggested Security Practices

In addition to the guidelines discussed in the previous section, some other suggested security practices come into play. We cover these in this section:

▶ It's a good idea to turn on all the object and property rights when assigning the Supervisor object. This ensures that an IRF will not accidentally remove a needed right. Even though assigning the Supervisor object implies all rights, These rights can be removed with an IRF if they are not enabled. For example, Toby is assigned the Supervisor, Browse, and Inheritable rights to the Organization object ACME. At the RESEARCH Organizational Unit object below ACME, Toby receives all rights through inheritance. When you use the Effective Rights button to check Toby's rights at RESEARCH, you see that all rights are in effect. At the RESEARCH container, the IRF is modified to block the Supervisor object and All Properties rights. Now when you cfmck on Toby's effective rights at RESEARCH, he has only the Browse object right and Read and Compare All Properties rights. Even if you enable all the rights for Toby at ACME, the IRF at RESEARCH will still remove his Supervisor right. However, he will retain the other rights, including the Write right to RESEARCH's Object Trustees property, which permits Toby to modify the trustee list and IRF of RESEARCH to recover his rights.

▶ An account created when a new tree is created has the default name *Admin* and receives full rights to the entire tree. A good practice is to rename this account so unauthorized persons do not attempt to guess this account's password to gain access to your network.

NDS Security Implementations 259

➤ When you need to have a user with the same rights as the Admin account, do not set the user security equal to the Admin account. Imagine a situation in which a user, Chester, has been set security equal to the Admin. When the Admin user is on vacation or out of town, Chester can perform the various necessary administrative duties. However, suppose Chester is modifying various user accounts and accidentally deletes Admin from his Security Equal To property. When Chester goes to view the next user account he is scheduled to work on, he receives a message that he's unauthorized to read the trustee list. Puzzled, Chester attempts to read the trustee list of the [Root] object and receives the same message. If no other user has Supervisor rights, Chester will have to wait until Admin returns to correct the situation.

➤ If you need a user to have the same rights as the Admin account, add that user to the trustee lists of all appropriate objects and explicitly grant the rights for each trustee assignment.

➤ Change the Admin password on a regular basis. However, be aware that some applications are "tied" to the Admin password and may not function as expected when you change the password. Part of your network documentation should include any of these situations and specifics on the procedures for rectifying them.

➤ Don't use the Admin account for regular, daily activities. Reserve this account and use it for only those cases where rights to the entire tree are needed. In some cases, the password may be secured and used only when necessary. In any case, there should be at least one account with full rights to the entire tree. This is necessary for enterprise-wide actions, such as creating partitions.

➤ Create at least one account that has the same rights as the Admin account. This acts as a safety net in case something happens to the Admin account's rights. If you do not want these accounts visible to users, modify the IRFs to block the Browse right. Add the accounts to the appropriate object's trustee lists rather than using the Security Equal To property.

➤ Create another account for each administrator and use those accounts for daily administrative duties. Do not set these accounts' security equal to the Admin account. Place the accounts on the appropriate trustee lists and assign the necessary rights. The Admin account can create and configure the administrator accounts. You can also block visibility of these accounts by setting their IRFs to block the Browse right.

➤ Add the Admin account and each of the accounts that need full rights to the entire tree to the trustee lists of all containers, [Root], and all servers with all object rights and All Properties rights enabled. This prevents any IRFs from interfering with the account's rights.

Administration

The separate NDS and file system-security systems offer flexibility in dividing up administrative duties. A network can have NDS administrators who are responsible for maintaining all the NDS objects and no rights on the servers' file systems, other than those an ordinary user has. There can be file system administrators who have all rights in the file system for tasks such as installing software and performing backups and restores. These users have no administrative rights in NDS other than those applicable to an ordinary user.

The NDS hierarchy and security system allow some administrative tasks to be handled centrally and some to be distributed. Of course, if you're the only administrator, your role is the central administrator. However, if your network consists of several administrators who are responsible for particular areas of the network, you can divide up the tasks. Container administrators are useful for handling daily tasks on a branch of the tree and relieving the central or enterprise administrator. For example, a container administrator can handle the tasks of creating and maintaining user accounts for a container and subcontainers. These administrators will have full rights to a branch of the tree but no administrative rights at any higher levels.

Centralized Administration

Some tasks must be handled by an enterprise administrator who has full rights to the tree, no matter how large or small the network. These centralized tasks include the following:

➤ **Installing the first server in a new tree** As mentioned earlier, the Admin account is created when you create a new tree, and it has full rights to the entire tree. Installing the first server, naming the tree, and setting the Admin's password is the job of the enterprise administrator.

➤ **Creating the upper levels of the tree** The Organization and the first-level Organizational Units should be created by the enterprise administrator. If the network includes a wide area network (WAN), the enterprise administrator may also need to create the next level of Organizational Units.

➤ **Renaming a tree** This requires an enterprise administrator account with rights to the entire tree and is accomplished with the DSMERGE utility, which is run on the server. The process for renaming the tree is very simple; however, there may be serious ramifications if you rename a tree. Services that are already installed and running may be linked to a tree name, and renaming the tree can render these services nonfunctional. You'll need to adjust workstations where the client software is configured for Preferred Tree rather than Preferred Server.

➤ **Partitioning** The NDS database can be divided into logical divisions called *partitions*. Copies, or *replicas*, of these partitions can be distributed around the network on various servers. Partitioning and replication are covered in Chapter 17, and these operations need to be performed by an enterprise administrator.

➤ **Synchronizing** In a NetWare 5 network, time is very important. It's critical that all servers in the network have the same time for NDS to function properly. Depending on the size of the network, the default strategy for synchronizing time may need to be changed or modified. This type of activity requires an enterprise administrator.

➤ **Creating administrator accounts** An enterprise administrator must create and maintain any container administrator accounts. The enterprise administrator may also have to specify what type of network activities these accounts should perform.

➤ **Upgrading** The enterprise administrator needs to coordinate upgrades of servers, applications, and/or clients. Although container administrators can handle the actual implementation of these tasks, planning and scheduling should be centrally organized and administered.

➤ **Auditing** NetWare 5 gives you the ability to audit a variety of events. The auditing environment needs an enterprise account for initial setup and configuration.

➤ **Installing additional servers** New server installation in an existing tree needs to be centrally coordinated, because it can affect replica numbers, time synchronization, and network traffic.

Distributed Administration

As mentioned in the previous section, the structure of NDS allows some network administrative tasks to be distributed. In these situations, container administrators need to have sufficient rights to manage a branch of the tree. This approach is particularly useful in larger organizations, and it provides a mechanism to allow users' needs to be addressed and resolved quickly.

Container administrators can perform a number of tasks, including the following:

- **Creating user accounts** The container administrators can be responsible for creating and managing accounts in their containers and subcontainers.

- **Managing users' passwords** Even when container administrators do not have all NDS rights on the containers, they can manage users' passwords through the use of Selected Properties rights assignments.

- **Managing file-system security and application installations** Container administrators with full system rights on all servers in their containers can manage the file-system security for users as well as manage application installations.

- **Managing backup strategies and systems for servers** This task can include restoring data if the need arises. However, restoring data that may affect the rest of the network (for example, NDS restoration) is a job that should be coordinated and supervised by the enterprise administrator.

- **Subdividing container administrator activities** Activities are subdivided using Organizational Role objects, which can be configured to change users' passwords when necessary. If this is configured through Selected Properties, the Organizational Role objects will not receive more unnecessary rights.

- **Maintaining login scripts of objects in their administrative branch** Container administrators can maintain the login scripts of the objects in their particular locations.

- **Monitoring the performance of servers** Container administrators can monitor server performance in their containers and track any errors. It's also important to monitor disk space usage. The container administrator may also be responsible for upgrading application and client software, as well as handling server upgrades—after the enterprise administrator has scheduled the operating system modification.

Password Manager

One of the tasks a container administrator, Organizational Role, or User object may need to do is change users' passwords. NetWare 5 includes a property called Password Management that allows you to configure an environment in which a user's password can be changed without requiring the Supervisor right. If you make a user a trustee of a container and assign the Read, Write, and Inheritable rights to the Password Management property, the user will then be able to change any user's password in that container. This is useful for help desk personnel when the help desk person does not to know the old password and needs to change it. You can also set other related password properties, depending on your needs (for example, Intruder Lockout Reset). The Read and Write rights on this property allow a user to unlock an account that has been disabled through intruder lockout settings. However, you need to make sure that the locked accounts have not been tampered with.

Print-Related Tasks

Users who are responsible for queue-based printer servers need to be an operator of the print server. If more than one user needs this ability, you can use an Organizational Role object and add this object to the print server's Operator property. These users can then load the print server and bring it down when necessary.

In some cases, users are responsible for managing the jobs in a queue-based printing environment. Adding these users or an Organizational Role object as print queue operators allows these users to modify, delete, and reorder the print jobs in the queue.

Novell Distributed Print Services (NDPS) printing has similar administrative tasks to queue-based printing. If you place a User or Organizational Role object as the operator of the NDPS Printer object, the user can modify, delete, reorder, copy, and move print jobs.

> **EXAM ALERT**
> Make sure you can distinguish between a task that requires an enterprise administrator and tasks that can be performed by a container administrator, a password manager, or a Printer object operator.

Guidelines For Creating Container Administrators

Here are some guidelines for networks that incorporate container administrators:

➤ Use an Organizational Role object when more than one user needs container administrator rights. For safety reasons, add one or two of the organizational role occupants as a trustee of the container. This provides a safety net if the Organizational Role object's rights are compromised.

➤ Add the enterprise administrator accounts as trustees of the containers and enable all rights. This provides a degree of fault tolerance, especially in situations where only one user is the container administrator.

▶ If you do not want container administrators to manage the file system, assign them all rights except Supervisor. This prevents the Supervisor object right from being inherited to the Server object and giving all rights to that server's file system. If the container administrator needs all NDS rights, assign Supervisor at the container and add the container administrator as a trustee of the Server objects without assigning Supervisor.

▶ Do not configure a container administrator as the security-equal of another container administrator. Either use an Organizational Role object or add the container administrators as trustees of the container and assign the necessary rights to each trustee object.

▶ You can set up a container administrator that has administrative rights only on objects he or she creates. Assign the Browse, Create, and Inheritable object rights and the Read and Compare property rights for the administrator of the container. Container administrators can create objects in the container, and they are added as trustees of these objects. The container administrator is assigned the Supervisor right (and the Inheritable right for containers) on these objects.

Creating A Container Administrator

Follow these steps to create a container administrator:

1. Make sure your enterprise accounts are trustees of the container with all rights enabled.

2. Create the Organizational Role object.

3. Make the Organizational Role object a trustee of the container.

4. Enable the appropriate NDS rights: Supervisor, Browse, Create, Delete, Rename, and Inheritable object rights or Browse, Create, Delete, Rename, and Inheritable object rights. The Inheritable right must be enabled so the Organizational Role object can administer objects in the container, as shown in Figure 16.1.

5. To prevent the container administrators from modifying the ACL or IRF of the container, assign the Read right to the Object Trustees property of the container. However, make sure somebody can still administer and change this property before modifying it.

6. If the container administrator does not have Supervisor object right on the Server objects, assign the necessary file system rights for the Organizational Role object.

NDS Security Implementations

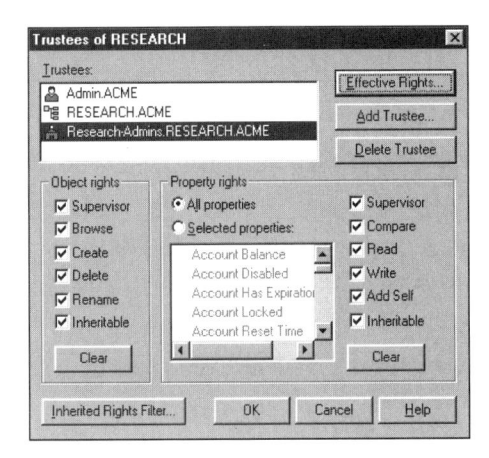

Figure 16.1 Notice that all the rights are checked in this Trustees Of RESEARCH dialog box.

7. Add the users as occupants of the Organizational Role object. Also, assign one or two occupants as explicit trustees of the container with matching rights. This provides fault tolerance for the organizational role occupants.

Notice that the occupants of the Organizational Role object are added last. Whenever you make a change in NDS or file-system security, these changes are effective immediately. If a user is logged in and the changes apply to this user, he or she will notice them immediately. By adding the occupants last, you prevent the user's rights from jumping around as you make changes to the Organizational Role object's rights when setting up the container administrators.

Exclusive Container Administrator

An exclusive container administrator is a type of container administrator that's rare in most networks but may be necessary in certain high-security arenas. With an exclusive container administrator, there's a very restrictive or a completely restrictive IRF on the container that allows the inheritance of only a few or no rights. In this situation, fault tolerance is very important. Make sure the enterprise administrators are trustees of the container with all rights enabled. This prevents the IRF from revoking the enterprise administrators' rights. If this is not done and the exclusive container administrator removes his or her trustee assignment or deletes the account, you may have a branch of the tree that is inaccessible and unmanageable. It may even be invisible. If you want to prevent users from seeing containers, use an IRF and block only the Browse right. This will not affect any administrators with administrative rights from managing the containers.

You can also create an exclusive container administrator in which only that person has rights. This is very rare and very risky. The steps for performing this configuration are as follows:

1. Make the top-secret user a trustee of the container with all object and all property rights enabled.

2. Modify the container's IRF to allow Browse and Read to All Properties to flow through. This will allow all users to see the objects but not to administer them. You can also block all rights.

3. Modify the top-secret User object's trustee list so the User object has all rights to the top-secret User object.

4. Remove the enterprise administrators as trustees of the top-secret User object.

5. Remove the enterprise administrators as trustees of the container.

> **TIP** The Supervisor right cannot be blocked with an IRF unless there's at least one trustee of the object with the Supervisor right. However, after you've assigned the trustee and blocked the Supervisor with an IRF, the branch can still become inaccessible. If the trustee rights are revoked, the trustee entry is removed, or the trustee's account is deleted, that branch of the tree is unmanageable.

Practice Questions

Question 1

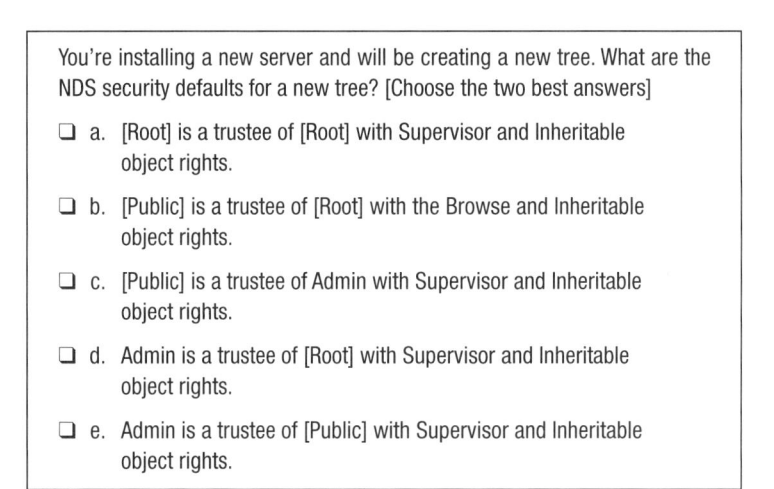

> You're installing a new server and will be creating a new tree. What are the NDS security defaults for a new tree? [Choose the two best answers]
>
> ❑ a. [Root] is a trustee of [Root] with Supervisor and Inheritable object rights.
>
> ❑ b. [Public] is a trustee of [Root] with the Browse and Inheritable object rights.
>
> ❑ c. [Public] is a trustee of Admin with Supervisor and Inheritable object rights.
>
> ❑ d. Admin is a trustee of [Root] with Supervisor and Inheritable object rights.
>
> ❑ e. Admin is a trustee of [Public] with Supervisor and Inheritable object rights.

The correct answers are b and d. Making the topmost object in the tree a trustee of itself does not gain anything. Therefore, answer a is incorrect. If [Public] is assigned Supervisor right to the Admin user, anybody can administer the Admin object. Therefore, answer c is incorrect. Having the Admin as a trustee of [Public] does not gain the Admin user any administrative rights on the tree. Therefore, answer e is incorrect.

Question 2

When a new container is created, the container is added as a trustee of itself with certain rights enabled. Which rights are assigned by default? [Choose the two best answers]

- ❑ a. The Read Selected Property right to the container's Login Script property
- ❑ b. The Read Selected Property right to the container's Net Address property
- ❑ c. The Read right to All Properties
- ❑ d. The Write Selected Property right to the container's Print Job Configuration (Non NDPS) property
- ❑ e. The Read Selected Property right to the container's Print Job Configuration (Non NDPS) property

The correct answers are a and e. Containers do not have Net Address properties because they do not represent a physical or software network resource. Therefore, answer b is incorrect. There are no rights assigned through All Properties. Therefore, answer c is incorrect. Because answer e is correct, answer d is incorrect.

Question 3

One of the container administrators in your network will be installing a new server. What are the default NDS trustee assignments for a new server? [Choose the two best answers]

- ❑ a. The [Public] object is granted the Read All Properties right.
- ❑ b. Server is granted the Supervisor object right.
- ❑ c. Admin is granted the Supervisor object right.
- ❑ d. The [Public] object is granted the Read Selected Property right to the Messaging Server property.
- ❑ e. Server is granted the Write Selected Property right to the Net Address property.

The correct answers are b and d. The [Public] object is not granted any All Properties rights, only the Selected Property Read right to the Messaging Server property. Therefore, answer a is incorrect. Admin is not made a trustee of a new server by default. Therefore, answer c is incorrect. The server trustee assignment is not made through a Selected Property assignment but via All Properties, as in answer b. Therefore, answer e is incorrect.

Question 4

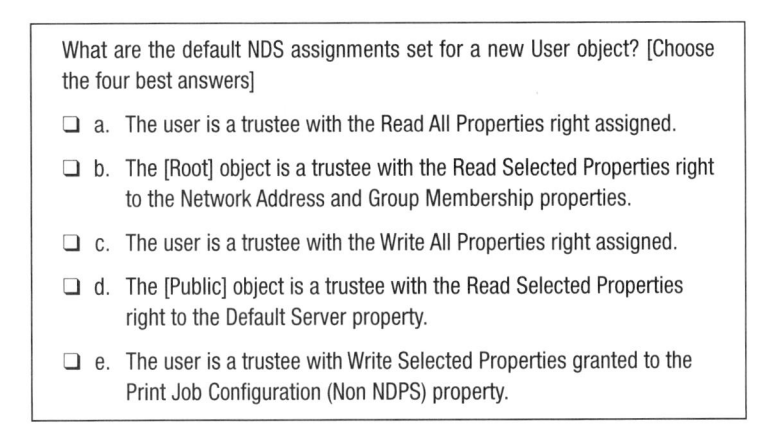

> What are the default NDS assignments set for a new User object? [Choose the four best answers]
>
> ❑ a. The user is a trustee with the Read All Properties right assigned.
> ❑ b. The [Root] object is a trustee with the Read Selected Properties right to the Network Address and Group Membership properties.
> ❑ c. The user is a trustee with the Write All Properties right assigned.
> ❑ d. The [Public] object is a trustee with the Read Selected Properties right to the Default Server property.
> ❑ e. The user is a trustee with Write Selected Properties granted to the Print Job Configuration (Non NDPS) property.

The correct answers are a, b, d, and e. Because answer e is correct, answer c makes no sense and is therefore incorrect.

Question 5

> In a heterogeneous environment, it may be necessary to set some specific NDS rights so users can access needed resources. What do you need to do to allow a user to properly access a Directory Map object?
>
> ○ a. Make the user a trustee of the Directory Map object and assign the Read All Properties right.
>
> ○ b. Make the user a trustee of the Directory Map object and assign the Browse object right.
>
> ○ c. Make the user a trustee of the Directory Map object and assign the Browse All Properties right.
>
> ○ d. Make the user a trustee of the Directory Map object and assign the Browse Selected Properties right to the Path property.
>
> ○ e. Make the user a trustee of the Directory Map object and assign the Read Selected Properties right to the Path property.

The correct answer is e. The user is a trustee of the Directory Map object, but rights are not assigned through All Properties. Therefore, answer a is incorrect. The user is not granted any object rights to the Directory Map object. Therefore, answer b is incorrect. Browse is an object right, not a property right. Therefore, answers c and d are incorrect.

Question 6

> You need to create some additional administrator accounts with the same rights as the enterprise administrator. You want to make sure there's sufficient fault tolerance in case of accidents and ensure that there's somebody with sufficient rights to manage the network when the enterprise administrator is on vacation. Which of the choices presented follows good NDS security guidelines? [Choose the two best answers]
>
> ❑ a. Add the Admin user to each of the new administrator account's Security Equal To property.
>
> ❑ b. Create an Organizational Role object and add that object to the [Root] trustees list and enable all rights.
>
> ❑ c. Add one of the occupants of the Organizational Role object as a trustee of [Root] and enable all rights.
>
> ❑ d. Add the Organizational Role object to the trustee list of the Admin object and enable all rights.
>
> ❑ e. Add the Organizational Role object to the Security Equal To property of the Admin user.

The correct answers are b and c. It's not recommended to assign NDS administrative rights through a Security Equal To setting. Therefore, answer a is incorrect. Adding the Organizational Role object to the trustee list of the Admin object does not gain any administrative rights on the tree. Therefore, answer d is incorrect. For the same reasons why answers a and d are incorrect, answer e is incorrect.

Question 7

> Which of the following are tasks that container administrators can perform without the intervention of the enterprise administrators? [Choose the two best answers]
>
> ❑ a. Creating subcontainers
>
> ❑ b. Modifying existing user account information, such as passwords, that resides under the [Root] object
>
> ❑ c. Performing file system backups and restores
>
> ❑ d. Creating partitions for any of their subcontainers
>
> ❑ e. Adjusting the time on their servers for daylight saving time on and off dates

Chapter 16

The correct answers are a and c. There are no objects directly under [Root], and container administrators do not have rights at the [Root] object. Therefore, answer b is incorrect. Partitioning is an enterprise administrator task no matter what level the partition. Therefore, answer d is incorrect. Enterprise administrators are responsible for network time and time synchronization. Therefore, answer e is incorrect.

Question 8

Which of the following are tasks that need to be performed by an enterprise administrator? [Choose the three best answers]

- ❑ a. Use DSNAME to rename the tree
- ❑ b. Adjust the network time synchronization design
- ❑ c. Create and manage server volume data
- ❑ d. Create and manage container administrators
- ❑ e. Enable NetWare 5 auditing

The correct answers are b, d, and e. DSNAME is not a utility, and DSMERGE is used to rename a tree. Therefore, answer a is incorrect. A container administrator can handle volume data can be handled by a container administrator. Therefore, answer c is incorrect.

NDS Security Implementations 273

Question 9

You've been contracted to set up the NDS security for a midsized network that includes a WAN with local users at each location responsible for their portion of the network. Based on the following information and Figure 16.2, select the best strategy that will satisfy your client's needs. [Choose the best answer]

➤ .CN=ADMIN.O=ACME has Supervisor object and All Properties rights to [Root].

➤ .CN=LEE.OU=SALES.O=ACME has the Write Selected Property right to the .OU=SALES.O=ACME Fax Number property.

➤ .OU=RESEARCH.O=ACME is a trustee of .OU=RESEARCH.O=ACME and is granted the Read Selected Property right to the Login Script property.

➤ [Public] object is a trustee of [Root] with the Browse object right assigned.

➤ There's an IRF on HR that blocks the Browse right.

➤ Able and Toby are on the .CN=RESEARCH-ADMINS.OU=RESEARCH.O=ACME occupant list.

➤ Able and Toby need to be able to administer all the objects in the RESEARCH container.

(continued)

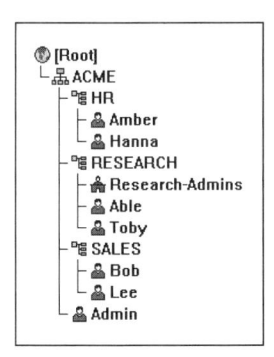

```
[Root]
└─ ACME
   ├─ HR
   │  ├─ Amber
   │  └─ Hanna
   ├─ RESEARCH
   │  ├─ Research-Admins
   │  ├─ Able
   │  └─ Toby
   ├─ SALES
   │  ├─ Bob
   │  └─ Lee
   └─ Admin
```

Figure 16.2

Question 9 (continued)

○ a. Assign ADMIN as a trustee of the RESEARCH container and enable all the object and property rights. Grant Able and Toby Supervisor rights to the ACME container so they receive Supervisor rights through inheritance where they need them in the RESEARCH container.

○ b. Assign ADMIN as a trustee of the RESEARCH container and enable all the object and property rights. Grant Toby and Able the Supervisor-equivalent right to the Admin object so they can administer the RESEARCH container.

○ c. Grant Able and Toby Supervisor rights to the RESEARCH container so they receive Supervisor rights where they need them in the RESEARCH container.

○ d. Assign ADMIN as a trustee of the RESEARCH container and enable all the object and property rights. Grant the Organizational Role object, RESEARCH-ADMINS, all rights to the RESEARCH container so Toby and Able will receive Supervisor rights to manage objects in the RESEARCH container. Grant Able and Toby Supervisor rights to the RESEARCH container so they receive Supervisor rights where they need them in the RESEARCH container.

○ e. Assign ADMIN as a trustee of the RESEARCH container and enable all the object and property rights. Grant the Organizational Role object, RESEARCH-ADMINS, all rights to the RESEARCH container so Toby and Able will receive Supervisor rights to manage objects in the RESEARCH container.

The correct answer is d. Granting Supervisor rights to the ACME container will give Able and Toby the needed rights to RESEARCH and also to SALES and HR. Nothing in the specs indicate they need Administrative rights to SALES or HR. Therefore, answer a is incorrect. There's no such thing in NetWare 5 as a Supervisor-equivalent right. This is a play on words that refers to NetWare 3.x's supervisor equivalencies and NetWare 5's Security Equal To property. Therefore, answer b is incorrect. Answer c is correct, except that there's no provision for fault tolerance. The ADMIN account could be locked out of administering the RESEARCH branch of the tree. Therefore, answer c is not the best choice. The same reason applies to answer e, which is correct, but answer d provides for more suggested fault tolerances. This question is tricky because, by themselves, answers c and e are okay, but answer d is more thorough and highlights all the suggested guidelines for fault tolerance. There's also information in the specs that's not necessary to reach the correct conclusion.

Need To Know More?

The Help available with NetWare Administrator addresses some of the suggested NDS security guidelines.

The online documentation shipped with NetWare 5 also covers NDS security.

www.novell.com/documentation/idx_nds.html is the main page for Novell's Web-based documentation for NDS. The subsections "NDS Concepts And Planning" and "NDS Object Administration" cover NDS security and implementation.

www.novell.com/products/nds is the Novell Web site for NDS that covers a range of NDS-related topics.

www.novell.com/products/wpnds.html points to Novell's "NDS White Paper," which covers topics such as the advantages of NDS and NDS's background.

http://developer.novell.com/research/appnotes.htm is Novell's Web site that offers most of the articles published in *AppNotes*, Novell's technical journal, during the past nine years. Several NDS-related articles have been published over the last few years. This site is searchable across all posted articles. The following articles are of particular interest:

➤ "Learning And Applying The Rules Of NDS Security," a classic for NDS security, is located at **http://developer.novell.com/research/appnotes/1997/august/02/index.htm**.

➤ "Implementing NDS-Enabled Solutions At Clemson University, Part 2," which covers a real-world implementation of NDS that incorporates NDS security guidelines, is located at **http://developer.novell.com/research/appnotes/1998/august/a3frame.htm**.

➤ "Protecting Your Network Against Known Security Threats," which covers many areas of network security and includes NDS security issues, is located at **http://developer.novell.com/research/appnotes/1997/november/a6frame.htm**.

http://developer.novell.com/research/devnotes.htm is Novell's Web site for software developers. One of the resources is the journal, *Developer Notes*, which often runs NDS-related articles that do not deal exclusively with programming and code design. This site is searchable across all posted articles.

NDS Partitions And Replicas

Terms you'll need to understand:
- Partitions
- Replicas
- Master replica
- Read/write replica
- Read-only replica
- Subordinate reference
- Parent partition
- Child partition

Techniques you'll need to master:
- Defining Novell Directory Services (NDS) partitions
- Comparing different types of replicas
- Understanding when subordinate references are created

The Novell Directory Services (NDS) database contains all the objects and data that represent the users and resources in your network. NDS is used for authenticating the user's initial access to the network. NDS is also involved after the user's initial login to verify access to resources. When an authenticated user attempts to access a resource, NDS is called up to verify the user's right to access the resource.

A NetWare 5 network cannot function if NDS is inaccessible or damaged. It's very important that NDS is always accessible and healthy. In this chapter, we briefly cover NDS partitioning and replication, which is addressed in more depth in the *Exam Cram for NDS Design And Implementation CNE* book. NDS health, maintenance, and troubleshooting are addressed in the next two chapters.

Partitions And Replicas In A New Tree

For a user to log into a NetWare 5 network and use the network resources, the system must be able to access NDS to verify and fulfill the user's request. If you have more than one server in your network, you can place a copy of the database on another server for fault tolerance. If your network involves a wide area network (WAN), placing portions of the database on servers on either side of a WAN link can reduce network traffic and cost. Copying and relocating the database is accomplished through NDS partitions and replicas.

When a new NDS tree is installed, the [Root] is automatically created, and all objects the administrator creates reside below it—Organization, Organizational Role, Admin, Server, Volume, and other leaf objects. At this time, there's only one copy of the database on the first server installed.

Novell uses the term *partitioning* to refer to the process of dividing the database into logical divisions. The term *logical* is used because when you view the database with NetWare Administrator or browse with Network Neighborhood, you have no indication whether the database is in one piece or in several pieces. Partitioning is one of the tasks an enterprise administrator plans and implements. In addition, partition changes do not occur frequently. When you install a new tree, the entire database is in one logical division or partition. This partition includes all objects in the NDS tree, and only one partition exists—unless you divide up the database into smaller partitions or merge trees.

Partitions have names so you can distinguish them from each other. The name a partition receives is the same name as the topmost object in the partition. Therefore, the name of the partition in a new tree is [Root] because that's the top object in the database. Every NDS database has a [Root] partition, and it may have other partitions as well.

NDS Partitions And Replicas

NDS stores its data in a hidden directory on the SYS volume _NETWARE. After you install the first server in a new tree, this directory contains all the NDS data for that tree. Novell uses the term *replica* to refer to files that contain the data for a partition. There are four types of replicas—master, read/write, read-only, and subordinate reference.

The first original copy of a partition is called the *master replica*. Therefore, in our new server (see Figure 17.1), the entire database is in one partition—[Root]. The collection of files that make up the entire database is the master replica. In the example shown in Figure 17.1, the ACME-SRV server holds the master replica of the [Root] partition.

If you have one server in a tree, that server holds the entire database. However, if you have more than one server in a tree, you might want to put a copy of the database on another server for fault tolerance. Suppose the ACME-SRV server is one of six servers in the tree and it's the only one that contains a copy of the database. If ACME-SRV goes down, nobody can access any resource on any of the other five servers. However, if you place a copy of the database on another server in the tree (for example, RESEARCH-SRV) and then ACME-SRV goes down, users can still use the copy on RESEARCH-SRV to access the network and any other resources that are not dependent on ACME-SRV.

Copies of NDS can be stored as different replica types. As mentioned previously in this section, the first original copy of the database is the master replica of [Root]. A master replica contains all the data in the partition; it can be used for authentication, and it's a writable copy, which means changes can be written directly to the replica (for example, changing a property value). If you want a complete, writable copy of a partition, create a *read/write replica*. In the example, you can put a read/write replica of [Root] on RESEARCH-SRV. You can have multiple read/write copies of a partition, but only one master replica. The major difference between the master and read/write copies is that certain NDS tasks must be performed on the master replica. The *Exam Cram for NDS Design And Implementation CNE* covers tasks specific to the master replica.

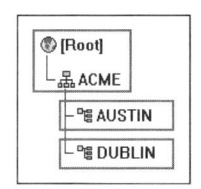

Figure 17.1 The ACME-SRV server holds the master replica of the [Root] partition.

> **TIP:** Whenever a change is made to NDS, it must be sent to all other copies of the partition that include the item changed. Wherever the change was recorded, that replica sends the change to the other replicas. For example, you change the phone number of a User object by making that change to a read/write replica. The read/write replica sends the change to all other replicas. The change does not have to go to the master replica first. When a change occurs, NDS sends only the changed data, not the entire object.

Another replica type is the *read-only replica*. This replica contains a complete copy of the partition, but changes originating from a client cannot be written directly to a read-only replica. This replica type cannot be used for login authentication because during login, the date and time of the login is written to NDS. You can have several read-only replicas per master replica.

> **TIP:** NDS design guidelines do not suggest using read-only replicas. They have the same data as the master replica and the read/writes of the replica, and they're part of a synchronization cycle that may lead to unnecessary traffic.

There's a fourth type of replica called *subordinate reference*. These replicas do not contain a complete copy of the partition and cannot be used for login or resource access verification. They are created automatically and are basically pointers that indicate where a complete copy of the partition exists. Subordinate references are covered in the following section.

> **EXAM ALERT:** Be able to compare and contrast master, read/write, and read-only replicas and know which ones can be used for logins and changes.

Partitioning NDS

As mentioned in the previous section, *partitions* are logical divisions of the database. The NDS database operates and appears as a single entity, whether it's in one partition or ten. Imagine that you have an NDS tree with two Organizational Unit objects—AUSTIN and DUBLIN—below the Organization object, ACME (refer to Figure 17.1). The resources and users in the two Organizational Unit objects are connected by a WAN link that crosses thousands of miles. You want to divide the database along these geographical boundaries

NDS Partitions And Replicas   281

to improve performance and to reduce network traffic across the WAN link. However, before you start "chopping up" the database, you need to know a few rules for creating partitions.

A partition's top boundary is always a single container, and any leaf objects and subcontainers below it are considered part of the partition until another partition is encountered or the end of the tree is reached, whichever occurs first. In the ACME example, two partitions can be created—one on each of the Organizational Unit container boundaries. The result of that division leaves three partitions: [Root], AUSTIN, and DUBLIN.

> *Note:* *The* Exam Cram for NDS Design and Implementation CNE *covers NDS design guidelines, which include partitioning. Some of the more important reasons for partitioning the database include geographical considerations (WAN), the number of objects in a container, and performance optimization for servers and clients.*

If there are three servers in DUBLIN and two servers in AUSTIN, we can place copies of the DUBLIN partition on the DUBLIN servers. For the AUSTIN servers, we can place copies of the AUSTIN partition on the AUSTIN servers. For fault tolerance and performance, we can place a copy of [Root] on another server in AUSTIN and on one in DUBLIN. See Figure 17.2 for an illustration of this process.

> **TIP** NDS does not contain information about the server's files and directories. NDS contains Volume objects that store some information about the volume but nothing about the volume's data. Therefore, replicating NDS does *not* replicate volume data. This is a separate service handled by Novell Replication Services (NRS).

Servers	Replicas		
	[Root]	AUSTIN	DUBLIN
ACME-SRV	Master		
AUS-DATA-SRV	Read/Write	Master	
AUS-APPS-SRV		Read/Write	
DUB-SRV	Read/Write		Master
DUB-DATA-SRV			Read/Write
DUB-APPS-SRV			Read/Write

Figure 17.2 Partitioning and placing replicas on the servers.

Chapter 17

In the example, the [Root] partition has two partitions below it: AUSTIN and DUBLIN. We can say that the [Root] partition is the parent of the AUSTIN and DUBLIN partitions, and both AUSTIN and DUBLIN are children of [Root]. This terminology is important for defining subordinate reference replicas. Note that on the ACME-SRV server, there's a copy of [Root], a parent, but no copies of the child partitions (AUSTIN and DUBLIN). This configuration creates two subordinate references on ACME-SRV, one for each child. The subordinate reference is basically a pointer that indicates where full copies of the child partitions reside (that is, servers with the master and read/write replicas). Subordinate references occur automatically, and the only way you can control their placement is via the servers on which you place the parent and child partitions.

In Figure 17.3, a subordinate reference also occurs on the AUS-DATA-SRV server. This server has a copy of the parent and one child (AUSTIN), but not the other child (DUBLIN); therefore, a subordinate reference is created for DUBLIN. For the same reason, a subordinate reference for AUSTIN is generated on the DUB-SRV server.

> **TIP**
> Parents need to know where their children are at all times. If a server has a replica of a parent partition and the children are not on the same server, leave a note (subordinate reference) that tells the parent where the children are.

> **EXAM ALERT**
> If you're presented with a drawing of a NDS tree with partition boundaries, be sure you're able to determine which are legal and illegal boundaries. Understand the conditions under which subordinate references are generated and that they are created automatically, unlike read/write and read-only replicas.

	Servers	Replicas		
		[Root]	AUSTIN	DUBLIN
[Root] └ ACME	ACME-SRV	Master	Subordinate Reference	Subordinate Reference
	AUS-DATA-SRV	Read/Write	Master	Subordinate Reference
├ AUSTIN	AUS-APPS-SRV		Read/Write	
└ DUBLIN	DUB-SRV	Read/Write	Subordinate Reference	Master
	DUB-DATA-SRV			Read/Write
	DUB-APPS-SRV			Read/Write

Figure 17.3 Subordinate reference replicas.

Practice Questions

Question 1

There are a number of reasons why a network administrator might partition the database. Which of the following statements defines NDS partitioning?

- a. Partitions are logical divisions of the database. Copies of the database, called *replicas*, can be stored on different volumes on a server to provide fault tolerance.
- b. Partitions are logical divisions of the database. Copies of the database, called *replicas*, can be stored on servers in another tree to provide fault tolerance.
- c. Partitions are logical divisions of the database. Copies of the database, called *replicas*, can be stored on different servers to provide fault tolerance.
- d. Partitions are logical divisions of the database. Partitioning should only be done when the network crosses a WAN link.
- e. Partitions are logical divisions of the database. Partitioning should be done only when the network does not cross a WAN link.

The correct answer is c. NDS stores its information in a hidden directory on the SYS volume and not on other volumes. Therefore, answer a is incorrect. You cannot store one tree's replicas in another tree. Therefore, answer b is incorrect. The presence of a WAN link is one reason to partition, but it's not the only reason. Therefore, answer d is incorrect. One of the NDS partitioning guidelines is to partition along geographical boundaries. Therefore, answer e is incorrect.

Question 2

The ACME-TREE administrator wants to partition the tree but is not sure where the boundaries can reside. Which of the following are legal partition boundaries? [Choose the three best answers]

- a. [Root]
- b. O=ACME
- c. CN=ACME-SRV
- d. OU=RESEARCH.O=ACME
- e. CN=ACME-SRV_SYS.OU=RESEARCH.O=ACME

Chapter 17

The correct answers are a, b, and d. Servers are not legal partition boundaries because they are leaf objects, not containers. Therefore, answer c is incorrect. The Volume object in NDS is a leaf object and is not a permitted partition boundary. Therefore, answer e is incorrect.

Question 3

The network administrator of ACME-TREE decides that more than one copy of each partition is a good idea. Which of the following contains correct combinations of replicas? [Choose the two best answers]

- ❏ a. The master replica of [Root] and master replica of ACME are on ACME-SRV. A read/write of ACME is stored on RESEARCH-SRV, and a master of SALES is stored on SALES-SRV.
- ❏ b. The master replica of [Root] and master replica of ACME are on ACME-SRV. A read/write of ACME and a read/write of [Root] are stored on RESEARCH-SRV.
- ❏ c. The master replica of [Root] and master replica of ACME are on ACME-SRV. A read/write of ACME is stored on ACME-SRV.
- ❏ d. The master replica of [Root] and master replica of ACME are on ACME-SRV. A master of ACME and a master of [Root] are stored on RESEARCH-SRV.
- ❏ e. The master replica of [Root] and master replica of ACME are on ACME-SRV. A subordinate reference of ACME and a subordinate reference of SALES are stored on RESEARCH-SRV.

The correct answers are a and b. A server cannot hold more than one copy of the same partition on a server, even if they're different replica types. Therefore, answer c is incorrect. You cannot have more than one copy of a master replica. Therefore, answer d is incorrect. Subordinate references are created automatically, and ACME and SALES are not parent partitions. Therefore, answer e is incorrect.

Question 4

What are four different types of NDS replicas? [Choose the four best answers]

- ❏ a. Master
- ❏ b. Read-only
- ❏ c. Subordinate reference
- ❏ d. [Root]
- ❏ e. Read/write

NDS Partitions And Replicas 285

The correct answers are a, b, c, and e. [Root] is not a type of partition. Therefore, answer d is incorrect.

Question 5

> Which of the following types of NDS replicas can be used for login authentication?
>
> ○ a. [Root], master, read/write
> ○ b. Master, read-only
> ○ c. Master, read/write
> ○ d. Master, read-only, subordinate reference
> ○ e. Read/write, read-only

The correct answer is c. [Root] is not a partition type. Therefore, answer a is incorrect. Read-only replicas cannot be used for login because the client cannot write to them. The login process stamps the date and time in the User object properties. Therefore, answers b and e are incorrect. Subordinate references cannot be used for authentication because they do not contain a complete copy of the partition. Therefore, answer d is incorrect.

Question 6

> The network administrator partitions the database into three partitions. The master replica of [Root] is stored on the ACME-SRV server. The master replica of ACME is stored on the ACME-SRV server. A read/write replica of ACME is stored on the RESEARCH-SRV server. You're running NetWare Administrator from the SYS:\PUBLIC directory on RESEARCH-SRV. Which of the following statements describes what you see in NetWare Administrator?
>
> ○ a. Because you're running NetWare Administrator on RESEARCH-SRV, you can view only the contents of the ACME partition.
> ○ b. Because you're running NetWare Administrator on RESEARCH-SRV, you can view the contents of the entire tree but only after you log into ACME-SRV.
> ○ c. You can view the entire tree in NetWare Administrator.
> ○ d. You can view the entire tree in NetWare Administrator, and there's a green box indicating a partition next to each container that's a partition boundary.
> ○ e. You won't be able to view any objects until you run NetWare Administrator on ACME-SRV.

Chapter 17

The correct answer is c. Because answer c is correct, answer a is incorrect. It's not necessary to log into another server to view the tree. Therefore, answer b is incorrect. NDS Manager, not NetWare Administrator, displays a green box next to each container that marks a partition boundary. Therefore, answer d is incorrect. Because answer c is correct, answer e is incorrect.

Question 7

According to Figure 17.4, on which server or servers will subordinate references occur?

Trick question

○ a. ACME-SRV

○ b. RESEARCH-SRV

○ c. SALES-SRV

○ d. ACME-SRV and RESEARCH-SRV

○ e. There are no subordinate references

The correct answer is c. ACME-SRV has complete copies of all three partitions: one parent and two children. Therefore, answer a is incorrect. RESEARCH-SRV has a copy of a partition, but it's not a parent, so no subordinate references are created. Therefore, answer b is incorrect. Because answers a and b are incorrect, answer d is incorrect. Because answer c is correct, answer e is incorrect. This question is labeled "tricky" because you must be very comfortable with the rules determining when subordinate references occur. The question is really more difficult than it is tricky.

[Root]
└ ACME
   ├ RESEARCH
   │ └ RESEARCH-SRV
   └ SALES
      └ SALES-SRV

Servers	Replicas		
	[Root]	RESEARCH	SALES
ACME-SRV	Master	Read/Write	Read/Write
RESEARCH-SRV		Master	
SALES-SRV	Read/Write		Master

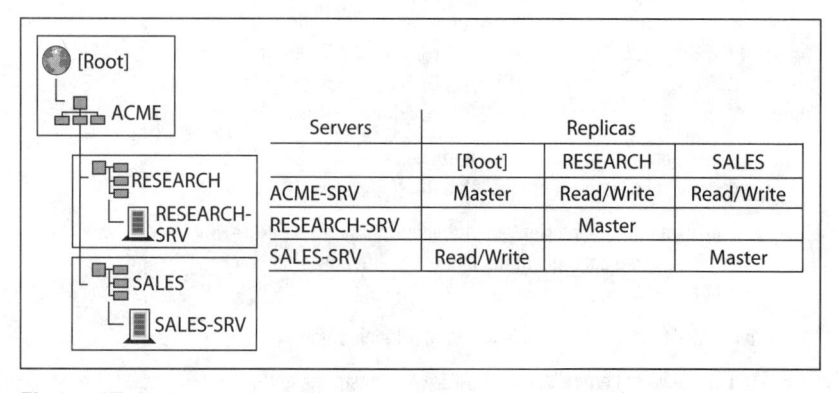

Figure 17.4

Need To Know More?

http://developer.novell.com/research/appnotes/1998/august/a3frame.htm is where you can find "Implementing NDS-Enabled Solutions At Clemson University, Part 2." This article covers a real-world implementation of NDS that incorporates NDS partitions and replicas.

www.novell.com/products/nds is the Novell Web site for NDS. It covers a range of NDS-related topics.

www.novell.com/documentation/idx_nds.html is the main page for Novell's Web-based documentation for NDS. The subsection "NDS Database Management" covers NDS partitions and replicas.

NDS Preventive Maintenance And Utilities

Terms you'll need to understand:
√ Replica
√ Novell Directory Services (NDS) Manager
√ DSREPAIR
√ DSTRACE
√ Partition root object
√ DS.NLM
√ Transaction Tracking Services (TTS)

Techniques you'll need to master:
√ Describing examples of simple and complex NDS changes
√ Defining the functions of NDS Manager, DSREPAIR, and DSTRACE
√ Identifying NDS preventive maintenance procedures
√ Specifying the proper procedures for retaining NDS health when a server is scheduled to be down

Novell Directory Services (NDS) is a database that contains all the information about your network resources and access rights. As with any other database, various procedures should be performed to maintain a healthy system, reduce errors, and make the database more efficient and reliable.

In this chapter, we first cover the basics of NDS synchronization and replication, which help to determine whether a problem is present or only a normal or transient event. We also cover the various NDS preventive maintenance procedures that reduce the likelihood of errors. In addition, we discuss the proper procedures for handling planned server downtime.

NDS Replication And Synchronization

Before we discuss NDS maintenance, you need to understand a little about NDS synchronization. NDS is a distributed, replicated database, and all the servers that hold replicas must distribute changes and synchronize the database information. Because of communication speeds, acknowledgments, and varying amounts of data, NDS is a loosely consistent database. At any single point in time, the data may not be exactly the same in all replicas, because it takes time for data to be replicated and synchronized. The amount of time it takes for a change to be replicated and synchronized depends on a number of factors, including the type of NDS change, the size of the partition, and the number of servers in the replica ring. NDS errors, troubleshooting, and recovery are covered in Chapter 19.

> **TIP:** You need to understand that replication and synchronization delays may not indicate a problem with NDS. If changes are taking place, such as partitions being merged or a large number of objects being created, unknown objects may appear in NDS. These objects will have a yellow circle with a question mark in the center. The presence of these icons does not necessarily mean corruption.

NDS changes are categorized as either simple or complex. Simple changes are such things as changing a User object's telephone number. This change affects one object and takes little time to replicate and to synchronize all replicas. Another example of a simple change is creating a partition, which is nothing more than creating logical boundaries in your tree. Because the information is already replicated around the network, creating a partition just "draws" the logical boundaries.

Complex changes to the NDS database take more time to perform and replicate. An example of a complex change is merging two partitions in a case where the replicas of each original partition reside on different servers. Before the merge starts, each server receives a copy of the other partition (if it's not already present). This transfer of data takes time to complete. An outline of the steps involved in a partition merge is listed here:

1. The replicas that will be involved in the merge are identified and their locations are noted.

2. Copies of each partition are sent to servers that do not hold replicas of the partition. The result is that each server that held one of the two partitions now holds a copy of both partitions.

3. The merging of the data proceeds. When the merge is completed, each server containing the replicas involved in the join holds a replica that contains the combined information.

> Make sure you're comfortable with describing the process of a complex change in NDS. Many more items and steps are involved, but for our purpose, this is all that needs to be addressed.

Utilities

NetWare 5 includes utilities for viewing, configuring, and repairing NDS. These include NDS Manager, DSREPAIR, and DSTRACE. NDS Manager is a Windows-based application that presents a graphical view of NDS partitions and replicas. You can use NDS Manager to create partitions and place replicas on selected servers. The utility allows you to check partition continuity (as shown in Figure 18.1) and synchronization, and it includes repair tools. You can also use NDS Manager to remove a server from a tree.

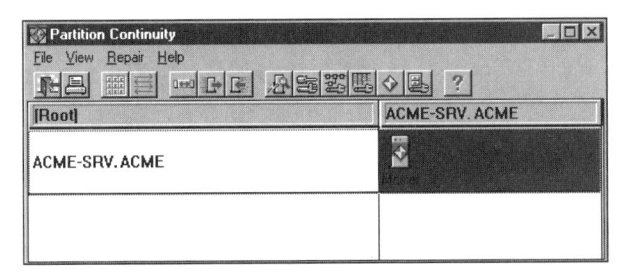

Figure 18.1 The NDS Manager's Partition Continuity dialog box.

Chapter 18

> **TIP:** To run NDS Manager from the NetWare Administrator Tools menu, copy the NMSNAP32.DLL file from the SYS:PUBLIC\WIN32 directory and paste it into the SYS:PUBLIC\WIN32\SNAPIN directory. Then restart NetWare Administrator. The NDS Manager option will appear in the Tools menu.

DSREPAIR is a NetWare Loadable Module (NLM) that runs on the NetWare 5 server. This utility has many features and functions—it's not just a repair application, as its name may imply. DSREPAIR can be used to determine which replicas reside on a server and their synchronization status, as well as to trigger replica synchronization. The utility has several advanced options for performing NDS repair procedures (see Figure 18.2).

You'll see that several advanced features in DSREPAIR are unavailable when loading the utility by executing DSREPAIR at the server command prompt. To go immediately to the DSREPAIR advanced options, enter "DSREPAIR -A" at the server console.

> **TIP:** Be aware that many of the additional features available with the **-A** option can cause serious damage to your network if not used properly.

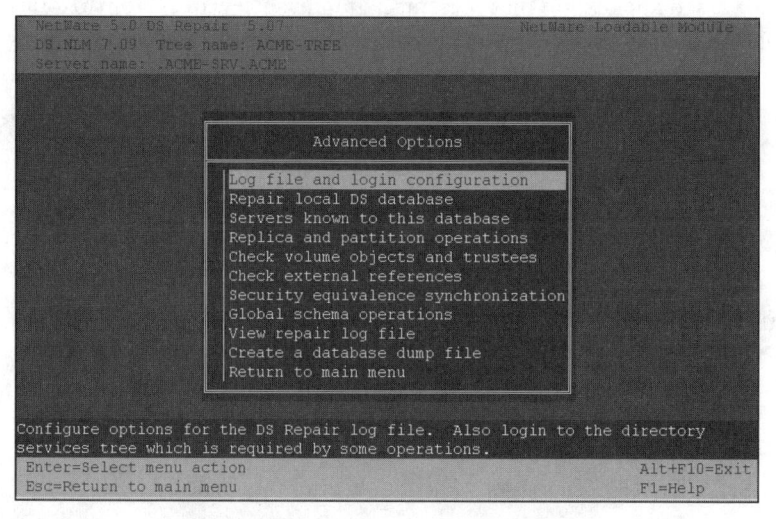

```
NetWare 5.0 DS Repair 5.07                    NetWare Loadable Module
DS.NLM 7.09   Tree name: ACME-TREE
Server name: .ACME-SRV.ACME

                    Advanced Options
          ┌────────────────────────────────────────┐
          │ Log file and login configuration       │
          │ Repair local DS database               │
          │ Servers known to this database         │
          │ Replica and partition operations       │
          │ Check volume objects and trustees      │
          │ Check external references              │
          │ Security equivalence synchronization   │
          │ Global schema operations               │
          │ View repair log file                   │
          │ Create a database dump file            │
          │ Return to main menu                    │
          └────────────────────────────────────────┘

Configure options for the DS Repair log file. Also login to the directory
services tree which is required by some operations.
Enter=Select menu action                              Alt+F10=Exit
Esc=Return to main menu                               F1=Help
```

Figure 18.2 The DSREPAIR Advanced Options menu.

NDS Preventive Maintenance And Utilities 293

The third utility is DSTRACE, which in NetWare 5 refers to a **SET** command and an NLM. Executing the command **SET DSTRACE = ON** or **SET NDS TRACE TO SCREEN = ON** at the server console opens a Directory Service screen. This NDS screen allows you to watch NDS synchronization events. DSTRACE.NLM is a new utility added to NetWare 5 that has numerous features and commands for monitoring almost any aspect of NDS activity. The DSTRACE Console screen allows you to monitor the synchronization process and to view any errors that may occur. Other applications of the utilities covered in this section can be found in Chapter 19.

Preventive Maintenance Procedures

NDS is a loosely consistent database, and at any time, all replicas might not have the same information in all their copies. The NDS data files are open and accessible when the server is up and running, and changes and synchronization events can occur at any time specified by the system. Because NDS is being used and modified constantly, you must perform various preventive maintenance procedures to help reduce the likelihood of database inconsistencies. Here are some symptoms of NDS inconsistencies:

➤ **Unable to view an object's details** You may receive an error message when attempting to access the object in NetWare Administrator.

➤ **Unknown objects appear in NetWare Administrator** The appearance of an unknown object that isn't the result of a normal, transitive operation *may* indicate an inconsistency in the database. An unknown object appears as a yellow circle with a question mark in the center.

➤ **Inability to access or use a replica** Master and read/write replicas can be used for authentication. If you're suddenly unable to log into NDS through your preferred server containing the needed replicas, this may indicate an inconsistency in the database.

It's important to note that you might never see inconsistencies in NDS. A well-designed NDS tree, along with preventive maintenance procedures, helps reduce the likelihood of database inconsistencies. In this section, we cover some of these NDS preventive maintenance items.

> **ALERT:** You may encounter a description of a series of events that defines a scenario. Although there are many more items and events that can lead to NDS inconsistencies, you should at least be familiar with the items addressed in this chapter.

Replica Placement

Part of your NDS design is determining partition boundaries and replica placement. The number of replicas you have and where you place the replicas in respect to each other has a big impact on user access to network resources. You need to have enough replicas to provide an efficient and fault-tolerant environment so the users can use the network's resources. Novell suggests that you maintain three copies of each partition for fault tolerance. Your design may dictate more than three copies of a partition to increase performance, but too many replicas can lead to excessive NDS synchronization traffic. This increase in traffic and delay in information transfer can lead to inconsistencies in the database.

> *Note:* Partition boundaries and replica placement design is addressed in the Exam Cram for NDS Design and Implementation CNE.

Managing Partition Operations

Creating, deleting, and merging partitions is an administrative task that needs to be handled centrally. If a network includes several administrators with full rights to the NDS tree, the probability of attempted simultaneous partition operations increases. This can create inconsistencies in the database and cause significant problems. Therefore, it's imperative that you coordinate and centralize for whom and/or where the partition operations are initiated. This may include permitting partition operations from only one workstation. As a preventive measure, NetWare 5 will lock a partition when you're changing its boundaries, so simultaneous actions should be practically impossible. However, it's a good idea to centralize and coordinate partition operations.

If the central administrator determines that container administrators are to perform scheduled partition operations, these administrators need to have the Supervisor object right to the partition root object, which is the topmost object in the partition. In addition, if you want to merge a partition with its parent partition, you need to have Supervisor rights to both the parent and child partitions. In general, partition operations do not occur on a regular basis; to avoid any potential problems, the account used to perform the operations should have full rights to the entire tree.

Grant fewer rights to the container objects to those container administrators whom you do not want performing partition operations. You can assign the Browse, Create, Delete, and Rename object rights and Supervisor rights to All Properties. Also configure the Read right to the Object Trustees property through Selected Properties. This provides the container administrator with all the necessary rights to administer the container but not with the ability to alter the container's trustees and/or Inherited Rights Filter (IRF) to gain Supervisor object rights.

Partition operations take some time to complete, ranging from a few minutes to a few hours. Operations such as merging a partition typically take much more time than creating a partition. When these lengthy operations are being processed, the user can still use the partition to gain access to network resources. However, you should avoid changing, adding, or deleting objects until the partition operation is complete.

Backing Up NDS

Backing up NDS should be part of your protection scheme even when your network has the recommended three copies of every partition. Backing up NDS is even more important if the network consists of only one server, because there are no replicas of the database online. Backing up a server's file system does not back up NDS. Even though NDS data is stored on the server, it's very important that your backup software can back up and restore NDS.

You should perform a backup of NDS prior to a partition merge or creating a new partition. Although backing up NDS does not back up partition boundaries, the NDS backup will contain all the object data of the database. Although you'll probably never have to restore NDS from your backup, it's still important to have a backup of the database as a vital part of your disaster recovery plans.

If correcting synchronization problems or re-creating a replica from a valid replica does not resolve the NDS errors, restoring NDS is recommended as a last resort. Restore NDS when it's indicated in documented NDS troubleshooting procedures or as instructed by Novell Support Services. You may never encounter a situation in which you need to restore NDS from a backup if you have replicas of your database distributed around the network.

NDS Version

In a NetWare 5 network that contains more than one server, all servers need to be running the same version of NDS. Versions may become out of sync if NetWare 5 Support Packs or updated NDS components are applied only to some servers rather than to all.

NDS Manager provides a method for remotely updating NDS on the NetWare 5 servers in your tree. You can find out which version of DS.NLM (Directory Services) is running on all your servers using NDS Manager. If you've applied a newer version of DS.NLM to one of the servers, you can distribute this to the other servers with NDS Manager. Any new features in the newest version will be unavailable until all the servers that hold replicas are running the same version of DS.NLM. You cannot, however, update across operating system versions. For example, you cannot update a NetWare 4.11 server with a NetWare 5 version of NDS. The updated DS.NLM is available at no charge from Novell's Support Connection Web page (http://support.novell.com).

To determine the version of DS.NLM running on the servers in your tree and to update DS.NLM, follow these steps:

1. In NDS Manager, choose Preferences from the Object menu and select the NDS Update Options tab.

2. Select the Entire Subtree (Current Container And Down) option under the Search For NDS Servers To Include section. This allows you to display all the servers and the NDS version for each machine. Click on OK.

3. Navigate and select the server that contains the updated DS.NLM.

4. Select Update from the NDS Version menu item under the Object menu.

5. In the NDS Version Update window, change the context at the top to the [Root] object.

6. Under the Servers area, all the found servers and their NDS versions are displayed.

7. You can move the server you want to update to the Target Server area or use the Select All Servers With NDS Versions Older Than Source button.

8. When you have the window configured, click on OK, and the update process will begin.

Don't Let The SYS Volume Run Out Of Disk Space!

NDS stores its data in a hidden directory on the SYS volume, and it's very important for NDS health and integrity that the SYS volume never run out of disk space. The contents of the hidden directory (SYS:_NETWARE) are protected with Transaction Tracking Services (TTS), which keeps track of all completed and incomplete transactions. If TTS detects incomplete transactions that have occurred from an event such as a sudden shutdown, any NDS changes are rolled back to the last complete transaction and incomplete entries are automatically deleted.

One of the symptoms of a SYS volume that's very low on disk space is the shutdown of TTS. This shutdown protects the NDS data by closing the database

NDS Preventive Maintenance And Utilities

so no changes can occur. The server will send messages that it's running out of disk space. If you see a message stating that TTS has been shut down, SYS is rapidly approaching no remaining storage space. Here are a number of practices that help reduce the likelihood of the SYS volume space running out:

- Increase the minimum disk space requirement for delivering a warning message. Although this will not prevent space from running out, it will give you more time to work with before the system shuts down. This value is viewed and set with either MONITOR.NLM or by modifying a SET parameter at the server console. The value is expressed in disk allocation units, and the default is 256. When the server encounters 256 or less, it will begin broadcasting warning messages. The range is from 0 to 1000000. To increase the minimum disk space requirement, enter the following at the server console:

  SET VOLUME LOW WARNING THRESHOLD = <new value>

- Make sure the queue-based print queues are not stored on the SYS volume. In contrast to NetWare 3.x, you have the ability to store the print queues on any volume.

- Store the Novell Distributed Print Services (NDPS) database on another volume so SYS space is not used to hold users' print jobs.

- Store user files and applications on a volume other than SYS.

- If a server is already low on SYS volume space, do not add a replica to that server.

- Never disable TTS manually. If you disable TTS on a server, the database is shut down and any replicas stored on that server are unavailable.

> **TIP** Novell suggests monitoring the size of CD-ROM index files (SYS:\CDROM$$.ROM) because they may be several megabytes in size. However, NetWare 5 does not support CD-ROMs as traditional NetWare volumes but as NSS volumes that do not create index files.

Planned Server Downtime

There are times when you'll need to bring down a server that contains replicas. NDS is designed to handle periods of downtime. Any changes that occur that need to be replicated to the unavailable server are queued up. When the server

Chapter 18

comes online, the changes are sent to the server and applied in the proper order based on timestamps.

When a server detects that the server it's trying to contact is unavailable, it uses a back-off algorithm so changes are not sent until the unavailable server comes back online. The disconnected server will also periodically request changes when it hasn't received any NDS information for a specified period. This helps to resynchronize the unavailable server when it comes back online.

If you need to bring a server down for more than a few days, be sure to do the following to prevent NDS inconsistencies:

➤ Move any replicas off the server before bringing the server down.

➤ Do not perform any partition operations while the server is down.

➤ Do not perform a lot of object changes or deletions.

Bringing a server down permanently also requires a set of procedures to prevent NDS errors from occurring. These procedures are also applicable in situation in which the SYS volumes will be replaced and the information is not restored from backup:

➤ Move any replicas off the server to other servers.

➤ Remove NDS from the server. At the server console, enter "NWCONFIG" and select Directory Options. From the options displayed, choose Remove Directory Servers From This Server. You'll be prompted to authenticate to NDS before removing the NDS data. This is the preferred method of removing the server from the tree, because it also removes any associated Volume objects. When this is complete, use NDS Manager to remove the Server object from the tree.

> **TIP:** You can unconditionally remove NDS from the server by typing "NWCONFIG –DSREMOVE" at the server console. You'll still receive the prompts, but you'll remove NDS no matter what. This option should be used with great care.

> **ALERT:** Notice that you remove NDS and the associated Volume objects with NWCONFIG from the server console. Server objects, on the other hand, are removed with NDS Manager, not NetWare Administrator.

Practice Questions

Question 1

Which of the following are regarded as simple NDS changes? [Choose the two best answers]

- a. Creating a partition
- b. Merging two partitions
- c. Changing the phone numbers for 500 User objects in a container
- d. Removing replicas from a server
- e. Changing the fax number of a User object

The correct answers are a and e. Merging and changing property values for many objects at the same time are considered to be complex changes. Therefore, answers b and c are incorrect. Removing replicas from a server is not considered an NDS change because you're simply deleting a copy of a portion of the database and not altering the contents. Therefore, answer d is incorrect.

Question 2

Which of the following utilities can be used to create NDS partitions?

- a. NetWare Administrator
- b. DSMERGE
- c. NDS Manager
- d. Partition Manager
- e. DSTRACE

The correct answer is c. NetWare Administrator cannot be used to create or view partition information. Therefore, answer a is incorrect. DSMERGE is used to merge two trees and to rename a tree. Therefore, answer b is incorrect. There is no Novell application called Partition Manager. Therefore, answer d is incorrect. DSTRACE is used to monitor NDS activities. Therefore, answer e is incorrect.

Question 3

A week ago you partitioned the database and distributed the replicas across three servers. Since then, the network has not been used much because of the annual company meeting. Upon returning to work, you notice several objects in NDS that have a yellow circle with question mark icon. What do you do to fix this problem?

○ a. Make sure the proper snap-ins are configured in the SnapIn directory under the SYS:\PUBLIC directory.

○ b. Remove all read/write replicas from the servers and add read-only replicas.

○ c. Do nothing, because these are normal objects.

○ d. Begin the process of NDS troubleshooting for NDS inconsistencies.

○ e. Reinstall DS.NLM to make sure the proper version is installed to view these objects.

The correct answer is d. The objects with a yellow circle question mark appearing in NDS after a week of inactivity indicate inconsistencies in the database. Therefore, answers a, b, and c will not help the situation and are incorrect. Reinstalling NDS will not help, because the problem lies in the data managed by NDS. Therefore, answer e is incorrect.

Question 4

Novell recommends that you have duplicate copies of your partitions for fault tolerance and performance. What's the recommended number of replicas for a partition to provide fault tolerance?

○ a. Every server in the tree should have a copy of the [Root] partition and three copies of any other partitions.

○ b. There should be three copies of each partition.

○ c. There should be three copies of the [Root] partition and two copies of all the other partitions.

○ d. As long as you have a reliable backup-and-restore strategy, there's no need for more than one copy of each partition.

○ e. There should be three copies of each partition on three designated servers.

The correct answer is b. Because answer b is correct, answers a and c are incorrect. A reliable backup-and-restore strategy for NDS is a preventive procedure that has nothing to do with the number of replicas recommended for fault tolerance. Therefore, answer d is incorrect. The three copies of each partition should be distributed on more than three servers. Therefore, answer e is incorrect.

Question 5

What rights are necessary to create a partition?

- a. Supervisor file system rights to the server from which you're running NDS Manager
- b. The Supervisor object right to the [Root] object and the partition's child container
- c. The Supervisor object right to the Object Trustees property
- d. The Supervisor object right to the partition root object
- e. All NDS and file system rights to the entire tree and all servers in the tree

The correct answer is d. You do not need to have file system rights to create a partition. You need file system rights to add a replica to a server. Therefore, answer a is incorrect. Rights are not needed to a child partition when creating a partition. You need to have rights to the parent and child partitions when merging the two partitions. Therefore, answer b is incorrect. Object rights can't be granted to properties; property rights would be assigned instead. Therefore, answer c is incorrect. You do not need to have full rights to everything to create a partition. Therefore, answer e is incorrect.

Chapter 18

Question 6

You should restore NDS from a tape backup under certain conditions. Which of the following would satisfy those conditions? [Choose the three best answers]

- ❏ a. The network has only one server and the SYS volume has crashed.
- ❏ b. The network has multiple servers but the read/write replica on one server is damaged.
- ❏ c. The network has multiple servers, half of which are experiencing serious NDS errors. Novell Technical Support has recommended that you remove NDS from those servers and restore from backup.
- ❏ d. You can restore NDS at any time when the network is not busy so users can continue accessing resources.
- ❏ e. The readme file in the most current Support Pack for NetWare 5 suggests restoring NDS from tape backup if the system fails during installation of the Support Pack.

Trick! question

The correct answers are a, c, and e. If one server has a damaged read/write replica, remove the replica from the server and add it back again. Adding a replica will copy the master replica information, and as long as that is healthy, the copy will be also. Therefore, answer b is incorrect. The statement in answer d is true, but the question asks for the best answers (the reason why this is a trick question). It's recommended that the system be backed up during off-hours whenever possible. Therefore, answer d is incorrect.

Question 7

Which NetWare 5 utility allows you to monitor and update DS.NLM across different servers in your tree?

- ○ a. NDS Repair
- ○ b. DSTRACE
- ○ c. DSREPAIR
- ○ d. NetWare Administrator
- ○ e. NDS Manager

The correct answer is e. There is no such utility as NDS Repair. Therefore, answer a is incorrect. DSTRACE and DSREPAIR are used to monitor and/or perform other NDS-related tasks, but they do not allow you to update DS.NLM across multiple servers. Therefore, answers b and c are incorrect. NetWare Administrator does not include any options to update DS.NLM. Therefore, answer d is incorrect.

Question 8

> NDS stores its data on the SYS volume, and it's important that the SYS volume does not run out of disk space. Which of the following is a symptom of low remaining disk space on SYS that has an impact on NDS?
>
> ○ a. TTS has been enabled.
>
> ○ b. The server that's running low on disk space begins an automatic purge of deleted files and, if the server contains a read/write replica of any partitions, those are deleted to recover disk space.
>
> ○ c. The server issues an internal command to stop processes and broadcasts a message indicating that the server is down.
>
> ○ d. TTS has been disabled.
>
> ○ e. The server automatically dismounts the volume that's running out of space when the number of free disk allocation units reaches 256 or less.

The correct answer is d. Because answer d is correct, answer a is incorrect. The system will begin purging deleted data files, but will not delete any replica information. Therefore, answer b is incorrect. The server may eventually stop processing and halt, but it cannot broadcast messages after it is down. Therefore, answer c is incorrect. When the number of remaining disk allocation units reaches 256 or less, TTS will be disabled, but the volume is not automatically dismounted. Therefore, answer e is incorrect.

Question 9

> Your company has recently acquired another company, and you've begun the consolidation process of network resources. You need to remove a server from the tree, and you want to ensure that NDS does not become corrupted. Which of the following is the best tactic for your task?
>
> ○ a. Make sure all replicas in the tree are synchronized. Change any replicas on the server you'll be removing to read-only so no changes are made to the data. Use NDS Manager to remove the Server object from the tree. Remove the associated Volume objects with NetWare Administrator.
>
> ○ b. Make sure all replicas in the tree are synchronized. Remove any replicas from the server you'll be removing. Use NDS Manager to remove the Server object from the tree. Remove the associated Volume objects with NetWare Administrator.
>
> ○ c. Make sure all replicas in the tree are synchronized. Remove any replicas from the server you'll be removing. Use NWCONFIG to remove NDS from the server. Use NDS Manager to remove the Server object from the tree.
>
> ○ d. Make sure all replicas in the tree are synchronized. Remove any replicas from the server you'll be removing. Use NWCONFIG to remove NDS from the server. Use NetWare Administrator to remove the Server object from the tree.
>
> ○ e. Make sure all replicas in the tree are synchronized. Remove any replicas from the server you'll be removing. Use NWCONFIG to remove NDS from the server. Use NDS Manager to remove the Server object and the associated Volume objects from the tree.

The correct answer is c. This question is tricky because you need to know which utility is used to remove a Server object from the tree (NDS Manager) and which utility is used to remove NDS from the server (NWCONFIG). The other statements do not list the correct utilities. Therefore, answers a, b, d, and e are incorrect.

Need To Know More?

- **http://developer.novell.com/research/appnotes.htm** is Novell's Web site where you can find most of the AppNotes (from Novell's technical journal *AppNotes*) for the past nine years. Several NDS-related articles have appeared during the last few years. This site is searchable across all posted articles.

- **http://developer.novell.com/research/devnotes.htm** is Novell's Web site for software developers. It includes the journal *Developer Notes*, which often runs NDS-related articles that are not strictly related to programming and code design. This site is searchable across all posted articles.

- **www.novell.com/products/nds** is Novell's Web site for NDS. It covers a range of NDS-related topics, including references to good practices for healthy NDS trees.

- **www.novell.com/products/nds/wpnds.html** points to Novell's NDS white paper, which covers items such as the advantages of NDS and NDS background.

NDS Troubleshooting And Recovery

Terms you'll need to understand:
- √ Novell Directory Services (NDS) Manager
- √ Partition Continuity
- √ DSREPAIR.NLM
- √ **SET DSTRACE**
- √ DSTRACE.NLM

Techniques you'll need to master:
- √ Identifying symptoms of NDS inconsistencies
- √ Outlining the steps for removing a crashed server from the tree
- √ Recognizing three examples of NDS errors
- √ Repairing NDS
- √ Defining the repair options in NDS Manager
- √ Identifying some of the options in DSREPAIR.NLM

In a NetWare 5 network, Novell Directory Services (NDS) may become inconsistent or corrupted over time. NDS stores its data in a hidden directory, SYS:_NETWARE and can suffer damage when the system becomes unstable or a hardware failure occurs. Errors can also appear as a result of an administrator's actions—intentional or otherwise. You need to be able to recognize NDS errors when they occur and to use some of the tools to either diagnose the problem or collect data requested by other parties.

In this chapter, we examine some symptoms of inconsistencies in the NDS database and address the procedures for cleaning up NDS after a server crash. We also present some sample NDS errors, provide guidelines for repairing NDS, and identify the tools used for repairing and viewing NDS events.

NDS Inconsistencies

As we discussed in previous chapters, it's the nature of replicated, distributed databases such as NDS to contain information that's loosely consistent. At any single point in time, a replica may not have exactly the same information as the other copies. When a change occurs in a replica, it takes time for that information to be dispersed to all the replicas and for the information to be synchronized. Prolonged database inconsistencies outside the expected delay factors can result in a situation in which the replicas cannot be synchronized. The information in the replicas is now dissimilar and distorted. The recommended actions and procedures to take when database information is not synchronized across the replicas include identifying the inconsistency, developing a monitoring or repair strategy, and performing corrective actions when indicated.

Inconsistencies in the NDS database can produce a variety of symptoms. The following list shows some examples of inconsistencies that impact users:

➤ **A user is attempting to log in with an account using the proper password, but the system does not accept the password** If intruder detection is enabled for the user's container, the user's account may become locked after repeated attempts.

➤ **The time it takes to log into the network is unusually long** If there are no other conditions on the network that are responsible for the login delay, the problem may be corrupted NDS information. In this situation, NDS may not be able to resolve or deliver the information requested by the client.

➤ **Previous modifications to the database are no longer present** If sufficient time has passed after the modifications to allow for replication delays and the data is still not present, the database may be corrupted or the information may not have been replicated properly.

NDS Troubleshooting And Recovery   **309**

▶ **NDS rights previously configured for trustees have disappeared or are altered** This can also be the result of corrupted information in the database or information not being replicated after an expected amount of time.

▶ **The user is experiencing inconsistent performance and reported errors cannot be duplicated** These problems are probably the most difficult type to deal with. If all other factors have been ruled out, investigate possible NDS problems.

Another symptom of NDS inconsistencies is the presence of unknown object types in NetWare Administrator. Sometimes when you're creating a partition or merging partitions, unknown objects appear temporarily. These objects are represented by a yellow circle icon with a question mark in the center that appears next to the object. If these objects are still present after the expected time for the partition operation to be completed, the database may be corrupted and the information unreliable.

There are other situations that produce unknown objects that do not disappear over time. When a server has been removed from the tree with NDS Manager, the server's Volume objects are still present in the tree, but their references to the server are no longer valid. These Volume objects appear as unknown objects. Deleting these unknown Volume objects is part of the necessary cleanup after you remove a server from the tree. If the deleted server was a planned removal, the proper procedure is to remove NDS from the server with NWCONFIG.NLM before removing the server from the tree. This removes the associated Volume objects. If the removed server was the result of a crash or another unexpected activity, the unknown Volume objects need to be removed manually using NetWare Administrator.

Objects that appear with a white rounded square icon with a question mark in the center do not indicate unknown or corrupted objects. This question mark icon appears when the workstation running NetWare Administrator is unable to locate the proper snap-ins for the object or does not have the necessary Registry entries. For example, let's say the network is using Z.E.N.works Policy Packages to manage workstations. The NDS schema was extended to include the new Z.E.N.works objects when you installed Z.E.N.works. When you go to another workstation, the Z.E.N.works-related objects appear as white question marks in squares, but the objects appear properly on your workstation. In this case, the problem resides in the other workstation. Snap-ins for NetWare Administrator dynamic link library (DLL) files are located in the SYS:\PUBLIC\WIN32\SNAPINS directory. If the workstation can access the snap-in files but the objects do not display properly, the workstation's Registry might not contain the necessary information.

If the NDS database is unable to properly synchronize the data, the system generates error messages. By monitoring these messages, you can discover the problem. If you cannot determine what's causing the problem, you need to gather additional information that can be used by Novell Support Services in providing a solution. There are several ways in which you can monitor for error messages, and each provides information a bit differently. When troubleshooting a problem, you may need to use more than one tool to collect the information you need.

NDS Manager provides a mechanism for gathering information at a workstation. The utility allows you to view the partition boundaries and the location of the replicas graphically. If you suspect that the information in the replicas is not consistent, you can select the suspected partition and run Check Synchronization from the Object menu. The resulting information displays a count for the value All Processed=No. When there are no problems, this value is zero. The All Processed=No value indicates the number of times a synchronized event has failed. However, this does not report all instances of synchronization errors.

NDS Manager displays the synchronization information from the first replica it contacts, not from all the replicas of the selected partition. To check all replicas of a partition, you need to perform a Partition Continuity check. To do this, select the partition and choose Partition Continuity from the Object menu. This process contacts all replicas in the replica ring and checks for synchronization errors. Any errors are displayed as exclamation points in yellow "yield signs" over the server icon. When you double-click on the error indicator, you see a display of status information. The information may contain an error code. If you select the blue question mark icon next to the error number, the Help file opens to the specified error code description.

> **EXAM ALERT**
>
> Make sure you know the procedure for performing both a Check Synchronization and Partition Continuity check in NDS Manager.

The Partition Continuity window is a separate window from the main NDS Manager screen and has a different menu. The Repair menu includes a subset of commands identical to those found in DSREPAIR.NLM. Before using any items in the Repair menu, check the online documentation and Help files for specific conditions under which you should use the specific Repair menu item. If you apply a Repair menu item incorrectly, it can lead to NDS database corruption.

NDS Manager is a good tool for performing a quick check on the health of NDS. If you need to get more details about suspected NDS errors, you can use the **DSTRACE SET** parameter and the DSTRACE NetWare Loadable Module

NDS Troubleshooting And Recovery 311

(NLM). In previous versions of NetWare, DSTRACE was a **SET** command with a lot of options and switches for displaying NDS events. In NetWare 5, the **SET** parameter still exists, but all the diagnostic tools are in the new DSTRACE.NLM utility.

The **DSTRACE SET** parameter allows you to open a NDS screen to display synchronization information, including synchronization errors. You can use the NetWare Administrator Help file to look up error code information. To activate the NDS window, enter the following at the server's command prompt:

```
SET DSTRACE = ON
```

or

```
SET NDS TRACE TO SCREEN = ON
```

> *Note:* *You can also use the Server Parameters menu in MONITOR.NLM to view or change the value of the* **DSTRACE SET** *parameter.*

A separate NDS window opens when either one of these commands is executed. You can toggle to this screen and watch the synchronization traffic. Running this in the **ON** state for an extended period of time can have a negative impact on the server's performance. When you suspect an error, you can turn the **SET** parameter on and monitor the results. When you finish gathering information, issue the **SET** command again, using **OFF** rather than **ON**.

The DSTRACE.NLM introduced with NetWare 5 contains a lot of options and switches for displaying NDS activities and for interacting with NDS events. Entering "DSTRACE" at the server console loads the NLM into memory. Issuing "HELP DSTRACE" at the server console displays the ways in which you can use DSTRACE.NLM. Entering "DSTRACE" at the server console when DSTRACE is already loaded displays the DSTRACE Configuration information.

Unplanned Server Downtime

Hardware failure, among other things, can cause a server crash that results in unplanned server downtime. In this case, you're unable to do the tasks we addressed in Chapter 18 for planned server downtime. You must now perform procedures for manually removing the crashed server from the tree.

When a server crashes and the hard drive containing the SYS volume is no longer available, the effect is the same as removing a server from the tree. The recovery process involves removing the crashed server from the tree and removing all traces of its presence from NDS. After that, you can replace the damaged drive, reinstall NetWare 5, and replace the lost data. Here are the steps for removing a crashed server from the tree:

1. Using the Replica List documentation, determine which replicas were stored on the crashed server. If the server held any master replicas, you need to designate one of the read/write replicas on another server as the master replica by using DSREPAIR or NDS Manager.

2. Delete the Server object from the tree with NDS Manager.

3. Delete any of the crashed server's NDS Volume objects with NetWare Administrator.

4. Perform a Partition Continuity check with NDS Manager to determine the presence of any NDS errors. If -625 TRANSPORT FAILURE errors that refer to the crashed server occur for a long period of time, you may need to remove the crashed server from the replica ring or lists. You can do this by loading **DSREPAIR -A** at the server console. The **-A** switch provides more options, but you should use them with extreme care.

5. Once you've corrected any NDS errors, you can install the new hard disk and prepare to re-create the server.

6. Install NetWare 5 on the new or repaired server.

7. At the NDS configuration screen, install the server into the same tree that it was originally in.

8. Once the NetWare 5 installation is complete, you can add replicas to the new server.

9. Restore the recovered server's file system data for the affected volume or volumes from the data backup.

10. If the recovered server supports bindery services, verify the bindery context and reset it if necessary.

> Be comfortable with the order of actions performed in removing a server from the tree. Remember, NDS Manager is used to delete a Server object, and NetWare Administrator is used to delete Volume objects.

Examples Of Some NDS Errors

There are many codes that refer to events or failures in NDS. In this section, we cover three NDS errors. The first of these probably occurs at some time in most networks. The other two we hope you'll never see.

-625 TRANSPORT FAILURE

If servers that hold replicas of the same partition cannot contact each other, the environment reports -625 TRANSPORT FAILURE errors. Several things can account for the inability of the servers to contact each other. For example, the physical link between the two servers may be down. It may be that the physical network is fine, but there's a lot of traffic on the communication media. This error may also appear if one of the servers in a replica ring has the database locked by DSREPAIR or NDS Manager. Usually, -625 errors occur infrequently and disappear quickly. However, if these error codes are displayed frequently or last for long periods of time, you need to investigate your communication link or activities.

-701 SYNCHRONIZATION DISABLED

This error message appears when NDS synchronization has been disabled. This may be the result of an error in another application or software component that's interfering with synchronization. Synchronization on a server can be enabled at the server console.

-621 TRANSACTIONS DISABLED

NDS uses Novell's Transaction Tracking System (TTS) to keep track of completed and failed (or incomplete) transactions. If the system is suddenly shut down, there may be changes in NDS that were not completed before shutdown. When the system comes back up, any incomplete actions are rolled back to the last good complete transaction. This process helps to retain the integrity and reliability of the information in the database.

When the SYS volume begins to run low on disk space, the server begins broadcasting messages to all authenticated users. When the space gets critically low, TTS is disabled and the NDS database is closed. This is done to protect the NDS data stored on the SYS volume. When TTS is disabled, the server also broadcasts this fact to all authenticated users. At this point, the server is practically useless and may soon stop responding and/or operating. TTS can also be disabled if the database is so badly corrupted that it cannot be opened and used. When you resolve the problems that disabled TTS, you can enable TTS from the server console.

> You should know these three NDS error codes, their definitions, and the actions or situations that can generate them.

Fixing NDS

When errors occur in NDS that are not the result of a temporary situation and are not resolved in the expected amount of time, the database may need to be repaired. The repair actions you take are dependent on the type of NDS inconsistency. Here are a few guidelines for repairing NDS:

➤ One of the first procedures is to let the system run for a few hours and monitor NDS activity. Over time, the system may be able to synchronize and correct the problem itself. If you know that the errors are the result of a temporary condition that has been resolved, letting NDS repair itself is the proper procedure. For example, the link between two servers holding replicas has been down for a few hours for maintenance and the servers have been reporting -625 errors. In this case, when the link is back up, NDS synchronizes and reestablishes communication. Eventually, the information in both replicas will be consistent, and the -625 errors will disappear.

➤ While NDS errors are present, do not bring any servers down that hold replicas. Bringing a server down and making it unavailable to NDS prevents any NDS self-correction.

➤ While there are NDS errors present, do not attempt any partition operations. Doing so will probably make matters worse and make it even more difficult to repair.

> **EXAM ALERT:** Be able to describe the NDS repair guidelines discussed in the previous list.

The two utilities you can use to monitor and repair NDS are NDS Manager and DSREPAIR. In NDS Manager, you can select a partition and choose Partition Continuity from the Object menu. The resultant Partition Continuity window is separate from the main NDS Manager window and has its own menu options. The Repair menu contains a subset of the DSREPAIR commands. The following is a summary of the Repair menu items found in NDS Manager:

➤ **Assign New Master** Do *not* use this feature to change a replica type. Use it only when you're sure that the master replica is corrupted or destroyed by such things as the server holding a crashed and unrecoverable master replica. This operation converts an existing replica to a master of the selected partition.

NDS Troubleshooting And Recovery   315

▶ **Receive Updates** The selected replica on the server is overwritten with a copy of the data from the master replica. This operation needs to be used with care. If the master replica is damaged or has incorrect data, this is copied to another server and eventually will be copied to the other replicas. Initiating Receive Updates may also generate extra network traffic.

▶ **Remove Server** To remove a server that's no longer present from the tree, execute Delete Server from the Object menu in the main NDS Manager window. After a period of time, NDS removes all references to the deleted server from the tree. If the server's references are not deleted after a period of time, you may need to use the Remove Server option in the Repair menu. This removes the selected server from the replica list of the selected partition.

▶ **Repair Local Database** Use this option when you determine that the information in the database is corrupted. If the database cannot be repaired and/or it cannot be opened for access, you may have to delete the replica and replace it with a new read/write copy.

▶ **Repair Network Addresses** Each server contains a table that lists each server and its associated network address. This repair option compares the values of the server's network addresses in the selected replica with the values in the server's table. If there are discrepancies, the selected replica is repaired so the network address property values in the database are accurate.

▶ **Repair Replica** This operation checks the selected replica's information with the other replicas in the ring. If there are inconsistencies or errors, only the selected replica will be repaired.

▶ **Repair Volume Objects** This option compares the NDS Volume objects for the associated server with all mounted volumes on that server. If the NDS Volume object for a mounted volume is not found in the same container as the server, NDS attempts to create a Volume object for the unknown volume.

▶ **Send Updates** This operation sends the information from the selected replica to the other copies of the same partition, including the master replica. The data received by the sending server is combined with the data in each of the replicas.

▶ **Synchronize Immediately** NDS attempts to synchronize the information in the selected partition with all other servers that hold a replica of the partition.

▶ **Verify Remote Server IDs** Each item in the NDS database has a unique ID. This option checks the remote server's ID and compares that value with the data stored in the database. If there's an error or inconsistency, NDS attempts to repair the server IDs. This action does not lock the database, so it does not interfere with users attempting to access a resource.

> **EXAM ALERT**
> You should be able to identify what each of the Repair menu items in the previous list do.

The second utility for viewing and repairing NDS information is DSREPAIR, which is executed at the server console and contains the same repair options as NDS Manager, as well as many other options. Entering "DSREPAIR" at the server console displays an Available Options window. Here are the options:

▶ **Unattended Full Repair** This option performs any repair operations on replicas stored on the server that do not require intervention by you.

▶ **Time Synchronization** This operation contacts each server referenced in the server's replicas and gathers the version of DS.NLM, the time source type, and indicates whether the time is in sync.

▶ **Report Synchronization Status** This option presents the time of the last successful synchronization for each server referenced in the replicas stored on the server.

▶ **View Repair Log File** This choice allows you to view the DSREPAIR log information that's stored in SYS:SYSTEM\DSREPAIR.LOG.

▶ **Advanced Options Menu** This option (shown in Figure 19.1) produces additional menus that allow you to perform manual operations on the

```
         Replica Options, Partition: .[Root].
View replica ring
Report synchronization status of all servers
Synchronize the replica on all servers
Repair all replicas
Repair selected replica
Schedule immediate synchronization
Cancel partition operation
Designate this server as the new master replica
Display replica information
View entire partition name
Return to replica list
```

Figure 19.1 The DSREPAIR.NLM Advanced Options menu that's available when DSREPAIR is loaded.

NDS Troubleshooting And Recovery   317

```
Replica Options, Partition: .[Root].
View replica ring
Report synchronization status of all servers
Synchronize the replica on all servers
Repair all replicas
Repair selected replica
Schedule immediate synchronization
Repair time stamps and declare a new epoch
Cancel partition operation
Destroy the selected replica on this server
Designate this server as the new master replica
Display replica information
Delete Unknown leaf objects
View entire partition name
Return to replica list
```

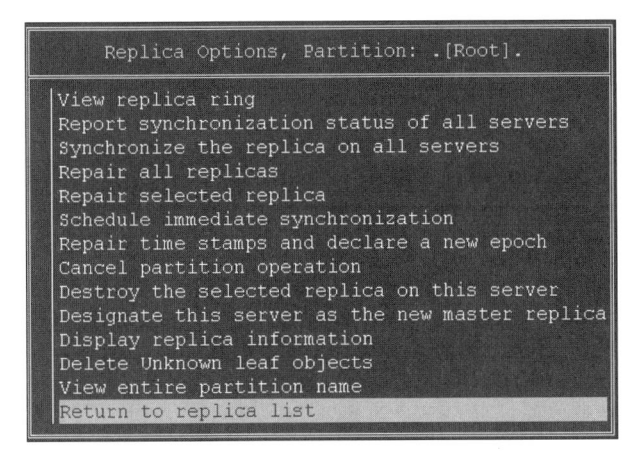

Figure 19.2 The DSREPAIR.NLM Advanced Options menu that's available when the **-A** switch is loaded.

NDS database. Be aware that if you load DSREPAIR with the -A option, you'll see more features in the Advanced Options menu (shown in Figure 19.2), all of which should be used with great care.

Practice Questions

Question 1

> Users are calling the help desk and reporting problems with the network. Which of the following complaints probably indicate inconsistencies in NDS? [Choose the three best answers]
>
> ❑ a. It's taking about five minutes to log in.
>
> ❑ b. When I go to change the phone number of a user in NetWare Administrator, there are white squares with question marks next to some of the items.
>
> ❑ c. This is the container administrator for the SALES container, and the trustee assignments I made yesterday for the WPUSERS group are no longer there.
>
> ❑ d. I can log into the NetWare 5 RESEARCH server, but when I go to access files on the HISTORY NetWare 3.x server, it indicates that my account is locked.
>
> ❑ e. When I try to change a user's fax number in NetWare Administrator, there are yellow circles with question marks next to some of the items.

The correct answers are a, c, and e. White square icons with question marks indicate that the workstation running NetWare Administrator cannot locate the snap-ins or the workstation's Registry entries don't contain the necessary information. Therefore, answer b is incorrect. The inability to access a NetWare 3.x server is not a problem with a NetWare 5 NDS tree. The NetWare 3.x bindery may have problems or the account may indeed be locked. Therefore, answer d is incorrect.

Question 2

> You have selected a partition in NDS Manager and chosen Check Synchronization from the Object menu. From the information presented in Figure 19.3, what do you determine?
>
> ○ a. All events have been synchronized and there have been no NDS errors.
>
> ○ b. There are eight NDS events pending synchronization and one event that has been completed.
>
> ○ c. The continuity of the partition is up to date for all copies of the partition's replicas.
>
> ○ d. There have been eight unsuccessful attempts to synchronize the database.
>
> ○ e. There have been eight successful attempts to synchronize the database.

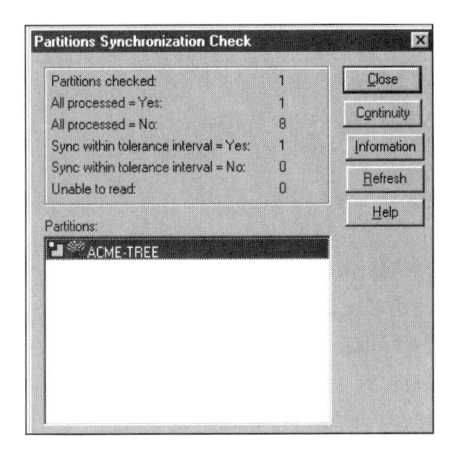

Figure 19.3

The correct answer is d. Because d is correct, answers a and e are incorrect. The All Processed=No value does not indicate events pending, but rather the number of times an NDS synchronization has failed to complete. Therefore, answer b is incorrect. Because there have been eight incomplete actions, the continuity of the partition is not up to date across all replicas. Therefore, answer c is incorrect.

Question 3

> Which of the following commands open and display NDS synchronization events in a NDS screen on the server? [Choose the two best answers]
>
> ❑ a. **SET DSTRACE = ON**
>
> ❑ b. **SET NDS TRACE TO SCREEN = ON**
>
> ❑ c. **DSTRACE -A**
>
> ❑ d. **DSTRACE ON**
>
> ❑ e. **SET DSTRACE TO SCREEN = ON**

The correct answers are a and b. DSTRACE is an NLM for viewing and interacting with NDS events, but using **-A** or **ON** does not open any information screen. Therefore, answers c and d are incorrect. Answer e has a syntax error (answer b shows the correct syntax). Therefore, answer e is incorrect.

Question 4

> Which of the following statements are true of DSTRACE in NetWare 5? [Choose the two best answers]
>
> ❑ a. DSTRACE is a **SET** parameter that allows you to view NDS synchronization events.
>
> ❑ b. DSTRACE is a utility that can be launched from NDS Manager to view NDS synchronization events.
>
> ❑ c. You can use the DSTRACE **SET** parameter's Advanced Options menu to view replica and partition information.
>
> ❑ d. The DSTRACE NLM contains options and switches for monitoring and interacting with NDS events.
>
> ❑ e. You can use the DSTRACE NLM's Advanced Options menu to view replica and partition information.

The correct answers are a and d. Both the DSTRACE NLM and the **SET** parameter can be run from the server console but not from a workstation running NDS Manager. Therefore, answer b is incorrect. **SET** parameters do not contain menu options. Therefore, answer c is incorrect. The DSTRACE NLM does not contain an Advanced Options menu (DSREPAIR does). Therefore, answer e is incorrect.

Question 5

> You have been called in to remove a crashed server from the tree. What's the proper order of actions to perform?
>
> 1. Delete the Server object from the tree with NDS Manager.
> 2. Determine which replicas were stored on the crashed server.
> 3. Perform a Partition Continuity check to make sure no NDS errors are present.
> 4. Remove the crashed server's Volume objects from the tree with NetWare Administrator.
>
> ○ a. 1, 4, 2, 3
> ○ b. 2, 1, 4, 3
> ○ c. 2, 4, 1, 3
> ○ d. 3, 1, 4, 2.
> ○ e. 3, 4, 1, 2

The correct answer is b. You should determine which replicas were stored on the crashed server; delete the Server object from the tree with NDS Manager; remove the crashed server's Volume objects from the tree with NetWare Administrator; and then perform a Partition Continuity check to make sure no NDS errors are present. All other answers have the incorrect order. Therefore, answers a, c, d, and e are incorrect.

Question 6

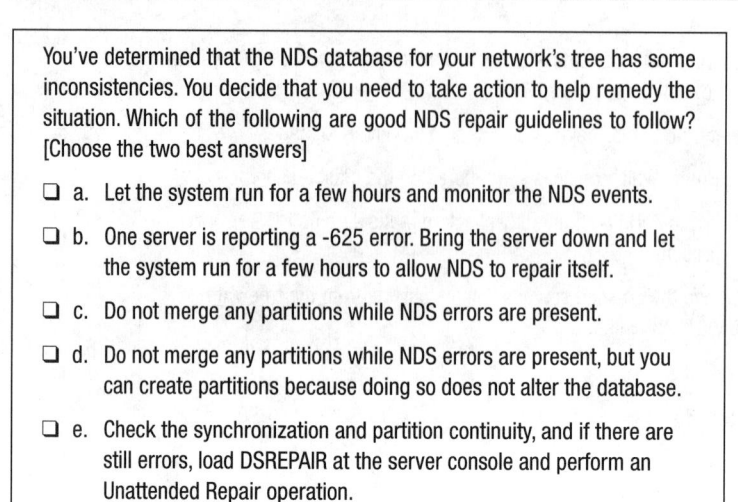

You've determined that the NDS database for your network's tree has some inconsistencies. You decide that you need to take action to help remedy the situation. Which of the following are good NDS repair guidelines to follow? [Choose the two best answers]

- ❑ a. Let the system run for a few hours and monitor the NDS events.
- ❑ b. One server is reporting a -625 error. Bring the server down and let the system run for a few hours to allow NDS to repair itself.
- ❑ c. Do not merge any partitions while NDS errors are present.
- ❑ d. Do not merge any partitions while NDS errors are present, but you can create partitions because doing so does not alter the database.
- ❑ e. Check the synchronization and partition continuity, and if there are still errors, load DSREPAIR at the server console and perform an Unattended Repair operation.

The correct answers are a and c. Bringing a server down that holds replicas prevents NDS from trying to repair itself. Therefore, answer b is incorrect. You should not perform any partition operations while NDS errors are present. Therefore, answer d is incorrect. Taking the action in answer e goes against what answer a states. Therefore, answer e is incorrect.

Question 7

> While visiting one of your company's offices that's connected to the network over a WAN link, you notice some unexpected messages on the server consoles. After loading the DSTRACE NLM on the ACME-DATA and ACME-MAIL servers, you notice some error messages. The local administrator points out that one of the servers, ACME-PS, keeps shutting down without any apparent reason. Extracts from the DSTRACE.LOG file contain the following information:
>
> ```
> 10:02:05   -621 ACME-PS
> 10:04:07   -625 ACME-DATA
> 10:04:32   -625 ACME-MAIL
> 12:00:45   -701 ACME-MAIL
> 12:57:02   -621 ACME-PS
> 13:10:27   -625 ACME-DATA
> 13:10:35   -625 ACME-MAIL
> ```
>
> The network is experiencing some problems that occur about every two hours. Some of the errors are occurring at unexpected intervals, and one event occurs when the daily backup begins at noon. With the information given to you by the local administrator and the DSTRACE.LOG file, what do you deduce?
>
> ○ a. ACME-PS is experiencing communication problems. TTS has been disabled on ACME-DATA. ACME-MAIL has had synchronization disabled and is experiencing communication problems.
>
> ○ b. ACME-MAIL is experiencing communication problems. TTS has been disabled on ACME-MAIL. ACME-PS has had synchronization disabled and is experiencing communication problems.
>
> ○ c. ACME-DATA and ACME-MAIL are experiencing communication problems. TTS has been disabled on ACME-PS. ACME-MAIL has had synchronization disabled.
>
> ○ d. ACME-DATA and ACME-MAIL are experiencing TTS-disabled events. Communication problems are indicated on ACME-PS. ACME-MAIL has synchronization disabled.
>
> ○ e. ACME-DATA and ACME-MAIL are experiencing communication problems. Synchronization has been disabled on ACME-PS. ACME-MAIL has had TTS disabled.

The correct answer is c. This question is tricky because you need to know the definition of the three error codes presented in this chapter (–625 TRANSPORT FAILURE, –621 TRANSACTIONS DISABLED, and –701 SYNCHRONIZATION DISABLED) along with some idea as to why the errors occur. ACME-PS is not experiencing communication problems, and TTS has not been disabled on ACME-DATA. Therefore, answer a is incorrect.

TTS has not been disabled on ACME-MAIL, synchronization has not been disabled on ACME-PS, and it's not experiencing communication problems. Therefore, answer b is incorrect. ACME-DATA and ACME-MAIL are not experiencing TTS disabled events, and communication problems are not indicated on ACME-PS. Therefore, answer d is incorrect. Synchronization has not been disabled on ACME-PS, and ACME-MAIL has not had TTS disabled. Therefore, answer e is incorrect.

NDS Troubleshooting And Recovery   325

Need To Know More?

http://developer.novell.com/research/appnotes.htm is where you can find the January 1999 issue of *AppNotes*, which contains the article "Troubleshooting NDS In NetWare 5 With DSREPAIR And DSTRACE."

http://support.novell.com is the Novell support Web site where you'll find the following TIDs. These contain related topics that may be of interest. Go to the Knowledgebase and perform a search using the TID number:

- TID 2945762   Synthetic Time In NetWare 5 When Booting

- TID 2913292   DS Health Check Procedures

- TID 2908056   Removing A Crashed Server From The NDS Tree

- TID 2942882   NW5-NetWare 5 Error Codes

DHCP Services

Terms you'll need to understand:

- √ Dynamic Host Configuration Protocol (DHCP)
- √ Domain Name System (DNS)
- √ DNS-DHCP Locator object
- √ DNSDHCP-GROUP Group object
- √ RootServerInfo Zone object
- √ DNS/DHCP Management Console
- √ DHCP Server object
- √ Subnet object
- √ Subnet Address Range (SAR) object
- √ IP Address object

Techniques you'll need to master:

- √ Understanding DHCP basics
- √ Installing DNS and DHCP Services on a NetWare 5 server
- √ Extending the NDS schema to support DNS and DHCP objects
- √ Installing the DNS/DHCP Management Console
- √ Configuring DHCP Services
- √ Specifying the various DHCP options
- √ Starting the DHCP Service
- √ Configuring the workstation to use DHCP Services

One of the most significant enhancements in NetWare 5 is the ability to have a pure Internet Protocol (IP) network without using Internetwork Packet Exchange (IPX) at all. For networks that support access to the Internet, the ability to perform all NetWare-related actions with the same protocol as the Internet helps reduce traffic and administrative overhead. However, one of the rules of IP is that all devices on the network must have unique numbers. This is in contrast to an IPX network where the client software detects the network address and uses its own network board address to indicate its identity.

In an IP network, the administrator must determine a plan and method to provide each device a unique address. This can be accomplished by either manual or automated configuration. Novell provides an automated process to deliver IP information to clients through the Novell DNS/DHCP Services. In this chapter, you'll learn the features of this product, how to set up and install the Dynamic Host Configuration Protocol (DHCP), and how to configure the client to use DHCP. Chapter 21 will address the same topic areas for the Domain Name System (DNS). Both of these services use the same tool for configuring DHCP and DNS. This chapter covers installing the DNS and DHCP components and management tool.

Overview Of DHCP

DHCP provides methods to deliver IP-related configuration information to clients or hosts on an IP network. This option is often very desirable to network administrators who otherwise would have to visit every user's workstation to manually configure the IP parameters, such as the IP address, subnet mask, default gateway, and so on. Using a DHCP Service, the network administrator can deliver all or some of these parameters to a workstation automatically when the system is started.

DNS/DHCP Services were available before the release of NetWare 5; however, in NetWare 5, the DNS/DHCP Services store the entire configuration information and data in Novell Directory Services (NDS). Because this information is integrated in NDS, wherever you have NDS replicas stored on the network, you also have all the DNS and DHCP information replicated. This provides fault tolerance and load balancing of the DNS and DHCP information without a separate, similar system needing to be maintained in another environment. In addition, all the administration and management is accessed through a centralized database—NDS.

IP specifications require that every host, or *node*, on an IP network has a unique address. This address consists of two pieces of information contained in one IP

DHCP Services

address: the common network address and the unique host address. Often, the host needs a gateway IP address, which is commonly the access point to the Internet. These gateways can be routers or firewalls that handle all the Internet-related traffic to and from the internal network. In addition, if the user is accessing the Internet, the workstation also needs the IP address of the DNS server, the domain name, and other DNS-related information.

The DHCP protocol consists of two components that enable the distribution of client-required IP information. The first component is a protocol that's used to deliver configuration parameters to a host, and the second component is a mechanism used to deliver network addresses to hosts. All this required IP information plus NDS-specific information, such as workstation context, can be delivered to the user through Novell DNS/DHCP Services.

> *Note: Specifics and details on IP addressing, subnet masks, and other IP issues are addressed in* Exam Cram for Networking Technologies CNE.

The architecture of DHCP is based on a client/server model. In this environment, designated DHCP servers deliver IP network addresses and other configuration information to hosts configured to request this information dynamically. To provide this service in a Novell IP network, you need to install and configure a DHCP server and set up the clients to retrieve IP information automatically.

DHCP uses three methods to distribute IP addresses to hosts. You, as the network administrator, can use one or all three of these methods in the network, and you can make changes to existing configurations:

- **Automatic allocation** In this mechanism, the DHCP Service assigns a permanent address to a client or host.

- **Dynamic allocation** This method delivers an IP address to a host, but only for a specified period of time. This is called a *lease*, and you configure it. If the workstation using a dynamically allocated address shuts down before the lease period has expired, the address is returned to the pool and is available for distribution to another host. This mechanism is the only one that allows a previously assigned address to be recycled. This method is applicable to user workstations, laptops, and other environments where there are a limited number of addresses available.

- **Manual allocation** This process provides a means for the network administrator to assign a specific address to a particular host. DHCP delivers this specific address to the indicated host.

330 Chapter 20

> Fault tolerance and load balancing of the DNS and DHCP information are present wherever NDS partitions that contain the DNS and DHCP objects are replicated.

DHCP And DNS Services Installation

When you install NetWare 5, all the necessary setup components and support files for DNS and DHCP are placed on the SYS volume. The necessary NetWare Loadable Modules (NLMs) for the services are put in the SYS:\SYSTEM folder, and the setup file for the management component is copied to the SYS:\PUBLIC\DNSDHCP directory.

Before you can set up Novell's DNS or DHCP Service, you must perform the following three tasks:

➤ Extend the NDS schema. When NetWare 5 is installed, the NDS schema does not contain DNS or DHCP object structure components. To create and manage DNS and DHCP components, the NetWare 5 tree's schema must be extended to incorporate these new objects.

➤ The workstation that will be managing the DNS and DHCP components must have the Novell Client installed. If the workstation does not have the Novell Client installed or is running a non-Novell NetWare service, the Novell Client will need to be installed. The workstation can be running either Windows 95/98 or Windows NT.

Note: For information on installing the Novell Clients, go to the online documentation that ships with NetWare 5 and search on "Installing NetWare Clients."

➤ To manage DNS and DHCP Services, the DNS/DHCP Management Console must be installed on workstations used to administer the environment. To view the objects in NetWare Administrator, the DNS and DHCP snap-ins need to be installed.

> You need to know the three required tasks that must be completed before you can configure DNS and DHCP Services.

DHCP Services **331**

Extend The NDS Schema

The NetWare 5 schema can be extended to include the DNS and DHCP objects in one of three ways:

➤ When NetWare 5 is installed, there's the option to install DNS and DHCP Services. If this option is selected, the schema is extended to include the new objects.

➤ Additional NetWare products, such as DNS and DHCP, can be added at any time through the NetWare GUI running on the server. To add additional products, follow these steps:

1. Select Install from the Novell button in the lower-left corner of the NetWare server GUI screen.

2. Click on New Product in the Installed Products window.

3. Specify the path to the source files in the Source Path window. This will be either the NetWare 5 installation CD-ROM or the location where the installation files are stored on your server.

4. Select the Novell DNS/DHCP Services product and click on Next.

5. In the Novell login screen, you need to authenticate to NDS with an account that has full rights to the [Root] object and, preferably, the entire tree.

6. Continue the installation as indicted in the next screen to finish.

➤ The schema can also be extended by running DNIPINST.NLM at the server console. To do so, follow these steps:

1. At the login screen presented, log in with an account that has full rights to the [Root] object and, preferably, the entire tree.

2. The next screen prompts you for the location of three DNS/DHCP objects that are created at the time the schema is installed. (These objects are discussed in the following section.) Press Enter to continue; the schema is then extended.

> **ALERT** You need to know the three ways to extend the schema for DNS and DHCP.

If you try extending the schema again on a tree that already has been extended, you receive a message indicating that the schema has already been extended.

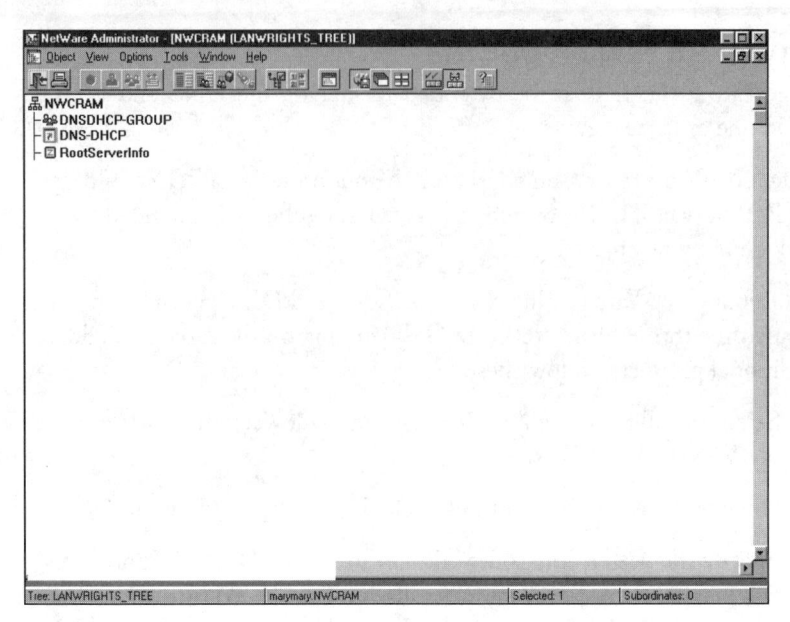

Figure 20.1 The three default objects that are created when the schema is extended for DNS and DHCP.

When the schema is extended for DNS and DHCP, three default objects are created. These three objects can exist only once per tree. These objects are discussed in the following list and shown in Figure 20.1:

➤ **Group object** The default name of this object is *DNSDHCP-GROUP*. It's a standard NDS Group object. Any servers in your tree that are designated as DNS or DHCP servers are automatically made members of this group. This group is also automatically made a trustee of the other DNS and DHCP objects so the other objects receive their needed NDS rights.

➤ **Locator object** The default name of this object is *DNS-DHCP*. It contains much of the information relating to DNS and DHCP Services so the management utility does not have to search the entire tree. The Locator object contains global defaults and DHCP options, and it lists all the DHCP and DNS servers, subnets, and zones in the tree. You can view the object in NetWare Administrator; however, you cannot configure this object, and it's not displayed in the management utility.

➤ **RootServerInfo Zone object** The default name of this object is *RootServerInfo*. Its main role is to point to DNS root servers on the Internet. This allows a user to resolve a name for a host that does not exist in your domain. For example, if you point your browser to **www.novell.com**, this object will allow the name to be resolved to the

DHCP Services

appropriate IP address. This example assumes you're not in the **novell.com** domain. If you don't have a means to reach these root name servers outside your domain, you need to have the entire Internet DNS database in your NDS tree.

At the time the schema is extended, the appropriate snap-ins for NetWare Administrator are also installed and placed in the SYS:\PUBLIC\WIN32\SNAPINS directory, which makes them accessible to NetWare Administrator. These snap-ins allow you to view the new DNS and DHCP objects in the tree but not to administer them. However, you can perform some NDS operations on the DNS/DHCP objects, such as moving and deleting them, but administration is handled by a separate management utility—the DNS/DHCP Management Console.

> **EXAM ALERT**
> You need to know the names of the three default DNS/DHCP objects. Also, know that there can be only one instance of these objects per tree. Know the role of the snap-ins for NetWare Administrator: They are used to view the DNS and DHCP objects, not to administer them.

DNS/DHCP Management Console

The last of the three tasks to accomplish before you can begin setting up DNS and/or DHCP Services is the installation of the DNS/DHCP Management Console, which is a Java application that provides a graphical interface used to configure, manage, and monitor DNS and DHCP objects. All the objects created and managed through the DNS/DHCP Management Console are NDS objects, and they will appear in NetWare Administrator. Once the console is installed, it can be launched from NetWare Administrator from the Tools menu or as a standalone application.

To access the DNS and DHCP information with the DNS/DHCP Management Console, the workstation must have the Novell Client software installed. Here are some additional workstation requirements to run the Management Console:

➤ 48MB memory minimum; 64MB memory recommended

➤ 8.5MB free disk space to store the Management Console files

The location of the DNS/DHCP Management Console setup utility, SETUP.EXE, is SYS:\PUBLIC\DNSDHCP\. To install the DNS/DHCP Management Console, run SETUP.EXE and follow these steps:

1. After acknowledging the license, you need to specify the location to store the utility on the workstation. The default location is C:\Program Files\Novell\DNSDHCP\.

Chapter 20

2. You have the option of installing the snap-in files if they have not already been installed. If you choose this option, you need to specify the location of the directory where NetWare Administrator is stored. The default location is SYS:\PUBLIC\WIN32.

3. Reboot the workstation if indicated.

When the installation is complete, a shortcut titled DNSDHCP is placed on the workstation that points to C:\Program Files\Novell\DNSDHCP\DNSDHCP.EXE, assuming the default installation location is chosen (see Figure 20.2).

> **EXAM ALERT**
> You need to know the path and name of the setup file for the Management Console and the default installation destination.

Configuring DHCP

Novell DHCP Services cannot be started until the environment is configured. These configuration requirements can be summarized as follows:

➤ A NetWare 5 server must be assigned as a DHCP server.

➤ The information you want delivered to a workstation must be set up.

➤ The DHCP Service must be started on the NetWare 5 server.

The first task in configuring the DHCP Service for a NetWare 5 network is designating a server to run the DHCP Service. After you configure a DHCP Server object, you can set up the subnets the server will service, the IP address ranges, and information specific to the DHCP server. The DHCP Server object can be created in an Organization, Organizational Unit, Country, or Locality object. Here are steps to configure a DHCP Server object and its options:

1. Run the DNS/DHCP Management Console (DNSDHCP.EXE) from the installation location on the workstation. The default path is C:\Program Files\Novell\DNSDHCP\.

2. Select the tree from the list of trees to which you're authenticated for the DHCP Service and then click on the Launch button. You have the

Figure 20.2 The DNS/DHCP Management Console shortcut icon.

DHCP Services

ability to manage all the DNS and DHCP Services in one tree or several trees from the same workstation.

In the upper-left area of the console window are two tabs: DNS Service and DHCP Service. You use these to change to the service you want to manage or administer. Each page in the DNS/DHCP Management Console has three panes:

- ► The left pane displays the objects that can be managed and the location of the objects in the service hierarchy.

- ► The right pane presents detailed information about the selected object.

- ► The bottom pane displays the DNS and DHCP servers that exist in the tree.

There's also a status bar at the bottom that displays information. The information displayed depends on which item is selected or what activity is occurring. The status bar may indicate the name of the selected item, the status of the current database action in progress, or the status of the selected service. The DNS/DHCP Management Console does not have a menu bar; it has a toolbar used to present the various options. As you pass the mouse over the toolbar items, the name of the tool is displayed, which indicates its action. To begin setting up DHCP, click on the DHCP Service tab.

3. Click on the Create button, shown in Figure 20.3, in the toolbar. You'll be presented with a window to specify the location of the DHCP Server object in the tree.

4. In the Create New DHCP Record dialog box (see Figure 20.4), select DHCP Server and click on OK.

5. Select your Server object in the Create DHCP Server dialog box (see Figure 20.5) and click on Create.

The DHCP Server object is created and the default name is DHCP_, followed by the name of the NetWare 5 server (for example, DHCP_ACME-SRV). Notice in the bottom pane of the DNS/DHCP Management Console that the DHCP Server object is displayed with a red X over the icon. This red X indicates the service has not been started on the server, as shown in Figure 20.6. When the service is running, the icon is presented without any lines over the icon.

336 Chapter 20

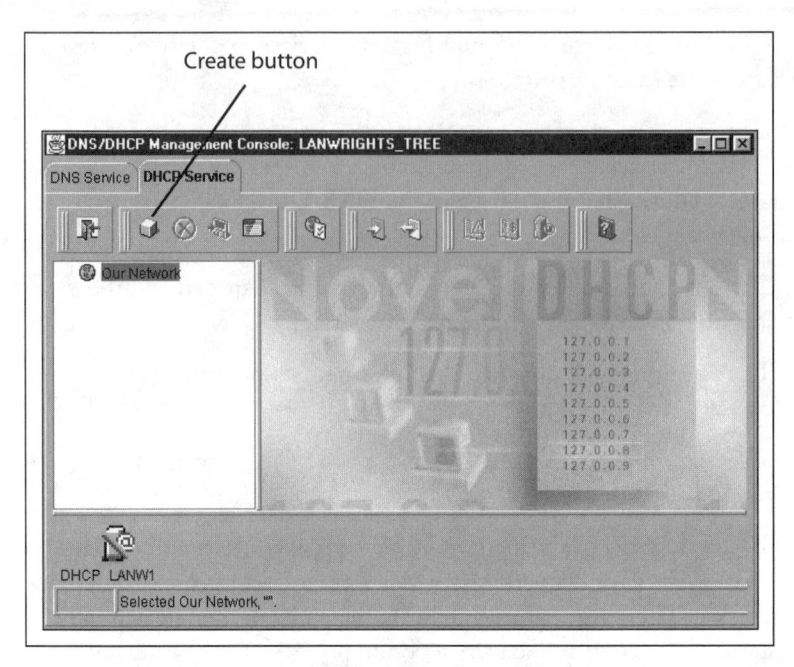

Figure 20.3 The Create button in the DNS/DHCP Management Console.

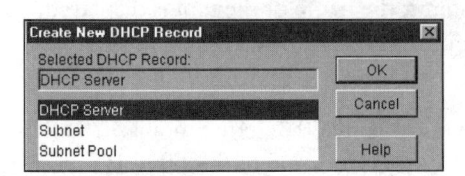

Figure 20.4 The Create New DHCP Record dialog box.

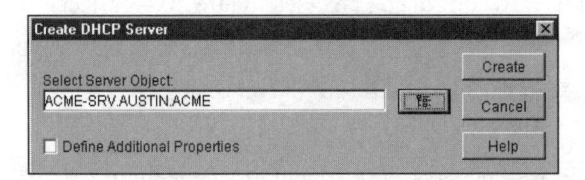

Figure 20.5 The Create DHCP Server dialog box.

Figure 20.6 The DHCP server icon indicating the service is not running.

DHCP Services

If you select the DHCP Server object in the bottom pane, the right pane will display the interface for configuring the DHCP Server object. These options include the following:

- **Set SNMP Traps Option** This option can be used by tools such as ManageWise. The options available are None (the default), Major Events, and All.

- **Audit Trail And Alerts Option** When this is configured, you can view the information by clicking on the View Events|Alerts button on the toolbar. The options available are None (the default), Major Events, and All.

- **Enable Audit Trail Log** By default, this option is not enabled. When this option is configured, you can view the information by clicking on the View Audit Trail Log button on the toolbar.

- **Mobile User Option** The options available are No Mobile User Allowed, Allow Mobile User But Delete Previously Assigned Address (the default), and Allow Mobile User But Do Not Delete Previously Assigned Address.

- **Ping** By default, this option is not enabled. This option specifies whether the DHCP server will ping the address it delivers to a client before giving the address out. If a response comes back from the ping, the DHCP server will not deliver to that address because it's already in use.

6. Once the DHCP Server object is configured, the next step is to specify the network address the DHCP Service will deliver. This is called a *DHCP Subnet object*. This is a container object that stores IP address configuration information that can be assigned to nodes. The DHCP Subnet object can exist in an Organization, Organizational Unit, Country, or Locality object. Click on the Create button. Then, from the presented list of object types in the Create New DHCP Record dialog box, choose Subnet and click on OK.

7. In the Create Subnet dialog box that appears (see Figure 20.7), specify the following:

    - **Subnet Name** The name of these objects must be unique throughout the entire tree.

    - **NDS Context** You can either enter or browse to the container in which you want this object to reside.

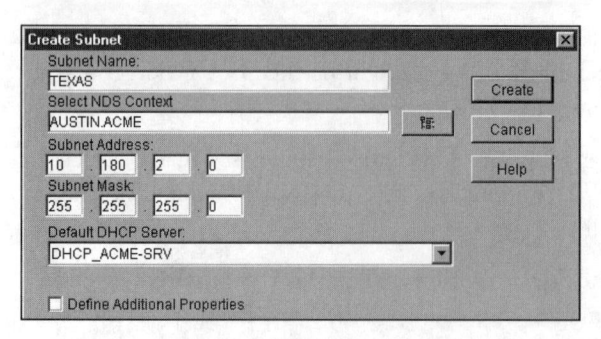

Figure 20.7 The Create Subnet dialog box.

➤ **Subnet Address** Here, you specify the network address that will be serviced by the DHCP server (for example, 10.180.2.0).

➤ **Subnet Mask** This is the subnet mask value that's used by the subnet address you've specified (for example, 255.255.255.0).

➤ **Default DHCP Server** This is the name of the DHCP server that will be servicing this IP network.

When you've entered these items, click on Create. If you experience any errors while creating this object, it's probably because of one of the following reasons:

➤ The name you entered for the Subnet object is already in use elsewhere in the tree.

➤ The subnet address you specified has already been configured for another Subnet object in the tree.

When you select the Subnet object in the left pane, you can also configure other DHCP subnet options in the right pane, including the following:

➤ DNS Zone For Dynamic Update (default is None)

➤ Domain Name

➤ Subnet Pool Reference (default is None)

➤ Default DHCP Server (default is the DHCP server you just created)

➤ Comments

➤ Lease Type (Permanent or Timed). Note that the timed default is three days, and you can enter the values for days, hours, and minutes

DHCP Services 339

➤ Set Boot Parameter Option (by default, this is not enabled). You can configure the server address, server name, and boot file name

8. The next item to configure is the DHCP Subnet Address Range (SAR) object or objects, which is where you specify the range of addresses that can be delivered to a client for the subnet. With the Subnet object selected, click on the Create button in the toolbar. From the displayed list of objects, select Subnet Address Range and then click on OK.

9. In the dialog box that appears, specify the subnet address range name and the start address. The *start address* is a range of contiguous addresses where you specify the starting and ending values. If you have values that are not contiguous, you need to create a SAR for each contiguous subrange. Values specified in one SAR cannot overlap any other SAR values. Once these items are configured, click on the Create button.

   There are also options that can be configured for the SAR object. These are accessed by selecting the SAR object in the left pane, and the options are then displayed in the right pane:

   ➤ Range Type, which includes Dynamic BOOTP (which stands for Bootstrap Protocol), Dynamic DHCP with Automatic Hostname Generation, Dynamic DHCP, Dynamic BOOTP, DHCP (the default), and Excluded

   ➤ Auto Hostname Starts With

   ➤ DNS Update Option (default is No Update)

   ➤ DHCP Server (default is the DHCP server you just created)

   ➤ Comments

10. If you have any addresses that need to be excluded or a host that needs a specific address you want to set, you need to configure IP Address objects. When you create a Subnet object, two IP Address objects are created automatically. These are both exclusions for the host address of 0 and 255. For example, if the Subnet object is 10.180.2.0 with a subnet mask of 255.255.255.0, the two exclusion IP addresses are for 10.180.2.0 and 10.180.2.255. These are necessary because some non-NetWare hosts and the IP components they're running cannot have host addresses ending in 0 or 255.

    IP Address objects you create must reside in a Subnet object, and their creation begins by selecting the Subnet object. Click on the Create button, and from the objects displayed in the Create New DHCP Record dialog box, choose IP Address and then click on OK.

340 Chapter 20

11. In the Create IP Address dialog box, specify the address and the assignment type: Exclusion or Manual. If you choose Manual, you need to fill in other values, such as the MAC address. When you've completed the information, click on Create.

12. Many IP configurations today allow multiple IP subnets to exist on the same physical network. This is supported by Novell's DHCP Services though the use of a *Subnet Pool object*. To create a subnet pool, you must first create a Subnet object for each network that will be in the pool. Select Our Network or a Subnet object and click on the Create button. Choose Subnet Pool from the available objects listed and click on OK.

13. Enter the name of the Subnet Pool object, specify the NDS context, and click on Create. Subnet Pool objects can be created in Organization, Organizational Unit, Country, or Locality containers.

14. Select the Subnet Pool object in the left pane and in the right pane use the Add button to select the Subnet objects for the network addresses that will be used on the same network segment.

> **EXAM ALERT**
>
> You need to know the process for creating all the DHCP objects in the DNS/DHCP Management Console application.

Once you've set up and configured the DHCP Service components, the next action is to start the service on the NetWare 5 server. At the server console, enter "DHCPSRVR" to load DHCPSRVR.NLM. This loads all the DHCP information that's stored in NDS into the server's cache. If you make any future configuration changes to the DHCP server, you'll need to start and stop the DHCP Service. You can do this by unloading and reloading the NLM on the server console. You can also choose the Start/Stop Service button in the DNS/DHCP Management Console toolbar. Figure 20.8 shows a sample DHCP Service configuration, including Subnet, SAR, IP Address, and Subnet Pool objects.

The last action to perform is setting up the client's workstation to use DHCP instead of a manually assigned number. If the IP protocol is not running on the workstation, you'll need to add the protocol. In the IP protocol configuration windows for Windows 95/98 or Windows NT, choose to obtain an IP address automatically. There may be other IP-related information you may need to configure at this time for your network. You may also need to reboot the machine to enable all the changes. To determine whether a Windows 95/98 client has received an IP address from your DHCP server, run WINIPCFG at the

DHCP Services **341**

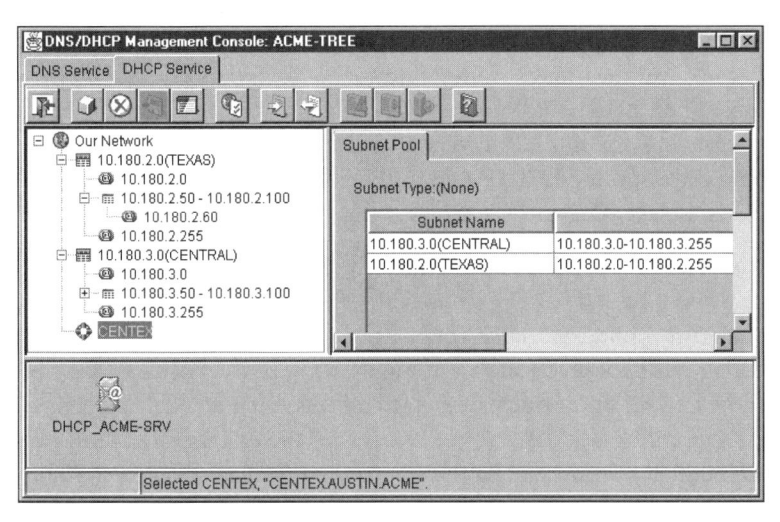

Figure 20.8 Sample DHCP Service configuration.

workstation. For Windows NT, enter "IPCONFIG /ALL" in a command-prompt window. If the utility reports an address of 0.0.0.0, the client did not receive an address. If the address listed is in the range of values supported by your DHCP server, you know the client found the DHCP server. You may also want to check to make sure the IP services you want are reachable using the PING utility or a Web browser.

Global DHCP Options

The DHCP Management Console also allows you to configure options that are global to the DHCP environment, not just to specific objects. There are basically two types of global options—those for administrative ease and those to deliver configuration information to the workstations.

The administrative options include items such as pinging an address before attempting to deliver it. If there are manually assigned IP hosts that are not indicated in the DHCP server's information as exclusions, the DHCP server would have no knowledge of these. In this case, pinging an address before it's delivered prevents the unsuccessful assignment of a number that's already in use. This option is set by selecting the DHCP server in the lower pane and then selecting or deselecting Ping Enabled in the right pane.

Information such as the NDS context, the preferred NetWare 5 server, the DNS server, and so on can also be configured in the DHCP Service and delivered to the clients at the same time they receive an IP address. The ability to deliver NDS information can greatly reduce the time the network administrator has to spend configuring each workstation for NDS information. Also, when users travel with a laptop that plugs in somewhere else in the network, this can help deliver the proper information to the clients based on their physical locations. These parameters can be set globally to apply to all DHCP servers in the tree or to specific DHCP servers. If the same information is configured globally and for a specific DHCP object, the value of the setting specified at the individual object takes precedence over the global value.

To set preferences globally, click on the Global Preferences button in the toolbar and select the Global DHCP Options tab in the right pane. If the item you want to configure is not listed, click on the Modify button. The Modify DHCP options dialog box appears, as shown in Figure 20.9. In the list of options displayed on the left, select the one you want to modify, click on Add, and modify the appropriate information in the bottom area of the dialog box. The Global DHCP Defaults tab in the Global Preferences pane allows you to configure exclusions for specific hardware addresses that apply to all the DHCP servers in the tree. There's also a DHCP Options Table tab available in the right pane that displays all the 87 options that have been defined. You can add to this list, delete items to make them unavailable, or modify any of the existing data.

Importing And Exporting DHCP Databases

One of the nice features of NetWare 5 DHCP Services is the ability to import DHCP information from another DHCP configuration. If the network has

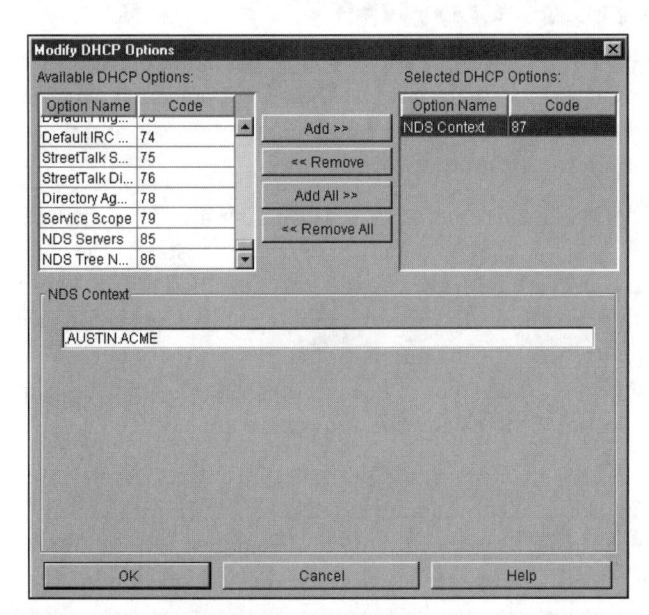

Figure 20.9 The Modify DHCP Options dialog box.

been using Novell DHCP version 2, you cannot upgrade "in place" to version 3, which is the version in NetWare 5. However, you can export the DHCP version 2 information to a file and then import the data into DHCP version 3 using the Import DHCP Database button on the toolbar. You can also use the same tool for importing a DHCP version 3 database into your environment.

The import tool will ask for the location of the database file and then display the subnets defined in the file. You can choose to import all or selected subnets and specify the NDS context in which the objects will reside. You're presented with a verify screen. If the information is correct, you can import the data. You may also be presented with dialog boxes to indicate which NetWare 5 server and/or DHCP server will service the subnets. If a subnet with the same parameters already exists in the tree, the subnet information will not be imported.

The DHCP information can also be exported by selecting the Export DHCP Database button on the toolbar. You'll be presented with a dialog box to specify the location of the file.

Practice Questions

Question 1

> What's the main function of the DHCP protocol?
> - a. To deliver NDS information to the workstation
> - b. To deliver IP-related information, such as the IP address, to the workstation
> - c. To deliver IPX-related information to the workstation
> - d. To deliver IP Compatibility Mode information to the workstation
> - e. To deliver IP-related information, such as the machine name, to the workstation

The correct answer is b. NDS information can also be delivered to the workstation, but it's not a major function and it's Novell specific. Therefore, answer a is incorrect. DHCP has nothing to do with IPX. Therefore, answer c is incorrect. DHCP does not deliver Compatibility Mode information to the workstation. This is handled by the Novell Client. Therefore, answer d is incorrect. The machine name is set through the local operating system of the workstation. Therefore, answer e is incorrect.

Question 2

> What are the three ways the DHCP protocol can distribute IP addresses? [Choose the three best answers]
> - a. Manual allocation
> - b. Exclusion allocation
> - c. Dynamic allocation
> - d. Automatic allocation
> - e. Static allocation

The correct answers are a, c, and d. Addresses that are excluded are handled by creating an IP Address object in a Subnet object. Therefore, answer b is incorrect. Static allocation is a made-up term and does not exist. Therefore, answer e is incorrect.

Question 3

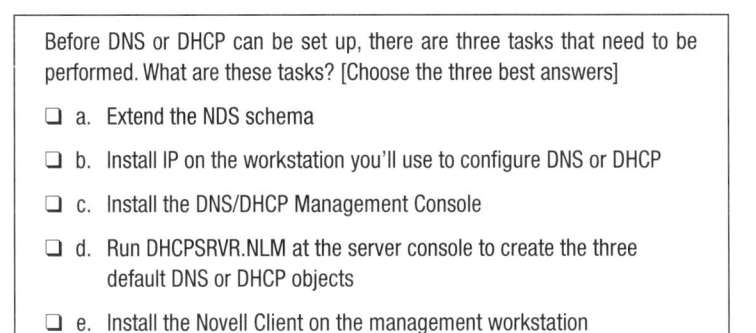

> Before DNS or DHCP can be set up, there are three tasks that need to be performed. What are these tasks? [Choose the three best answers]
>
> ❏ a. Extend the NDS schema
> ❏ b. Install IP on the workstation you'll use to configure DNS or DHCP
> ❏ c. Install the DNS/DHCP Management Console
> ❏ d. Run DHCPSRVR.NLM at the server console to create the three default DNS or DHCP objects
> ❏ e. Install the Novell Client on the management workstation

The correct answers are a, c, and e. Installing IP on the workstation is not one of the tasks Novell identifies. Therefore, answer b is incorrect. DHCPSRVR.NLM is the NLM run at the server console to start DHCP Service. It does not create any objects when it's run. Therefore, answer d is incorrect.

Question 4

> What are the three ways the NDS schema can be extended to incorporate DNS and DHCP objects? [Choose the three best answers]
>
> ❏ a. Run DNIPINST at the server console
> ❏ b. Install DNS and DHCP Services when you install a NetWare 5 server
> ❏ c. Choose Install in the NetWare GUI and select DNS and DHCP Services
> ❏ d. Run DNIPINST from a console prompt window on the management workstation
> ❏ e. Run DNSDHCP at the server console

The correct answers are a, b, and c. Because answer a is correct, answer d is incorrect. The DNSDHCP NLM or NCF file does not exist. Therefore, answer e is incorrect.

Question 5

What are the three default DNS/DHCP objects created when the schema is extended? [Choose the three best answers]

- ❏ a. DNS-DHCP Server object
- ❏ b. RootServerInfo Zone object
- ❏ c. DNSDHCP-GROUP Group object
- ❏ d. DHCP_*SERVERNAME* Locator object, where *SERVERNAME* is the name of the DHCP server
- ❏ e. DNS-DHCP Locator object

The correct answers are b, c, and e. There's no such default object as the DNS-DHCP Server object. Therefore, answer a is incorrect. When you create a DHCP server, the default is DHCP_, followed by the name of the server. This is not performed when the schema is extended but is something you configure. Therefore, answer d is incorrect.

Question 6

What's the path of the NetWare Administrator snap-ins?

- ○ a. SYS:\SYSTEM\WIN32\
- ○ b. SYS:\PUBLIC\WIN32\SNAPINS
- ○ c. SYS:\MGMT\WIN32\SNAPINS
- ○ d. SYS:\PUBLIC\MGMT\SNAPINS
- ○ e. SYS:\SYSTEM\WIN32\SNAPINS

The correct answer is e. The other pathnames are not the paths to the NetWare Administrator snap-ins. Therefore, answers a, b, c, and d are incorrect.

Question 7

> What are the requirements for running the DNS/DHCP Management Console? [Choose the three best answers]
>
> ❏ a. Novell Client software installed on the workstation
> ❏ b. NDS authentication to a NetWare 5 server in the tree
> ❏ c. Minimum of 48MB memory on the workstation
> ❏ d. 8.5MB free disk space on the SYS volume
> ❏ e. 8.5MB free disk space on the workstation

The correct answers are a, c, and e. You don't have to have a connection to the NetWare 5 tree to run the utility because all the files are on the workstation. Therefore, answer b is incorrect. Because answer e is correct, answer d is incorrect.

Question 8

> Where's the DNS/DHCP Management Console setup file located?
>
> ○ a. SYS:\SYSTEM\DNSDHCP\
> ○ b. SYS:\PUBLIC\DNSDHCP\
> ○ c. C:\Program Files\Novell\DNSDHCP\
> ○ d. C:\Program Files\DNSDHCP\
> ○ e. SYS:\PUBLIC\Novell\DNSDHCP

The correct answer is b. Answers a, c, d, and e are not valid paths to the DNS/DHCP Management Console setup file and are therefore incorrect.

Question 9

What are the three configuration requirements that must be performed for providing DHCP in the network? [Choose the three best answers]

- ☐ a. A NetWare 5 server must contain the workstation configuration information.
- ☐ b. The workstation must be configured to use DHCP.
- ☐ c. The DHCP Service must be started on a NetWare 5 server.
- ☐ d. The information to be delivered to a workstation must be configured.
- ☐ e. A NetWare 5 server must be assigned as a DHCP server.

The correct answers are c, d, and e. The server does not hold workstation configuration information. Therefore, answer a is incorrect. A workstation does not have to be configured to use DHCP for DHCP Services to run. Therefore, answer b is incorrect.

Question 10

Which of the following statements is true regarding Subnet objects?

- ○ a. The Subnet object contains information about the Global Subnet options.
- ○ b. The Subnet object contains the range of addresses available for delivery.
- ○ c. The Subnet object contains exclusion addresses.
- ○ d. The Subnet object defines a network address.
- ○ e. Only one instance of a Subnet object can exist in a tree at any one time.

The correct answer is d. Global Subnet options are not contained in a Subnet object. A Subnet object can have options, but these are not global. Therefore, answer a is incorrect. An SAR contains the range of addresses available for consumption. Therefore, answer b is incorrect. Exclusions are IP Address objects, not Subnet objects. Therefore, answer c is incorrect. There can be several instances of Subnet objects in the same tree. An example of this is a Subnet Pool object. Therefore, answer e is incorrect.

Question 11

> You've been contacted by the corporate IS department to upgrade the existing NetWare 4.11 network to NetWare 5 and retain all the existing services and configuration details. Because the NetWare 4.11 network is a recent install, all the existing servers are capable of supporting NetWare 5. Some of the servers will be running DHCP Services, NDPS services, and data backup. Which of the following is proper advice relating to DHCP Services?
>
> ○ a. Upgrade the servers using the NetWare 5 install program for an In-Place Upgrade. Selecting DNS/DHCP Services when installing the NetWare 5 server will create the default NDS objects and upgrade the DHCP 2 database to a DHCP 3 database.
>
> ○ b. Export the NetWare 4.11 DHCP information to a file. Upgrade the servers using the NetWare 5 install program for an In-Place Upgrade. Selecting DNS/DHCP Services when installing the NetWare 5 server will create the default NDS objects. Import the DHCP file you saved using the Management Console.
>
> ○ c. Export the NetWare 4.11 DHCP information to a file and edit the file to remove old, outdated information. Upgrade the servers using the NetWare 5 install program for an In-Place Upgrade. Selecting DNS/DHCP Services when installing the NetWare 5 server will create the default NDS objects. Import the DHCP file you saved using the Management Console.
>
> ○ d. Export the NetWare 4.11 DHCP information to a file. Upgrade the servers using the NetWare 5 install program for an In-Place Upgrade. Do not select DNS/DHCP Services when installing the NetWare 5 server because the export file contains all the information about the default objects. Import the DHCP file you saved using the Management Console.
>
> ○ e. Export the NetWare 4.11 DHCP information to a file. Upgrade the servers using the NetWare 5 install program for an In-Place Upgrade. Selecting DNS/DHCP Services when installing the NetWare 5 server will allow you to import the DHCP information contained in the file.

The correct answer is b. Upgrading to NetWare 5 does not upgrade DHCP 2 databases. Therefore, answer a is incorrect. If you need to change configuration information, this can always been done after the data is imported. Therefore, answer c is incorrect. The export file does not contain information about the default NDS objects. Therefore, answer d is incorrect. You cannot import DHCP information when you're installing the DHCP Service. Therefore, answer e is incorrect. This question is a bit tricky because you need to know that DHCP version 2 needs to be imported to convert it to DHCP version 3.

Question 12

> You have created a Subnet object for the network address 172.16.3.0. What exclusion address is created?
>
> ❍ a. 172.16.3.127 and 172.16.3.255
>
> ❍ b. 172.16.3.0 and 172.16.3.127
>
> ❍ c. 172.16.3.0
>
> ❍ d. 172.16.3.255
>
> ❍ e. 172.16.3.0 and 172.16.3.255

The correct answer is e. You must have two numbers—one ending in 0 and one in 255. Answers a, b, c, and d do not have these and are therefore incorrect.

DHCP Services   **351**

Need To Know More?

The DNS/DHCP Management Console has a Help button that includes brief descriptions of the DNS and DHCP Services. The Help file also includes information on how to create and configure the various DHCP-related objects.

http://info.internet.isi.edu:80/in-notes/rfc/files/rfc2131.txt contains an request for comment (RFC) titled "Dynamic Host Configuration Protocol."

http://developer.novell.com/research/appnotes/1998/april/a2frame.htm is the URL for the AppNotes article "Easing TCP/IP Network Management With Novell's DNS/DHCP Services."

http://developer.novell.com/research/appnotes/1998/november/a1frame.htm is the URL for the AppNotes article "Novell DNS/DHCP Services: Design Issues And Troubleshooting."

http://support.novell.com contains the following TIDs that relate to the topics covered in this chapter. At Novell's support Web site, go to the Knowledgebase and perform a search using the following TID numbers:

➤ TID 2943068   NW5 DHCP Configuration Hotstart

➤ TID 2944243   NW5 DHCP-Setup For Default Router (Gateway)

➤ TID 2941322   DNSDHCP-DHCP Server Redundancy Support

➤ TID 2945741   How To Remove DHCP 3.0 From A NW 5 Server?

www.novell.com/whitepapers/nw5/dns_dhcp.html is the URL for the white paper "Novell DNS/DHCP Services For NetWare 5," which gives a good overview of NetWare 5's DNS and DHCP Services.

DNS Services

Terms you'll need to understand:

- √ Domain Name System (DNS)
- √ Zone Transfer
- √ DNS server
- √ DNS Zone
- √ DNS resource record
- √ NAMED.NLM

Techniques you'll need to master:

- √ Understanding DNS basics
- √ Configuring DNS objects
- √ Starting DNS Services on a NetWare 5 server

In the last chapter, we covered the Dynamic Host Configuration Protocol (DHCP) Service—an automated service for distributing Internet Protocol (IP) addresses and information to workstations in a NetWare 5 IP network. Another feature of an IP network is the assignment of names to services and machines. Although people tend to remember names better than IP addresses, the IP network uses numbers to refer to hosts. One mechanism for resolving a machine name to its number is the Domain Name System (DNS). In this chapter, we cover the DNS Services provided with NetWare 5. The installation of DNS and the management tool used are the same as for the DHCP Services, covered in Chapter 20.

Overview Of DNS

The number of hosts providing services that users can access has increased with the explosive growth of Internet services and organizations with intranets. Each of these services has a unique IP number that's used to access the host. However, the numbers are not easy to remember. For example, if you want to access Novell's corporate Web site, it's probably easier for you to remember www.novell.com than 137.65.2.6.

The main role of DNS is to provide a method to access services through names. That is, the DNS Service provides a mechanism to resolve a hostname to an IP address. Another DNS Service feature provides a consistent namespace for referring to resources. This naming convention does not include network-specific terms such as routes, addresses, and so on, thus making the names easier to remember and to use. Another important aspect of DNS is a mechanism that handles database size and update frequency. To address this, the DNS database is distributed among Internet servers, and the information is cached locally to improve performance. Also, the DNS database is extensible, can store different types of information, and can be accessed by different protocols and management systems.

The DNS hierarchical namespace begins with a single domain at the top, called the *root domain*. The namespace is divided below the root domain into top-level domains, such as .com, .edu, .org, .mil, and .net. Below these top-level domains are subdomains. A subdomain typically reflects an individual company or organization, such as *acme*.com. Below this are typically the organization's hostnames that are running services, such as *www*.acme.com.

The DNS architecture has three major components:

▶ **Domain namespace and resource records** DNS is a hierarchical tree-structured namespace that contains data in resource records. Each node and leaf of the namespace contains information sets that are extracted by queries. A query includes the name of the item and the type of resource information. For example, a user on the Internet uses domain names to identify hosts that were obtained by a query to a DNS Service for the IP address of the associated host.

➤ **Name servers** Name servers are computers running programs that store the information about the domain tree's structure. Typically, a specific name server contains the complete information about a subset of the domain with references to other name servers that contain the rest of the domain information. Name servers that have the complete information for a part of the domain are said to be the *authority* for that portion of the namespace. The authoritative information is organized into units, called *zones*, and is automatically distributed to the name servers you specify to provide redundancy.

➤ **Resolvers** *Resolvers* are programs that extract information from the name servers, usually as a result of a request from a client. If the resolver cannot obtain the requested information from the domain's name servers, it continues to query for the information outside the domain.

A user refers to a host by its name, followed by the name of the domains above it in the hierarchy. The names are separated by dots (periods) to the top or the root. For example, *www.acme.com* is the name for a host named *www* in a company's *acme* domain. The last dot of the name (*.com*) refers to the root domain.

The domain namespace is divided into zones that contain all the information about the parts of the namespace. There are three types of DNS Zones:

➤ **Standard DNS Zone** The zone used to resolve hostnames to IP addresses.

➤ **IN-ADDR-ARPA** The zone used to resolve IP addresses to hostnames.

➤ **IP6.INT** The zone used for the new IPv6 information.

A DNS system consists of a master or primary name server that stores all the changes in the domain. This is typically a file that has a specific format called *Berkeley Internet Name Domain (BIND)*. There are also replica or secondary name servers that contain complete copies of the master name information. Replicas keep their information current by querying the master server. The master file has a serial number stored in the start of authority (SOA) record that lets the system know when changes have occurred. A replica name server checks the master's serial number when it queries the master name server. If the replica's value is lower than the master's value, a zone transfer takes place. The entire master file is copied to the replicas in a zone transfer.

Information about the DNS Zones is stored in several different types of resource records. The common ones are listed in Table 21.1.

In NetWare 5, DNS Services must be configured before they are activated. The two types of DNS name servers are represented in Novell Directory Services (NDS) as primary and secondary Zone objects. NetWare 5 servers are assigned to service a DNS Zone through DNS Zone objects. The tasks performed by the NetWare 5 server depend on the type of zone. If the server is servicing a primary Zone object, the tasks are the same as those of a master name server. If it's a secondary Zone object, the tasks are those of a replica name server. Here are the designated server tasks for a primary Zone object:

➤ It adds and deletes resource records.

➤ It handles queries to the NDS to resolve names to IP addresses.

➤ It updates zone serial numbers.

The designated server for a secondary Zone object receives zone transfers from a traditional master name server that's not storing the information in NDS.

> **EXAM ALERT**
>
> DNS is covered in depth in the *Exam Cram for Networking Technologies CNE*, also by The Coriolis Group. You need to be familiar with the basic DNS concepts covered in this chapter.

Table 21.1 The types of resource records.

Abbreviation	Type Of Resource Record	Description
A	Address	This is a common record type used to map machine names in the domain to IP addresses.
CNAME	Canonical name	This contains the canonical name of an alias.
MX	Mail eXchange	This stores Mail eXchange information, such as Simple Mail Transfer Protocol (SMTP) mail addresses to domain names equivalencies.
NS	Name server	This contains the authoritative name server for the domain.
PTR	Pointer	This stores pointers that refer to another part of the domain within an IN-ADDR-ARPA zone.

DNS Services **357**

Installing DNS

The details of installing DNS components are covered in Chapter 20. In this section, we review the main points. The NDS schema must be extended to contain the new DNS and DHCP objects. The schema can be extended by one of three ways:

- Installing DNS/DHCP services when installing NetWare 5
- Installing DNS/DHCP services using the NetWare 5 GUI on the server
- Running DNIPINST.NLM at the server console

After the schema is extended, three default DNS/DHCP objects are created. These objects can exist only once per tree:

- **DNS/DHCP Locator object** Contains DNS and DHCP information used by the Management Console for efficient access
- **DNS/DHCP Group object** A standard NDS Group object of which all DNS and DHCP objects are members
- **RootServerInfo Zone object** Holds information about the Internet root domain servers so names can be resolved outside your local domain

The NetWare Administrator snap-ins can be installed, depending on the procedure used to extend the schema. The snap-ins are placed in SYS:\SYSTEM\SNAPINS\.

The Java-based DNS/DHCP Management Console is not installed when the schema is extended. The installation program is copied to SYS:\PUBLIC\DNSDHCP and is called SETUP.EXE. The DNS/DHCP Management Console is installed, by default, in C:\Program Files\Novell\DNSDHCP\ and is called DNSDHCP.EXE.

As with DHCP, DNS objects and the associated data are stored in NDS. Whenever NDS partitions that contain DNS information are replicated, the data is also replicated. This provides fault tolerance and load balancing for your NetWare 5 DNS Services. Another advantage of using NDS to store DNS information is centralized management. You can access and make changes to DNS from any place in your network, which reduces the overhead associated with maintaining a separate DNS system and database.

> **EXAM ALERT**
> Don't forget the installation and setup details applicable to DNS. These topics are covered in Chapter 20.

DNS Configuration

As mentioned earlier, you must configure and activate DNS Services in a NetWare 5 network. The first task is to create a DNS Name Server object to specify the NetWare 5 server that will be providing the DNS Services. The procedure for creating the DNS Server object is as follows:

1. Run the DNS/DHCP Management Console (DNSDHCP.EXE) from the installation location on the workstation. The default path is C:\Program Files\Novell\DNSDHCP\.

2. From the list of trees, select the tree you're authenticated for the DNS Service and click on the Launch button. You can manage all DNS and DHCP services in one tree or several trees from the same workstation.

3. At the upper-left area of the console window are two tabs: DNS Service and DHCP Service. Click on the DNS Service tab to begin setting up DNS.

4. Select All Zones in the left pane and click on the Create button in the toolbar.

5. You'll see a window for specifying the type of object to create. Select DNS Server in the Create New DNS Record dialog box (see Figure 21.1) and click on OK.

6. Select your NetWare 5 Server object, specify the hostname, enter the domain name, and click on Create in the Create DNS Server dialog box (see Figure 21.2).

7. The default name of the new DNS Server object is DNS_, followed by the name of the NetWare 5 server (for example, DNS_ACME-SRV).

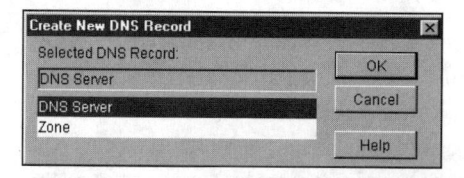

Figure 21.1 The Create New DNS Record dialog box.

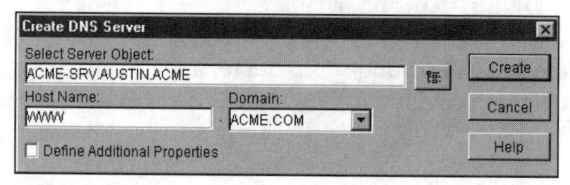

Figure 21.2 The Create DNS Server dialog box.

DNS Services

Notice in the bottom pane of the Management Console that the DNS Server object is displayed with a red X over the icon. This indicates that the service has not been started on the server.

8. Selecting the DNS Server object in the bottom-right pane displays the interface where you configure the DNS Server object. The configuration options for the DNS Server object include Zones, Forwarding List, No-Forward List, Options (including Event Log—None [default], Major Events, and All), and Enable Audit Trail Log (the default is not enabled).

   After you've configured DNS Server object, the next step is to create a DNS Zone object. Select All Zones in the left pane and click on the Create button on the toolbar.

9. Select Zone in the Create New DNS Record dialog box and click on OK.

   Note: A Zone object is a container type object that holds all the data for a single zone. It contains Resource Record Set objects and Resource Record objects. You can create several zones in your network that can be serviced by one server. The information stored by this object includes all the NDS servers that service the zone and the SOA.

10. Several items need to be configured in the Create Zone dialog box, as shown in Figure 21.3. After you enter this information, click on the Create button.

11. After you select the Zone object, the right pane shows items that can be configured for the zone. These include the following:

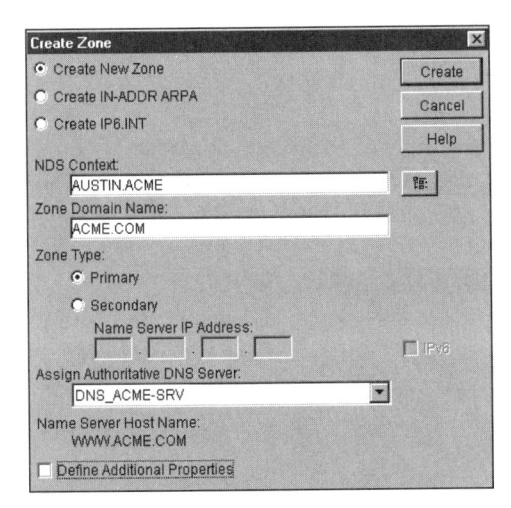

Figure 21.3 The Create Zone dialog box.

- **Authoritative DNS Servers** The default is the DNS server you just created.
- **Dynamic DNS Server** The default is the DNS server you just created.

On the SOA Information tab you can configure the following:

- **Zone Master** The default is your zone name.
- **E-Mail Address** The default is root.*yourdomain*.
- **Serial Number** The default is *yyyymmddnn*, where *y*=year, *m*=month, *d*=day, and *n*=sequence number.
- **Interval Values** Including Refresh (the default is 180 minutes), Retry (the default is 60 minutes), Expire (the default is 168 hours), and Minimum TTL (where TTL is the time to live and the default is 24 hours).

12. Once you create the DNS Zone object, the next task is to create the resource records. Select the zone you just created and click on the Create button on the toolbar.

13. In the Create New DNS Record dialog box, choose Resource Record and click on OK. The Create Resource Record dialog box shown in Figure 21.4 appears. Enter the necessary information in this dialog box.

Note: A resource record is a leaf-type object that contains the data type and information for a single resource record. These objects are placed in Resource Record Set objects. Once the resource record is created, it cannot be modified. If you need to make changes, the procedure is to delete the object and re-create it with the new values.

Figure 21.5 shows a sample DNS Service configuration displaying the Zone and Resource Record objects just created. After all the DNS objects and information have been created, you need to start the service. At the server console,

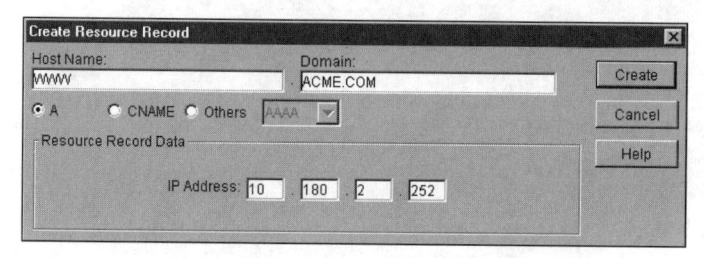

Figure 21.4 The Create Resource Record dialog box.

DNS Services 361

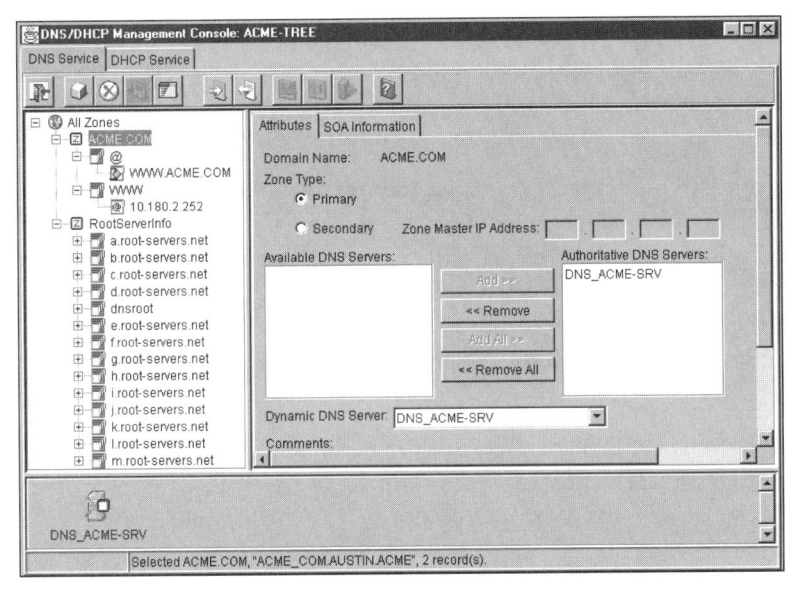

Figure 21.5 Sample DNS Service configuration displaying Zone and Resource Record objects.

enter "NAMED", which runs NAMED.NLM. If any changes are made to DNS after the service has started, you'll have to stop and restart the service.

Clients' workstations are the last things you need to take care of. You need to add the IP protocol on any workstations that aren't already running it. In the IP protocol configuration windows for Windows 95/98 or Windows NT, click on the DNS tab and enter in the name of the host, the domain name, and the IP number of the DNS server. You may need to configure other IP-related information for your network at this time. You may also need to reboot the machine to enable all the changes. Check to make sure the IP services you want are reachable using the PING utility or a Web browser to determine whether DNS is resolving the addresses.

> **EXAM ALERT**
> Know the process of creating all the DNS objects in the DNS/DHCP Management Console application and how to start the service on the NetWare 5 server.

Importing And Exporting DNS Databases

The DNS/DHCP Management Console can export and import DNS information. If the network has been using an earlier version of DNS for NetWare or another vendor's DNS Services, you can export the information to a BIND master file format. The BIND master file can be imported into the NetWare 5 DNS environment. If you attempt to import information for a zone that already exists, you'll receive an error, and the information will not be imported.

To import a BIND master file, click on the Import DHCP Database button on the DNS/DHCP Management Console toolbar. The import tool asks for the BIND file location and displays the zones defined in the file. You then specify the NDS context in which the objects will reside. You may be prompted to select the DNS server that will be used to manage the zone. The last screen displayed is a verify screen. If the information is correct, click on Import.

The DNS information can also be exported by selecting the Export DNS Database button on the toolbar. You'll be presented with a dialog box to specify the location of the BIND file.

Practice Questions

Question 1

What's the major function of the DNS Service?

○ a. To deliver a hostname to the workstation that's easier to remember than IP numbers

○ b. To provide a mechanism for resolving hostnames to IP addresses

○ c. To deliver NDS-specific information to the workstation

○ d. To deliver IP Compatibility Mode information to the workstation so the user can find the IP service

The correct answer is b. DNS is used to resolve hostnames, not to specify hostnames. Therefore, answer a is incorrect. NDS-specific information can be delivered to the workstation through NetWare 5 DHCP services. Therefore, answer c is incorrect. DNS and DHCP are not involved in Compatibility Mode information. Therefore, answer d is incorrect.

Question 2

What are the types of DNS Zones? [Choose the three best answers]

❑ a. IP6.INT

❑ b. Secondary

❑ c. IN-ADDR-ARPR

❑ d. Standard

❑ e. Primary

The correct answers are a, c, and d. Secondary and primary are types of name servers. Therefore, answers b and e are incorrect.

Question 3

What type of resource record is used to store a host's name and IP address so the host's name can be resolved?

○ a. PTR

○ b. MX

○ c. A

○ d. CNAME

○ e. NS

The correct answer is c. PTR records are used for pointers to refer to services outside the domain. Therefore, answer a is incorrect. MX records are for Mail eXchange information used by SMTP-based services. Therefore, answer b is incorrect. CNAME contains the canonical name of an alias. Therefore, answer d is incorrect. NS stores the authoritative name server for the domain. Therefore, answer e is incorrect.

Question 4

What is a DNS Zone object in the DNS Services for NetWare 5?

○ a. The DNS Zone object is a container-type object that holds all the data for a single zone.

○ b. The DNS Zone object contains the addresses of the primary name servers on the Internet.

○ c. The DNS Zone object contains the addresses of the secondary name servers on the Internet.

○ d. The DNS Zone object contains resource records for the information of all the IPv6 zones in the tree.

○ e. The DNS Zone object contains information about the various subnets in the tree.

The correct answer is a. The RootServerInfo Zone object contains information about the name servers on the Internet. Therefore, answers b and c are incorrect. There can be only one IPv6 zone in an NDS tree. Therefore, answer d is incorrect. DNS does not contain information about DHCP subnets. Therefore, answer e is incorrect.

Question 5

> What are the major components of DNS? [Choose the three best answers]
> - a. Resolvers
> - b. Arbitrators
> - c. Name Servers
> - d. DNS-DHCP Locator object
> - e. Domain namespace and resource records

The correct answers are a, c, and e. *Arbitrators* is a term that isn't used in DNS. Therefore, answer b is incorrect. The DNS-DHCP Locator object is an NDS-specific object for NetWare 5 DNS Services. Therefore, answer d is incorrect.

Question 6

> The DNS/DHCP Management Console can import DNS information from another DNS database. What's the required format for the file you want to import?
> - a. NAMED
> - b. BIND
> - c. DNS
> - d. ZONE
> - e. IPDNS

The correct answer is b. NAMED is the NLM that's run on the NetWare 5 server to start DNS Services. Therefore, answer a is incorrect. DNS resolves hostnames to IP addresses, it's not the name of the file format. Therefore, answer c is incorrect. ZONE is not a file format but rather a division of the DNS namespace. Therefore, answer d is incorrect. IPDNS is a made-up name. Therefore, answer e is incorrect.

Question 7

You've been requested to set up DNS Services on a new NetWare 5 network. What's the proper order of events?

1. Install the DNS/DHCP Management Console.
2. Run DNIPINST.NLM at the server console.
3. Create a DNS Zone object.
4. Run NAMED.NLM at the server console.
5. Create a DNS Server object.
6. Create a resource record.

- ○ a. 2, 5, 3, 6, 1, 4
- ○ b. 2, 1, 5, 3, 6, 4
- ○ c. 4, 1, 5, 3, 6, 2
- ○ d. 4, 5, 3, 6, 1, 2
- ○ e. 1, 2, 3, 4, 5, 6

The correct answer is b. This question requires you to remember the steps for installing the DNS/DHCP components from Chapter 20 and from this chapter.

DNS Services   **367**

Need To Know More?

The DNS/DHCP Management Console has a Help button that includes brief descriptions of the DNS and DHCP services. The Help file also includes information on how to create and configure the various DHCP-related objects.

http://info.internet.isi.edu:80/in-notes/rfc/files/rfc1034.txt contains a request for comment (RFC) titled "Domain Names: Concepts And Facilities." This RFC contains valuable information on the concepts and facilities of DNS.

www.novell.com/whitepapers/nw5/ contains the white paper "Novell DNS/DHCP Services For NetWare 5" that gives a good overview of NetWare 5's DNS and DHCP services.

http://developer.novell.com/research/appnotes/1998/april/02/index.htm includes the AppNotes article "Easing TCP/IP Network Management With Novell's DNS/DHCP Services." This article contains valuable information about Novell's DNS/DHCP Services.

http://developer.novell.com/research/appnotes/1998/november/01/index.htm contains the AppNotes articled "Novell DNS/DHCP Services: Design Issues And Troubleshooting." This article contains valuable information on design issues and troubleshooting as they relate to Novell's DNS/DHCP Services.

http://support.novell.com offers technical information documents (TIDs) that contain information related to the topic of this chapter. Go to the Knowledgebase and search using the following TID numbers:

➤ **TID 2943070** NW5 DNS Configuration Hotstart

➤ **TID 2941377** DNSDHCP Upgrading DNS 4.x To 5.x (With NW5)

➤ **TID 2943940** Converting DNS Data From 4.11 To NetWare 5

Netscape FastTrack Server

Terms you'll need to understand:
- √ World Wide Web
- √ Web server
- √ FastTrack Server
- √ NSWEB.NCF
- √ NSWEBDN.NCF
- √ ADMNSERV.NLM
- √ Server Administrator

Techniques you'll need to master:
- √ Defining the function of a Web server
- √ Installing Netscape FastTrack Server
- √ Configuring and using Netscape FastTrack Server
- √ Securing Netscape FastTrack Server

The World Wide Web has become one of the most cost-effective locations for companies to establish a presence. If a company is to be successful in its Internet endeavors, it must remember that performance is crucial to the success of every Web site. With this in mind, let's take a look at how Novell and Netscape have integrated the performance and stability of their products to provide a high-performance, reliable Web server solution—Netscape FastTrack Server on NetWare 5.

In this chapter, you'll learn about the function of a Web server in general, as well as how to install, configure, use, and secure Netscape FastTrack Server.

Defining The Function Of A Web Server

A Web server is an application that publishes information for use on the World Wide Web or internally within an intranet. The Web server application itself runs on an operating system such as NetWare 5 and can be used to publish various document types, including audio files, video files, executable files, Zip files, and graphics for public or internal company access.

Netscape FastTrack Server for NetWare is activated by loading several NetWare Loadable Modules (NLMs) on the NetWare 5 server. After the FastTrack Server is installed, a NetWare configuration file (NCF), NSWEB.NCF, is used to load the required NLMs. Figure 22.1 shows the contents of the NSWEB.NCF file.

> **ALERT** You type "NSWEB" at the server console to start FastTrack Server and "NSWEBDN" to stop it.

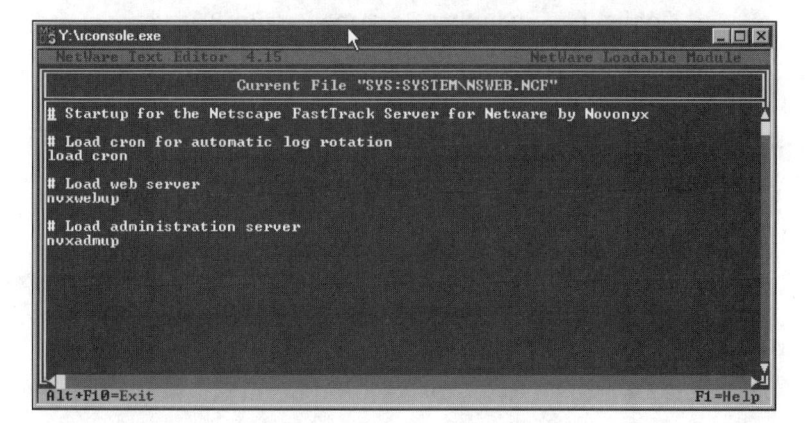

Figure 22.1 NSWEB.NCF contents.

The first NLM that's loaded by the NSWEB.NCF file is the NetWare scheduler NLM, CRON.NLM. The next module loaded in the Netscape FastTrack Server initialization process is NSHTTPD.NLM. The NSHTTPD.NLM module is the actual FastTrack Server component, and it's loaded with the -d switch, followed by the default document directory to initialize the Web site.

When the NSHTTPD.NLM module is loaded on the server, the following NLMs, which the Netscape Web server requires to run, are automatically loaded:

- **NETDB.NLM** This is the NLM for network database access.

- **CSSYSMSG.NLM** This is the NLM for the system message facility.

- **NSLCGI.NLM** This is the NLM for the Local Common Gateway Interface (LCGI) support library.

BTRIEVE.NLM is also loaded, unless another program on the server that requires Btrieve client/server database functionality has initialized the NLM.

The last line in the NSWEB.NCF file that's executed sets up the Administration Server component so the server can be administered from within a Web browser. The security modes that can be used with the Netscape FastTrack Server are discussed later in this chapter.

Netscape FastTrack Server Installation

The installation of a Netscape FastTrack Server system is performed from a client workstation that has a drive mapped to the SYS volume of the NetWare server that will be used as the Web server.

Installation Requirements

The client machine being used to configure and install Netscape FastTrack Server can be running either Windows 95/98 or Windows NT as the desktop operating system. The NetWare Client must be installed, and the Web browser in use on the client has to be Netscape Navigator version 3.x or higher in order to administer the Web server after the installation is complete.

The NetWare 4.11 (or higher) server, where Netscape FastTrack Server is being installed, must have at least 64MB of RAM and 100MB free space on the SYS volume. Also, long name space support must be added to any volume that will be used to host Web documents.

The Actual Installation

To begin the installation of Netscape FastTrack Server, map a drive to the SYS volume of the NetWare server where the Web server will be installed. Now, let's walk through the installation step by step:

1. Double-click on the SETUP.EXE FastTrack Server installation file from the client workstation. If you do not have a copy of FastTrack Server, it can be downloaded from Novell's Web site at **www.novell.com/products/netscape_servers/fastdl.html**.

2. The first screen displays the client resource requirements before the installation begins. Click on Finish to unpack the installation files and begin the installation.

3. Click on Next to continue past the warning to close all programs before beginning installation.

4. Read the license agreement and click on Yes.

5. Click on the Browse button, as shown in Figure 22.2, and select the drive letter you previously mapped to the SYS volume of the NetWare server as the installation drive. Alternately, after you click on Browse, you can click on Network to map a drive to the SYS volume as you're installing FastTrack Server.

6. You're asked for the Internet Protocol (IP) address and name of the server (hostname). Click on Next after you've entered the requested information.

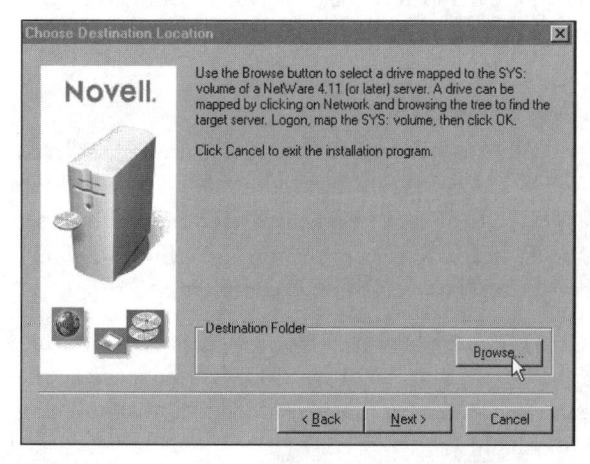

Figure 22.2 The Browse button in the Choose Destination Location dialog box.

Netscape FastTrack Server 373

7. The next box that appears asks you to enter the server port. The default is 80, which is the standard port number used by Hypertext Transfer Protocol (HTTP) services. You shouldn't change this unless you fully understand the ramifications.

8. In the next dialog box, specify the username and password of the account that will be used to administer the Web server. You must confirm the password before you can continue.

9. A dialog box with Lightweight Directory Access Protocol (LDAP) information is displayed next. You don't enter anything here; click on the Next button to continue.

10. When asked, indicate that you would like the appropriate command added to the AUTOEXEC.NCF file so FastTrack Server will be loaded automatically when the NetWare server is started.

11. A summary screen displays the choices you've made so far. Verify that the information is correct. (Use the Back button to make any corrections.) Click on the Next button to start copying files to your server. A bar graph indicating file copy progress is displayed.

12. After the files are copied to the server, you can view the readme file and launch the FastTrack Server. Click on the Finish button to exit the installation process. Netscape Navigator starts automatically if you've checked the Read Me checkbox.

> **TIP** It's a good idea to document all the configuration information for future access.

After you've completed these steps, you should test to make sure FastTrack Server has been installed properly. You can do this by restarting the NetWare server; FastTrack Server will be loaded automatically if NSWEB is in the AUTOEXEC.NCF file. Alternately, you can enter "NSWEB" at the server console.

> **EXAM ALERT** ADMSERV.NLM is executed at the server console to start the Administration Server.

FastTrack Server Basics

When the Netscape FastTrack Server is installed, administration can only be performed from a Web browser. Specifically, the client workstation being used to configure the server must have Netscape Navigator 3.x or higher as the Web browser. Once the appropriate Web browser has been launched, you can reach the FastTrack Server Administration Web site by typing "http://*Server IP:Admin Port*" in the Location field of the Web browser. *Server IP* is the IP address of the Web server—if DNS has been implemented, you could use the server's Domain Name System (DNS) name instead of the IP address. *Admin Port* is one of the parameters specified during installation and can be found at the server if you switch to the Netscape Web server screen.

If you attach with the correct port and IP address, you're prompted for the username and password that was entered during installation. When the correct username and password are entered, the Web browser will automatically be forwarded to the Web server's administration Web site—this is called the Administration Server home page and is shown in Figure 22.3.

In the bottom-left corner of the administration Web site, you'll see a button with your server's name on it. Immediately to the left of this button are On and Off buttons. These buttons are used to shut down the Web site(s) hosted by the Web server.

Clicking on the button with your server's name on it changes the Admin Preferences page to the Server Preferences page (see Figure 22.4).

Select View Server Settings in the left frame to view the current configuration (see Figure 22.5).

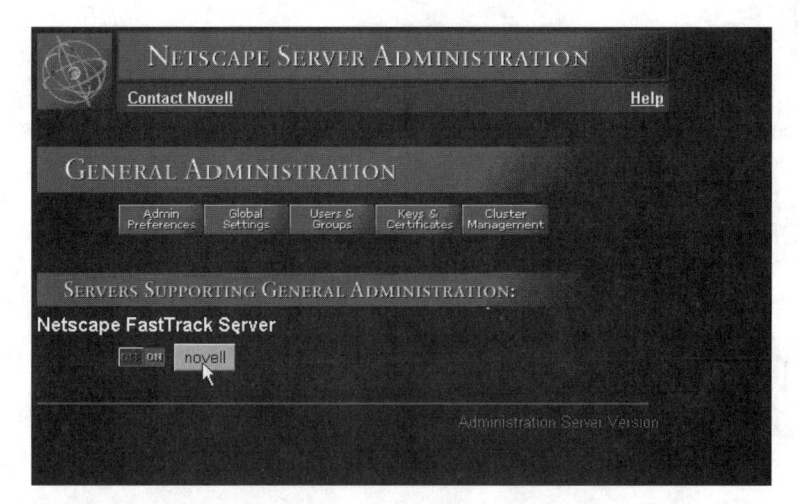

Figure 22.3 The Netscape FastTrack Server Administration Server page.

Netscape FastTrack Server **375**

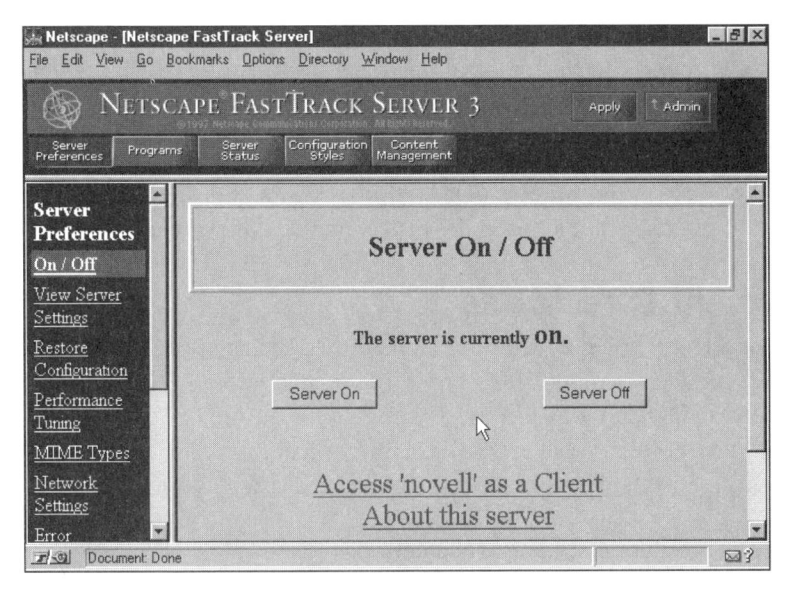

Figure 22.4 The Server Preferences page.

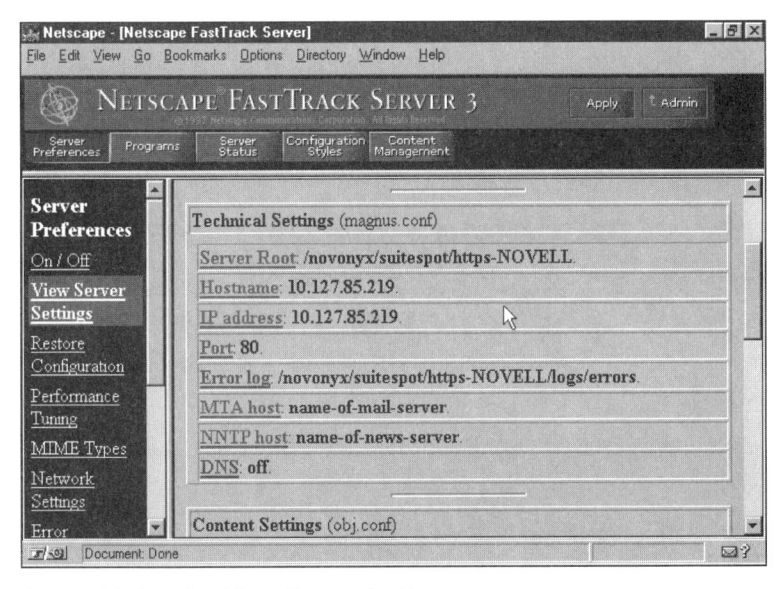

Figure 22.5 The View Server Settings page.

The server's configuration parameters can be changed on the View Server Settings page by clicking on the setting you want to view or modify. The corresponding configuration screen will appear and allow you to change the parameters. A few configuration options such as the port and the Web server name or IP address can be configured by selecting Network Settings.

376 Chapter 22

> **ALERT** The Netscape FastTrack Server is administered through a Web browser on the workstation. You can stop and start the server from the main Administrative page. Make sure you can navigate through the various pages for configuring the Netscape FastTrack Server. Remember that many pages require you to click on the Apply and Save buttons for changes to become effective and in place the next time the Web server is started.

Document Directories

Document directories are directories that hold the Web content. There can be only one primary document directory (the default is SYS:/NOVONYX/ SUITESPOT/DOCS), which is the directory users are directed to when they access the Web server. You access this directory by clicking on the Content Management button in the Server Administrator page, as shown in Figure 22.6.

> **ALERT** The default primary document directory is SYS:/NOVONYX/ SUITESPOT/DOCS. The location can be changed to any volume that supports the long name space.

You can create document directories in addition to the primary document directory. To create additional document directories, click on the Additional Document Directories selection in the left pane of the Content Management screen and provide the appropriate information.

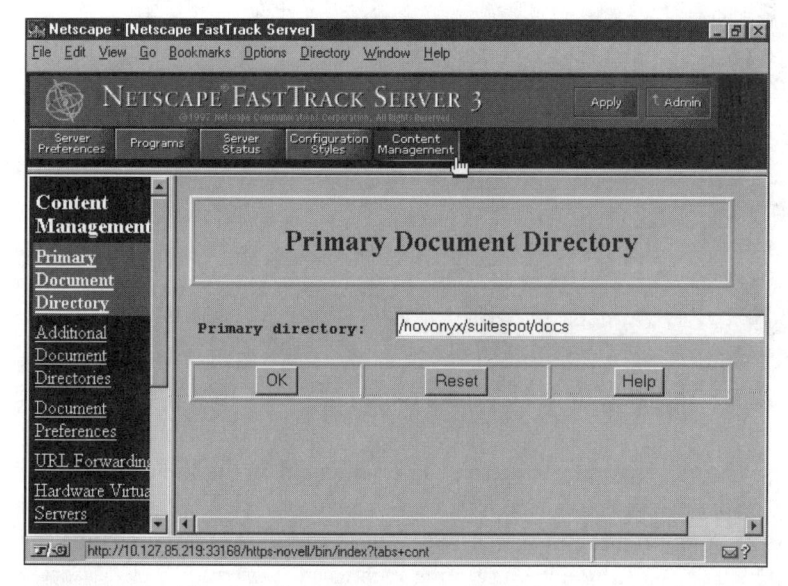

Figure 22.6 Viewing the Primary Document Directory in the Content Management screen.

To specify the default document that the user will see when he or she first accesses the Web server, select Document Preferences in the right pane of the Content Management screen. The names of the documents you want the Web server to search for within the Web site in response to Web browser requests are delimited by commas.

There can be several Web sites hosted on a single FastTrack Server, and users may choose to use different document names for their initial Web page, such as DEFAULT.HTM or INDEX.HTM. If a user decides to give his or her Web page a name that isn't specified in the Document Preferences selection, the user's initial Web page is only available if the URL in the Web browser is included in the initial Web page file name (for example, **http://www.myco.com/mypage.htm**).

Securing The FastTrack Server

When Netscape FastTrack Server is installed, it uses its own directory service to manage users and groups. Without any further configurations, this means that anyone using a Web browser can access the Web server's content files located in the SYS:/NOVONYX/SUITESPOT/DOCS directory and all its subdirectories. If you're designing a public access Web server, the default configuration is sufficient.

You can configure FastTrack Server to use Novell Directory Services (NDS) as a security authority. Configuring the Web server to use NDS instead of its own directory service allows access to content to be controlled by the NetWare file system security system rights assignments. The administrator can restrict rights to files and folders by using NDS objects as trustees and by specifying the necessary rights. This configuration of using NDS to determine access to the Web server content is called *binding* the Netscape FastTrack server to NDS.

To configure the Netscape FastTrack server to use NDS as a security provider, access the Administration Server and perform the following steps while attached to the Web server's administration Web site:

1. When you first attach to the Administration Server, click on the Global Settings button.

2. In the Obtain Directory Service From area, choose the radio button beside Novell Directory Services (as shown in Figure 22.7).

3. You'll see a notice about switching to NDS. Click on OK to continue.

4. Click on the Insert Context button to add the context that contains your users. Enter the context into the pop-up box and click on OK.

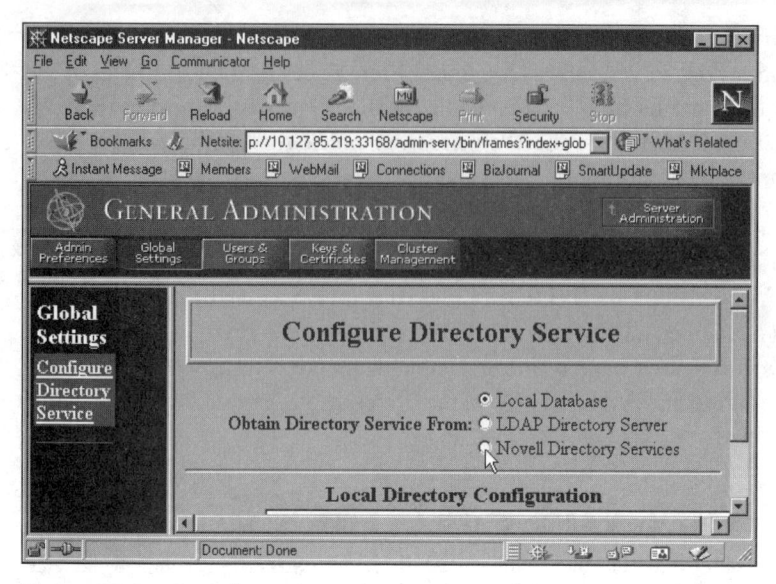

[Screenshot of Netscape Server Manager showing Configure Directory Service page with options: Local Database, LDAP Directory Server, Novell Directory Services]

Figure 22.7 Switching to NDS security mode.

5. Click on the Save Changes button. You'll see a message stating that you must restart the Administration Server before the changes will take effect.

6. At the NetWare server console, type "NSWEBDN" to stop FastTrack Server. After it's finished unloading, type "NSWEB" to start it again.

7. The users who access FastTrack Server must have valid NDS accounts in the context entered in Step 5. The users need to have a the minimum of Read and File Scan rights to the directory containing the Web documents. If this is the primary document directory, grant the user the Read and File Scan rights to this directory.

> **EXAM ALERT**
> The Netscape FastTrack server can be secured by binding to NDS. Access to Web content is then controlled through NDS.

Practice Questions

Question 1

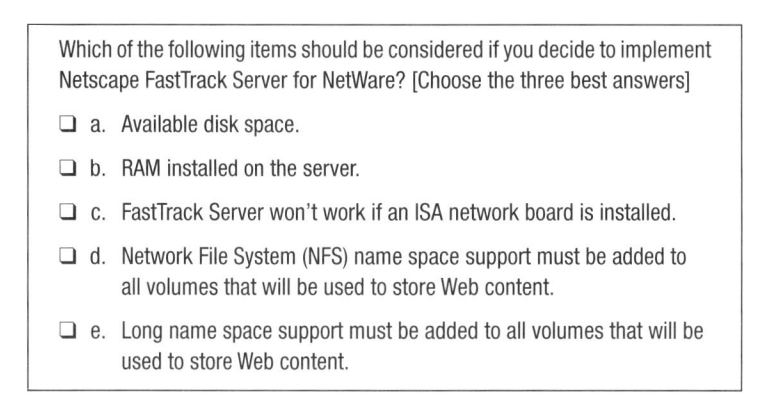

Which of the following items should be considered if you decide to implement Netscape FastTrack Server for NetWare? [Choose the three best answers]

- ❑ a. Available disk space.
- ❑ b. RAM installed on the server.
- ❑ c. FastTrack Server won't work if an ISA network board is installed.
- ❑ d. Network File System (NFS) name space support must be added to all volumes that will be used to store Web content.
- ❑ e. Long name space support must be added to all volumes that will be used to store Web content.

The correct answers are a, b, and e. As long as the Novell server where FastTrack Server is running supports the network board, the Netscape FastTrack Server should function just fine. Therefore, answer c is incorrect. The FTP service requires NFS name space support, and the only requirement for Web services is that the volumes hosting the Web content have long name space support. Therefore, answer d is incorrect.

Question 2

Which of the following sets of NLMs are loaded in the NSWEB.NCF file?

- ○ a. CRON.NLM, NS.NLM, and ADMSRV.NLM
- ○ b. NETDB.NLM, CSSYMSG.NLM, and NSHTTPD.NLM
- ○ c. NSHTTPD.NLM, CRON.NLM, and ADMSERV.NLM
- ○ d. ADMSERV.NLM, CRON.NLM, and CSSYMSG.NLM
- ○ e. None of the above

Trick question!

The correct answer is c. There is no NLM called NS.NLM or ADMSRV.NLM. Therefore, answer a is incorrect. NETDB.NLM and CSSYMSG.NLM are automatically loaded when NSHTTPD.NLM is loaded. This question asks which NLMs are loaded by the NSWEB.NCF file. Therefore, answer b is incorrect. The CSSYMSG.NLM is automatically loaded by NSHTTPD.NLM

380 Chapter 22

and is not loaded by the NSWEB.NCF file explicitly, as the question calls for. Therefore, answer d is incorrect. Answer e is incorrect because answer c is correct.

Question 3

> Which of the following statements about the Netscape FastTrack Server for NetWare is false?
>
> ○ a. FastTrack Server supports multiple file types, including graphics, sound, and video.
>
> ○ b. The port used by FastTrack Server can be changed.
>
> ○ c. You can use FastTrack Server to publish information stored on a Windows NT Server system.
>
> ○ d. FastTrack Server supports two security modes: one using NDS and the other using a scaled-down directory service.
>
> ○ e. You can shut down FastTrack Server remotely if required.

The correct answer is c. All other answers are supported by FastTrack Server. Therefore, answers a, b, d, and e are incorrect.

Question 4

> What information must be supplied and recorded in order to administer the Netscape FastTrack Server system once the installation is complete? [Choose the three best answers]
>
> ❑ a. Web server port
>
> ❑ b. Administration Web site port
>
> ❑ c. Administrative username
>
> ❑ d. Password

The correct answers are b, c, and d. The server port will be configured to 80, by default. Although you can change this value, it will not have an effect on the administration of the Web server. Therefore, answer a is incorrect.

Question 5

Which command is typed at the server console to shut down FastTrack Server?

- ○ a. **NSWEB -down**
- ○ b. **NSWEBDN**
- ○ c. **NSWEB**
- ○ d. **NSWEB -exit**

The correct answer is b. FastTrack Server is stopped by typing "NSWEBDN" at the server console. **NSWEB** starts FastTrack Server. Therefore, answer c is incorrect. **NSWEB -down** and **NSWEB -exit** are not valid commands. Therefore, answers a and d are incorrect.

Question 6

What's the default directory that stores the Web content files for FastTrack Server?

- ○ a. /NOVONYX/FASTTRACK/DOCS
- ○ b. /NOVONYX/SUITESPOT/DOCS
- ○ c. /NETSCAPE/FASTTRACK/DOCS
- ○ d. /SUITESPOT/FASTTRACK/DOCS

The correct answer is b. The primary document directory is located on the SYS volume in /NOVONYX/SUITESPOT/DOCS. All other directories listed are incorrect.

Need To Know More?

Grein, Randy and Pat Brown. *Exam Cram For NetWare 4.11 To 5 Update.* Certification Insider Press: Scottsdale, AZ, 1999. ISBN: 1-57610-355-2. Chapter 8 of this book covers Netscape FastTrack Server as it relates to the NetWare 4.11 to 5 Update test.

http://support.novell.com/servlet/Knowledgebase provides you with a search engine that will lead you to numerous articles on the subjects covered in this chapter. Search for "Netscape FastTrack Server."

www.novell.com/products/netscape_servers/fasttrack.html is the Netscape FastTrack Server for NetWare home page. From this Web site, you can access the FastTrack Server download.

www.novell.com/catalog/bg/bge34440.html is the Netscape FastTrack Server Product details page. This page provides you with numerous details about FastTrack Server.

FTP Services

Terms you'll need to understand:

- Transmission Control Protocol/Internet Protocol (TCP/IP) protocol suite
- File Transfer Protocol (FTP)
- Protocol
- Typeless naming
- Typeful naming

Techniques you'll need to master:

- Describing the File Transfer Protocol (FTP)
- Installing FTP services
- Configuring FTP services
- Starting/stopping FTP services
- Securing FTP services
- Using FTP services

This chapter describes the Novell File Transfer Protocol (FTP) server, how to manage its installation and configuration, and how to secure the files and folders it provides.

Defining The File Transfer Protocol (FTP)

FTP came to be in the late 1960s as part of the Advanced Research Projects Agency (ARPANET) venture between the Department of Defense and various educational institutions. The FTP protocol definition is actually part of the original Transmission Control Protocol/Internet Protocol (TCP/IP) protocol suite. It's the protocol responsible for transferring files to and from a local hard drive to an FTP server located on another TCP/IP-based network (such as the Internet). Its function is outlined in Request For Comment (RFC) 959.

> **Tip:** Because FTP is based on the TCP/IP protocol, the TCPIP.NLM module must be loaded on the NetWare server that will be using the FTP service.

The FTP protocol defines a file transfer method that allows files to be uploaded or downloaded from an FTP server by an FTP client. Virtually every operating system on the market supports an FTP client of some type—whether it's an actual FTP application or simply a Web browser depends on the operating system used. This makes the FTP protocol, as well as the implementation of FTP servers for file distribution, an important part of the Internet and a key component in file transfer capabilities between disparate operating systems.

By now, most users have at one time or another downloaded a file from the Internet, or perhaps uploaded a file to their company's FTP server. To provide a NetWare server with the ability to transfer files using the FTP protocol, a NetWare Loadable Module (NLM) called FTPSERV.NLM is loaded. This is the module for the NetWare FTP server program. Once the FTP server is initialized, up to 64 simultaneous connections can be established for uploading and downloading files.

> *Note: The FTPSERV.NLM is loaded when a user starts an FTP session with the NetWare server, which loads the INETD.NLM module. INETD.NLM activates FTPSERV.NLM when an FTP request is*

received. This process of an event triggering a service's activation is referred to as a daemon.

> **EXAM ALERT:** Be sure you understand the interaction between INETD.NLM and FTPSERV.NLM.

FTP Services Installation

You can add the FTP server component to the NetWare 4.x or 5.x operating system by installing the Unix Print Services for NetWare. The Unix Print Services for NetWare product is provided on the same CD-ROM as the NetWare 5 operating system.

The only prerequisite to entering "NWCONFIG" and beginning the installation is that Network File System (NFS) support must be added to any volumes that will host files published by the FTP server. To add NFS support to the volumes that will store FTP-related files, perform the following steps:

1. Type "NFS" at the server console.
2. Type "Add Name Space NFS to *Volume Name*", where *Volume Name* is the name of the volume that will be hosting files managed by the FTP server.

When the NFS name space has been added to volumes that will store FTP files, the installation can be started. The Unix Print Services product is installed using the NWCONFIG utility on the server. This means that for you to install Unix Print Services, the NetWare 5 operating system CD-ROM must be mounted as a volume on the NetWare server. If the server doesn't have a CD-ROM drive, the Unix Print Services' install files need to be copied to a volume on the NetWare server that will host the FTP service. The Unix Print Services product can be found at the following path on the NetWare 5 operating system CD-ROM:

`NetWare5:Products\NWUXPS`

After all the files have been copied to the server, you'll be asked whether the product should use Local Network Information Service (NIS) or Remote NIS. If you want to manage the NIS database from the local server, select Local NIS. If your company already has a NIS server in place and configured, you could choose Remote NIS. The primary function of NIS is to manage information regarding users and groups on the network; some organizations like to keep the administration of such information in a central location.

386 Chapter 23

> Be familiar with the location and name of the FTP services installation files.

FTP Configuration And Management Using UNICON

The management of Novell's FTP server is performed from within an application on the server called UNICON. UNICON can be used to stop, start, and change configuration options related to the FTP server. To start UNICON, simply type the following at the server's console:

UNICON

The screen shown in Figure 23.1 appears. Several NLMs that are required by UNICON are loaded, and you're prompted for a server name, username, and password.

The server name can either be the server's Domain Name System (DNS) name or the IP address of the server. The administrative username can be specified using a typeless or typeful distinguished name. Specify the appropriate information and press Enter to continue. You're presented with the UNICON main menu, which is shown in Figure 23.2.

> Configuration and administration of FTP services is done through a server-based utility—UNICON.NLM.

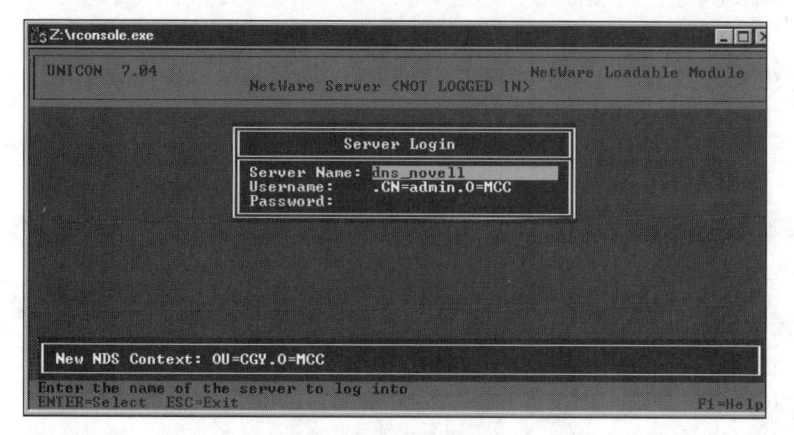

```
Z:\rconsole.exe
UNICON 7.04                                    NetWare Loadable Module
              NetWare Server (NOT LOGGED IN)

                      ┌─────── Server Login ────────┐
                      │ Server Name: dns_novell     │
                      │ Username:    .CN=admin.O=MCC│
                      │ Password:                   │
                      └─────────────────────────────┘




  New NDS Context: OU=CGY.O=MCC
Enter the name of the server to log into
ENTER=Select  ESC=Exit                                         F1=Help
```

Figure 23.1 The UNICON login screen.

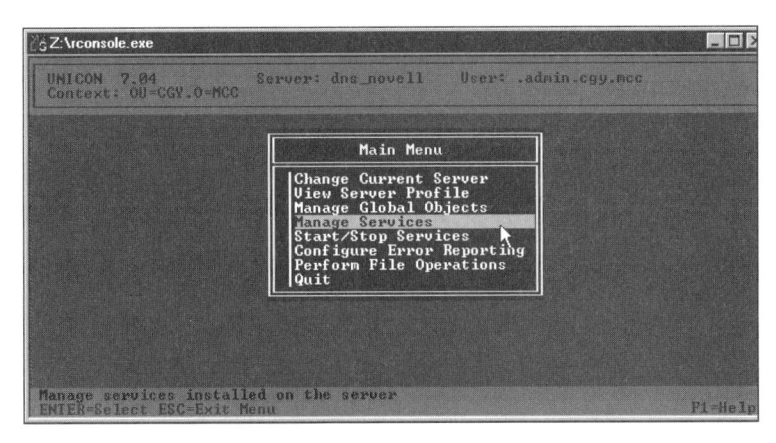

Figure 23.2 The UNICON Main Menu.

FTP Service Configuration

The Manage Services option, which is selected in Figure 23.2, is used to configure the services managed by UNICON, including the FTP service. To configure the FTP service, select Manage Services and press Enter. Then select the FTP service from the list of services provided and press Enter.

This takes you to the FTP Administration screen, where you can view the current connections to the FTP service, perform log file maintenance, restrict users from accessing the FTP service, and set the FTP server configuration parameters (see Figure 23.3).

Select Set Parameters and press Enter to view or set the FTP server configuration parameters. The FTP Server Parameters screen appears (see Figure 23.4).

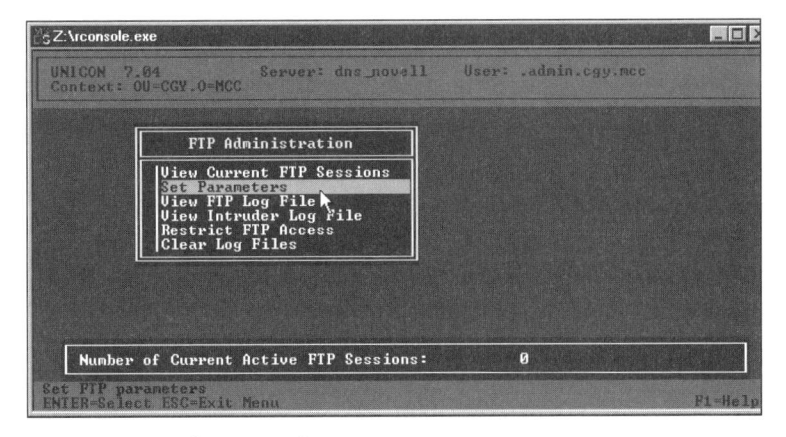

Figure 23.3 The FTP Administration screen.

388 Chapter 23

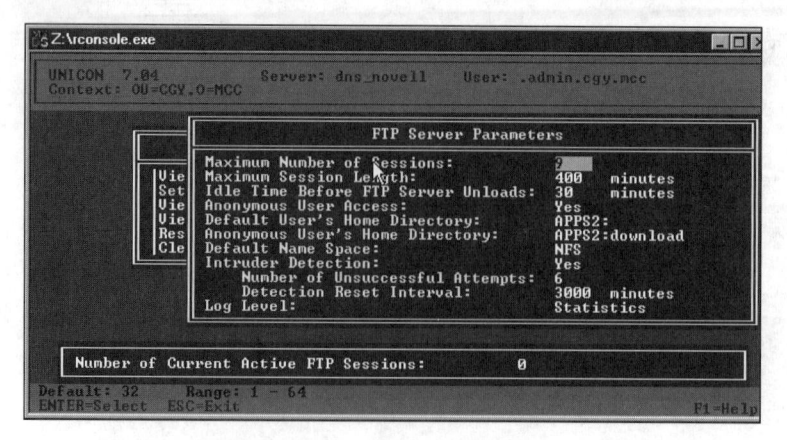

Figure 23.4 The FTP Server Parameters screen.

Each of the configuration options on the FTP Server Parameters screen is explained in the following list:

➤ **Maximum Number Of Sessions** This option specifies the maximum number of connections allowed to the FTP server. The range is from 1 to 64.

➤ **Maximum Session Length** This option configures the maximum amount of time a user can stay connected to the FTP server.

➤ **Idle Time Before FTP Server Unloads** This option indicates how long the server should remain awake if there are no FTP sessions in progress. If there are no sessions in progress for the time specified here, FTPSERV.NLM is unloaded. When a user attempts to FTP to the server, INETD.NLM reloads FTPSERV.NLM.

➤ **Anonymous User Access** This option specifies whether anonymous users will be allowed to access the files on the FTP site. If this option is set to No, all users will be required to provide a username and password to access the FTP site.

➤ **Default User's Home Directory** This option specifies the directory location that a user who has not logged in anonymously will be taken to if his or her corresponding User object in the NDS does not have a home directory specified.

➤ **Anonymous User's Home Directory** This option specifies the directory to which users who log on anonymously to the FTP server will be taken.

➤ **Default Name Space** This option indicates the namespace used to store and display files and directories. Network File System (NFS) allows

FTP Services 389

case-sensitive names and file names up to 255 characters. The DOS option forces conventional DOS restrictions, such as 8.3 naming and no case sensitivity.

➤ **Intruder Detection** This option is used to configure the system to detect intruders who are trying to guess login IDs and passwords. Set to Yes or No to turn intruder detection on or off, respectively. There are two other options available under Intruder Detection:

  ➤ **Unsuccessful Number Of Attempts** This option sets the number of times a user may log in incorrectly before intruder detection locks the account.

  ➤ **Detection Reset Interval** For an account to be locked by intruder detection, the unsuccessful login attempts must occur within the specified detection interval. For example, in Figure 23.4, the intruder detection system will only lock an account if the user logs in incorrectly six times within 3,000 minutes.

➤ **Log Level** This is the last configuration parameter available on the FTP Server Parameters screen. The FTP service currently supports four logging levels:

  ➤ **None** Disables logging of FTP-related activity

  ➤ **Statistics** Tracks the number of files copied to and from the FTP server

  ➤ **Logins** Records login information when users access the FTP site

  ➤ **File** Records a description of all FTP transactions

> **EXAM ALERT:** Notice that administration of FTP services uses UNICON, which is server oriented. Administration is not performed with a workstation utility.

Starting And Stopping The FTP Service

UNICON can also be used to start and stop the FTP service. To start or stop the FTP service, run UNICON and log in when prompted. When the main menu is displayed, select Start/Stop Services and press Enter. To start the FTP service that does not appear in the list of started (running) services (as shown in Figure 23.5), press the Insert key, select your FTP service, and hit Enter.

If you press Delete while a service is highlighted in the Running Services window, the service will be stopped. Other services can also be started by choosing Insert, selecting the service, and pressing Enter.

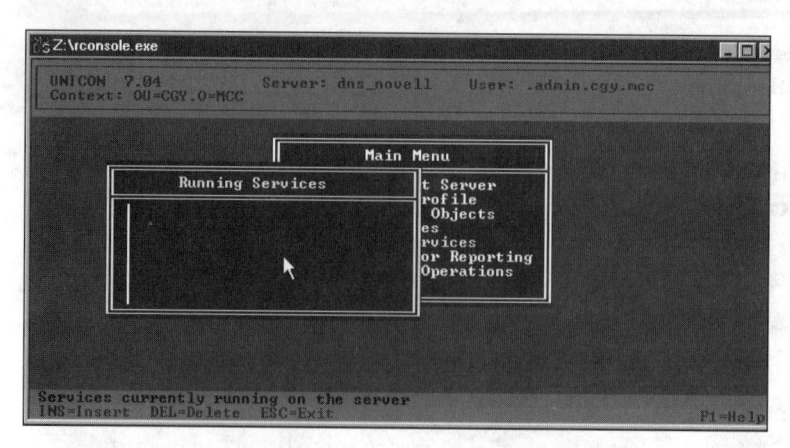

Figure 23.5 The Running Services window used to view, start, and stop FTP services.

Securing FTP Services

Once the FTP service is installed and configured, the last task is to ensure that the files and folders being exposed on the FTP site are secure. To secure the files, you have to implement file system restrictions on each individual who will be accessing the FTP server. When users log into the FTP server, their rights to the files and folders available on the FTP server are controlled through each User or Group object in the Novell Directory Services (NDS) database via NetWare Administrator. To configure restrictions on the files available to anonymous users, for example, you would set file system restrictions on the user called *anonymous* in NDS.

Using FTP Services

To use the newly installed FTP services, simply go to a client workstation and open a Web browser. Once you're in the Web browser, type a new address in the address/location URL box. The new address used should be the IP address of your Web server or the DNS name. Here's an example:

```
ftp://web_server_ip
```

In Figure 23.6, the appropriate entry is

```
ftp://10.127.85.219
```

FTP Services **391**

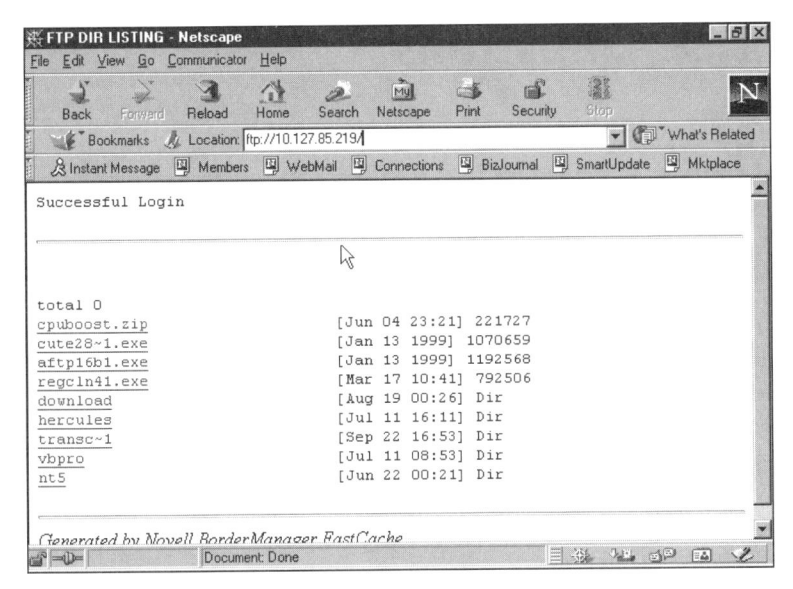

```
FTP DIR LISTING - Netscape
File  Edit  View  Go  Communicator  Help

Successful Login

total 0
cpuboost.zip              [Jun 04 23:21] 221727
cute28~1.exe              [Jan 13 1999] 1070659
aftp16b1.exe              [Jan 13 1999] 1192568
regcln41.exe              [Mar 17 10:41] 792506
download                  [Aug 19 00:26] Dir
hercules                  [Jul 11 16:11] Dir
transc~1                  [Sep 22 16:53] Dir
vbpro                     [Jul 11 08:53] Dir
nt5                       [Jun 22 00:21] Dir

Generated by Novell BorderManager FastCache
```

Figure 23.6 FTP access from a Web browser.

> A workstation browser can upload and download files to the FTP server.

Practice Questions

Question 1

Which of the following is a feature of the NetWare FTP server?

- ○ a. Integrated Lightweight Directory Access Protocol (LDAP) file system security management
- ○ b. Support for long file names through the use of the long name space
- ○ c. File system rights for FTP users can be administered from within NetWare Administrator
- ○ d. The ability to host up to 10,000 simultaneous connections
- ○ e. Connectivity with disparate systems using protocols other than TCP/IP

The correct answer is c. LDAP is a directory service access protocol that does not have file system access restriction capabilities. Therefore, answer a is incorrect. The NFS.NAM name space module provides long file name support on the FTP server. Therefore, answer b is incorrect. Currently, the FTP server is limited to a maximum of 64 connections. Therefore, answer d is incorrect. The FTP protocol is part of the TCP/IP protocol suite, which means that all systems using FTP to transfer files must use TCP/IP. Therefore, answer e is incorrect.

Question 2

What's the name of the NLM that provides FTP services on a NetWare 5 server?

- ○ a. HTTPD.NLM
- ○ b. INETD.NLM
- ○ c. FTPD.NLM
- ○ d. FTPSERV.NLM
- ○ e. FTPSRV.NLM

The correct answer is d. Answer a is incorrect because HTTPD.NLM is used by Netscape FastTrack Server. Answer b is incorrect because INETD.NLM activates FTPSERV.NLM when an FTP request is received, which is why this is a trick question. Answers c and e are incorrect because there are no NLMs called FTPD.NLM and FTPSRV.NLM.

FTP Services   393

Question 3

> Which of the following commands do you type at the server console to load the FTP service?
>
> ○ a. **UNICON**
> ○ b. **FTPSERV**
> ○ c. **FTPSRV**
> ○ d. **NSWEB -FTP**
> ○ e. None of the above

The correct answer is b. The UNICON utility can be used to start the FTP service, but it must be started via the menus in UNICON, as opposed to a console command. Therefore, answer a is incorrect. There is no NLM called FTPSRV. Therefore, answer c is incorrect. The NSWEB.NCF file is used to start FastTrack Server and can't be used to start the FTP service. Therefore, answer d is incorrect. Because answer b is correct, answer e is incorrect.

Question 4

> Which of the following NLMs must be loaded to receive an incoming FTP connection? [Choose the three best answers]
>
> ❑ a. INETD.NLM
> ❑ b. FTPSERV.NLM
> ❑ c. FTP.NLM
> ❑ d. BTRIEVE.NLM
> ❑ e. TCPIP.NLM

The correct answers are a, b, and e. There is no NLM called FTP.NLM. Therefore, answer c is incorrect. BTRIEVE.NLM is a client/server database NLM and does not have to be manually loaded for FTP functionality. Therefore, answer d is incorrect.

Question 5

When performing an installation of NetWare FTP services, which name space module must be loaded and added to all volumes hosting FTP files?

○ a. LONG.NAM

○ b. OS2.NAM

○ c. MAC.NAM

○ d. NFS.NAM

The correct answer is d. The LONG.NAM module provides long file name support for Windows-based machines accessing the NetWare server's files. Therefore, answer a is incorrect. The OS2.NAM name space module is used on pre-NetWare 5 servers to provide long file name capabilities. Therefore, answer b is incorrect. The MAC.NAM module is used to add support for storing Macintosh files on a NetWare volume. Therefore, answer c is incorrect.

Question 6

Which of the following statements about configuring the FTP server is true?

○ a. It's not possible to remotely administer the NetWare FTP service.

○ b. Administration must be performed on the server where the FTP service is running.

○ c. The file system access an FTP user is granted can be managed from within NetWare Administrator.

○ d. The FTP server can be shut down from within the NetWare Administrator.

The correct answer is c. The UNICON utility prompts for a server name when you first initialize it. If you specify a remote server that's hosting FTP services, it can also be administered as long as the servers are part of the same NDS tree. Therefore, answer a is incorrect. You can administer the FTP service when it's running or down. Therefore, answer b is incorrect. The FTP server can only be downed by unloading the appropriate NLMs at the server console or using UNICON. Therefore, answer d is incorrect.

Need To Know More?

http://support.novell.com/servlet/Knowleadgebase provides you with a search engine that leads you to numerous articles on the subjects covered in this chapter. Search for "FTP Service" to obtain information on these subjects.

www.novell.com/documentation is the Web site where you can access the same documentation that ships with the various NetWare products. Click on NetWare 5 and search for "FTP Service" to obtain information on these subjects.

NIAS Remote Access

Terms you'll need to understand:

- Novell Internet Access Server (NIAS)
- Remote access
- Plain Old Telephone Service (POTS)
- Integrated Services Digital Network (ISDN)
- xDSL (Generic Digital Subscriber Line)
- NIASCFG
- Asynchronous input/output (AIO)

Techniques you'll need to master:

- Understanding the features and requirements of NIAS
- Comprehending the technologies for remote access data transmission
- Installing and configuring NIAS remote access
- Understanding NIAS remote access security
- Using NIAS remote access

Productivity can be enhanced in any organization by providing dial-up access to the corporate local area network (LAN). The problem is that sometimes after you've weighed the productivity gain against the security risks, the decision to implement a remote access solution may not look as viable. Novell has approached this issue with the Novell Internet Access Server (NIAS), a product that covers the security concerns of implementing a remote access solution as well as offers superior performance and maintains support for a wide range of access methods. This chapter explains the key concepts related to installing, configuring, and managing NIAS.

Features And Requirements Of NIAS

The NIAS product has the capability to manage a single modem or a modem pool attached to a NetWare 5 server. When a user connects to NIAS from a remote dial-up connection, he or she is authenticated to Novell Directory Services (NDS). If the user's username and password are correct, he or she will be granted access to the NetWare server and all the resources available on the corporate network to which the user is connected.

There are a number of reasons why users might need to access resources remotely. Here are some examples of how NIAS can be used:

➤ An employee who needs to perform research from home could use the company's connection to the Internet or the corporate intranet.

➤ A user could dial into work and print documents so they are ready when he or she gets to work.

➤ A user could be granted secure dial-up access to retrieve company email or given the ability to run applications from home that are usually only available at work.

These are just a few ways NIAS could help increase productivity. In addition to the points in the previous list, it's important to remember that all users who attach to and access the network through NIAS will be authenticated to NDS. This means that any network resources that are being accessed through NIAS can be audited and secured using NetWare Administrator.

A good thing to remember about NIAS is that the remote access client, once connected to NIAS, will actually function as if it were on the LAN where the NIAS server resides. This includes access to most resources available on the LAN, within reason. Because of dial-up connectivity, limitations—such as whether a Plain Old Telephone Service (POTS), Integrated Services Digital

Network (ISDN), or frame relay connection is being made—can play a significant role in which tasks can be performed when the user is attached to NIAS from a remote access client. Larger applications and tasks that require high amounts of data transfer will not operate correctly over a slow connection. Connection speeds, benefits, and downfalls are discussed later in this chapter.

The requirements for running NIAS on a NetWare 5 server are minimal. The server that will run NIAS must have at least 5MB of memory above the memory required for the server. Novell has stated that NIAS will normally run using the minimum hardware configuration required to run NetWare 5. Remember that if other services, such as File Transfer Protocol (FTP) and Netscape FastTrack Server, are running or if there are several connections being hosted, additional hardware may have to be added to the server.

> Make sure you know the requirements to install NIAS and the role of NIAS in your networks.

Overview Of Technologies For Remote Access Data Transmission

Several data transmission choices are available on the market today—some more reliable and faster than others. The following descriptions explain the benefits and disadvantages of using each transmission type.

Plain Old Telephone Service (POTS)

The POTS, or regular dial-up line, is widely used today and provides the ability to transfer data at a maximum rate of 56Kbps. It's popular because of its worldwide existence and the fact that local connections are relatively inexpensive.

The downside of POTS lines is that in relation to other communication line speeds, connections are relatively slow. In addition, long distance charges may apply, and POTS lines can be subject to line instability. Modems attempt to maintain the connection during line interruptions, but disconnections still occur.

Integrated Services Digital Network (ISDN)

ISDN is a digital communication method that's used to transmit voice and data. ISDN comes in two flavors: Basic Rate Interface (BRI) and Primary Rate Interface (PRI).

Basic Rate Interface (BRI)

The most common form of ISDN used in the United States is the BRI format. This means that the modem or router making the ISDN connection uses two B, or *bearer*, channels, and one D, or *data*, channel. The B channels carry voice and data, and the D channel is used to carry control and signaling information.

When ISDN is implemented using the BRI format, each B channel supports a maximum transmission speed of 64Kbps. One channel is used for uploading data to a remote system, and the other is used for downloading data. This implementation of the BRI ISDN format guarantees that 64Kbps will be available for uploading, and 64Kbps will be available for downloading, because each channel is used for a separate task.

It's also possible to bond B channels using the NIAS Multilink Point-to-Point Protocol (MPPP) implementation. When MPPP is implemented on NIAS, the two B channels are treated as a single channel for either uploading or downloading. The combined bandwidth is 128Kbps in either direction. If a user is using 80Kbps of the 128Kbps available to download a file, there will be only 48Kbps available to a user who is uploading at the same time, because the two channels are treated as one.

Primary Rate Interface (PRI)

The PRI ISDN format is another implementation of ISDN in which 23 B channels and one 64Kbps D channel are implemented using a T1 line or 30 B channels and one D channel on an E1 line. T1 is implemented in Canada, the United States, and Japan. E1 lines are implemented in other countries, such as European countries. Their maximum transmission speeds are 1.544Mbps and 2.048Mbps, respectively.

Generic Digital Subscriber Line (xDSL)

Generic Digital Subscriber Line (xDSL, the x stands for *Generic*) is an emerging technology that uses traditional analog lines to provide high-speed data transfer rates of up to 8Mbps. xDSL technology uses the same two copper wires as a telephone and allows for the telephone service to coexist with data transmissions. One of the characteristics of xDSL is that it doesn't require dialing to establish a connection like a ISDN or POTS connection. Instead, the router listens for a signal and attaches to a switch at a predefined frequency. Once the connection has been established to a switch, it's permanent.

There are three main variations of the xDSL technology: Asymmetric DSL (ADSL), High bit-rate DSL (HDSL), and Splitterless DSL. Each implementation offers varying speeds and may require special equipment, which is usually supplied by your xDSL provider (such as the local telephone company, or telco). For example, ADSL supports downloads of up to 8Mbps, but the upload speed is slower. HDSL provides an equal amount of bandwidth for uploading and downloading.

As mentioned previously, the various implementations of xDSL are emerging technologies. Currently, the availability of xDSL technologies is one of the factors limiting their emergence. In order to implement ADSL, which provides the fastest downloads of the three, there must be a switch within five kilometers or three miles of the location where ADSL is being implemented. For most telephone companies, this means that they will have to upgrade their existing infrastructure, which takes time.

Several companies produce xDSL adapters. Once you've checked to see if your local telephone company supports xDSL, you can purchase an adapter for your Novell server and use NIAS to create the connection.

> Be comfortable with the basic descriptions and specifications of the various transmission technologies.

Installing And Configuring NIAS

When you're ready to configure the NIAS component on your NetWare 5 server, type "NIASCFG" at the server console. This command starts the configuration utility that's used to configure the various aspects of NIAS (see Figure 24.1).

If you select the Configure NIAS option and press Enter, you're asked which NIAS component you would like to configure. The first option is Remote

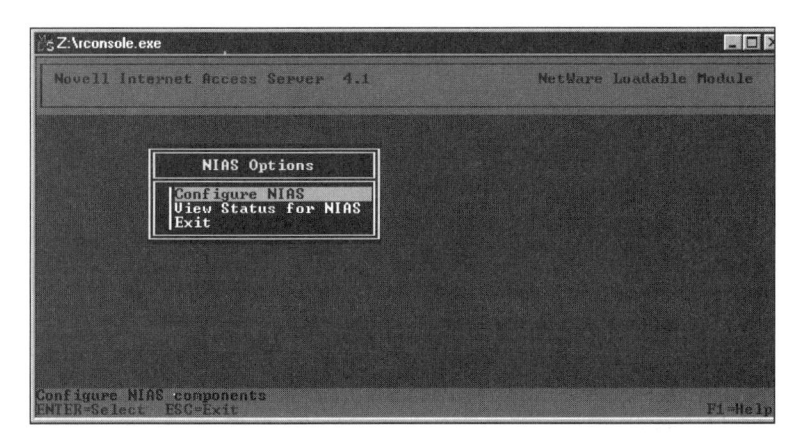

Figure 24.1 The NIAS Options screen.

Access, and it's used to configure connection aspects of NIAS, such as the type of connection. (We cover this option in detail in the following section.) The second option is Protocols And Routing. This option takes you into the Internetworking Configuration (INETCFG) utility, which is used to configure network boards, protocol support, and bindings.

> NIAS can be configured to support dial-in and remote access to the network.

Remote Access Configuration

As an example, we're going to configure remote access for an asynchronous device, such as a modem. To configure the remote access option on the server, follow these steps:

1. Select Remote Access and press Enter. Log into the server with the appropriate username and password.

2. Novell was thoughtful at this point: The next message displayed asks whether you would like instructions on how to configure the NIAS remote access component. If you choose Yes, the system displays a file that explains the configuration options available (see Figure 24.2). When No is chosen, the system will immediately continue with the NIAS configuration instead of displaying the configuration file.

3. Press Esc (if you read the instructions) after you've read the instructions or press Enter (if you didn't choose to read the instructions). The installation asks whether you have any synchronous adapters.

```
Z:\rconsole.exe                                              _ □ ×
Remote Access Configuration  4.1          NetWare Loadable Module
Context: [ROOT]

                    Configuration Instructions
BASIC REMOTE ACCESS SETUP AND CONFIGURATION INSTRUCTIONS

After you complete the product installation, remote access
runs these automated procedures so you can quickly and easily
set up and configure your remote access server for basic
operation. These automated procedures run the first time you
load NIASCFG and select the Remote Access option.

After you complete these procedures, you can use the remote
access configuration menu options to change the defined
settings or enter new settings. These instructions contain
four sections:

      * SETUP AND CONFIGURATION
      * REMOTE CLIENT ACCESS
      * CONFIGURATION REPORT

↑=Scroll Up  ↓=Scroll Down  PGUP  PGDN  HOME  END  ESC=Back    F1=Help
```

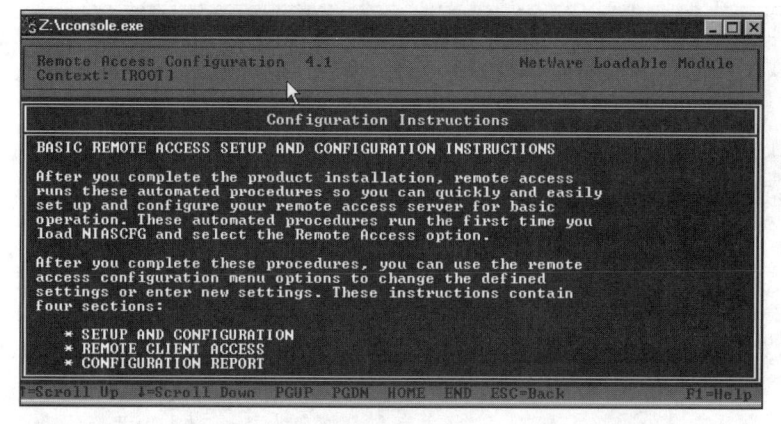

Figure 24.2 The Configuration Instructions screen for setting up and configuring remote access.

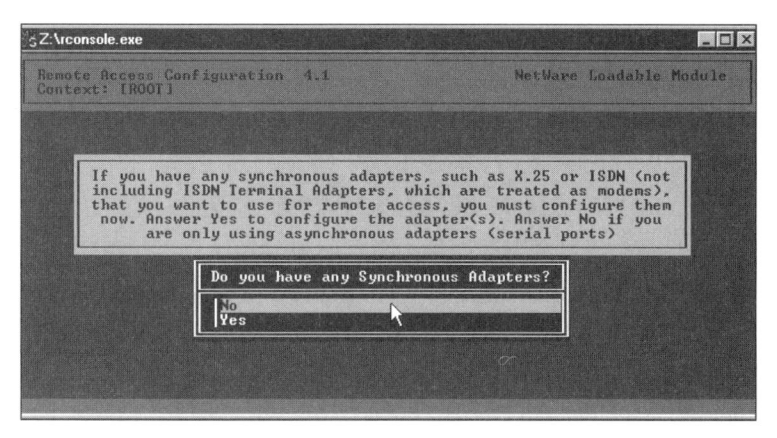

Figure 24.3 Selecting No in the Do You Have Any Synchronous Adapters? screen.

4. As shown in Figure 24.3, choose No, beacuse in this example, we're using a modem, which is an asynchronous device.

5. The system prompts you to configure your asynchronous input/output (AIO) port. Select your specific adapter from the list or choose the Other Board Not Listed Above option to insert the disk from your board manufacturer. In this example, we're using a modem, so choose the Serial Port (COMx) option (as shown in Figure 24.4).

6. When the configuration program indicates that the AIO driver was successfully loaded, press Enter. Then answer No to loading more AIO drivers.

    The system now detects the modem you're using and allows you to enter an IP address and subnet mask for the newly detected modem.

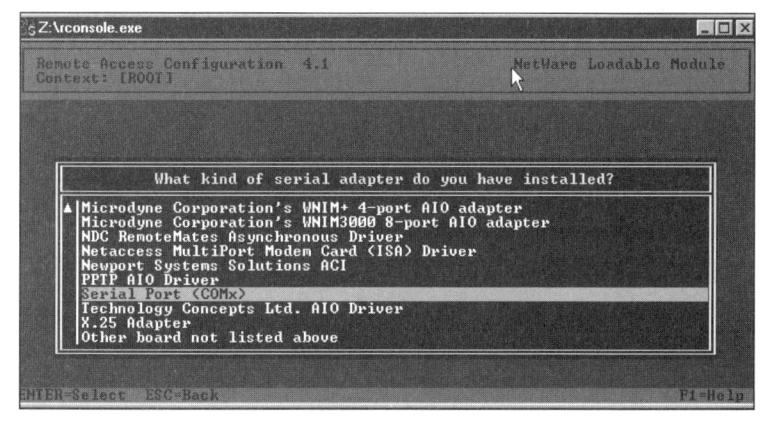

Figure 24.4 Choosing your adapter type.

404 Chapter 24

7. Configure a valid IP address range for the NIAS server to assign to clients when prompted.

8. Press Esc and save your changes. Don't enter a second address range unless it's required.

9. Configure an IPX external network address to allow remote access clients using IPX to connect.

10. Accept the defaults for all other configuration options and continue until the installation of the AIO device is complete.

11. The installation and configuration of your AIO device is complete when you see the screen depicted in Figure 24.5. You can now select the Configure Security option and press Enter to configure user access to the NIAS port. (Additional security methods are discussed in the following section.)

> **EXAM ALERT**
>
> Connections can be IP and/or IPX with security.

NIAS Remote Access Security

One of the benefits of using NIAS remote access within an organization is the enhanced level of security. As mentioned earlier in this chapter, remote access users gaining access to an organization's network through an NIAS server are required to log into NDS. This includes the ability to configure remote access connection options on a container group or a user-by-user basis.

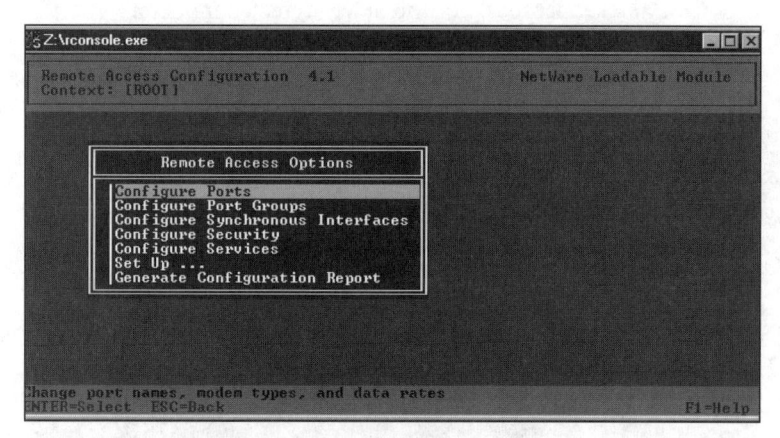

Figure 24.5 The Remote Access Options screen.

Configuring Security At The Container Level

Let's start with the NIAS remote access options that can be configured at the container level. The options configured at the container level affect all the users in the container. To configure the remote access options at the container level, do the following:

1. In NetWare Administrator, right-click on the container whose remote access you want to configure and choose Details.

2. Scroll down and choose the Remote Access property page (see Figure 24.6). The options available on the page include the following:

   ▶ **Idle Timeout** This option specifies how long a client can be idle before NIAS disconnects it.

   ▶ **IPX Parameters** This option allows for the IPX information assigned to a remote access client to be manually assigned.

   ▶ **IP Parameters** This option allows you to specify the following information:

      ▶ **Specify Domain Information** This option specifies the Domain Name System (DNS) server that remote access clients whose user IDs reside in that container should use.

      ▶ **Set Boot Parameters** This option allows a container-level server and boot file to be configured for remote-boot workstations.

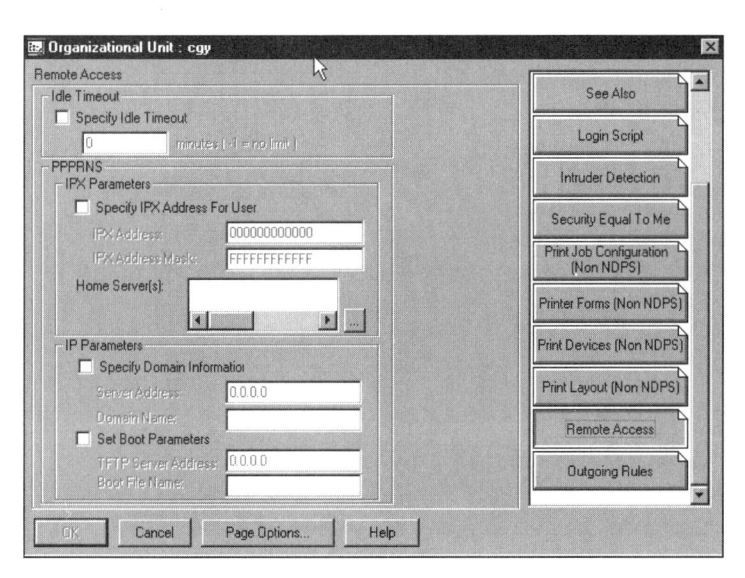

Figure 24.6 The Remote Access property page.

Configuring Security At The User Level

You can also use NetWare Administrator to enforce restrictions on individual users. To begin, double-click on a User object in NetWare Administrator, scroll down, and select the Remote Access-1 property page (see Figure 24.7).

The most significant restriction to remember under the User object's Remote Access-1 tab is the Dialback option. If you enable the Dialback option for a User object, the server will hang up on users when they call in and then call them back as a security precaution. This ensures that users are only dialing in from previously verified numbers.

The options available under the Remote Access-2 tab for the User object are similar to the options available on the container's Remote Access property page discussed in the previous section.

> **EXAM ALERT:** Make sure you understand how you secure NIAS access to your network with NDS.

Using NIAS Remote Access

To use NIAS to connect to a corporate network, the workstation acting as the remote access client must have Novell Client for Windows 95/98 or Windows

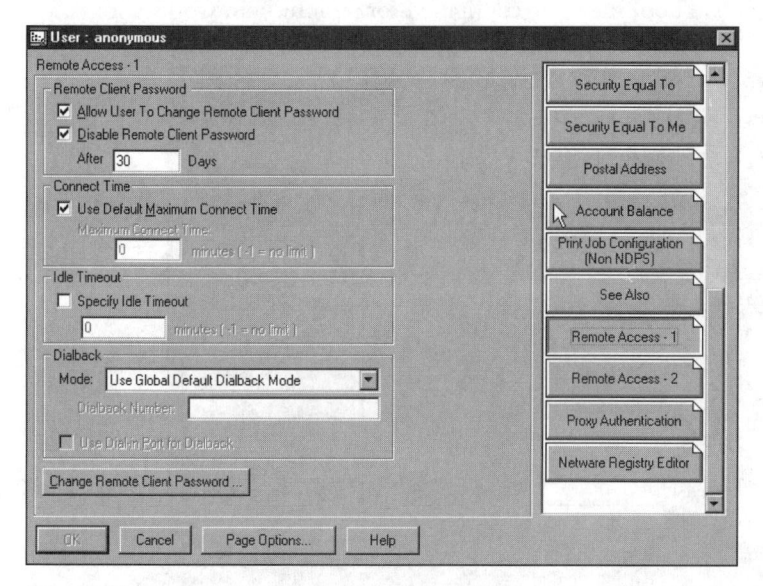

Figure 24.7 The User object's Remote Access-1 property page.

NT installed. Once the Novell Client has been added to the workstation, double-click on My Computer on the desktop and add a new dial-up connection. Configure the NIAS server's phone number as the number to dial, and then enter the appropriate username and password when prompted.

Practice Questions

Question 1

> Which of the following transmission types provides the fastest download speed?
>
> ○ a. xDSL
>
> ○ b. HDSL
>
> ○ c. ADSL
>
> ○ d. Splitterless DSL
>
> ○ e. None of the above. They all operate at about the same speed.

The correct answer is c. xDSL is the term used to refer to the group of DSL technologies as a whole. Therefore, answer a is incorrect. HDSL provides equal bandwidth for downloading and uploading. Therefore, answer b is incorrect. Splitterless DSL typically only achieves speeds of less than 1MB per second. Therefore, answer d is incorrect. Answer e is incorrect, because answer c is correct.

Question 2

> Which of the following are requirements for a client to attach to NIAS? [Choose the three best answers]
>
> ❏ a. 5MB of memory above the memory required to run the operating system.
>
> ❏ b. Novell Client must be installed.
>
> ❏ c. Dial-up networking must be installed on the client.
>
> ❏ d. The NIAS server must not perform any tasks other than managing remote access connections.
>
> ❏ e. Dial-up networking must be configured with the appropriate number and username/password.

The correct answers are b, c, and e. The question specifically asks for the requirements on the client, not the server. Therefore, answers a and d are incorrect.

Question 3

Which of the following technologies will allow for the fastest transfer speeds?

- ○ a. The technology that uses 23 B channels and one 64Kbps D channel
- ○ b. The technology that uses 30 B channels and one D channel
- ○ c. A dial-up modem connected to a telco
- ○ d. ISDN implemented in a BRI format
- ○ e. HDSL

Trick! question

The correct answer is b. The PRI format of ISDN implemented on a T1 line is described in answer a, which provides 1.544Mbps transfer rates. Therefore, answer a is incorrect. Dial-up modems max out at 56Kbps. Therefore, answer c is incorrect. Bonding the B channels when using BRI ISDN provides a maximum speed of 128Kbps. Therefore, answer d is incorrect. HDSL achieves speeds of 1.544Mbps in both directions—uploading and downloading. Therefore, answer e is incorrect. This is a trick question because it requires that you know that 30 B channels and one D channel translates to the ISDN PRI format implemented over an E1 line. This implementation is capable of 2.048Mbps.

Question 4

What's the appropriate step to begin the installation/configuration of NIAS on a NetWare 5 server?

- ○ a. Run NWCONFIG and select product options to install the NIAS product.
- ○ b. Type "startx" at the server console and install the NIAS product through the GUI interface.
- ○ c. Load the NIASCFG utility on the server and begin configuring the NIAS service.
- ○ d. Run the **NIASCFG** console command to begin the configuration.
- ○ e. None of the above. You must purchase the product first.

The correct answer is c. The NIAS product ships with NetWare 5 and does not have to be installed separately. Therefore, answer a is incorrect. The GUI interface is not used to install and configure NIAS. Therefore, answer b is incorrect. NIASCFG is an NLM, not a console command. Therefore, answer d is incorrect. Answer e is incorrect because answer c is correct.

Question 5

> What are two ways that NIAS security can be implemented? [Choose the two best answers]
>
> ❏ a. Using NDS Manager
>
> ❏ b. Using NetWare Administrator
>
> ❏ c. Using the **NIASCFG** command
>
> ❏ d. It can be set through INETCFG
>
> ❏ e. Using the NIASCFG utility

The correct answers are b and e. NDS Manager can't be used to set NIAS security. Therefore, answer a is incorrect. There is no command called **NIASCFG**. Therefore, answer c is incorrect. INETCFG is used to manage network devices and protocols. Therefore, answer d is incorrect.

Need To Know More?

You can access help for NetWare Administrator and the NIASCFG utility by pressing F1. The Help file will explain the various topics related to the configuration and security aspects of NIAS, depending on which screen you're on when F1 is pressed.

www.novell.com/documentation/lg/nw5/docui/index.html is the Novell online documentation Web site. Search for "NIASCFG," and you'll find in-depth information on the utility and each option that can be configured via NIASCFG.

http://support.novell.com/servlet/Knowledgebase contains a wide range of technical documents that discuss NIAS. On the Web site, choose the NetWare product category in Step 1. Technical Information Documents (TIDs) is selected, by default, in Step 2. Finally, search for NIAS in Step 3 to find a plethora of information related to NIAS.

25

Additional Novell Services

Terms you'll need to understand:

- GroupWise Administration Module
- GroupWise client
- Message transfer system
- Message store
- Directory store
- Document store
- Message Transfer Agent (MTA)
- Post Office Agent (POA)
- NetWare Management Agent
- Z.E.N.works
- Novell Internet Access Server (NIAS) 4.1
- Network Address Translation (NAT)
- SAMDRV.DLL and MSSAMSRV.DLL
- Domain Object Wizard
- Mailbox Manager for Exchange

Techniques you'll need to master:

- Outlining the basic features of GroupWise
- Describing the basic path of a message in GroupWise
- Outlining the basic features of ManageWise
- Describing the basic features of a firewall
- Outlining the basic features of BorderManager
- Outlining the basic features of NDS for NT
- Describing the sequence of events for processing a Windows NT security event in NDS for NT

Novell produces other products that can be used on networks to enhance and extend their services. In this chapter, we'll cover four products that can be installed on a NetWare 5 network—GroupWise, ManageWise, BorderManager, and Novell Directory Services (NDS) for NT. Here's a description of each:

- **GroupWise** A popular product that provides email, calendaring, and workgroup services.

- **ManageWise** This product is designed to provide network management services, including documentation and monitoring functions.

- **BorderManager** A complete firewall and proxy product that's commonly used as a interface between a company's network and the Internet.

- **NDS for NT** A great product for networks that have a few Windows NT Servers providing services but don't want the extra overhead of maintaining additional accounts. NDS for NT allows you to maintain one account for both NDS and NT.

GroupWise

GroupWise 5 is a messaging system that's integrated with NDS and can be administered with NetWare Administrator. GroupWise has several features in addition to email, including the following:

- Calendaring
- Internet access
- Remote access
- Scheduling
- Shared folders
- Task management
- Threaded conferencing
- Workflow

The snap-ins to NetWare Administrator that allow viewing and management of the GroupWise system are also referred to as the *GroupWise administration module*. Figure 25.1 shows various features of GroupWise running in NetWare Administrator. With the GroupWise administration module in NetWare Administrator, you can perform the following tasks:

- Add, remove, and modify GroupWise user properties and preferences
- Configure and change the GroupWise system environment

Additional Novell Services 415

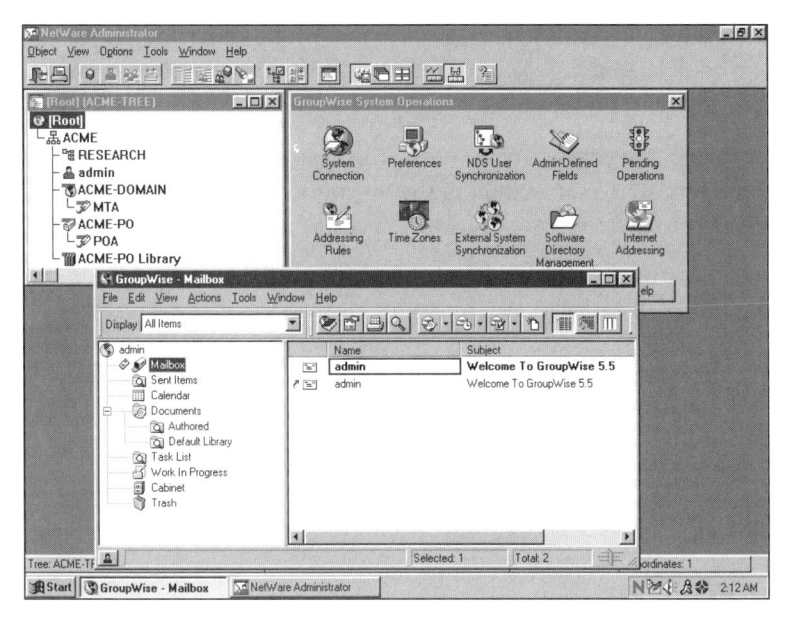

Figure 25.1 Various features of GroupWise running in NetWare Administrator.

- ➤ Perform maintenance on the GroupWise message store
- ➤ Execute GroupWise system diagnostics
- ➤ Manage and distribute the GroupWise client components

Before you can manage GroupWise from NetWare Administrator, you must perform two tasks:

- ➤ **NDS schema** To view and manage the GroupWise elements, you must extend the NDS schema.
- ➤ **GroupWise administration module** The GroupWise related snap-ins for NetWare Administrator must be installed for the GroupWise administration module.

GroupWise 5 consists of several components: GroupWise client, message transfer system, administration program, message store, directory store, and document store. Here's a summary of the basic types of events in a GroupWise system using most of these components:

1. GroupWise information for a user is modified by the administrator using NetWare Administrator and is stored in the directory store database.

2. A user creates and sends a message with the GroupWise client. The address book is used to locate the recipient, and this process accesses the directory store information.

3. The message transfer system sends the message to the recipient's message store. The information in the directory store is used by the message transfer system to indicate the path to use to move the message.

4. The recipient uses the GroupWise client to read the messages located in the recipient's message store.

> Make sure you can list the features of GroupWise and the basic process of how messages are handled.

In the following sections, we detail the various GroupWise components.

GroupWise Client

The GroupWise client enables the user to interact with the GroupWise system. The client is available for a mixture of desktop operating systems: Windows 3.x, Windows 95/98, Windows NT Workstation, Macintosh, and Unix. Actions the user can perform with the GroupWise client include the following:

➤ Accessing and managing documents in the GroupWise library

➤ Creating personal calendars

➤ Creating, sending, and receiving email messages

➤ Managing his or her mailbox for incoming and outgoing messages

➤ Scheduling meetings with other GroupWise users

Message Transfer System

The message transfer system is a key component of GroupWise. This system handles the movement of messages between the sender and the recipient. The GroupWise messaging system consists of two main components:

➤ Message Transfer Agent (MTA)

➤ Post Office Agent (POA)

If the message is crossing geographical locations, one or more of these processes may exist in the complete transfer of the message. In addition, if the message is destined for outside the GroupWise system, such as the Internet, gateways are also included in the message delivery path.

Administration Program

The GroupWise administration program or module is accessible within NetWare Administrator and is provided by snap-ins. This program provides the interface for managing the various GroupWise items, and it cannot be run separate from NetWare Administrator.

The Message, Directory, And Document Stores

The message store holds messages for users so they can access their messages at convenient times. The contents of the message store are located on a server or servers that can be accessed with the GroupWise client. When a GroupWise user sends a message to another user, a copy of the message is stored in the message store. This type of message architecture is called *store-and-forward*. The messages are stored in a database and large attachments are stored as files.

To enable GroupWise to operate efficiently, a separate directory is used to store GroupWise user information, such as names, departments, and telephone numbers. This directory may also contain information about the user's location. This directory store is a distributed database that's stored at several locations so it's readily available to the GroupWise users. Whenever there's a change to the directory store database, the information is sent to the other copies of the database through a process called *directory synchronization*. Whenever a component in GroupWise needs directory information, the directory store is accessed, not NDS.

The directory store provides message-routing information that's used by the message transfer system to determine how messages are delivered to the recipients, and it provides GroupWise address book information that allows users to efficiently search for other GroupWise users.

For example, here's a typical course of events that demonstrates the role of the directory store in a single-domain, single-post office GroupWise system:

1. A GroupWise object is created, modified, or deleted in NetWare Administrator.

2. The changed information is stored in NDS. If there are NDS replicas for the corresponding portion of the NDS tree, the changes are sent to the NDS replicas.

3. The GroupWise domain administrative input queue receives an administrative message from NetWare Administrator when the changes occur.

4. The MTA takes the administrative message and updates the GroupWise directory store.

5. Any changes to user NDS properties, such as a user's telephone number, are automatically synchronized between NDS and GroupWise.

The document store component is unique to GroupWise and does not exist in other similar software. This component allows workgroup users to manage shared documents and files. The documents are stored and managed from GroupWise libraries. A common use of this component is in the legal industry to track changes in documents that are handled by several individuals.

ManageWise

ManageWise is a comprehensive package that allows you to manage mixed networks of various desktop operating systems and server operating systems. For example, you can monitor NDS information as well as NetWare and Windows NT Server events and operations. ManageWise is used for the following tasks:

- Managing and monitoring servers
- Managing and analyzing network traffic
- Managing and taking inventory of network assets
- Enabling virus protection for the entire network
- Managing user desktops

> *Note:* *User desktops can be handled with ManageWise through the implementation of Z.E.N.works (Zero Effort Networks). A copy of Z.E.N.works is provided with ManageWise. For more information on Z.E.N.works, see the online documentation at www.novell.com/documentation/lg/zen/docui/index.html.*

The various functions that ManageWise includes are provided through a graphical interface called the *ManageWise Console* (see Figure 25.2). These ManageWise features are covered in the following sections.

Managing And Monitoring Servers

ManageWise can be configured to monitor and manage servers. On a NetWare server, more than 2,000 server conditions can be periodically or continuously monitored. This information can be useful for analyzing trends, bottlenecks, and performance values. Some of the server management features available in ManageWise include the following:

- **Multiple server monitoring** By installing ManageWise on several servers, you can compare their performances and optimize their settings from a single location.

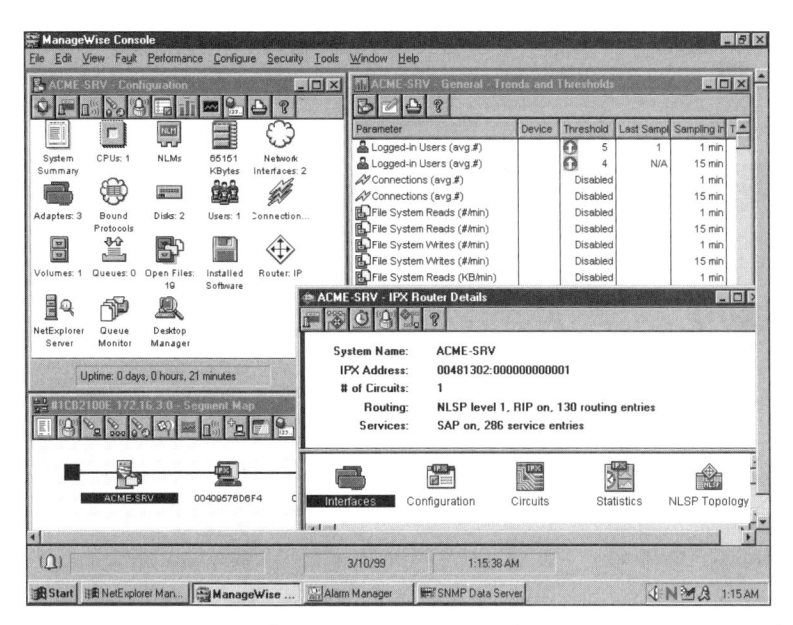

Figure 25.2 Various functions running on the ManageWise Console.

➤ **Continuous monitoring** For around-the-clock management, ManageWise allows you to monitor devices 24 hours a day, 7 days a week. This information can be used for trend analysis and for tracking down problems before they reach dangerous levels.

➤ **Server optimization** With the information collected by ManageWise, you can optimize the servers for their specific services.

➤ **Print queue management and monitoring** Print queue usage and information can be monitored and managed with ManageWise. Usage information can be presented in tabular or graphical format.

Managing And Analyzing Network Traffic

ManageWise includes the NetWare LANalyzer Agent, which is used to analyze network traffic. The information collected with the LANalyzer Agent software can be used to develop network traffic trends and to troubleshoot network traffic-related issues. ManageWise supports the Internet Protocol (IP), Internetwork Packet Exchange (IPX), Systems Network Architecture (SNA), and AppleTalk network protocols. The network traffic features available with ManageWise include the following:

➤ **Traffic analysis** You can sort the collected network traffic information to display the network entities producing the most traffic. You can monitor and capture network packets to determine which activities are creating the greatest demand.

➤ **Troubleshooting** Network packets can be captured and displayed to help troubleshoot connectivity issues. Duplicate network addresses, packet errors, and service and transmission media problems can also be detected with ManageWise.

Managing And Taking Inventory Of Network Assets

With ManageWise asset management and inventory, you can collect hardware and software component information that you can use for troubleshooting, documenting, and forecasting network trends. These features are handled by the NetExplorer software component and include the following:

➤ **Automatic discovery** You can configure ManageWise to automatically discover and collect information on the network's servers, workstations, and routers.

➤ **Network maps** The information collected can be displayed as graphical maps of the network. Items on the map are directly linked to tools so you can monitor and manage the various devices. An internetwork map displays an overview of the network's topology. A segment map presents all the devices located on a specified network segment. A custom map can be used to document the wide area network (WAN) and key service providers and elements.

➤ **Asset inventory** ManageWise detects hardware and software components of the devices it discovers. The components include processor type and speed, physical memory installed, and software applications for both servers and workstations. You also have the ability to customize items you want to scan as well as the desired information.

➤ **Network address management** ManageWise can present a table of all network address in use for IP and IPX, which can be useful for resolving duplicate addresses.

Enabling Virus Protection For The Entire Network

ManageWise includes a virus protection component that can be applied to the entire network. The anti-virus components can be applied to servers or workstations, or both. The ManageWise virus protection features include the following:

➤ **Scanning** ManageWise uses both pattern-based scanning to identify known viruses and rules-based algorithms to locate virus-like behavior as well as viruses designed specifically to hide from scanners.

➤ **Configurable scanning actions** You can configure ManageWise to scan when files are transferred to and/or from the server, to scan workstations at login, and to scan servers at specific times. Checking for viruses at login is a useful feature for mobile users with laptops who log into your network.

➤ **Actions** ManageWise can be configured to perform a variety of actions on infected files when a virus is detected—quarantine, rename, clean, and delete.

> **ALERT** Make sure you can list the basic features of ManageWise.

BorderManager

In recent years, more and more networks have included the capability for users to access the Internet from their desktops. However, bringing the Internet to a network also brings along security risks. To help reduce these security problems, network administrators install firewalls between the Internet and the company's network.

The term *firewall* is derived historically from the use of brick walls placed between wood houses to prevent the spread of fire. In a network, a firewall provides a mechanism to control both inbound and outbound access between networks. This helps reduce unauthorized access to a company's intranet from the Internet or any external network. A firewall can be used between a company's networks in addition to foreign networks. It can also be used to control which resources users can access on the Internet.

Firewalls commonly contain one for more of the following components:

➤ **Application gateways** These are also referred to as *application-level proxies*. These gateways provide access control at the Application layer of the Open Systems Interconnection (OSI) model and are generally considered to be the most secure type of firewall. Control can also include implementations at the Presentation layer of the OSI model.

➤ **Circuit gateways** These are also referred to as *circuit-level proxies*. Circuit gateways function at the Session layer of the OSI) model to verify that the TCP or UDP requests are valid. A gateway can replace the IP address of the requester with its own IP address before allowing access to the company's network. The gateway can also include routing policies that are based on protocols such as the Hypertext Transfer Protocol (HTTP).

▶ **Packet-filtering routers** These are also referred to as *screening routers* and are used to restrict inbound traffic. They prevent access by filtering out unauthorized IP addresses and port numbers.

BorderManager's name is based on its role—providing border management between a company's private corporate network and the public Internet. Services provided by BorderManager include the following:

▶ Controlling and monitoring a company's Internet access. This includes both inbound and outbound traffic.

▶ Improving Internet access performance by providing accelerators.

▶ Controlling access to Internet content for users based on the service requested and/or information content, as shown in Figure 25.3.

The firewall components in BorderManager include many functions, which are covered in the following paragraphs.

Novell Internet Access Server (NIAS) 4.1 provides routing and connectivity services. The version of NIAS in BorderManager replaces NetWare Connect 2 and NetWare MultiProtocol Router (MPR) 3.1 and has improved functions over NIAS 4. NIAS functions include the following:

▶ **IPX gateway** Similar to NAT, this gateway can translate IPX addresses to addresses permissible on the external network.

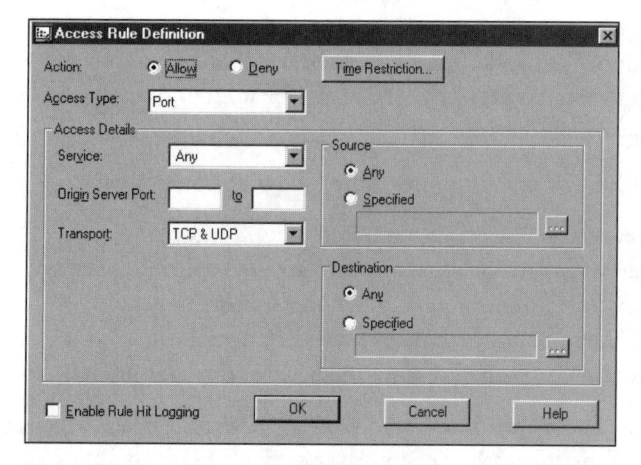

Figure 25.3 A sample BorderManager rules setup.

Additional Novell Services

- **Multiprotocol routing** Allows you to route various types of protocols.

- **Network Address Translation (NAT)** Many networks use IP addresses on their network machines that are not registered on the Internet. NAT provides the ability to translate an unregistered IP address to a registered IP address that can be used on the Internet. NAT functions at the Network layer of the OSI model.

  Note: Network Address Translation is also referred to as Network Address Translator.

- **Packet filtering** This operates at the Transport, Network, and Data Link layers of the OSI model.

Remote access to a network is provided by BorderManager with NIAS Remote Access. This service allows users to access their company's network from a dial-up connection.

IP Gateway software in BorderManager functions at the Application, Session, and Network layers of the OSI model and provides two services:

- **IPX to IP Gateway** This allows IPX-only network clients to access an IP network.

- **IP to IP Gateway** This is used by NetWare 5 networks that are using the Compatibility Mode Driver. This gateway translates unregistered internal IP address to registered IP addresses.

Proxy cache software services place a user's Internet requests in memory cache. This improves Internet content access performance because the user's browser can pull the information from memory, which is faster than obtaining the information from the source server on the Internet. Proxy caches typically function at the Presentation and Application layers of the OSI model. A proxy cache can increase performance when it's configured as one of the following three types of proxies:

- **Hierarchical proxy cache** This type of cache allows the administrator to place multiple caches in the network that store frequently accessed information. These are particularly useful in a WAN when placed at strategic Internet access points, because they provide users Web content information from cache instead of retrieving it from the source Web server.

- **HTTP accelerator** This is also referred to as a *Web server accelerator* or *reverse proxy*. These types of proxies are placed between the company's intranet Web servers and the users. When this information is placed in a reverse proxy cache, delivery of the information to the users is considerably faster than retrieving the information from storage—95 to 100 percent of Web site content is cacheable.

➤ **Standard proxy cache** This is also referred to as a *client accelerator*. When configured as a standard proxy cache, BorderManager uses its memory to store Web pages that are frequently accessed by the users. This improves user performance, especially when the Internet is congested.

The Virtual Private Network (VPN) feature in BorderManager allows an organization to create secure connections between its intranets across the Internet. Using NIAS 4.1 tunneling and several layers of encryption, an IPX or IP single point-to-point link appears as a tunnel, which can be used at full speed over T1 and T3 lines. This is a cost-effective solution for organizations because BorderManager provides secure networks without having to support expensive, dedicated private lines. The initial secure network-to-network link is established using Diffie-Hellman public key, private key encryption. VPNs operate at the Application, Presentation, Session, Transport, Network, and Data Link layers of the OSI model.

By incorporating the following functions in BorderManager, you can provide a complete firewall for a network:

➤ A packet-filtering gateway (by implementing NAT and the packet-filtering functions of NIAS 4.1)

➤ Circuit-level gateway functions (when the IP gateway is configured)

➤ Application gateway services (when the proxy cache is configured)

➤ VPN

> **EXAM ALERT:** Make sure you can list the basic features of BorderManager and know how BorderManager can be configured as a firewall.

NDS For NT

Many Novell networks include a mixture of different application server operating systems, such as Windows NT and Unix. Each of these environments includes its own security system, which needs to be maintained in addition to the NDS network. This can lead to additional administrative overhead and management costs. NDS for NT allows you to place Windows NT domains in the NDS tree. This provides a single access point for managing both the NDS and Windows NT worlds. When NDS for NT is installed, the NDS schema is extended, and NDS can accept and process all Windows NT domain requests that originate from other Windows NT Server clients, Windows NT Workstation clients, and other clients.

NDS for NT enables the administration of components of a mixed network from a single database—NDS. This allows for simpler administration of users, and eliminates the need to synchronize different databases and disparate databases that become unsynchronized. NDS for NT also removes the need for Windows NT domain trusts and also allows you to use NetWare 5 user templates to create new accounts and to modify existing accounts. NDS maintains the proper password format for each operating system, so the user only needs to authenticate to NDS.

NDS for NT is a different solution than Novell Administrator for NT, which synchronizes accounts between the Windows NT database and NDS. In this product, the administrator needs to maintain separate accounts in NDS and Windows NT. In addition, domain trusts may need to be created and maintained with Novell Administrator for NT. NDS for NT allows you to set up access to resources in different Windows NT domains without the need for trusts. Also, whenever NDS is replicated across different servers, fault tolerance is present for users to gain access to NDS and Windows NT services.

Moving user accounts in Windows NT domains is not as simple as it sounds. The account needs to be re-created in the destination domain and deleted in the source domain. In addition, any resource permissions and files need to be re-created and/or moved to the destination domain. With NDS for NT, Windows NT domains are treated like groups. All you need to do is to assign the existing NDS account rights in the destination domain and remove the permissions in the source domain. Furthermore, you can assign a single user operator role with NDS for NT, which cannot be accomplished through NDS operator groups.

When a network using NDS for NT removes an account from NDS, all permissions to the Novell and Windows NT environments disappear. Because only one instance of the account was present, no additional Windows NT accounts are available that would allow unauthorized access to the Windows NT environment.

Windows NT applications that depend on domain services occur as if NDS for NT was not present. When a request to a domain occurs, NDS for NT redirects the request to NDS instead of the Windows NT database. The application is unaware of NDS for NT because the information returned from NDS is in the proper format the application expects.

NDS for NT contains several components that allow you to maintain and manage Windows NT domains in NDS. These are SAMSRV.DLL, Domain Object Wizard, Novell Client for NT, NetWare Administrator, and Mailbox Manager for Exchange. We discuss these components in the following sections.

The SAMSRV.DLL Component

In a Windows NT domain, the accounts are stored in a database, and communications to and from the database occur through a component called SAMSRV.DLL. Applications that need to communicate with the database, such as User Manager For Domains and NETLOGON, make a request to SAMLIB.DLL. Then, SAMLIB.DLL communicates with SAMSRV.DLL using remote procedure calls (RPCs). If the application is running on the same machine where the accounts are stored, the RPCs occur internally. If the application is running on another machine, the RPCs are sent across the network to the Windows NT Server where the accounts reside. SAMDRV.DLL then accesses the account database, which is referred to as the *SAM* or *Security Accounts Manager*.

When NDS for NT is installed, the Microsoft-provided file SAMSRV.DLL is renamed to MSSAMSRV.DLL, and a new Novell-provided SAMSRV.DLL file is installed. Now when an application makes a request to the SAM database, the request is passed to SAMLIB.DLL, then to SAMDRV.DLL, and then to NDS (instead of the Windows NT SAM database). All security information and access requests are now handled in NDS—all through the replacement of one file on the Windows NT machine.

The proper order in which to install NDS for NT is on all the Windows NT primary domain controllers (PDCs) first and then on the backup domain controllers (BDCs). Furthermore, you don't need to install NDS for NT on Windows NT member servers because they're already members of a domain that's incorporated in NDS. To maintain the integrity of the environment, every time the Windows NT Servers running NDS for NT are restarted, the shutdown process checks to make sure the Novell version of SAMSRV.DLL is present. If it isn't, it's copied onto the server so it's available when the Windows NT Server is started.

The Domain Object Wizard Component

The Domain Object Wizard is run automatically when the Windows NT Server is rebooted after NDS for NT is installed. When it's run for the first time, it extends the NDS schema to allow Windows NT domains to exist in NDS. The tool is also used to migrate the domains from Windows NT into NDS. The wizard allows you to specify where in NDS the domain object resides. You can also associate existing NDS accounts with Windows NT domain accounts. The Domain Object Wizard is also responsible for renaming the Microsoft-provided SAMSRV.DLL file and installing the Novell-provided SAMSRV.DLL file. When NDS for NT is installed with the location defaults, the tool can be accessed from the Start menu. You can also remove NDS for NT from the Windows NT Server by running the Domain Object Wizard at any time (see Figure 25.4).

The Other Components

Every Windows NT Server running NDS for NT must also run Novell Client for NT. If the client is not already installed, the NDS for NT installation process will install the client.

For NetWare Administrator to properly view and manage the domain objects in NDS, snap-ins for NetWare Administrator must be present. These are installed the first time NDS for NT is installed in the tree.

The final component in NDS for NT is the Mailbox Manager for Exchange. Exchange is an email, scheduling, and workgroup application that runs on Windows NT Servers. Instead of managing another set of accounts in the Exchange database, NDS for NT includes the Mailbox Manager for Exchange, which allows you to manage all Exchange account information in NDS. Any changes made in NetWare Administrator are automatically synchronized with the Exchange database on the Windows NT Server.

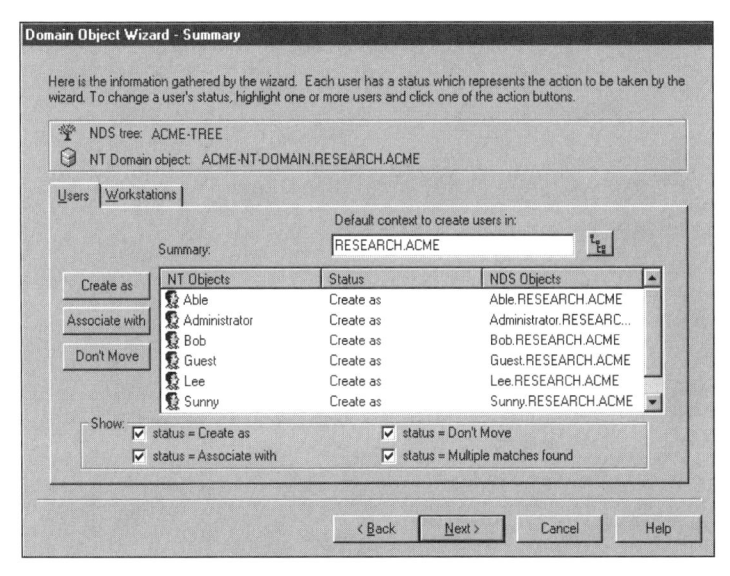

Figure 25.4 NDS for NT's Domain Object Wizard.

Chapter 25

> **TIP:** With the current release of NDS for NT, if you, as an administrator, make a change to an Exchange account with the Microsoft-provided Exchange managers, the information will not be synchronized with NDS. You can, however, manually synchronize the information between Exchange and NDS.

> **EXAM ALERT:** Make sure you can list the features of NDS for NT. In addition, make sure you can describe the process of events that occurs when a request is made to the SAM database when NDS for NT is running.

Practice Questions

Question 1

> Which of the following is a major feature of ManageWise?
> - a. It's used to deliver a hostname to the workstation so the agent can locate the workstation.
> - b. It's used to monitor server events, not workstation activities.
> - c. It's used to manage NetWare and Windows NT Server events.
> - d. It's used to deliver virus information messages to network users.
> - e. It's used to incorporate Windows NT domains in NDS so they can be easily managed.

The correct answer is c. Hostnames are not delivered to workstations by any product features discussed in this chapter. Therefore, answer a is incorrect. ManageWise can be used to monitor server and workstation events. Therefore, answer b is incorrect. Information about viruses can be delivered with GroupWise. Therefore, answer d is incorrect. Managing Windows NT domains is a feature of NDS for NT. Therefore, answer e is incorrect.

Question 2

> Which of the following is a major feature of GroupWise?
> - a. It's used for the management of Exchange's message store from NetWare Administrator.
> - b. It's used to schedule appointments with other GroupWise users.
> - c. It's used to create a VPN for the secure delivery of email through the Internet.
> - d. It's used to manage Windows NT groups from within NDS.
> - e. It's used to cache frequently accessed Web pages to improve message delivery.

The correct answer is b. GroupWise includes an Exchange gateway for delivering messages between the systems, and one of NDS for NT's components allows for the management of Exchange from NDS. Therefore, answer a is incorrect. VPNs are created with BorderManager. Therefore, answer c is incorrect. Management of Windows NT groups in NDS is one of the features of

NDS for NT. Therefore, answer d is incorrect. Caching of Web content is another feature of BorderManager. Therefore, answer e is incorrect.

Question 3

Which of the following is a major function of BorderManager?
- ○ a. It's used to provide IP-to-IP gateway services.
- ○ b. It's used to cache frequently accessed document store files for improved performance.
- ○ c. It's used to provide virus detection services at the border of the corporate network and the Internet.
- ○ d. It's used to monitor software running on the user workstations to prevent unauthorized access to the Internet.
- ○ e. It's used to provide an interface between NDS and Windows NT accounts.

The correct answer is a. BorderManager does not cache GroupWise document store information. Therefore, answer b is incorrect. Virus detection services are provided with ManageWise. Therefore, answer c is incorrect. Software monitoring is another feature of ManageWise. Unauthorized Internet access is monitored at the BorderManager service, not at an end-user application. Therefore, answer d is incorrect. Management of Windows NT accounts is handled with NDS for NT. Therefore, answer e is incorrect.

Question 4

Which of the following is a major function of NDS for NT?
- ○ a. It has the ability to manage NDS partitions in Windows NT directory services.
- ○ b. It's used to incorporate Windows NT workstations into NDS for easier management of the workstations.
- ○ c. It's used to provide a mechanism to synchronize user accounts between NDS and NT.
- ○ d. It's used to incorporate Windows NT domains into NDS to reduce the administrative overhead of duplicate accounts in Windows NT and NDS.
- ○ e. It's used to provide a mechanism to migrate Windows NT Servers to NetWare 5 servers.

Additional Novell Services **431**

The correct answer is d. Windows NT does not a have "directory services" in the same sense as NetWare 5. Therefore, answer a is incorrect. Incorporating Windows NT workstations is a function of the Novell Administrator for NT product. Therefore, answer b is incorrect. Synchronizing accounts is another feature of Novell Administrator for NT, and NDS for NT eliminates the duplication of Windows NT accounts. Therefore, answer c is incorrect. NDS for NT is not a migration tool for server operating systems. Therefore, answer e is incorrect.

Question 5

What's the role of the directory store in GroupWise?

- ○ a. It's used to store all documents so changes and editors can be tracked.
- ○ b. It's the location where users go to request more storage space for their email and attachments.
- ○ c. It's a distributed database of GroupWise user information.
- ○ d. It holds all user messages so the user can access and read the messages at a convenient time.
- ○ e. It processes the transfer of messages between sender and recipient.

The correct answer is c. The document store manages shared documents and files to track changes. Therefore, answer a is incorrect. There is no place within GroupWise to request additional storage space. Therefore, answer b is incorrect. The message store holds messages for users. Therefore, answer d is incorrect. The message transfer system is responsible for moving messages. Therefore, answer e is incorrect.

Question 6

What's the role of SAMSRV.DLL on a Windows NT Server running NDS for NT?

- ○ a. It's used to handle the management of the Windows NT SAM stored on the Windows NT Server.
- ○ b. It's used to redirect Windows NT SAM requests to NDS for processing.
- ○ c. It's used to import Windows NT domain information into NDS.
- ○ d. It's used to redirect NDS requests to the Windows NT SAM for processing.
- ○ e. It extends the schema of the Windows NT domain so NDS information can be stored on the Windows NT Server.

The correct answer is b. NDS for NT eliminates the need to manage the Windows NT SAM database. Therefore, answer a is incorrect. The Domain Object Wizard allows you to import Windows NT domain information into NDS. Therefore, answer c is incorrect. Because answer b is correct, answer d is incorrect. Windows NT does not have a schema to extend. Therefore, answer e is incorrect.

Question 7

What can the LANalyzer Agent in ManageWise do?

- ○ a. Periodically discover network elements
- ○ b. Scan for viruses and perform the configured action
- ○ c. Analyze network traffic to develop trends for troubleshooting
- ○ d. Redirect ManageWise SNMP traps to the ManageWise Console
- ○ e. Analyze the network topology and protocols

The correct answer is c. The NetExplorer component of ManageWise performs the network entities search. Therefore, answer a is incorrect. Virus scanning is performed by another element of ManageWise. Therefore, answer b is incorrect. LANalyzer does not redirect SNMP traps to the ManageWise Console. Therefore, answer d is incorrect. LANalyzer can be used to analyze network protocols but not network topology. Therefore, answer e is incorrect.

Question 8

> What are some of the components of a firewall? [Choose the three best answers]
> - a. Packet-filtering router
> - b. NIAS 4.1
> - c. Circuit gateways
> - d. Application gateways
> - e. Z.E.N.works

The correct answers are a, c, and d. NIAS 4.1 is an implementation in BorderManager, not a generic piece of software. Therefore, answer b is incorrect. Z.E.N.works is a component used to manage workstations. Therefore, answer e is incorrect.

Question 9

> At which layers of the OSI model does a VPN operate?
> - a. Session, Transport, Presentation, Application
> - b. Physical, Session, Transport, Presentation, Application
> - c. Data Link, Network, Session, Presentation, Application
> - d. Network, Transport, Session, Presentation, Application
> - e. Data Link, Network, Transport, Session, Presentation, Application

The correct answer e. Because answer e is correct, all the other choices are incorrect.

Question 10

How can a proxy cache improve Internet access for users?

○ a. Frequently accessed Web pages are placed in the proxy cache server memory.

○ b. It has the ability to open up more than one port for increased access speed.

○ c. Frequently accessed Web pages are stored on the proxy cache server.

○ d. It can create a secure port for the secure transfer of data.

○ e. It allows the filtering of specific information.

The correct answer is a. Opening additional ports is not a function of a proxy cache server. Therefore, answer b is incorrect. Because answer a is correct, answer c is incorrect (plus, storing Web pages on disk defeats the purpose of memory cache). VPNs handle secure connections for data transfer. Therefore, answer d is incorrect. Filtering of information is not handled by a proxy cache server but by packet-filtering components. Therefore, answer e is incorrect.

Question 11

What's the purpose of the message store in GroupWise?

○ a. To handle and process the delivery of messages from sender to recipient

○ b. To store messages so they can be read at a later time

○ c. To store the rules for delivery of messages to specific users

○ d. To store forwarded messages that you can then delete at a later date

○ e. To hold messages that cannot be delivered because of addressing errors

The correct answer is b. Delivery of messages is handled by the Message Transfer Agent. Therefore, answer a is incorrect. Delivery path information is stored in the directory store. Therefore, answer c is incorrect. The message store does not store forwarded messages or undeliverable messages only—it stores all messages. Therefore, answers d and e are incorrect.

Question 12

> Which of the following services are available in ManageWise?
>
> ○ a. Virus protection, discovery of network components, and management of Windows NT Server domains
>
> ○ b. Virus protection, management of multiple servers, and management of Windows NT Server domains
>
> ○ c. Virus protection, management of desktops, network traffic analysis, and management of Windows NT Server domains
>
> ○ d. Virus protection, management of desktops, network traffic analysis, server management and monitoring, and inventory of network assets
>
> ○ e. Virus protection, management of Windows NT Server domains, network traffic analysis, server management and monitoring, and inventory of network assets

The correct answer is d. Management of Windows NT domains is a feature of NDS for NT. Therefore, answers a, b, c, and e are incorrect.

Question 13

You have recently installed BorderManager on a new NetWare 5 server to create a firewall between the company's network and the Internet. GroupWise was installed a month ago, but recently users have complained that their email is very slow. Since that time, you have installed ManageWise and have collected traffic information for one week. With this information, you decide to subdivide the network to add a third logical network. Users are no longer complaining about slow access, but users accessing the Windows NT fax server are complaining about having to log into the fax server again. You first decide to run NetWare Administrator from SYS:\PUBLIC\WIN95 to synchronize NDS and NT domain account information. When you expand the container where the domain object resides, you notice the domain object's icon is different. It's now a rounded square with a question mark, and when you double-click on it to get details, nothing happens. You suspect there may be some problems. Which of the following actions do you take?

○ a. Run DSREPAIR on the server console that holds replicas of the partition where the domain object resides.

○ b. Run the version of NetWare Administrator supplied with GroupWise to view the domain objects properly.

○ c. Install NDS for NT again so the schema is extended for viewing and managing the Windows NT domain objects properly.

○ d. Reinstall GroupWise, because after NDS for NT is installed, you need to reinstall any additional Novell products so their information is properly registered in NDS.

○ e. Run NetWare Administrator from the SYS:\PUBLIC\WIN32 directory.

The correct answer is e. Object icons with a yellow circle usually indicate an NDS error or inconsistency. Therefore, answer a is incorrect. The version of NetWare Administrator for GroupWise does not display the NDS for NT objects. Therefore, answer b is incorrect. The schema for NDS cannot be re-extended. Therefore, answer c is incorrect. It would be very impractical to have to reinstall all your server applications. Therefore, answer d is incorrect. This question is tricky because you need to remember the symptoms of NDS problems, that the version of NetWare Administrator for GroupWise does not show NDS for NT objects and that the directory for the NetWare 5 common utilities is SYS:\PUBLIC\WIN32.

Need To Know More?

www.novell.com/catalog/bg/bge14315.html contains a detailed description of NDS for NT 2.

www.novell.com/catalog/bg/bge34190.html contains information about BorderManager Enterprise Edition 3.

www.novell.com/catalog/bg/bge44602.html contains a detailed description of GroupWise 5.5.

www.novell.com/catalog/bg/bge54102.html contains information about ManageWise 2.6.

www.novell.com/catalog/qr/sne14315.html contains the Product Brief for NDS for NT 2.

www.novell.com/catalog/qr/sne34190.html contains the Product Brief for BorderManager Enterprise Edition 3.

www.novell.com/catalog/qr/sne44602.html contains the Product Brief for GroupWise 5.5.

www.novell.com/catalog/qr/sne54102.html contains the Product Brief for ManageWise 2.6.

Sample Test

In this chapter, we provide pointers to help you develop a successful test-taking strategy, including how to choose proper answers, how to decode ambiguity, how to work within the Novell testing framework, how to decide what you need to memorize, and how to prepare for the test. At the end of the chapter, we include 73 questions on subject matter pertinent to Novell Test 050-640, "NetWare 5 Advanced Administration." Good luck!

Questions, Questions, Questions

There should be no doubt in your mind that you're facing a test full of specific and pointed questions. NetWare 5 Advanced Administration is a form exam that consists of 73 questions that you can take up to 105 minutes to complete. This means you must study hard so you can answer as many questions as possible correctly, without resorting to guesses.

> *Note:* *We expect Novell to change this test to an adaptive format eventually. See Chapter 1 for more information on adaptive testing.*

For this exam, questions belong to one of six basic types:

- Multiple-choice questions with a single answer
- Multiple-choice questions with multiple answers
- Multipart questions with a single answer
- Multipart questions with multiple answers
- Operate a simulated NetWare console or utility interface
- Pick one or more spots on a graphic

Always take the time to read each question at least twice before selecting an answer, and always look for an Exhibit button as you examine each question. Exhibits include graphics information related to a question. An exhibit is usually a screen capture of program output or GUI information that you must examine to analyze the question's contents and formulate an answer. The Exhibit button brings up graphics and charts used to help explain a question, provide additional data, or illustrate page layout or program behavior.

Not every question has only one answer; many questions require multiple answers. Therefore, it's important to read each question carefully to determine how many answers are necessary or possible, and to look for additional hints or instructions when selecting answers. Such instructions often occur in brackets, immediately following the question itself (as they do for all multiple-choice, multiple-answer questions).

Simulation questions can be a mixed blessing. These task-oriented questions allow you to demonstrate your abilities to complete a certain task or to apply some analysis or management technique. The NetWare Administrator utility appears particularly often in NetWare 5 simulation questions because it's the nerve center for NetWare administration. This means it's essential for you to spend some time familiarizing yourself with the key administration and management tools in NetWare 5 so you'll be ready when simulations show up in test questions.

Picking Proper Answers

Obviously, the only way to pass any exam is to select enough of the right answers to obtain a passing score. However, Novell's exams are not standardized like the SAT and GRE exams, and they can sometimes be quite a bit more challenging. In some cases, questions can be hard to follow or filled with technical vocabulary, and deciphering them can be difficult. In those cases, you may need to rely on answer-elimination skills. Almost always, at least one answer out of the possible choices for a question can be eliminated immediately because it matches one of these conditions:

➤ The answer does not apply to the situation.

➤ The answer describes a nonexistent issue, an invalid option, or an imaginary state.

➤ The answer may be eliminated because of the question itself.

After you eliminate all answers that are obviously wrong, you can apply your retained knowledge to eliminate further answers. Look for items that sound correct but refer to actions, commands, or features that are not present or not available in the situation that the question describes.

If you're still faced with a blind guess among two or more potentially correct answers, reread the question. Try to picture how each of the possible remaining answers would alter the situation. Be especially sensitive to terminology; sometimes the choice of words (*remove* instead of *disable*) can make the difference between a right answer and a wrong one.

Only when you've exhausted your ability to eliminate answers, and you're still unclear about which of the remaining possibilities is correct, should you guess at an answer (or answers). Guessing gives you at least some chance of getting a question right; just don't be too hasty when making a blind guess.

Decoding Ambiguity

Novell exams have a reputation for including straightforward questions. You won't have to worry much about deliberate ambiguity, but you will need a good grasp of the technical vocabulary involved with NetWare and related products to understand what some questions are trying to ask. In our experience with numerous Novell tests, we've learned that mastering the lexicon of Novell's technical terms pays off on every exam. The Novell tests are tough but fair, and they're deliberately made that way.

However, you need to brace yourself for one set of special cases. Novell tests are notorious for their use of double negatives and similar circumlocutions, such as

"What item is not used when creating a <insert your favorite task here>?" Our guess is that Novell includes such Byzantine language in its questions because it wants to make sure examinees can follow instructions to the letter, no matter how strangely worded those instructions might be. Although this may seem like a form of torture, it's actually good preparation for those circumstances where you have to follow instructions from technical manuals or training materials, which are themselves not quite in the same ballpark as great literature or even plain English. Even though we've been coached repeatedly to be on the lookout for this kind of stuff, it still fools us from time to time. So you need to be on the lookout yourself and try to learn from our mistakes.

The only way to beat Novell at this game is to be prepared. You'll discover that many exam questions test your knowledge of things that are not directly related to the issue raised by a question. This means that the answers from which you must choose, even incorrect ones, are just as much a part of the skill assessment as the question itself. If you don't know something about most aspects of administering NetWare 5, you may not be able to eliminate obviously wrong answers because they relate to a different area of the operating system than the one that's addressed by the question at hand. In other words, the more you know about administering NetWare in general, the easier it will be for you to tell a right answer from a wrong one.

Questions often give away their answers, but you have to read carefully to see the clues that point to those answers. Often, subtle hints appear in the question text in such a way that they seem almost irrelevant to the situation. You must realize that each question is a test unto itself and that you need to inspect and successfully navigate each question to pass the exam. Look for small clues, such as the mention of utilities, services, and configuration settings. Little things like these can point at the right answer if properly understood; if missed, they can leave you facing a blind guess.

Because mastering the technical vocabulary is so important to testing well for Novell, be sure to brush up on the key terms presented at the beginning of each chapter. You may also want to read through the Glossary at the end of this book the day before you take the test.

Working Within The Framework

The test questions appear in random order, and many elements or issues that receive mention in one question may also crop up in other questions. It's not uncommon to find that an incorrect answer to one question is the correct answer to another question, or vice versa. Take the time to read every answer to each question, even if you recognize the correct answer to a question immediately.

That extra reading may spark a memory or remind you about a networking feature or function that helps you on another question later in the exam.

Review each question carefully; test developers love to throw in a few tricky questions. Often, important clues are hidden in the wording or special instructions. Do your best to decode ambiguous questions; just be aware that some questions will be open to interpretation.

You might also want to use the piece of paper or the erasable plastic sheet that you were provided to jot some notes about questions that contain key information.

> Don't be afraid to take notes on what you see in various questions. Sometimes, what you record from one question—especially if it isn't as familiar as it should be or reminds you of the name or use of some utility or interface details—can help you with other questions later in the test.

Deciding What To Memorize

The amount of memorization you must undertake for an exam depends on how well you remember what you've read and how well you know the software by heart. If you're a visual thinker and can see drop-down menus and dialog boxes in your head, you won't need to memorize as much as someone who's less visually oriented. The tests will stretch your recollection of NetWare 5 concepts, tools, and technologies.

At a minimum, you'll want to memorize the following types of information:

➤ The upgrade and migration options for NetWare 5

➤ The features and functions of queue-based printing

➤ The basics of the NetWare 5 Java console's layout and its functions

➤ The backup and restore features of NetWare 5

➤ The basics of NDS security

➤ The Netscape FastTrack Web Server's features, functions, and utilities

If you work your way through this book and try to exercise the various capabilities of NetWare 5 that are covered throughout, you should have little or no difficulty mastering this material. Also, don't forget that The Cram Sheet at the front of the book is designed to capture the material that's most important to memorize; use this to guide your studies as well. Finally, don't forget to obtain and use Novell's Test Objectives for Course 570 as part of your planning and preparation process.

Preparing For The Test

The best way to prepare for the test—after you've studied—is to take at least one practice exam. We've included one here in this chapter for that reason; the test questions are located in the pages that follow. (Unlike the preceding chapters in this book, the answers don't follow the questions immediately; you'll have to flip to Chapter 27 to review the answers separately.)

Give yourself no more than 105 minutes to take the exam, keep yourself on the honor system, and don't look at earlier text in the book or jump ahead to the answer key. When your time is up or you've finished the questions, you can check your work in Chapter 27. Pay special attention to the explanations for the incorrect answers; these can also help to reinforce your knowledge of the material. Knowing how to recognize correct answers is good, but understanding why incorrect answers are wrong can be equally valuable.

Taking The Test

Relax. Once you're sitting in front of the testing computer, there's nothing more you can do to increase your knowledge or preparation. Take a deep breath, stretch, and start reading that first question.

There's no need to rush—you have plenty of time. If you can't figure out the answer to a question after a few minutes, though, you may want to guess and move on to leave more time for remaining unanswered questions. Remember that both easy and difficult questions are intermixed throughout the test in random order. Because you're taking a form test, you should watch your time carefully: Try to be one-quarter of the way done (18 questions) in at least 26 minutes, halfway done (37 questions) in at least 52 minutes, and three-quarters done (55 questions) in 78 minutes.

Set a maximum time limit for questions, and watch your time on long or complex questions. If you hit your time limit, you need to guess and move on. Don't deprive yourself of the opportunity to see more questions by taking too long to puzzle over answers, unless you think you can figure out the correct answer. Otherwise, you're limiting your opportunities to pass.

That's it for pointers. Here are some questions for you to practice on.

Question 1

NetWare 5 includes a new backup product and services. One of the components is referred to as a *host server*. What are the roles and/or functions of the host server? [Choose the two best answers]

- a. The physical backup device is attached to the host server.
- b. The backup data is stored on specially configured NSS volumes.
- c. The host server runs the Target Service Agents (TSAs) for all device types that can be backed up.
- d. NWBACK32.NLM is executed from the SYS:\SYSTEM directory and is used to set up and submit the backup jobs.
- e. The backup NLMs, such as SBCON and QMAN, are run on the host server.

Question 2

The DHCP protocol includes the ability to distribute IP addresses to requesters. Which of the following are valid methods for delivering IP addresses? [Choose the three best answers]

- a. Static allocation
- b. Dynamic allocation
- c. Manual allocation
- d. Automatic allocation
- e. Exclusion allocation

Question 3

NetWare 5 supports both the traditional file system and Novell Storage Services (NSS). Which of the following are advantages of the traditional file system over NSS? [Choose the four best answers]

- ❑ a. TTS cannot be used on NSS volumes.
- ❑ b. Disk suballocation can be enabled and disabled on traditional volumes but not on NSS volumes.
- ❑ c. NetWare 5 auditing can be enabled only for traditional NetWare volumes.
- ❑ d. Volume compression is a feature that's supported on traditional NetWare volumes.
- ❑ e. For fault tolerance, traditional volumes support disk mirroring whereas NSS volumes do not.

Question 4

When setting up a queue-based printing environment, what are the roles of the NDS Printer objects? [Choose the four best answers]

- ❑ a. Configuring who receives printer error messages
- ❑ b. Specifying printer operators and printer users
- ❑ c. Monitoring the status of the printer
- ❑ d. Specifying the connection types of the printer
- ❑ e. Prioritizing printer usage

Question 5

Administration of NDS can be divided into two categories. Which of the following answers describe tasks that should be performed by an enterprise NDS administrator? [Choose the three best answers]

- ❑ a. Manage the file systems of servers located in the various Organizational Unit containers
- ❑ b. Rename the tree with the DSNAME.NLM utility
- ❑ c. Manage and configure the network time synchronization strategy
- ❑ d. Configure and enable auditing of NDS and file system events
- ❑ e. Create and manage container administrators

Sample Test   **447**

Question 6

The NetWare 5 network you've been assigned to manage while the NDS administrator is on vacation is showing symptoms of NDS inconsistencies. You decide to perform some actions to eliminate the problems. Which of the following answers provides good NDS repair guidelines?

○ a. Two servers holding read/write replicas of the [Root] partition are reporting -625 errors. These two servers should be brought down to allow the rest of the system to correct itself.

○ b. Merging of partitions should not be performed while there are NDS problems. However, a partition can be created because there's no structural change to the database.

○ c. Let the system run for a few hours and monitor NDS activity during that time frame.

○ d. Use NDS Manager to check synchronization and partition continuity. If there are still errors, load DSREPAIR on a server not reporting errors and perform an unattended repair.

○ e. Change the master of the [Root] partition to a read-only replica because inconsistent NDS information cannot be written to those partition types.

Question 7

You've downloaded an HTML file that contains code that refers to a Java utility you want to run on your NetWare 5 server. Which of the following is the correct command for displaying the Java utility?

○ a. **JAVA DATA:\JAVAUTILS\WEBVIEW.HTML**

○ b. **DISPLAY DATA:\JAVAUTILS\WEBVIEW.HTML**

○ c. **APPLET DATA:\JAVAUTILS\WEBVIEW.HTML**

○ d. **JAVA APPLET DATA:\JAVAUTILS\WEBVIEW.HTML**

○ e. **DATA:\JAVAUTILS\WEBVIEW.HTML**

Question 8

The Widgets company has decided to upgrade its NetWare 4.11 servers to NetWare 5. The ACME-DATA server being upgraded has the following specifications:

- 166MHz Pentium processor
- 96MB RAM
- 50MB DOS partition
- 500MB SYS volume with 100MB free

Which of the following is the correct way to upgrade the ACME-DATA server?

○ a. Bring the server down and run INSTALL.BAT from the NetWare 5 installation CD-ROM.

○ b. Free up space on the SYS volume so at least 200MB is free. Then bring the server down and run INSTALL.BAT from the NetWare 5 installation CD-ROM.

○ c. Free up space on the SYS volume so at least 200MB is free. Run the Migration Wizard from a workstation and upgrade the NetWare 4.11 files to NetWare 5.

○ d. Free up space on the SYS volume so at least 200MB is free. Mount the NetWare 5 installation CD-ROM on the server and run INSTALL.BAT located at the root of the CD-ROM.

○ e. Bring down the server and increase the size of the NetWare partition. Then run INSTALL.BAT from the NetWare 5 installation CD-ROM.

Question 9

Which of the following is a function of NIAS?

❍ a. Network Information Attribute Services is configured so clients can access the network remotely.

❍ b. Novell Internet Access Services is used to set up a gateway to the Web server provided in NIAS.

❍ c. Novell Internet Access Services in NetWare 5 is used with NetWare Connect to allow clients remote access to the network.

❍ d. Novell Internet Access Server is used with ManageWise to monitor Internet access and usage.

❍ e. Novell Internet Access Server, which is provided with NetWare 5, can be configured to allow clients remote access to the network.

Question 10

One of Novell's suggested guidelines for replicas is to have more than one copy of each partition. Which of the following contains a recommended combination of replicas? [Choose the two best answers]

❑ a. A master replica of [Root] and a master replica of ACME are on ACME-SRV. A read/write replica of ACME is stored on ACME-SRV.

❑ b. A master replica of [Root] and a master replica of ACME are on ACME-SRV. A read/write replica of ACME is stored on RESEARCH-SRV, and a master replica of SALES is stored on SALES-SRV.

❑ c. A master replica of [Root] and a master replica of ACME are on ACME-SRV. A read/write replica of ACME and a read/write replica of [Root] are stored on RESEARCH-SRV.

❑ d. A master replica of [Root] and a master replica of ACME are on ACME-SRV. A master replica of ACME and a master replica of [Root] are stored on RESEARCH-SRV.

❑ e. A master replica of [Root] and a master replica of ACME are on ACME-SRV. A subordinate reference of ACME and a subordinate reference of SALES are stored on RESEARCH-SRV.

Question 11

Time zone information is typically stored in which NetWare 5 configuration file?

○ a. STARTUP.NCF

○ b. CONFIG.NCF

○ c. TIMEZONE.NCF

○ d. AUTOEXEC.NCF

○ e. CONFIG.SYS

Question 12

Which of the following options load the Netscape FastTrack Administrative Server? [Choose the two best answers]

❑ a. Executing ADMNSERV at the NetWare 5 server that runs the Netscape FastTrack Server

❑ b. Entering **http://ACMEWEB.ACME.COM:20098** as the URL in your Web browser, where 20098 refers to the Netscape FastTrack Server administrative port

❑ c. Running the ADMNSERV application on your workstation

❑ d. Entering **APPLET ACME.ACME.COM:20098** at the NetWare 5 server that runs the Netscape FastTrack Server

❑ e. Entering **ftp://ACMEWEB.ACME.COM:20098** as the URL in your Web browser, where 20098 refers to the Netscape FastTrack Server administrative port

Question 13

Which of the following satisfies the requirements for migrating a NetWare 3.x server to NetWare 5? [Choose the four best answers]

❑ a. 96MB of RAM on the NetWare 5 server

❑ b. An existing NetWare 5 network

❑ c. Pentium Pro processor on the NetWare 5 server

❑ d. IP connection between the NetWare 3.x server and the NetWare 5 server

❑ e. IPX connection between the NetWare 3.x server and the NetWare 5 server

Question 14

NetWare 5 gives you the capability to view and change values of the **SET** parameters. Which of the following methods allow you to view and change values of the **SET** parameters? [Choose the two best answers]

❑ a. SERVMAN.NLM

❑ b. MONITOR.NLM

❑ c. INSTALL.NLM

❑ d. NWSET.NLM

❑ e. The **SET** command

Question 15

There are four types of NDS replicas. Which two replica types can be used for authentication? [Choose the two best answers]

❑ a. Read-only

❑ b. Master

❑ c. Read/write

❑ d. Subordinate reference

❑ e. [Root]

Question 16

To administer DNS and DHCP in NetWare 5, the NDS schema must be extended. Which of the following are the three valid ways to extend the NDS schema? [Choose the three best answers]

❑ a. Install DNS and DHCP Services when the NetWare 5 server is installed.

❑ b. Choose Install in the NetWare 5 GUI and select Novell DNS/DHCP Services.

❑ c. Run DNIPINST in a console prompt window on your workstation.

❑ d. Run DNSDHCP at the NetWare 5 server console.

❑ e. Run DNIPINST at the NetWare 5 server console.

Question 17

DNS consists of three major components. What are they? [Choose the three best answers]

- a. Arbitrators
- b. Resolvers
- c. Domain name space and resource records
- d. DNS-DHCP Locator object
- e. Name servers

Question 18

You've performed some scheduled maintenance on the NetWare 5 network over the weekend. On Monday morning, users are complaining that logging into the server is extremely slow. Which of the following **SET** parameters probably needs to be increased?

- a. Minimum Service Processes
- b. Minimum Packet Receive Buffers
- c. Maximum Packet Receive Buffers
- d. Maximum Service Processes
- e. Allow LIP

Question 19

Which of the following are disadvantages of the NetWare 5 In-Place Upgrade when deciding to upgrade a NetWare 3.x server? [Choose the three best answers]

- a. Block suballocation cannot be enabled for existing volumes.
- b. Volume compression cannot be enabled for existing volumes.
- c. NSS cannot be used for any volumes.
- d. IP cannot be enabled and configured until after the upgrade is complete.
- e. Storage device drivers, such as AHA1540.DSK, cannot be used.

Question 20

In which directory are the NetWare 5 common administrative utilities located?

○ a. SYS:\PUBLIC

○ b. SYS:\SYSTEM

○ c. SYS:\PUBLIC\WIN95

○ d. SYS:\PUBLIC\WIN32

○ e. SYS:\SYSTEM\PUBLIC

Question 21

What's the default location of the primary document directory for the Netscape FastTrack Server?

○ a. SYS:\PUBLIC\NOVONYX\SUITESPOT\DOCS

○ b. SYS:\NOVONYX\SUITESPOT\DOCS

○ c. SYS:\JAVA\NOVONYX\SUITESPOT\DOCS

○ d. SYS:\NSFTS\NOVONYX\SUITESPOT\DOCS

○ e. SYS:\NETSCAPE\SUITESPOT\DOCS

Question 22

Which of the following commands loads ConsoleOne on a NetWare 5 server?

○ a. **STARTX**

○ b. **CONSOLEONE**

○ c. **STARTC1**

○ d. **C1START**

○ e. **JAVA C1**

Question 23

You've just completed an In-Place Upgrade. What are some of the post-upgrade tasks you should perform? [Choose the three best answers]

❏ a. Upgrade the client software on the Windows 95 machines to at least version 2.2.

❏ b. Modify any login scripts so the new names of the NetWare 5 users are placed in the **MAP** statements.

❏ c. Convert the old queue-based printing environment to NDPS because the pre-NetWare 5 queue-based printers will not operate in NetWare 5.

❏ d. Make sure the name of the new NetWare 5 server is placed in all login script **MAP** statements so the system doesn't have to rely on the Message Server property of the User object.

❏ e. Upgrade the client software on the Windows NT machines to at least version 4.50.

Question 24

Which NetWare 5 feature allows the storage of very large files—as large as 4TB?

○ a. Traditional NetWare file system

○ b. FAT32

○ c. Long name space

○ d. Novell Storage Services (NSS)

○ e. Consumers

Sample Test   455

Question 25

Which of the following best describes a NetWare 5 print queue?

○ a. A NetWare 5 print queue is a mapped drive letter created on the user's workstation that points to the queue on the server.

○ b. A NetWare 5 print queue is a directory created on the user's workstation that holds the print files before printing.

○ c. A NetWare 5 print queue is defined as a bindery-based object, so it's compatible with NetWare 4.x.

○ d. A NetWare 5 print queue is a specialized volume created to hold the print files so there's no risk of running out of space on the SYS volume.

○ e. A NetWare 5 print queue is a directory created on the server that holds the print files before printing.

Question 26

You've received an email from a container administrator indicating that the Long Term Cache Hit value is 76 percent on one of the servers. What's the significance of this value? [Choose the two best answers]

❑ a. It represents the cumulative percentage of requests for data that's in cache.

❑ b. It represents the total number of requests for data that's in cache.

❑ c. A value below 90 percent indicates that the server is not too busy fulfilling cache requests.

❑ d. A value below 90 percent indicates that more memory is needed.

❑ e. The value should be as close to 0 percent as possible, which indicates that the server is not too busy fulfilling cache requests.

Question 27

Changes to NDS are categorized as simple and complex. Which of the following are examples of simple NDS changes? [Choose the two best answers]

- ❏ a. Merging two partitions
- ❏ b. Changing the phone number for 500 User objects in a container through the use of a Template object
- ❏ c. Creating a partition
- ❏ d. Removing replicas from a server
- ❏ e. Changing the fax number of a User object

Question 28

Which of the following complaints are probable signs of NDS inconsistencies? [Choose the three best answers]

- ❏ a. When I go to change the phone number of a user in NetWare Administrator, there are these white squares with question marks next to some of the items.
- ❏ b. This is the container administrator for the SALES container. The trustee assignments I made yesterday for the WPUSERS group are no longer there.
- ❏ c. I can log into the NetWare 5 RESEARCH server, but when I go to access files on the HISTORY NetWare 3.x server, it indicates that my account is locked.
- ❏ d. It's taking about five minutes to log in.
- ❏ e. When I go to change the fax number of a user in NetWare Administrator, there are these yellow circles with question marks next to some of the items.

Question 29

A network administrator must perform three tasks before setting up NetWare 5 DNS or DHCP Services. What are these tasks? [Choose the three best answers]

- ❑ a. Make sure IP is installed and configured on the workstation used to configure DNS or DHCP.
- ❑ b. Extend the NDS schema for DNS and DHCP objects.
- ❑ c. Run DHCPSRVR.NLM at the server console to create the three default DNS and DHCP objects.
- ❑ d. Install the DNS/DHCP Management Console.
- ❑ e. Install the Novell Client on the management workstation.

Question 30

There are three types of DNS Zones. What are they? [Choose the three best answers]

- ❑ a. Secondary
- ❑ b. IN-ADDR-ARPA
- ❑ c. Primary
- ❑ d. Standard
- ❑ e. IP6.INT

Question 31

Which type of actions can the LANalyzer agent in ManageWise perform?

- ○ a. Scan for viruses and perform the configured action
- ○ b. Redirect ManageWise SNMP traps to the ManageWise Console
- ○ c. Periodically discover network elements
- ○ d. Analyze network traffic to develop trends and for troubleshooting
- ○ e. Analyze the network topology and protocols

Question 32

NetWare 5's protected address space feature offers several benefits. Which of the following are some of those benefits? [Choose the two best answers]

- ❏ a. Inactive code is placed in a swap file to free up physical memory resources.
- ❏ b. As soon as the modules within an address space are unloaded, the address space is terminated by the operating system.
- ❏ c. The operating system is protected from the failure of an application running in a protected address space.
- ❏ d. Modules are not allowed access to resources outside their own address space.
- ❏ e. Inactive data is placed in a swap file to free up physical memory resources.

Question 33

NetWare includes a feature that allows you to optimize the communication between clients and servers. This system reduces the number of acknowledgments and allows up to 64K of data to be sent. Which of the following matches this description?

- ○ a. Packet receive buffers
- ○ b. Reserved buffers
- ○ c. LIP
- ○ d. Packet burst
- ○ e. Event control blocks

Question 34

You've been called in to assist in configuring IP on a NetWare 5 server. Which server console command can you use to determine the current server protocol configuration?

- ○ a. **IPCON**
- ○ b. **CONFIG**
- ○ c. **NWCONFIG**
- ○ d. **INSTALL**
- ○ e. **MONITOR**

Question 35

What's the name of the utility for configuring and managing NetWare 5 FTP services?

○ a. Netscape FastTrack Server

○ b. FTPCON

○ c. UNICON

○ d. WEBSRV

○ e. NIAS

Question 36

On which of the following servers can you use the NetWare 5 In-Place Upgrade? [Choose the three best answers]

❏ a. NetWare 4.10

❏ b. Windows NT 3.51

❏ c. NetWare 2.2

❏ d. NetWare 4.11

❏ e. NetWare 3.11

Question 37

Which of the following statements satisfy the NetWare 5 SYS volume requirements? [Choose the two best answers]

❏ a. The amount of memory required to support the SYS volume is dependent on the size of the volume and any additional name spaces.

❏ b. The minimum size of the NetWare 5 SYS volume has to be at least 500MB.

❏ c. The INSTALL.NLM utility is used to view the SYS volume configuration information.

❏ d. The minimum size of the NetWare 5 SYS volume has to be at least 5,000MB.

❏ e. The NetWare 5 SYS volume can either be a traditional NetWare volume or a NSS volume.

Question 38

Which of the following are correct definitions of NSS storage groups? [Choose the two best answers]

- ❑ a. Storage groups represent specific types of physical devices, such as CD-ROMs and hard drives.
- ❑ b. Storage groups allow you to mount the server's DOS partition as a NetWare volume.
- ❑ c. Storage groups are created from the storage deposits discovered by the NSS providers and registered by the NSS consumers.
- ❑ d. Once storage groups are defined, you can create NSS volumes.
- ❑ e. Storage groups represent the space already occupied by the DOS partition and NetWare partitions, so the space cannot be used by NSS.

Question 39

What's the name of the workstation utility used to configure a backup and/or restore session in NetWare 5?

- ○ a. SBACKUP
- ○ b. NetWare Administrator
- ○ c. SBCON
- ○ d. NWBACK32
- ○ e. NetWare Backup/Restore

Question 40

Which NDS rights are necessary to allow a user to see a NDS object and to rename the object?

- ○ a. Browse and Rename
- ○ b. Read and Modify
- ○ c. File Scan and Modify
- ○ d. Read and Rename
- ○ e. Browse and Modify

Question 41

You've been out of town for a week. When you return, you notice that several objects in NetWare Administrator have a yellow circle with a question mark icon next to them. What's the proper procedure for fixing the problem?

○ a. Remove all read/write replicas from the servers and add read-only replicas.

○ b. Make sure the proper snap-ins are configured in the Snap-In directory under the SYS:\PUBLIC directory.

○ c. Reinstall DS.NLM to make sure the proper version is installed to view these objects.

○ d. Begin the process of NDS troubleshooting for NDS inconsistencies.

○ e. Do nothing. These are normal objects.

Question 42

A NetWare 5 server has crashed in the production tree and is not salvageable. The following actions must be performed:

1. Delete the Server object from the tree with NDS Manager.
2. Determine which replicas are stored on the crashed server.
3. Perform a continuity check to make sure no NDS errors are present.
4. Remove the crashed server's Volume objects from the tree with NetWare Administrator.

In which order should you perform these actions?

○ a. 2, 1, 3, 4

○ b. 1, 2, 3, 4

○ c. 2, 1, 4, 3

○ d. 1, 2, 4, 3

○ e. 4, 3, 2, 1

Question 43

What's the required format for importing DNS information into the NetWare 5 DNS environment?

- ○ a. NAMED
- ○ b. IPDNS
- ○ c. ZONE
- ○ d. BIND

Question 44

Which of the following are options that can be used with the **SWAP** command? [Choose the three best answers]

- ❑ a. **MIN**
- ❑ b. **DEL_SPACE**
- ❑ c. **MAX**
- ❑ d. **ADD_SPACE**
- ❑ e. **MIN_Free**

Question 45

You can configure a proxy cache to improve Internet access for users. Which of the following is a feature of a proxy cache?

- ○ a. It opens more than one port for increased access speed.
- ○ b. Frequently accessed Web pages are placed in the proxy cache server memory.
- ○ c. It creates a secure port for the secure transfer of data.
- ○ d. Frequently accessed Web pages are stored on the proxy cache server.
- ○ e. It allows the filtering of specific information so frequently accessed Web pages have priority.

Question 46

A pure IP NetWare 5 network has been installed, and you need to configure remote access to the server console. Which of the following files allows this type of remote console access?

○ a. RSPX

○ b. REMOTE

○ c. RCONAG6

○ d. NIAS

○ e. RCONSOLE

Question 47

What are the three ways the Netscape FastTrack Server can be stopped? [Choose the three best answers]

❏ a. Executing NSWEBDN at the server console

❏ b. Clicking on the Off button next to the server name on the Administration Server page

❏ c. Executing NSWEB at the server console

❏ d. Shutting down the Netscape FastTrack Administration Server

❏ e. Clicking on the Server Off button on the Server Manager page

Question 48

Which of the following protocols can be configured when using the In-Place Upgrade to upgrade a NetWare 4.11 server? [Choose the two best answers]

❏ a. IP

❏ b. ARP

❏ c. TCP

❏ d. IPX

❏ e. SPX

Question 49

Your company has decided to migrate its Novell 3.x servers to NetWare 5, and you want to use the Novell Upgrade Wizard. Which of the following scenarios is correct?

○ a. Load the NetWare 5 GUI screen on the server and choose the Upgrade Wizard from the Tools menu.

○ b. Access the NetWare 5 server console from a workstation and run the Upgrade Wizard from the remote console menus.

○ c. Run the Upgrade Wizard from a Windows NT workstation running Novell Client 4.50.

○ d. Run the Upgrade Wizard from a Windows 95 workstation running the Novell VLM client.

○ e. Run WIZARD.BAT from a DOS prompt on a Windows 95 workstation.

Question 50

Which of the following are migrated when using an across-the-wire migration to upgrade a NetWare 3.x server?

○ a. File trustee information, user accounts, and groups

○ b. File trustee information, user accounts, groups, and passwords

○ c. File trustee information, user accounts, groups, passwords, and account restrictions

○ d. File trustee information, user accounts, groups, and account restrictions

○ e. File trustee information, user accounts, groups, and account restriction (except for password properties)

Question 51

NetWare 5 file compression is designed not to interfere with daily activities. Which of the following statements concerning the default volume compression settings are correct? [Choose the two best answers]

❑ a. The server begins compressing files starting at 6:00 A.M.

❑ b. If the server determines that compressing the file will reduce the file's size 20 percent or greater, the file will be marked for compression.

❑ c. If a file has not been accessed for a month and the amount of disk savings is at least 20 percent, the file will be compressed during the next compression cycle.

❑ d. Volume compression cannot be enabled on a volume that's configured with disk suballocation.

❑ e. The server will stop compressing files when all the marked files have been compressed or at 12:00 A.M., whichever comes first.

Question 52

Which of the following is the proper definition of a NSS provider?

○ a. NSS providers scan the server's hard disk space to locate unused space.

○ b. NSS providers allow the SYS volume to use NSS because the providers support TTS.

○ c. NSS providers are separate NLMs that are installed to register free space with NSS storage areas.

○ d. NSS providers are added to the workstation connection software so the administrator can manage NSS volumes.

○ e. NSS providers scan the server's memory and determine which file blocks are in RAM and register this information with NSS.

Question 53

Which of the following is the proper syntax for loading the SALES-PS print server that is located in the .OU=AUSTIN,O=ACME container?

- ○ a. **PSERVER .SALES-PS.ACME.AUSTIN**
- ○ b. **PSERVER .SALES-PS.AUSTIN.ACME**
- ○ c. **PSERVER .SALES-PS.SALES.ACME**
- ○ d. **PSERVER ACME-PS**
- ○ e. **LOAD PSERVER .SALES-PS.AUSTIN.ACME.Root**

Question 54

Judy has been assigned the Browse and Inheritable rights to the OU=TEXAS.O=ACME container. She is also a trustee of O=ACME with the Create, Delete, Rename, and Inheritable rights. What are Judy's effective rights at OU=TEXAS.O=ACME?

- ○ a. Browse
- ○ b. Browse, Create, Delete, and Rename
- ○ c. Create, Delete, and Rename
- ○ d. Browse, Delete, Rename, and Read All Properties
- ○ e. Supervisor

Question 55

What are the default assignments of a newly created container object to itself? [Choose the two best answers]

- ❏ a. The Read Selected Property right to the container's Print Job Configuration (Non NDPS) property
- ❏ b. The Read Selected Property right to the container's Net Address property
- ❏ c. The Read right to All Properties
- ❏ d. The Write Selected Property right to the container's Print Job Configuration (Non NDPS) property
- ❏ e. The Read Selected Property right to the container's Login Script property

Sample Test **467**

Question 56

Which rights are required to create a partition?

○ a. The Supervisor object right to the Object Trustees (ACL) property

○ b. The Supervisor object right to the partition [Root] object

○ c. The Supervisor file system rights to the server from which you're running NDS Manager

○ d. The Supervisor object right to the [Root] object and the partition's child container

○ e. All NDS and file system rights to the entire tree and all servers in the tree

Question 57

Which NetWare 5 utility can you use to view and update DS.NLM on different servers in the tree?

○ a. NDS Repair

○ b. DSREPAIR

○ c. NDS Manager

○ d. NetWare Administrator

○ e. DSTRACE

Question 58

When you extend the schema to support NetWare 5 DNS and DHCP Services, three NDS objects are created. What are they? [Choose the three best answers]

❏ a. RootServerInfo Zone object

❏ b. DHCP_*SERVERNAME* Locator object (where *SERVERNAME* is the name of the DHCP server)

❏ c. DNS-DHCP Server object

❏ d. DNSDHCP-GROUP Group object

❏ e. DNS-DHCP Locator object

Question 59

Three items must be configured to provide NetWare 5 DHCP Services. What are they? [Choose the three best answers]

- ❑ a. The workstation must be configured to use DHCP.
- ❑ b. A NetWare 5 server must be set up to contain the workstation configuration information.
- ❑ c. A NetWare 5 server must be assigned as a DHCP server.
- ❑ d. The information to be delivered to a workstation must be configured.
- ❑ e. The DHCP Service must be started on a NetWare 5 server.

Question 60

Hostnames and IP addresses are stored in which type of resource record?

- ○ a. PTR
- ○ b. MX
- ○ c. A
- ○ d. CNAME
- ○ e. NS

Question 61

The following actions must be taken to set up DNS Services on a NetWare 5 network:

1. Install the DNS/DHCP Management Console.
2. Run DNIPINST.NLM at the server console.
3. Create a DNS Zone object.
4. Run NAMED.NLM at the server console.
5. Create a DNS Server object.
6. Create an A resource record.

In which order should you perform these actions?

○ a. 2, 5, 3, 6, 1, 4
○ b. 2, 1, 5, 3, 6, 4
○ c. 4, 1, 5, 3, 6, 2
○ d. 4, 5, 3, 6, 1, 2
○ e. 1, 2, 3, 4, 5, 6

Question 62

What's the purpose of the SAMSRV.DLL file on a Windows NT Server system that's being managed with NDS for NT?

○ a. To handle the management of the Windows NT SAM stored on the Windows NT Server system
○ b. To redirect Windows NT SAM requests to NDS for processing
○ c. To import Windows NT domain information into NDS
○ d. To redirect NDS requests to the Windows NT SAM for processing
○ e. To extend the schema of the Windows NT domain so NDS information can be stored on the Windows NT Server system

Question 63

What's the role of the message store in GroupWise?

○ a. To handle and process the delivery of messages from sender to recipient

○ b. To store messages so they can be read later

○ c. To store the rules for delivery of messages to specific users

○ d. To store forwarded messages that you can then delete later

○ e. To hold messages that cannot be delivered because of addressing errors

Question 64

What's the first procedure that should be enabled to create a more secure network?

○ a. Enable auditing of NDS and file system events

○ b. Restrict physical access to servers and network resources except to authorized personnel

○ c. Lock the file server console with the MONITOR utility

○ d. Require that all accounts have passwords with a minimum of six characters in length

○ e. Install BorderManager servers at locations where your network interfaces with the Internet

Question 65

Migrating a NetWare 3.x server to a NetWare 5 server with an across-the-wire migration has several advantages. Which of the following are among those advantages? [Choose the four best answers]

- ❏ a. There's virtually no chance of data loss because the original files and bindery remain on the NetWare 3.x servers.
- ❏ b. The Novell Upgrade Wizard allows you to verify the project configuration before the migration.
- ❏ c. You can migrate a NetWare 3.11, NetWare 3.12, and a NetWare 3.2 server to one NetWare 5 server.
- ❏ d. Migrated data can be placed on NSS volumes.
- ❏ e. There's virtually no chance of data loss because an across-the-wire migration makes a backup of the NetWare 3.x bindery and data files.

Question 66

Which of the following is a correct statement about the Novell Upgrade Wizard and across-the-wire migration?

- ❍ a. The Novell Upgrade Wizard checks for conflicts and problems before the actual migration of information occurs.
- ❍ b. You have the option of moving the NetWare 3.x print configuration to NetWare 5, but it must be converted to NDPS to exist in the NetWare 5 network.
- ❍ c. The Novell Upgrade Wizard is a graphical tool that runs from a workstation. It can be used to upgrade NetWare 2.2 and NetWare 3.2 servers to NetWare 5.
- ❍ d. The destination container and/or directories must exist before using the Novell Upgrade Wizard.
- ❍ e. An across-the-wire migration is the only upgrade path for a NetWare 3.x server when you want the SYS volume to be a NSS volume.

Chapter 26

Question 67

NSS volumes offer several advantages over traditional NetWare volumes. What are some of these advantages? [Choose the three best answers]

- ❏ a. Files of up to 8TB can be stored on a NSS volume.
- ❏ b. You can have any number of NSS volumes on a NetWare 5 server.
- ❏ c. NSS volumes can be as large as 8TB.
- ❏ d. Because of the large file and volume sizes, NSS volumes take longer to mount.
- ❏ e. Additional memory may be required to support the larger NSS volumes and files.

Question 68

Which of the following is a description of a NSS consumer?

- ○ a. A NSS consumer scans the server's hard disk space to locate unused space.
- ○ b. A NSS consumer represents the entries on a file or directory ACL and specifies the rights the user (or consumer) has at that location.
- ○ c. A NSS consumer groups the storage deposits the NSS providers have discovered into storage groups.
- ○ d. A NSS consumer allows you to define the sizes and names of the NSS volumes.
- ○ e. A NSS consumer registers the free space found by the NSS provider so other systems cannot claim the same space.

Question 69

Which type of backup best fits the following pattern? On Wednesday, the backup takes a long time. Thursday's backup time is short. Backups performed on Friday through Tuesday are taking longer and longer each day, but they do not take as long as Wednesday's backup.

- a. Incremental backup
- b. Differential backup
- c. Full backup
- d. Normal backup
- e. Designated backup

Question 70

John is a trustee of OU=AUSTIN.O=ACME with the Supervisor and Inheritable rights assigned. He's also a trustee of O=ACME with the Browse right. What are John's effective rights to the SYS:\PUBLIC directory on the CN=PROD-SVR.OU=AUSTIN.O=ACME server?

- a. Read and File Scan.
- b. Read, Write, Create, Erase, Modify, File Scan, and Access Control.
- c. Browse and Read.
- d. Supervisor, Read, Write, Create, Erase, Modify, File Scan, and Access Control.
- e. John has no rights in the file system unless they are explicitly granted in the file system.

Question 71

In a multicontext environment, it may be necessary to set some specific NDS rights so users can access their needed resources. What would you need to do to allow a user to properly access a Profile object?

- ○ a. Make the user a trustee of the Profile object and assign the Read All Properties right.
- ○ b. Make the user a trustee of the Profile object and assign the Browse object right.
- ○ c. Make the user a trustee of the Profile object and assign the Browse All Properties right.
- ○ d. Make the user a trustee of the Profile object and assign the Browse Selected Properties right to the Script property.
- ○ e. Make the user a trustee of the Profile object and assign the Read Selected Properties right to the Script property.

Question 72

Which of the following is a symptom of running out of disk space on the SYS volume that may affect NDS?

- ○ a. TTS has been enabled.
- ○ b. The server that's running low on disk space begins an automatic purge of deleted files. Also, if the server contains read/write replicas of any partitions, those are deleted to recover disk space.
- ○ c. The server issues an internal command to stop processes and broadcasts a message indicating that the server is down.
- ○ d. TTS has been disabled.
- ○ e. The server automatically dismounts the volume that's running out of space when the number of free disk allocation units reaches 256 or less.

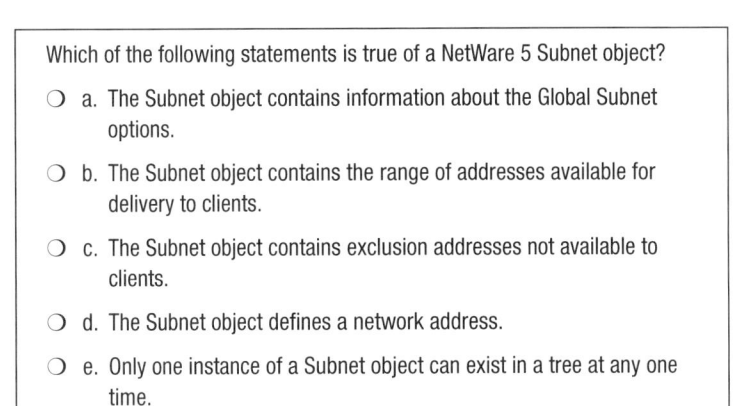

Question 73

Which of the following statements is true of a NetWare 5 Subnet object?

- ❍ a. The Subnet object contains information about the Global Subnet options.
- ❍ b. The Subnet object contains the range of addresses available for delivery to clients.
- ❍ c. The Subnet object contains exclusion addresses not available to clients.
- ❍ d. The Subnet object defines a network address.
- ❍ e. Only one instance of a Subnet object can exist in a tree at any one time.

Answer Key

1. a, e
2. b, c, d
3. a, c, d, e
4. a, c, d, e
5. c, d, e
6. c
7. c
8. b
9. e
10. b, c
11. d
12. a, b
13. a, b, c, e
14. b, e
15. b, c
16. a, b, e
17. b, c, e
18. b
19. a, b, e
20. d
21. b
22. d
23. a, d, e
24. d
25. e
26. a, d
27. c, e
28. b, d, e
29. b, d, e
30. b, d, e
31. d
32. c, d
33. d
34. b
35. c
36. a, d, e
37. a, b
38. c, d
39. d
40. a
41. d
42. c
43. d
44. a, c, e
45. b
46. c
47. a, b, e
48. a, d
49. c
50. c
51. b, c
52. a
53. b
54. a
55. a, e
56. b
57. c
58. a, d, e
59. c, d, e
60. c
61. b
62. b
63. b
64. b
65. a, b, c, d
66. a
67. a, b, c
68. e
69. b
70. d
71. e
72. d
73. d

Question 1

The correct answers are a and e. The backup data is not placed onto a NSS volume but on some type of mobile media. Therefore, answer b is incorrect. The TSAs are run on each of the devices that contain information that will be backed up. For example, to back up a NetWare 3.12 server, TSA312 is run on the NetWare 3 server, not the NetWare 5 server. Therefore, answer c is incorrect. The NWBACK32.EXE application runs on the workstation, and there is no NWBACK32.NLM file located in the SYS:\SYSTEM directory. Therefore, answer d is incorrect.

Question 2

The correct answers are b, c, and d. There's no such thing as static allocation. Therefore, answer a is incorrect. If you need to exclude addresses, you must create an IP Address object in the corresponding Subnet object. Therefore, answer e is incorrect.

Question 3

The correct answers are a, c, d, and e. The ability to use or not use suballocation is determined when the volume is created. It cannot be removed or added to a volume that is already created and mounted. Therefore, answer b is incorrect.

Question 4

The correct answers are a, c, d, and e. Configuring error message reception, monitoring printer status, specifying connection types, and prioritizing printer usage are all functions of the NDS Printer objects. The Print Queue object is used to specify who can operate and use the associated printers. Therefore, answer b is incorrect.

Question 5

The correct answers are c, d, and e. These three tasks are within the scope of an enterprise NDS administrator's tasks. Managing the file systems of servers contained in Organizational Units is typically a role of the container administrator. Therefore, answer a is incorrect. Renaming the tree is a task of the enterprise administrator, and the utility used to rename a tree is DSMERGE.NLM— there is no DSNAME.NLM utility. Therefore, answer b is incorrect.

Question 6

The correct answer is c. Bringing down servers that hold replicas does not give NDS the chance to try to repair itself. Therefore, answer a is incorrect. While NDS problems exist, partition operations of any type should not be performed. Therefore, answer b is incorrect. Running DSREPAIR while there are still NDS inconsistencies on servers that are not reporting errors will not help. Therefore, answer d is incorrect. Read-only replica data cannot be changed by network administrators, but NDS will send changes to read-only replicas. In addition, changing the partition type will not help problems and should not be done while there are NDS problems. Therefore, answer e is incorrect.

Question 7

The correct answer is c. The terms used in the other options—JAVA DATA, DISPLAY DATA, and JAVA APPLET—do not exist. Therefore, answers a, b, and d are incorrect. Entering the text in answer e has no meaning by itself. Therefore, answer e is incorrect.

Question 8

The correct answer is b. There must be at least 200MB free on the SYS volume to use the In-Place Upgrade option. Therefore, answer a is incorrect. The Migration Wizard is not used in an In-Place Upgrade. Therefore, answer c is incorrect. The server must be down to run INSTALL.BAT for an In-Place Upgrade. Therefore, answer d is incorrect. The problem is not the size of the NetWare partition but the amount of free space on the SYS volume. Therefore, answer e is incorrect.

Question 9

The correct answer is e. There is no such thing as Network Information Attribute Services. Therefore, answer a is incorrect. A Web server is not part of the NIAS package, and NIAS stands for Novell Internet Access Server. Therefore, answer b is incorrect. NIAS in NetWare 5 replaces NetWare Connect and NIAS stands for Novell Internet Access Server. Therefore, answer c is incorrect. NIAS is a component of BorderManager, not ManageWise. Therefore, answer d is incorrect.

Question 10

The correct answers are b and c. A server cannot hold more than one copy of a partition. Therefore, answer a is incorrect. There cannot be more than one copy of a master replica. Therefore, answer d is incorrect. Subordinate references are created automatically, and you cannot have a subordinate reference on a server where another copy of the partition exists. Therefore, answer e is incorrect.

Question 11

The correct answer is d. AUTOEXEC.NCF usually contains time zone information. STARTUP.NCF is a NetWare 5 configuration file that typically contains the commands to load the storage device drivers, to set the values of some **SET** parameters, and to load support for name spaces. Therefore, answer a is incorrect. The CONFIG.NCF and TIMEZONE.NCF files do not exist. Therefore, answers b and c are incorrect. CONFIG.SYS is a configuration file used by DOS-based operating systems and is not used by NetWare 5. Therefore, answer e is incorrect.

Question 12

The correct answers are a and b. **ADMNSERV** is a NLM that's run at the server console. Therefore, answer c is incorrect. The **APPLET** command is used to execute Java code embedded in an HTML document. Therefore, answer d is incorrect. Answer e refers to an FTP service, not a Hypertext Transfer Protocol (HTTP) service, that's needed to access the Netscape FastTrack Administrative Server. Therefore, answer e is incorrect.

Question 13

The correct answers are a, b, c, and e. An across-the-wire migration between a NetWare 3.x server and a NetWare 5 server requires an IPX connection. Therefore, answer d is incorrect.

Question 14

The correct answers are b and e. SERVMAN.NLM is the name of the utility for viewing and changing **SET** parameters in versions prior to NetWare 5. Therefore, answer a is incorrect. INSTALL.NLM has been replaced in NetWare 5 with NWCONFIG.NLM. Therefore, answer c is incorrect. NWSET.NLM does not exist. Therefore, answer d is incorrect.

Question 15

The correct answers are b and c. Read-only replicas cannot be modified by a client when authenticating to record the data, time, and client's network address. Therefore, answer a is incorrect. Subordinate references do not contain complete copies of a partition and cannot be used for authentication. Therefore, answer d is incorrect. [Root] is a partition, not a replica type. Therefore, answer e is incorrect.

Question 16

The correct answers are a, b, and e. DNIPINST is a NLM and is not run at a workstation console prompt. Therefore, answer c is incorrect. A DNSDHCP command, file, or configuration file does not exist. Therefore, answer d is incorrect.

Question 17

The correct answers are b, c, and e. An arbitrator is not a component that exists in DNS. Therefore, answer a is incorrect. The DNS-DHCP Locator object is a special NDS object used in NetWare 5's implementation of DNS services. Therefore, answer d is incorrect.

Question 18

The correct answer is b. The Service Processes values should only be changed if the server is incrementing the number of allocated service processes to the point where the maximum is reached. Therefore, answers a and d are incorrect. The Maximum Packet Receive Buffers setting should only be increased on busy servers or if the number of currently allocated cache buffers is reaching the current maximum value. Therefore, answer c is incorrect. LIP is only a factor in routed networks. Therefore, answer e is incorrect.

Question 19

The correct answers are a, b, and e. NSS can be used for new volumes created on the upgraded server. Therefore, answer c is incorrect. IP can be enabled and configured during the upgrade process. Therefore, answer d is incorrect.

Question 20

The correct answer is d. SYS:\PUBLIC contains the common utilities typically used by clients such as MAP. Therefore, answer a is incorrect.

SYS:\SYSTEM is where most of the server NLM and configuration files are stored. Therefore, answer b is incorrect. SYS:\PUBLIC\WIN95 contains administrative utilities for backward compatibility. Therefore, answer c is incorrect. There is no such directory as SYS:\SYSTEM\PUBLIC for utilities. Therefore, answer e is incorrect.

Question 21

The correct answer is b. The other locations listed do not exist by default and therefore do not store documents for Netscape FastTrack Server. Therefore, answers a, c, d, and e are incorrect.

Question 22

The correct answer is d. **STARTX** is the command to load the NetWare 5 GUI. Therefore, answer a is incorrect. **CONSOLEONE** and **STARTC1** are not valid commands. Therefore, answers b and c are incorrect. **JAVA C1** is not an option for loading Java or ConsoleOne at the server console. Therefore, answer e is incorrect.

Question 23

The correct answers are a, d, and e. Because answer d is correct and there is no reason to put all the new usernames in **MAP** statements, answer b is incorrect. Queue-based printers, whether created before upgrading to NetWare 5 or after, are compatible with NDPS. Therefore, answer c is incorrect.

Question 24

The correct answer is d. The traditional NetWare file system cannot store files as large as 4TB. Therefore, answer a is incorrect. FAT32 is used by Windows 95/98, not by NetWare 5. Therefore, answer b is incorrect. Long name space allows for the storage of files with long names, independent of their sizes. Therefore, answer c is incorrect. Consumers are a component of NSS. Therefore, answer e is incorrect.

Question 25

The correct answer is e. Print queues have no interaction or correlation with mapped drive letters. Therefore, answer a is incorrect. A NetWare 5 print queue is created on the server, not the workstation. Therefore, answer b is incorrect.

Answer Key 483

The NetWare 5 print queue can be defined as a bindery-based object, but this is not for compatibility reasons with NetWare 4.x. Therefore, answer c is incorrect. Because answer e is correct, answer d is incorrect.

Question 26

The correct answers are a and d. The total number would be expressed as a percentage, not as a raw number. Therefore, answer b is incorrect. The Long Term Cache Hit value is not an indicator of how busy or idle the server is. Therefore, answers c and e are incorrect.

Question 27

The correct answers are c and e. Merging a partition with its parent is considered a complex NDS change. Therefore, answer a is incorrect. Although changing a single value (as in the correct choice e) is not complex, changing 500 User objects at one time is considered a complex change. Therefore, answer b is incorrect. Removing replicas from a server is not considered a NDS change because you're simply deleting a copy of a portion of the database and not altering the contents. Therefore, answer d is incorrect.

Question 28

The correct answers are b, d, and e. An icon that's a white square with a question mark in the middle does not indicate an unknown object. These icons typically appear when the NetWare Administrator snap-ins cannot be accessed. Therefore, answer a is incorrect. Accessing files on a NetWare 3.x server has no interaction with NDS. Therefore, answer c is incorrect.

Question 29

The correct answers are b, d, and e. Setting up IP on the management workstation is not one of the tasks Novell identifies. Therefore, answer a is incorrect. DHCPSRVR.NLM is executed at the server console to start the DHCP services after the environment has been configured. Therefore, answer c is incorrect.

Question 30

The correct answers are b, d, and e. Primary and secondary are types of DNS name servers. Therefore, answers a and c are incorrect.

Question 31

The correct answer is d. Virus scanning is performed by another element of ManageWise. Therefore, answer a is incorrect. LANalyzer does not redirect SNMP traps to the ManageWise Console. Therefore, answer b is incorrect. The NetExplorer component of ManageWise performs the network entities search. Therefore, answer c is incorrect. LANalyzer can be used to analyze network protocols but not network topology. Therefore, answer e is incorrect.

Question 32

The correct answers are c and d. Answers a and e describe NetWare 5's virtual memory operation. Therefore, answers a and e are incorrect. To return the address space to the operating system, you must use the **UNLOAD** command with the name of the address space at the server console to terminate usage of the address space. Therefore, answer b is incorrect.

Question 33

The correct answer is d. Packet receive buffers and reserved buffers are not used in acknowledgments. Therefore, answers a and b are incorrect. LIP is useful if there are non-Novell routers in the environment. Therefore, answer c is incorrect. Event control blocks is another term for packet receive buffers. Therefore, answer e is incorrect.

Question 34

The correct answer is b. **IPCON** is not a NetWare 5 command. Therefore, answer a is incorrect. NWCONFIG is a utility that can be used to configure IP and is not a command to return the information on the server console. Therefore, answer c is incorrect. INSTALL is a NLM that existed in pre-NetWare 5 versions and has been replaced with NWCONFIG. Therefore, answer d is incorrect. **MONITOR** can be used to determine the protocol information, but it's not a command for returning the information on the server console. Therefore, answer e is incorrect.

Question 35

The correct answer is c. Netscape FastTrack Server is used to provide HTTP services. Therefore, answer a in incorrect. FTPCON and WEBSRV are made-up names. Therefore, answers b and d are incorrect. NIAS is used to configure

Answer Key   485

remote access to the network and to provide gateway services. Therefore, answer e is incorrect.

Question 36

The correct answers are a, d, and e. Non-Novell servers cannot be upgraded with the In-Place Upgrade. Therefore, answer b is incorrect. NetWare 2.2 servers must first be upgraded to at least NetWare 3.x before you can use the In-Place Upgrade. Therefore, answer c is incorrect.

Question 37

The correct answers are a and b. INSTALL.NLM is the name of a pre-NetWare utility that's replaced with NWCONFIG.NLM. Therefore, answer c is incorrect. The minimum size of the NetWare 5 SYS volume is 500MB, not 5,000MB. Therefore, answer d is incorrect. The SYS volume must be a traditional NetWare volume. Therefore, answer e is incorrect.

Question 38

The correct answers are c and d. One of the advantages of NSS is the elimination of volumes' linkage to specific physical devices. Therefore, answer a is incorrect. Storage groups have no involvement in the server's DOS partition. Therefore, answer b is incorrect. Storage groups represent free space, not occupied space. Therefore, answer e is incorrect.

Question 39

The correct answer is d. SBACKUP is the name of the backup and restore NLM that runs on a NetWare 3.x or NetWare 4.x server. Therefore, answer a is incorrect. You can view the SMS objects in NetWare Administrator, but you cannot configure a backup session. Therefore, answer b is incorrect. You can configure a backup or restore session with SBCON; however, SBCON runs on the server, not on a workstation. Therefore, answer c is incorrect. NetWare Backup/Restore is another name for SBCON. Therefore, answer e is incorrect.

Question 40

The correct answer is a. Read, Modify, and File Scan are file system rights, not NDS rights. Therefore, answers b, c, d, and e are incorrect.

Question 41

The correct answer is d. The presence of yellow circle with question mark icons indicates NDS inconsistencies. Removing all read/write replicas from the servers, adding read-only replicas, and reinstalling DS.NLM to make sure the proper version is installed to view these objects will do nothing to remedy the situation. Therefore, answers a and c are incorrect. Whether the proper snap-ins are available will not help with inconsistent NDS data. Therefore, answer b is incorrect. These icons indicate NDS inconsistencies. Therefore, answer e is incorrect.

Question 42

The correct answer is c. You should determine which replicas are stored on the crashed server; delete the Server object from the tree with NDS Manager; remove the crashed server's Volume objects from the tree with NetWare Administrator; and finally, perform a continuity check to make sure no NDS errors are present. All other answers are not in the correct sequence and are therefore incorrect.

Question 43

The correct answer is d. NAMED is the name of the NLM for starting the DNS services. Therefore, answer a is incorrect. IPDNS is a made-up name. Therefore, answer b is incorrect. ZONE is a division of the DNS name space and is not a file format. Therefore, answer c is incorrect.

Question 44

The correct answers are a, c, and e. The other two answers, b and d, are made-up options and are therefore incorrect.

Question 45

The correct answer is b. Opening additional ports is not a function of a proxy cache server. Therefore, answer a is incorrect. VPNs handle secure connections for data transfer. Therefore, answer c is incorrect. Storing on disk defeats the purpose of memory cache. Therefore, answer d is incorrect. Filtering of information is not handled by a proxy cache server but rather by packet-filtering components. Therefore, answer e is incorrect.

Answer Key

Question 46

The correct answer is c. RSPX and REMOTE use the IPX protocol. Therefore, answers a and b are incorrect. NIAS is used to configure remote access to the network, not to server consoles. Therefore, answer d is incorrect. RCONSOLE is the name of the utility for accessing a server console on a workstation. Therefore, answer e is incorrect.

Question 47

The correct answers are a, b, and e. NSWEB starts up the Netscape FastTrack Server. Therefore, answer c is incorrect. Shutting down the Administration Server does not shut down Web services for users. Therefore, answer d is incorrect.

Question 48

The correct answers are a and d. ARP and TCP are protocols in the IP suite, and SPX is a protocol in the IPX suite. These protocols do not need to be configured or are provided by another service. Therefore, answers b, c, and e are incorrect.

Question 49

The correct answer is c. The Upgrade Wizard is a workstation utility. Therefore, answer a is incorrect. The Upgrade Wizard is not available from a remote console screen. Therefore, answer b is incorrect. You need to use the Novell Client version 2.2 or higher on a Windows 95 workstation. Therefore, answer d is incorrect. There is no such file as WIZARD.BAT in reference to the Upgrade Wizard. Therefore, answer e is incorrect.

Question 50

The correct answer is c. Answers a, b, d, and e do not contain all the information that is migrated and are therefore incorrect.

Question 51

The correct answers are b and c. The start time for compression is 12:00 A.M. and the end time is 6:00 A.M. Therefore, answers a and e are incorrect. Volume compression and disk suballocation can both be enabled on a volume. Therefore, answer d is incorrect.

Question 52

The correct answer is a. The SYS volume cannot be a NSS volume, and the providers have nothing to do with TTS. Therefore, answer b is incorrect. NSS providers are separate NLMs, but they're not used to register the space. Registration of free space is done by the consumers. Therefore, answer c is incorrect. NSS providers are NLMs running on the server. Therefore, answer d is incorrect. Providers do not perform any actions on the server's memory. Therefore, answer e is incorrect.

Question 53

The correct answer is b. The other answers do not contain the proper syntax necessary to load the SALES-PS print server. Therefore, answers a, c, d, and e are incorrect.

Question 54

The correct answer is a. A trustee assignment for Judy at a subordinate object to O=ACME overwrites her inherited rights flowing down from O=ACME. Therefore, answers b and c are incorrect. Non-Supervisor object rights do not imply any property rights. Therefore, answer d is incorrect. The Supervisor right was never indicated in the scenario. Therefore, answer e is incorrect.

Question 55

The correct answers are a and e. Containers do not have Net Address properties, because they do not represent a physical or software network resource. Therefore, answer b is incorrect. There are no default rights assigned through All Properties. Therefore, answer c is incorrect. Because answer e is correct, answer d is incorrect.

Question 56

The correct answer is b. The first answer does not specify the object where you might need the Supervisor right. Therefore, answer a is incorrect. You do not need file system rights to create partitions, but you may need them to add replicas. Therefore, answer c is incorrect. Rights are not needed to a child partition when you're creating a partition. Therefore, answer d is incorrect. You do not need rights to the entire tree to create a partition. Therefore, answer e is incorrect.

Question 57

The correct answer is c. There is no utility called NDS Repair. Therefore, answer a is incorrect. DSREPAIR and DSTRACE can be used to monitor NDS activity but cannot be used to update DS.NLM. Therefore, answers b and e are incorrect. NetWare Administrator does not contain any features for viewing or updating DS.NLM. Therefore, answer d is incorrect.

Question 58

The correct answers are a, d, and e. DHCP_*SERVERNAME* Locator object is the default name used when a DHCP server is created. Therefore, answer b is incorrect. There's no such thing as the DNS-DHCP Server object created by default. Therefore, answer c is incorrect.

Question 59

The correct answers are c, d, and e. A workstation does not have to be configured to use DHCP servers for the DHCP server to run. Therefore, answer a is incorrect. The NetWare 5 server does not store workstation configuration information. Therefore, answer b is incorrect.

Question 60

The correct answer is c. PTR records are used for pointers to refer to services outside the domain. Therefore, answer a is incorrect. MX records are for Mail Exchange information used by SMTP-based services. Therefore, answer b is incorrect. CNAME contains the canonical name of an alias. Therefore, answer d is incorrect. NS stores the authoritative name server for the domain. Therefore, answer e is incorrect.

Question 61

The correct answer is b. To set up DNS Services on a NetWare 5 network, you have to run DNIPINST.NLM at the server console; install the DNS/DHCP Management Console; create a DNS Server object; create a DNS Zone object; create an A resource record; and run NAMED.NLM at the server console. Answers a, c, d, and e are not in the correct order and are therefore incorrect.

Question 62

The correct answer is b. NDS for NT eliminates the need to manage the Windows NT SAM database. Therefore, answer a is incorrect. The Domain Object Wizard allows you to import Windows NT domain information into NDS. Therefore, answer c is incorrect. SAMSRV.DLL redirects Windows NT SAM requests to NDS, not NDS requests to the Windows NT SAM. Therefore, answer d is incorrect. Windows NT does not have a schema to extend. Therefore, answer e is incorrect.

Question 63

The correct answer is b. Delivery of messages is handled by the Message Transfer Agent (MTA). Therefore, answer a is incorrect. Delivery path information is stored in the directory store. Therefore, answer c is incorrect. The message store does not store forwarded messages or undeliverable messages only but rather all messages. Therefore, answers d and e are incorrect.

Question 64

The correct answer is b. Answers a, d, and e are all good security practices, but none of them represent the number one action. Therefore, answers a, d, and e are incorrect. The SCRSAVER.NLM file is used in NetWare 5 to lock the file server console. Therefore, answer c is incorrect.

Question 65

The correct answers are a, b, c, and d. The Novell Upgrade Wizard does not make backup copies of the NetWare 3.x bindery and data files, but they're left intact on the NetWare 3.x server. Therefore, answer e is incorrect.

Question 66

The correct answer is a. NetWare 5 networks can contain both NDPS and queue-based print configurations. Therefore, answer b is incorrect. The Novell Upgrade Wizard cannot be used to upgrade NetWare 2.2 servers. Therefore, answer c is incorrect. The destination container and/or directories can be created with the Novell Upgrade Wizard. Therefore, answer d is incorrect. The SYS volume must be a traditional NetWare volume; it cannot be a NSS volume. Therefore, answer e is incorrect.

Answer Key **491**

Question 67

The correct answers are a, b, and c. One of the advantages of NSS is very fast volume mount times regardless of the volume size. Therefore, answer d is incorrect. Another advantage of NSS is the low memory overhead to support any size NSS volume. Therefore, answer e is incorrect.

Question 68

The correct answer is e. NSS providers scan the hard disks for free space. Therefore, answer a is incorrect. Consumers are not involved in file-system security. Therefore, answer b is incorrect. The NSS consumers are not involved in the creation of storage groups. Therefore, answer c is incorrect. NSS consumers are not involved in the definition of the NSS volume names and sizes. Therefore, answer d is incorrect.

Question 69

The correct answer is b. In an incremental backup, the backup time on each day would be about the same but never as long as the full backup, which begins the cycle. Therefore, answer a is incorrect. A full backup would take approximately the same time each day. Therefore, answer c is incorrect. Normal and designated backups do not exist. Therefore, answers d and e are incorrect.

Question 70

The correct answer is d. In the scenario presented, John receives the Supervisor object right to the Server object through inheritance. This gives him all file system rights on that server. Therefore, answers a, b, and e are incorrect. Browse is a NDS object right. Therefore, answer c is incorrect.

Question 71

The correct answer is e. The user is a trustee of the Profile object, but rights are not assigned through All Properties. Therefore, answer a is incorrect. The user is not granted any object rights to the Profile object. Therefore, answer b is incorrect. Browse is an object right, not a property right. Therefore, answers c and d are incorrect.

Question 72

The correct answer is d. TTS would be disabled, not enabled. Therefore, answer a is incorrect. The system will begin purging deleted data files but will not delete any replica information. Therefore, answer b is incorrect. The server may eventually stop processing and halt, but it cannot broadcast messages after it's down. Therefore, answer c is incorrect. When the number of remaining disk allocation units reaches 256 or less, TTS will be disabled, but the volume is not automatically dismounted. Therefore, answer e is incorrect.

Question 73

The correct answer is d. Global Subnet options are not contained in a Subnet object. A Subnet object can have options, but these are not global. Therefore, answer a is incorrect. An SAR contains the range of addresses available for consumption. Therefore, answer b is incorrect. Exclusions are IP Address objects, not Subnet objects. Therefore, answer c is incorrect. There can be several instances of Subnet objects in the same tree. An example of this is a Subnet Pool object. Therefore, answer e is incorrect.

Appendix A
SET Parameters

In most situations, you won't be required to modify any of the server's configuration parameters. However, to increase the performance of the server, you may want to change some of the server's parameters. The **SET** command is one way of modifying your server's configuration parameters. You can also view and modify these **SET** values by choosing Server Parameters in the MONITOR utility. The **SET** command is executed from the server's console.

The **SET** command uses the following syntax:

```
SET parameter = value
```

The following parameter categories are available for configuration using the **SET** command:

- ➤ Communications
- ➤ Directory caching
- ➤ Directory services
- ➤ Disk
- ➤ Error handling
- ➤ File caching
- ➤ File system
- ➤ Licensing services
- ➤ Locks
- ➤ Memory

Appendix A

- Miscellaneous
- Multiprocessor
- NetWare Core Protocol (NCP)
- Service Location Protocol (SLP)
- Time
- Transaction tracking

The **SET** command can be used in three different ways: without a parameter, with a parameter but with no value, and with both a parameter and a value.

When you run the **SET** command without a parameter, a menu appears with all the available parameter categories (each is assigned a number). When you select the number to the right of the category a list of the parameters for the category is displayed. For each of the parameters, the current value, the range of values that can be entered, and the default value of the parameter are listed. Executing the **SET** command with a parameter (but without a value) displays all the information previously outlined but without the default value (a brief explanation, the current value, and the value range). Finally, typing the **SET** command with both a parameter and a value reconfigures the parameter with the entered value. In addition, you can also type **HELP SET** *parameter* at the server console to receive additional information.

The values configured with the **SET** command are volatile. This means that any configured values are lost when the server is rebooted, unless the specific **SET** command is executed in either the AUTOEXEC.NCF or STARTUP.NCF file. **SET** parameters that can reside in the AUTOEXEC.NCF file can be executed at the server console and are in effect immediately. **SET** parameters that must be executed in the STARTUP.NCF file cannot be modified by typing the **SET** command at the server console. You'll receive a message indicating that the parameter could not be set.

As you can imagine, we could dedicate several chapters to all the possible parameters and their values. However, in this appendix, we cover just the main parameter categories and their definitions. A complete list of all the available parameters can be found in the NetWare documentation. Simply search for "SET parameters" or go to the Reference section and click on Utilities Reference|Utilities. Then scroll down until you see SET and click on it.

Communications

The communication parameter category includes parameters that deal with how NetWare handles its communication buffers, for example, Compatibility

Mode settings and load balancing. There are two types of communication buffers that deal with watchdog packets and packet receive buffers.

Watchdog packets are used by the operating system to make sure that a station is still connected to the server. If the server doesn't "hear" from a workstation within a set amount of time, it will send one of these watchdog packets to the workstation. The server will wait a predetermined amount of time (which you can control); then it will send another watchdog packet. The server has a maximum number of watchdog packets that it sends out to the workstation. Once this limit is met, the server terminates its connection with the workstation in question.

The packet receive buffers specify how much of the server's memory is assigned to store packets as they are received.

Directory Caching

The directory caching category simply deals with how NetWare stores (caches) frequently used directory information in memory. You have the ability to control what makes a directory a frequently used directory, how long a directory should be cached, and how much RAM is set aside for directory information caching.

Directory Services

As you've probably guessed, the directory services category deals with Novell Directory Services (NDS) and how NetWare controls it. Some of the parameters include the ability to control the NDS synchronization intervals and restrictions, the bindery context, and the intervals used to clean up NDS.

Disk

The disk category contains parameters that are used to control Hot Fix redirection, disk reads and writes, and disk mirroring/remirroring information. This is a category that you would not normally have to modify because NetWare is very efficient in controlling its disks.

Error Handling

This category controls how NetWare responds to an abend (abnormal end) or uncooperative NetWare Loadable Modules (NLMs). You can also control the size of the error logs and what actions that server must complete should the error logs exceed this defined size.

File Caching

As with directory caching, file caching allows you to control how much memory resources NetWare will allocate to frequently used files. The file cache buffer size is also controlled in this category. The file cache buffer size controls the number of files that will be cached in memory.

It's important to note that some of the NDS database is also stored in the file cache. Therefore, anytime you want to improve the performance of NDS on your NetWare server, you would do so through the file caching category and the SET command. You can also add more physical memory to the server to allow more caching of data.

File System

As you would expect, the file system category deals with how NetWare controls its file systems. Some of these parameters include controlling file compression, the purging of files, and warnings about volume capacities.

Licensing Services

As the name implies, this category simply deals with NetWare licensing. You can control information such as how licenses are searched for in the NDS tree.

Locks

NetWare uses locks to control who has access to files and to protect files from being accessed when not necessary. Using the parameters in this category, you can control the number of open files that the server can have, as well as the number of files an individual workstation can open. Also configured here is the number of record locks the server and workstations can have.

Memory

This category simply allows for the configuration of how memory is handled by the system. It includes how "garbage collection" is handled, how much virtual memory is used, and how much memory below the 16MB level is reserved for device drivers.

Miscellaneous

This heading simply contains some of the configuration items that cannot be grouped into the other categories, or ones that do not have enough options to merit their own category. These include the following:

- Controlling password security features
- Controlling the kernel and scheduler
- Controlling how alerts are handled
- Using some of the built-in developer options
- Informing the server how to handle invalid parameters

Multiprocessor

The multiprocessor category simply allows you to control secondary processors (processors other than the main installed processor). You can configure the system to auto load the secondary processors; if this value is entered in the STARTUP.NCF file, the secondary processors will be loaded during startup. Also available is the option to control how the processors handle threads for load balancing.

NetWare Core Protocol (NCP)

The NCP category includes the ability to control NCP packets, Transport Control Protocol (TCP) keep-alive packets, and the size of the TCP window, as well as to allow for large Internet packet support. Modifying some of these parameters will increase the speed at which the server can process NCP packets.

Service Location Protocol (SLP)

This category simply allows you to control how the Service Location Protocol (SLP) finds and sends information about some of the services available on the network. You can configure information such as maximum retry values, maximum transfer unit (MTU) values, and whether to use broadcast packets or multicast packets.

Time

For a NetWare network to operate efficiently with multiple servers, it requires the time on all of the servers to be synchronized. The time category allows for control over how synchronization takes place and how different time zones are handled. It's not uncommon to have servers in different time zones in the same NDS tree.

Transaction Tracking

The Transaction Tracking System (TTS) category in NetWare simply ensures that all data is written to disk properly. It tracks all transactions and then commits them to the databases when processor cycles are available. Available options include the maximum number of transactions that can be stored in memory and the maximum amount of time a transaction can be cached before it must be written to disk.

Appendix B
Commands And Utilities Tables

There are many console commands and utilities available that you can execute on a NetWare server. Tables B.1 and B.2 in this appendix look at some of the most common console commands and utilities available to you and briefly explains the action performed by each of them. For more information on a specific command or utility, or for a complete listing of these commands and utilities, check the NetWare 5 documentation under the Utilities subheading.

Table B.1 Commands you can run at the NetWare 5 server console.

Command	Action
ADD NAME SPACE	Allows you to store non-DOS files and directories on a NetWare volume (such as Windows 95/98/NT long file names and Macintosh files).
ALERT	Allows you to enable/disable console alerts and control how they're displayed.
ALIAS	Allows you to define commonly used commands and command strings to simplify their entry.
BIND	Links a protocol with a network board. This must be done for communication to take place.
CLEAR STATION	Terminates a connection between the server and a workstation.
CONFIG	Displays some basic information about the server, including up time, network boards and their binding information, and the name of the Novell Directory Services (NDS) tree.

(continued)

Appendix B

Table B.1 Commands you can run at the NetWare 5 server console (continued).

Command	Action
CONLOG	Allows you to log the messages sent to the console screen.
CPUCHECK	Displays the type of processor installed in the server.
DISABLE LOGIN	Stops users (and workstations) from logging onto the server. This command is useful if you're making modifications to the server and do not want logins to interfere.
DISMOUNT	Dismounts a NetWare volume so it's no longer available to the server.
DISPLAY INTERRUPTS	Displays the interrupts in use by the server.
DOWN	Shuts down the server's services, closes all files, and exits to DOS.
ENABLE LOGIN	Allows users to log onto the system after a **DISABLE LOGIN** command has been issued.
ENABLE TTS	Enables the Transaction Tracking System (TTS) on the server.
INITIALIZE SYSTEM	Enables the server to run as a multiprotocol router. It does this before loading the NETINFO.CFG file.
LANGUAGE	Allows you to change the language used for the NLMs to be loaded next.
LIST DEVICES	Lists all the storage devices installed and detected by the system, including hard disks and CD-ROM drives.
LOAD	Loads an NLM. The .NLM extension is not required. The **LOAD** command is no longer necessary in NetWare 5.
MEMORY	Displays the total server memory.
MEMORY MAP	Maps out which operating system is controlling the memory.
MIRROR STATUS	Gives you a status of any mirrors that might exist on your server.
MODULES	Displays all the loaded modules currently running on the server.
MOUNT	Mounts a NetWare volume so it's accessible by the server.

(continued)

Commands And Utilities Tables

Table B.1 Commands you can run at the NetWare 5 server console (continued).

Command	Action
NAME	Displays the server name.
PROTECT	A command that loads NLMs into the protected area of the server's memory.
PROTECTION	Displays the NLMs loaded into the protected memory area.
PROTOCOL	Displays all the currently configured protocols.
RESET SERVER	Shuts down the server and performs a warm reboot of the server's hardware.
RESTART SERVER	Shuts down the server and then immediately reboots it.
SCAN ALL	Scans a Small Computer System Interface (SCSI) bus for the attached devices.
SECURE CONSOLE	Locks some of the configuration features, such as the server date and time, to prevent them from being changed.
SPEED	Displays the speed of the processor installed in the server.
START PROCESSORS	Allows you to start secondary processors installed in the server.
STOP PROCESSORS	Allows you to stop secondary processors installed in the server.
SWAP	Allows you to display and modify the swap files used by the server.
TIME	Displays and configures server time and daylight saving status.
TRACK ON/OFF	A command that can be used to display all Routing Information Protocol (RIP) information as it's received and sent by the server.
UNBIND	Breaks the relationship between a protocol and a network board.
UNLOAD	Unloads an NLM from the server.
VOLUMES	Displays all the mounted volumes.

Table B.2 Utilities you can run from the NetWare 5 server console.

Utility	Action
DSDIAG	Allows for the diagnosis of current NDS information and for the documentation of the NDS structure.
DSMERGE	Merges two different trees into a single NDS tree. This utility can also be used to rename an NDS tree.
DSREPAIR	Fixes problems that might exist in the NDS tree.
FILTCFG	Allows you to configure filters for the Transport Control Protocol/Internet Protocol (TCP/IP), Internetwork Packet Exchange (IPX), and AppleTalk protocols.
INETCFG	A utility for configuring network information, including protocols and network boards.
IPXCON	Monitors IPX information through the server console.
IPXPING	Checks for the connection between two systems using the IPX protocol.
JAVA	Enables Java on the NetWare server.
KEYB	Allows you to modify the keyboard the server is using.
MONITOR	A useful utility that allows for a wide range of system-monitoring options.
NCMCON	A utility that allows for the configuration of plug-and-play boards.
NPRINTER	Loads and installs a NetWare printer.
NSS	Allows you to load/unload the Novell Storage Services (NSS) module.
NWCONFIG	A versatile configuration utility that allows you to control many components of the server.
PING	A utility that can be used to check connections between two systems.
RCONAG6	A tool that allows you to remotely manage your server using the RConsoleJ application.
RCONPRXY	Creates a RConsoleJ proxy server on a NetWare 5 server.
REMOTE	Used to allow remote control of the server from a workstation.
REMOVE	Removes the configuration of several different configuration options.
RSPX	This utility is used with **REMOTE** to allow RCONSOLE to run over the Sequenced Packet Exchange (SPX) protocol.

(continued)

Commands And Utilities Tables

Table B.2 Utilities you can run from the NetWare 5 server console (continued).

Utility	Action
SCRSAVER	Executes a screensaver. This used to be included in the MONITOR utility, but it now uses NDS security.
SPXCONFIG	Is used to configure the SPX protocol.
TCPCON	A utility used to monitor TCP/IP traffic on the server.
TECHWALK	Records the NetWare configuration information.
TIMESYNC	Synchronizes the time between servers.
TPING	A simplified PING program. It PINGs the host and then exits.
UPS_AIO	Allows you to configure how the server will interact with an uninterruptible power supply (UPS).
VIEW	Allows you to view the contents of a file from the console. However, it does not allow for editing.
VREPAIR	Repairs problems that may occur in NetWare volumes.

Appendix C
Sample
Configuration Files

NetWare uses several configuration files to control how the server is configured. Some of these files are analogous to how DOS uses the CONFIG.SYS and AUTOEXEC.BAT files. NetWare configuration files end with the .NCF extension. By default, two different files are created: STARTUP.NCF and AUTOEXEC.NCF. The easiest way to edit these two files is to use the NWCONFIG console utility.

The NetWare configuration files can be created with any file-editing tool (such as the EDIT tool from either DOS or the command console). Similar to the way DOS handles BAT files, NetWare executes the commands listed in an NCF file in the order in which they're entered. You can create several NCF files to simplify some of your administration tasks.

Controlling Which Commands Are Executed

Usually, you'll want all the commands that exist in NCF files to be executed. Some situations, however, require that the operator be prompted to accept a module being loaded. For example, you may find that a specific NetWare Loadable Module (NLM) conflicts with another that's currently running on the system. If you load the second NLM with the first in memory, the server may experience an abend (abnormal end). To prevent this, you should place a message in one of your NCF files informing the operator that the first NLM must be unloaded before the second is loaded.

Appendix C

To configure a NCF file to pause and ask the operator for input, you would enter the following command:

`? something.nlm`

Once this command is reached in the NCF file, the server will prompt the operator with the following prompt:

`something.nlm? y`

The system will now pause for 10 seconds and wait for user input. If no such input is entered, the system will choose the default value of *yes* and continue loading the module. You can configure both the default value and the amount of time the server is to wait for input.

To change the default answer that the server will use, simply place either a *y* or an *n* directly after the question mark. Here's an example:

`?n something.nlm`

This will automatically choose the answer *no* after the wait time expires.

> **TIP:** You can also configure the default answer for the entire system by modifying the Command Line Prompt Default Choice parameter.

Configuring the timeout is a slightly different process. Again, you can configure it using the Command Line Prompt Time Out parameter in the Miscellaneous category. Another way to configure this value to use the MONITOR utility. Execute the utility (by entering the command **MONITOR**), choose the Server Parameters|Miscellaneous option, and then choose the Command Line Prompt Time Out parameter.

STARTUP.NCF

The STARTUP.NCF file loads drivers, including disk drivers and name spaces, and some **SET** parameters that must be executed for the NetWare server to successfully start up. It's executed when you run SERVER.EXE from DOS (either automatically or manually). The STARTUP.NCF file is usually found in the C:\NWSERVER directory (or the directory in which you chose to install NetWare).

Sample Configuration Files

The following is a sample STARTUP.NCF file:

```
LOAD IDEHD.CDM
LOAD IDECD.CDM
LOAD IDEATA.HAM PORT=1F0 INT=E
LOAD IDEATA.HAM PORT=170 INT=F
```

AUTOEXEC.NCF

The AUTOEXEC.NCF file is executed once the STARTUP.NCF file is loaded. It completes the following tasks in order:

- Configures the server time, time zone, and time server type
- Specifies the bindery context
- Sets the server name
- Specifies the server's unique ID value
- Loads the network board drivers and binds the protocols
- Loads other NLM programs
- Loads the graphical interface for NetWare 5

The following is a sample AUTOEXEC.NCF file:

```
SET TIME ZONE = MST7MDT
SET DAYLIGHT SAVINGS TIME OFFSET = 1:00:00
SET START OF DAYLIGHT SAVINGS TIME = (APRIL SUNDAY FIRST 2:00:00 AM)
SET END OF DAYLIGHT SAVINGS TIME = (OCTOBER SUNDAY LAST 2:00:00 AM)
SET TIMESYNC TYPE = SINGLE
SET DEFAULT TIME SERVER TYPE = SINGLE

SET BINDERY CONTEXT = O=ORGANIZATION

# NOTE: THE PRECEDING TIME ZONE INFORMATION MENTIONED
# SHOULD ALWAYS PRECEDE THE SERVER NAME.
# WARNING!!
FILE SERVER NAME FS1
# WARNING!!
# IF YOU CHANGE THE NAME OF THIS SERVER, YOU MUST UPDATE
# ALL THE LICENSES THAT ARE ASSIGNED TO THIS SERVER. USING
# NWADMIN, DOUBLE-CLICK ON A LICENSE OBJECT AND CLICK ON
# THE ASSIGNMENTS BUTTON. IF THE OLD NAME OF
# THIS SERVER APPEARS, YOU MUST DELETE IT AND THEN ADD THE
# NEW SERVER NAME. DO THIS FOR ALL LICENSE OBJECTS.
```

Appendix C

```
SERVERID 92C964B
load conlog  maximum=100
SEARCH ADD SYS:\JAVA\BIN
; Network driver LOADs and BINDs are initiated via
; INITSYS.NCF. The actual LOAD and BIND commands
; are contained in INITSYS.NCF and NETINFO.CFG.
; These files are in SYS:ETC.
sys:etc\initsys.ncf
#LOAD IPXRTR
#LOAD PCNTNW.LAN PCI SLOT=2 FRAME=ETHERNET_802.2  NAME=PCNTNW_1_E82
#BIND IPX PCNTNW_1_E82 NET=FB52F63F
#LOAD IPXRTRNM
#LOAD TCPIP
#LOAD PCNTNW.LAN PCI SLOT=2 FRAME=ETHERNETII   NAME=PCNTNW_1_EII
#BIND IP PCNTNW_1_EII ADDR=11.0.0.3 MASK=255.0.0.0
MOUNT ALL

SEARCH ADD SYS:\JAVA\NWGFX
SYS:\SYSTEM\NMA\NMA5.NCF
LOAD BROKER "FS1_BROKER.Organization"

# BEGIN SAS/PKI (ADDED BY SASI)
LOAD SAS
LOAD PKI
# END SAS/PKI (ADDED BY SASI)

LOAD DSCAT.NLM
LOAD NLDAP.NLM

#RCONAG6.NLM is required by Console Manager in ConsoleOne and
by RConsoleJ
LOAD SPXS
LOAD RCONAG6 <Your Password Here> 2034 16800
STARTX.NCF
```

Glossary

access control list (ACL)—A list of objects (trustees) that have been granted or denied rights to perform operations on a particular object. Also called the *Object Trustees property* and the *Object Trustees (ACL) property*.

Access Control right—A file system right that allows users to make changes to files, directories, and trustee assignments.

across-the-wire migration—An upgrade method provided with NetWare 5 that leaves the NetWare 3.x source servers intact and "copies" the bindery and data files across the network to a NetWare 5 server. This method also allows you to migrate several NetWare 3.x servers onto a single NetWare 5 server.

American Standard Code for Information Interchange (ASCII)—The eight-bit character system that's standard for transferring data between systems.

Application object—The fundamental NDS object employed by the Application Launcher to efficiently and seamlessly deploy applications to users at workstations in the NDS tree.

architecture—The logical design of a system.

auto load printer—A printer attached to the server running the print server software.

AUTOEXEC.NCF—A NetWare server boot file.

Automatic Client Upgrade (ACU)—A utility that allows you to upgrade Novell Client for Windows 95/98, Windows NT, and Windows 3.x software automatically. The Windows 3.x version contains the NWDETECT, NWSTAMP, and NWLOG applications.

balanced tree (B-tree)—An efficient organizational structure used by Novell Storage Services (NSS) that allows it to retrieve file blocks that are not in the server's memory within four processor cycles.

Berkeley Internet Name Daemon (BIND)—Originally created by the University of California at Berkeley, BIND is a DNS server file format widely used by Internet Service Providers (ISPs) and hosts.

bindery—The flat database used in NetWare 3.x and earlier versions to contain User, Group, Print Server, and Print Queue objects. An NDS container can emulate a 3.x bindery, thus allowing services to establish a bindery connection for backward compatibility.

block suballocation—The process that allows partially filled disk data blocks to be segmented in 512-byte segments to recover empty space. These empty subblocks can then store small files or portions of files as needed.

Bootstrap Protocol (BOOTP)—This protocol gives a network node the ability to request IP address configuration. Unlike DHCP, this is a one-time configuration.

BorderManager—A complete firewall and proxy product that's commonly used as an interface between a company's network and the Internet.

btrieve—One of the first database programs created for networks. Btrieve was purchased by Novell and used in NetWare 2.x, 3.x, 4.x, and 5. It's still widely used by networks and applications around the world.

catalog—A flat-file database that holds information gathered from the NDS database.

Certificate Authority (CA)—A cryptographic verification form used to identify a person or other entity, such as a corporation.

child—Any object that receives information from a parent object or resides below a parent object.

Common Gateway Interface (CGI)—Server-side scripts that interact with input from a user, usually via a Web browser.

common name—The actual name you assign to a NDS leaf object (as opposed to an object's distinguished name).

Console Manager—A graphical Java applet that can run on the server console and on a Windows workstation that has the Java Runtime Environment (JRE) installed. Console Manager allows you to access server console screens on a workstation.

ConsoleOne—The NetWare management utility that uses a Java GUI environment to allow you to perform basic administrative functions on NDS objects, access the file system, and edit NetWare configuration files in a Java text editor. ConsoleOne can be run on the server or on a workstation.

consumer—This application registers the free space to be managed by Novell Storage Services (NSS) so other storage file systems cannot claim the same space. It's also called a *NSS consumer*.

container administrator—The administrator that controls local administrative activities for container objects, such as modifying user accounts and configuring access to objects in container.

container object—An NDS object that can contain or hold other objects—in contrast to leaf objects, which cannot.

context—An object's location in the NDS directory structure.

controlled access printer—A printer that can be used only by NDS-authenticated users with sufficient rights. Controlled access printers have corresponding NDS objects. Contrast this with *public access printers*, which have no security and no corresponding NDS objects.

Country objects—Objects that can exist only between the [Root] object and an Organization object. The Country object is used to designate a country as a valid NDS container object for wide area networks (WANs) that employ a geographical NDS design. It can only have a valid two-letter international country code, such as *US*, as its name. Country objects only need to exist in NDS if another X.500 directory system requires it.

current context—This is a workstation setting that specifies where in the NDS directory to look for objects. For example, if the workstation context is set to be OU=RESEARCH.O=ACME and a user logins as FRED, the system will look for a valid FRED object in the RESEARCH container.

digital persona—How a user is represented on a network.

Directory Services—Another way to refer to NDS.

disk blocks—The individual storage units for data on a drive.

disk thrashing—A term used to define excessive hard drive activity, where the disk's mechanical components are moving constantly to fulfill the disk read and write requests.

DNS Zone—The division of domain name spaces that contain all the information about the parts of the name space. There are three types of DNS Zones: Standard DNS Zone, IN-ADDR-ARPA, and IP6.INT.

DNS/DHCP Group object—The default DNS/DHCP object that's a standard NDS Group object of which all DNS and DHCP objects are members.

DNS/DHCP Locator object—The default DNS/DHCP object that contains DNS and DHCP information used by the Management Console for efficient access.

domain name server (DNS)—Machines that convert domain names (for example, zyxyx.com) to IP addresses using databases of hostnames and IP addresses.

Domain Name System (DNS)—A naming service utilized by the Internet that translates hostnames into IP addresses.

drive mapping—A drive association created using a workstation-based map utility (such as the Novell **MAP** command) that associates a drive letter with a directory or subdirectory on a hard drive. The drive letter association provides a way for the operating system to access files that reside on the hard drives of completely different operating systems.

Dynamic Host Configuration Protocol (DHCP)—A protocol that assigns dynamic, or temporary, IP configuration to workstations.

dynamic link library (DLL) files—Files that are libraries of executable code linked to applications when the applications are run, rather than being compiled with a program's executable. These files may be shared by several applications because they're linked dynamically and exist as independent files on the hard drive.

effective rights—The rights you actually have in a given location in NDS or the NetWare file system. They are determined by adding all the rights you've received by whatever means and subtracting all rights that have been revoked by the Inherited Rights Filter (IRF) or blocked by explicit assignments.

enterprise administrator—The administrator that controls tree name, partition and replication strategies, and time synchronization.

Ethernet—A networking technology characterized by its unique encapsulation of data (packet type), network board design, supported topology, and media type.

Ethernet cards—Network boards that provide Ethernet services for computers.

Fiber Distributed Data Interface (FDDI)—A network communications protocol characterized mainly by its use of fiber media for data transmission.

File Transfer Protocol (FTP)—A TCP/IP protocol used to transfer data between remote machines.

FILER—A utility used to manage NetWare volumes and files.

forced run—An Application Launcher feature that allows you to enforce the loading of programs, files, patches, and utilities on a user's workstation when he or she logs in. No user intervention is allowed; therefore, a user cannot prevent the running of the installation.

graphical user interface (GUI)—An operating environment that uses icons and buttons rather than commands to perform certain functions.

Group object—A NDS object designed to represent groups of users in the NDS tree and to the NetWare operating system. Changes made to a Group object are passed on to all members of the group automatically.

GroupWise—A popular product developed by Novell that provides email, scheduling, calendering, and workgroup services. GroupWise uses NDS to store configuration information.

Help Requester—A NetWare client-side program used to aid and support users on the network. It allows end users to access help resources.

Hierarchical Storage Management (HSM)—A data storage system that manages the movement of files between more expensive but faster media, such as hard drives, to less expensive but slower media, such as tapes, based on frequency of access. The process is generally transparent to the user.

host server—Normally denotes the location of the backup services, host adapter, and storage for a network.

hostname—The recognizable DNS name of a machine on a TCP/IP network.

Hot Plug PCI—A hardware specification that allows "hot swapping" of Peripheral Component Interconnect (PCI) cards so a machine doesn't have to be shut down when a new card is installed or removed.

Hypertext Markup Language (HTML)—The page description language used on the Web.

Hypertext Transfer Protocol (HTTP)—The standard set of rules that defines how Web servers communicate with Web clients (browsers).

Inheritable object property—A property that's enabled by default and allows object rights in the NDS tree to flow down the tree or to be inherited by subordinate containers and the objects in them.

Inheritable property right—A property that's enabled by default and allows property rights in the NDS tree to flow down the tree or to be inherited by subordinate containers and the objects in them.

Internetwork Packet Exchange (IPX)—This protocol was modeled after Xerox Corporation's Internetwork Packet protocol, XNS. It is the NetWare protocol that operates at the Network layer of the OSI model. IPX is sometimes used to include the entire protocol suite.

Internetwork Packet Exchange/Sequences Packet Exchange (IPX/SPX)—This is the native protocol stack for NetWare networks. SPX provides reliable connections and operates on the Transport layer, relying on IPX for lower-level network functions.

Java—Sun Microsystems' cross-platform programming language.

Java applet—A program written in Java that runs within a Java-compatible browser.

Java application—A standalone application written in Java that's executed in the Java environment. Java applications do not need a browser.

Java bean—A small piece of Java code written to perform a specific function.

Java class—A full-blown application that's written in Java.

Java Virtual Machine (JVM)—A virtual, or *nonphysical*, computer that executes Java code. The JVM provides hardware and operating system independence for Java applications.

kernel—The base of most operating systems. The kernel provides just the core functions deemed critical for the operating system. Further functionality is added by additional program modules.

LAN driver—A file containing software code that provides a communication link between the operating system and the network board.

leaf objects—A class of NDS objects that represents actual resources in the NDS tree and does not contain other NDS objects.

load balancing—A method for raising efficiency on a network by splitting up information packets over multiple connection paths.

local area network (LAN)—A collection of computers and other networked devices that fits within the scope of a single physical network. LANs provide the building blocks for internetworks and wide area networks (WANs).

login script—A set of instructions that the network client executes during the login process.

LPD—Line printer daemon, or LPD, is a standard for print services on TCP/IP networks and is analogous to NPRINTER in the NetWare world.

ManageWise—This product is designed to provide network management services, including documentation and monitoring functions.

manual load printer—A printer attached to something besides the server running the print services, such as a printer attached to a workstation and connected directly to the network.

master replica—The original copy of a partition that's used for authentication and partition merging and creation.

Media Access Control (MAC) address—A unique address that is hard-coded (or soft-coded) into a network board that distinguishes it from all other network boards.

Message (MSG) files—Files that contain system or error messages.

multiprocessor—More than one CPU on an individual machine. Multiprocessor systems come in several architectures, including symmetric multiprocessing (SMP) and asymmetric multiprocessing.

multiprocessor support—The ability to utilize multiple CPUs on a system.

multitasking—The ability to handle several tasks, generally giving the impression of simultaneous execution. Multitasking is managed either by time-slicing execution between processes, multiple processors, or a combination of the two.

multithreading—The ability to run multiple threads within a program or computation.

native IP—Novell's term for its implementation of the NetWare Core Protocol (NCP) and other high-level NetWare protocols over TCP/IP without the use of an IPX stub.

NDS for NT—A product for networks that have a few Windows NT Servers providing services but don't need the extra overhead of maintaining additional accounts. NDS for NT allows you to maintain one account for both NDS and Windows NT.

NDS object—Any object in the NDS tree. NDS objects can be divided into the subtypes [Root], container, and leaf.

NDS tree—The entire hierarchical Novell Directory Services (NDS) database of objects. If you have access to more than one tree, you must be authenticated to each tree to gain access to its resources.

NetWare 5 installation program—The application used to install NetWare 5 on a system.

NetWare Administrator—NetWare's graphical utility for managing NDS databases. Also called *NWAdmin*, although it's not a trademarked term. The executable for NetWare Administrator is NWADMIN32.EXE and is located in the SYS:\PUBLIC\WIN32 directory.

NetWare Backup/Restore—The application used to store and reload backups of NetWare servers and workstations files and data.

NetWare file system—NetWare's system of storing, manipulating, securing, retrieving, and otherwise managing files on disk drives connected to NetWare servers.

NetWare GUI—The graphical user interface utilized in NetWare. See also *graphical user interface (GUI)*.

NetWare Loadable Module (NLM)—One of several types of NetWare server executables; the other types include CDM, HAM, LAN, and NAM. Each executable has a specific function, with the NLM being the most general form.

Network Time Protocol (NTP)—An Internet standard for providing time synchronization. This protocol enhancement for TCP uses authoritative time servers to provide network time information through a hierarchy of time servers. NTP is similar but not identical to the timesync protocol for NetWare 4, which is still provided for NetWare 5 IPX servers.

Novell Directory Services (NDS)—Novell's directory service that stores information on the network resources and regulates their access. NDS is a hierarchical distributed database that is X.50x compliant.

Novell Distributed Print Services (NDPS)—A service that provides administrators the ability to control printing through NDS. It also provides bidirectional communications between control points, management applications and workstations, and network printers.

Novell Internet Access Server (NIAS)—A product that covers the security concerns of implementing a remote access solution while offering superior performance and maintaining support for a wide range of access methods.

Novell Licensing Services (NLS)—NLS manages licensed applications, such as NetWare 5, in the NDS database.

Novell Storage Services (NSS)—An enhanced file system that overcomes many of the limitations of the traditional NetWare file system.

Novell Upgrade Wizard—The workstation application used to set up and perform across-the-wire migrations.

object classes—General types of objects in the NDS tree differentiated by their schema. Organization and Country are two different classes of objects. Each object class has a different set of properties that designate its purpose. The set of properties defines the object class.

Object Trustees property—The property of an object that lists the trustees of an object in its ACL. Also called the *Object Trustees (ACL) property* and simply *ACL*.

Open Systems Interconnection (OSI) reference model—The standard model for network protocols. It contains the following layers: Physical, Data Link, Network, Transport, Session, Presentation, and Application. Often called simply the *OSI model*.

Organization objects—The class of container object that contains the subordinate objects that represent the resources of a specific organization in the NDS tree.

parent—Also called the *parent object*. This is simply a term for an object that stores other objects.

Point-To-Point Protocol (PPP)—A protocol developed by the Internet Engineering Task Force (IETF) to provide a more comprehensive dial-up alternative to the Serial Line Internet Protocol (SLIP).

Policy Package—Z.E.N.works NDS objects that allow you to create and maintain Workstation objects in the NDS tree. These policies are grouped into packages according to the types of objects (such as container, User, and Workstation objects) that the policies can be associated with.

Port Handler—A component of queue-based printing that provides communication between the Print Device Subsystem and the printer.

preemption—This is a processing technique that provides the system instant access to the processor.

preemptive multitasking—An operating system feature that allows the CPU to control when applications may execute. Preemptive multitasking provides some protection from poorly behaved applications but is characterized by higher processing overhead.

print queue—The temporary storage location (logical and/or physical) for documents sent to the printer but waiting to be printed.

Printer object—An object in the NDS structure symbolizing a physical printer.

processes—In the NetWare operating system, the number of simultaneous threads that may execute. Each process takes a small amount of RAM for thread stack space and other storage locations, which is offset by the greater efficiency under heavy load. The number of processes is controlled by admin-configurable settings accessed on the command line or the MONITOR utility.

Profile object—An NDS object that contains a common login script that executes for a set of users (assigned to the object) that exists in different containers or for a subset of users within a container.

protocol—A rule used to define the procedures to follow as data is transmitted or received.

provider—The NSS application that manages storage objects and scans all the storage devices to locate free space.

Pure IP—A new feature of NetWare 5 that allows you to run a network without IPX.

queue-based printing—The NetWare printing system that allows you to manage a network printing environment. You must configure three objects in NDS to use queue-based printing: the print queue, the printer, and the print server objects.

RConsoleJ—A utility used to access the server console screens on *remote* servers with IP or IPX.

read-only replica—A complete copy of a NDS partition that cannot be used for authentication.

read/write replica—A complete copy of a NDS partition. You can have several read/write replicas, and they can be used for authentication.

Redundant Array of Inexpensive Disks (RAID)—Multiple drives linked together via hardware or software, used to increase reliability. There are six recognized levels of RAID, with additional levels being developed. The exact features are highly dependent on the RAID level used.

Remote Console (RCONSOLE.EXE)—The utility used to access your NetWare server console over SPX and asynchronous connections.

remote control—A Z.E.N.works feature that allows a workstation to watch and interact with another workstation. Both users see each others' activities.

replica ring—The group of servers that stores copies of an NDS partition.

resource record—A leaf-type object that contains the data type and information about domain names.

RootServerInfo Zone object—The default DNS/DHCP object that holds information about the Internet root domain servers so names can be resolved outside your local domain.

suballocation 519

Routing Information Protocol (RIP)—A protocol that allows routers to communicate and inform each other of routes to available networks. RIP is available on TCP/IP and IPX but has generally been superceded by the Interior Gateway Protocol (IGP) and Open Shortest Path First (OSPF) on TCP/IP, and the NetWare Link Services Protocol (NLSP) on IPX.

SBackup Console (SBCON)—This NLM is used to perform backups and restorations of network data.

scheduling—The process of timing the transfer of data or actions.

Sequenced Packet Exchange (SPX)—In the IPX/SPX protocol suite, this protocol provides reliable data transfer between nodes and is roughly equivalent to the TCP protocol. SPX is characterized by a connection setup, ensuring data receipt and session termination.

server administrator—The person who maintains and configures the server.

server console—The NetWare 5 screen used by the network administrator to interact with and monitor the server.

Server object—An object that's created automatically whenever you install a server into NDS. It represents the physical server as an object in the NDS tree.

Service Advertising Protocol (SAP)—A protocol used by IPX to broadcast information on available services. SAP is characterized by limited scalability countered by easy configuration.

SLP Directory Agent—An agent that builds a table of services from SAP and NDS for use by IP clients, as well as to advertise IP services to IPX clients.

spooler—A temporary file location on a hard drive or in RAM, usually used for output such as printing. *Spool* is an abbreviation for Simultaneous Peripheral Operation On Line. There's little practical distinction between a spooler and print queue.

STARTUP.NCF—One of the two boot files for the NetWare server.

storage group—Free space on a drive or drives controlled by NSS.

Storage Management Services (SMS)—Novell's suite of services that allows information on NetWare volumes to be archived and retrieved. Typically, SMS is used to send data to and retrieve data from a tape drive.

suballocation—The means by which Novell maximizes both performance and available storage. NetWare traditional file system volumes use suballocation to break down unused portions of larger blocks (that contain a segment of data but leave an unused and otherwise wasted piece of disk space) into smaller 512K blocks; therefore, data can be written to the smaller blocks.

subnet mask—The 32-bit number that separates an IP address into node and network components.

subordinate reference replica—A subordinate reference replica is not a complete copy of the partition. It's created automatically on servers that have a complete replica of a parent partition but not its children. It cannot be used for authentication.

Supervisor object right—The right that allows you to perform any and all actions on an object. This right can be blocked by the Inherited Rights Filter (IRF).

Supervisor right—The unrestricted right to perform any operation on any file or directory for which the right is granted. This right cannot be blocked by the IRF.

SYS volume—The mandatory name of the first volume on a NetWare file server. The SYS volume must be a traditional NetWare volume.

target—The term used to identify the entity or item that can have its information backed up and restored to with NetWare 5's Backup and Restore system.

Target Service Agent (TSA)—The software or service that the target must be running to communicate with the backup service.

TCP/IP (Transmission Control Protocol/Internet Protocol)—Created by the Advanced Research Projects Agency (ARPA), this transmission protocol suite is the standard used for Internet communications.

Template object—This leaf object creates a boilerplate of information. This template is then used to create users or to modify existing user accounts. The Template object can contain information such as home directory paths, email accounts, and group memberships, along with many other properties.

threads—A logical program component that allows multitasking and may run separately from other modules on a system. Also referred to as an *executable object*. Typically, a single program consists of many modules that create, run, and destroy operation threads as needed.

topology—The physical layout of a network. Examples are star, ring, and bus.

traditional NetWare volume—A NetWare volume that uses a 32-bit interface and file allocation tables (FATs) to organize the storage space. The size of the files on a traditional NetWare volume is limited to a maximum of 4GB each, and volumes can be no larger than 1TB each.

Transaction Tracking System (TTS)—A system that prevents the corruption of data through tracking logical transactions from start to finish. TTS is the embedded tracking system in NetWare servers and is used for basic system integrity in NDS and other Btrieve functions.

trustee—Objects with the rights to access certain network resources. A trustee is defined as an object in the access control list (ACL) that has access to an object. There are six different objects that can be designated as trustees: Users, Groups, Organizational Roles, containers, [Root], and [Public].

typeful naming—Used in distinguished naming of NDS objects, where the object class is referred to before naming the object (for example, CN=MARYB.OU=AUSTIN.O=ACME). Generally, you only need to use typeful naming when typeless naming is not permitted.

typeless naming—Used in distinguished naming of NDS objects, where the object class is not referred to and the syntax of the distinguished name is trusted to identify the object correctly (for example, MARYB.AUSTIN.ACME).

Unicode—Standardized by the Unicode Consortium, Unicode is a 16-bit system used to encode characters and letters from many different languages.

Uniform Resource Locator (URL)—An addressing system used to locate files on a network or the Internet (for example, **www.zyxyx.com**).

Unix—An interactive time-sharing operating system developed in 1969 by a hacker to play games. This system developed into the most widely used industrial-strength computer operating system in the world, and it ultimately supported the birth of the Internet.

User Datagram Protocol (UDP) packet—An Internet transmission protocol that uses IP, but without the tracking of the data package (as with TCP).

User object—An NDS object representing an individual user containing personal information and access rights.

Video Electronics Standards Association (VESA)—A group committed to the standardization of VGA monitors.

Video Graphics Adapter (VGA)—The minimum standard for modern monitors. VGA displays at up to 640 by 480 pixels at 16 colors. Super VGA adheres to no one standard but expands on the number of pixels, colors, or both.

virtual memory—A method of emulating physical memory with drive space.

volume—The fundamental unit of NetWare server storage space. A *Volume object* is an NDS object that represents the corresponding physical volume.

VREPAIR—A NetWare utility used on traditional NetWare volumes to fix volume problems and remove name space entries from the file allocation table (FAT) and directory entry table (DET).

Web server—Any server that provides information to the World Wide Web.

wide area network (WAN)—An internetwork that connects multiple sites, where a third-party communications carrier, such as a public or private telephone company, is used to carry network traffic from one location to another. WAN links can be quite expensive, and are charged on the basis of bandwidth, so few such links support the same bandwidth as that available on most LANs.

Workstation Import Policy—A set of rules for naming Workstation objects and their location in NDS when they are created.

Workstation objects—NDS objects that represent workstations attached to your network and enable you to manage them efficiently.

World Wide Web—A group of servers interconnected to provide information via the Internet.

X-Windows—A graphical environment commonly seen in Unix and Linux. ConsoleOne is an X-Windows environment.

Xerox Network Services (XNS)—The basis of IPX. XNS utilizes a different encapsulation format than Ethernet.

Z.E.N.works (Zero Effort Networks)—A group of utilities for administrators that's used to increase the ease of most network management tasks by making them centrally available.

Index

Bold page numbers indicate sample exam questions.

-701 SYNCHRONIZATION DISABLED errors, 313
-621 TRANSACTIONS DISABLED errors, 313
-625 TRANSPORT FAILURE errors, 313

A

Access Control List. *See* ACL.
ACL, 236, 242
Across-the-wire migration, 16, 29–45, **464**
    advantages, 30–31, **40, 471**
    disadvantages, 31
    options, 30–32
    protocols, 31–32
    requirements, 32, **40**
    resources, 45
    Upgrade Wizard. *See* Novell Upgrade Wizard.
ACU, 30, **39**
Adaptive tests, 4–5
    test-taking strategy, 7–8
ADD NAME SPACE console command, 499
Add Self property right, 235
Address space, protected, **458**
Admin account, rights, 258–260
Admin user, new trees, 254
Administration, 260–263
    centralized, 260–261
    container administrators. *See* Container administrators.
    distributed, 261–263
    enterprise administrators, **271, 272, 446**
    GroupWise, 417
Aggressive mode, suballocation, 51
AIO.NLM file, 181
ALERT console command, 499
ALIAS console command, 499
All Properties property rights, 237
Ambiguous exam questions, 441–442

Applets. *See* Java applets.
Application directories, 88, **94**
Application installations, managing, 262
Application-level proxies, 421, **433**
Asymmetric DSL, 400–401
Auditing, 261
Authority, DNS, 355
Auto load printers, 102, 108
AUTOEXEC.NCF file, 148, 149, **450,** 507–508
    pound sign, 173–174, **186**
Automatic Client Upgrade. *See* ACU.

B

B channels, 400
Background, NetWare GUI, 161
Backing up files and NDS, 119–140, 121, **136, 295, 302**
    backing up servers, 127–130
    configuring sessions, **134**
    managing strategies and systems, 262
    resources, 140
    restoring data, 131–133, **137, 302**
    rights needed, 124–125, **137**
    SMS components and guidelines, 125–127, **135, 136**
    strategies, 120–125, **138**
    types of backups, 123–124
    Windows workstations, 122, 130–131, **134**
Backup engine, 122, 123
Balanced trees, NSS volumes, 63
Basic rate interface. *See* BRI.
Bearer channels, 400
Berkeley Internet Name Domain. *See* BIND.
BIND console command, 355, 362, 499
Block suballocation, traditional volumes, 50–52, **54**
Blue screen interface, 192
BorderManager, 421–424, **430, 433, 434, 436**
    NIAS, 422–423
    resources, 437

BRI, 400
Browse object right, 234, **460**
Browsers
    ConsoleOne GUI, 170
    Web browsers, FastTrack Server administration, 376
B-trees, NSS volumes, 63
Buffers, file cache, 219
Burst gap time, 224
Burst window size, 224

C

C1START.NCF file, 169, **453**
C worthy interface, 192
Cache hits, 195, **455**
Caches, monitoring utilization, 194–196, **198, 199, 200**
.CDM, file name extension, 143–144, **152**
CD9660.NSS module, 65
CD-ROM consumers, NSS volumes, 64
CD-ROMs
    monitoring size of index files, 297
    MOUNTING AS VOLUMES, 86
    NSS volume support, 65, **75**
CDROM$$.ROM directory, 86
Centralized administration, 260–261
Children
    backing up, 125
    partitions, 282
Choose Destination Location dialog box, 372
Circuit-level proxies, 421–422, **433**
Classes, Java, 158
CLEAR STATION console command, 499
Client accelerator, BorderManager, 424
Clients
    GroupWise, 416
    SMS, 125
Cluster size, 50
Commands. *See also specific commands.*
    console, 146–147, **153**, 493–497
    controlling execution, 505–506
Communications, SET parameters, 494–495
Compare property right, 235
Complex changes, NDS, 290, **456**
Compression, **465**
    system speed, **201**
    traditional volumes, 52, **56**
Confidence, 9
CONFIG console command, 499
Configuration files, 505–508
    shortcuts, 179, **186**

Configuration Files object, ConsoleOne GUI, 172–173
CONLOG console command, 500
Console commands, 146–147, **153**
Console Manager, 174–175, **185, 188**
CONSOLE1.EXE file, 169
ConsoleOne, 168–180, **187**
    adapting to user's needs, 179–180
    interface, 169–171
    My Server object, 171–176, **185**
    network management from server console, 176–179, **188**
    resources, 189
    starting, 169, **453**
Consumer, NSS volumes, 64, **74**
Container administrators, 263–266, **272**
    creating, 264–265
    exclusive, 265–266
    subdividing activities, 262
Container level security, NIAS, 405
Containers, new, NDS default rights, 254–255, **268, 466**
Context menus, ConsoleOne GUI, 171
Copying partitions, 261
CPUCHECK console command, 500
Crashes, 311–312
    recovering from, **320, 461**
Create button, DNS/DHCP Management Console, 335, 336
Create DHCP Server dialog box, 335, 336
Create DHCP Server icon, 335, 336
Create DHCP Server object, configuring, 337
Create DNS Server dialog box, 358
Create New DHCP Record dialog box, 335, 336
Create New DNS Record dialog box, 358
Create object right, 234
Create Print Queue dialog box, 101, 102
Create Resource Record dialog box, 360
Create Subnet dialog box, 337–338
Create Zone dialog box, 359–360
Custom device modules, 144, **152**
Custom directories, 87–89
Custom volumes, 84

D

D channels, 400
Data channels, 400
Data fragments, 51
Databases. *See* DHCP; DNS; NDS.

Delete object right, 234
Deleted files, recovery, 88, **92**
DELETED.SAV directory, 86
DETs, 49
DHCP, 327–351
    architecture, 329
    configuring, 334–341, **348, 468**
    global options, 341–342
    importing and exporting databases, 342–343, **349**
    installing, 330–334, **345, 457**
    IP address distribution, 329, **344, 445**
    protocol, 329, **344**
    resources, 351
DHCP Subnet object, 337–339, **348, 350, 475**
DHCPSRVR.NLM file, 340
Differential backup, 124, **473**
Digital tape drives, backing up, 121
Directories, 82–83
    custom, 87–89
    structure, 82–83, 89–90
    system-created, 84–87
Directory caching, 220–221
    SET parameters, 495
Directory entries, number of files stored on volumes, 51
Directory entry tables. *See* DETs.
Directory Map objects, 256, **270**
Directory Services, **SET** parameters, 495
Directory store, GroupWise, 417
Directory synchronization, GroupWise, 417
DISABLE LOGIN console command, 500
Disk, **SET** parameters, 495
Disk blocks, traditional volumes, 50, **57, 58**
Disk drivers, 143–144, **152**
    NetWare GUI, **164**
Disk mirroring, 68
Disk striping, 68
Disk subsystems, 218–219
Disk thrashing, 50, 205
Disk usage, optimizing, 217–221
DISMOUNT console command, 500
DISPLAY INTERRUPTS console command, 500
Display Properties configuration tool, 160–161
Distinguished name. *See* DN.
Distributed administration, 261–263
DN, print servers, 107, 108
DNA/DHCP Management Console, 330
DNIPINST.NLM file, 331

DNS, 353–367, **363**
    architecture, 354–356, **365, 452**
    configuration, 358–361
    domain levels, 354
    importing and exporting DNS databases, 361–362, **365, 462**
    installing, 330–334, 357, **366, 457, 469**
    resources, 367
    zones, 355–356, **363, 364, 457**
DNS/DHCP Management Console
    global options, 341–342
    installing, 333–334, **347**
    requirements for running, **347**
    shortcut icon, 334
Document directories, FastTrack Server, 376–377, **453**
Document store, GroupWise, 418
Domain Name System. *See* DNS.
Domain namespace, 354–356
    zones, 355–356
Domain Object Wizard, NDS for NT, 426–427
DOS, configuring network printers, 109
DOS consumers, NSS volumes, 64
DOS partitions, 48
    backing up, 121, **134, 136**
    NSS volumes, 63, 65–66, **76, 79**
DOWN console command, 500
Downtime
    planned, 297–298
    unplanned, 311–312
DSDIAG utility, 502
DSMERGE utility, 260–261, 502
DS.NLM file, 296
DSREPAIR utility, 291, 292, 316–317, 502
DSTRACE utility, 291, 293, 311, **320**
Dynamic Host Configuration Protocol. *See* DHCP.

E

EDIT.NLM utility, 150
Effective rights, 238–239, **247, 248, 251, 466, 473**
    NDS and file system security compared, 243–244
EIDE technology, 218
ENABLE LOGIN console command, 500
ENABLE TTS console command, 500
Encrypted passwords, 184
Enhanced Integrated Drive Electronics. *See* EIDE technology.

Error handling, **SET** parameters, 495
ETC directory, 86, **91**
Exam
    assessing readiness, 2
    layout and design, 5–7
    memorizing for, 443
    preparing for, 444
    taking, 444
Exam questions
    ambiguous, 441–442
    picking answers, 441
    strategies for handling, 9, 440
    tips, 442–443
    types, 440
Exam situation, 3–5
Exhibits, 3, 7
Exporting
    DHCP databases, 342–343, **349**
    DNS databases, 361–362

F

FastTrack Server, 369–382
    activating, 370–371, **450**
    document directories, 376–377, **453**
    function, 370–371, **380**
    installing, 371–373, **379**, **380**
    resources, 382
    security, 377–378
    shutting down, **380**, **463**
FastTrack Server Administration Server page, 374
FATs, 49
File allocation tables. *See* FATs.
File cache buffers, 219
File caching, 219–221
    SET parameters, 496
File system, **SET** parameters, 496
File system design, 81–95
    components, 82–83
    creating system and custom volumes, 83–84
    custom directories, 87–89
    directory structures, 89–90
    resources, 95
    system-created directories, 84–87
    traditional, 82–83
File system rights, **245**
File system security
    managing, 262
    NDS security compared, 243–244
File Transfer Protocol. *See* FTP service.

Files, backing up. *See* Backing up files and NDS.
FILTCFG utility, 502
Firewalls, 421–424, **430**, **433**, **434**
Folders, shortcuts, 179–180, **186**
Form tests, 3–4
    test-taking strategy, 7, 8
Free API, 205, **211**
FTP Server Parameters screen, 387, 388
FTP service, 383–395
    configuring, 387–389, **394**
    installation, 385–386, **393**, **394**
    management using UNICON, 386–387, **459**
    resources, 395
    security, 390
    starting and stopping, 389, **393**
    using, 390
FTPSERV.NLM file, 384–385, **392**
Full backup, 123

G

Garbage collection routine, 205, **210**
Generic Digital Subscriber Line. *See* xDSL.
Graphical user interface. *See* GUI; NetWare GUI.
Group object, extending schema for DNS and DHCP, 332, **346**, **357**, **467**
GroupWise, 414–418, **429**
    administration program, 417
    backing up data, 122, **134**
    client, 416
    message, directory, and document stores, 417–418, **434**
    message transfer system, 416
    resources, 437
GroupWise administration module, 414
GUI
    ConsoleOne, 169–171
    NetWare. *See* NetWare GUI.

H

.HAM, file name extension, 143–144, **152**
Hardware failure, 311–312
Help, JAVA.NLM file, **164**
HELP console command, 146, **153**
Hierarchical Storage Management. *See* HSM.
High bit-rate DSL, 400–401
Home directories, 87–88

Host adapter modules, 144, **152**
Host servers, backing up, 121, **445**
HSM, 69
HTML documents, Java applets defined as part of, 158–159
Hypertext Markup Language. *See* HTML documents.

I

IBM-formatted partitions, NSS volumes, 63
IDE technology, 218
Importing
    DHCP databases, 342–343
    DNS databases, 361–362, **365, 462**
Incremental backup, 123–124
Industry Standard Architecture. *See* ISA network boards.
INETCFG utility, 402, 502
Inheritable object right, 234
Inheritable property right, 235
Inheritance, NDS and file system security compared, 243
Inherited rights, 236, **247**
    changing and blocking, 239–241, 257–258
Inherited Rights Filter. *See* IRF.
Inherited Rights Filter dialog box, 240
INITIALIZE SYSTEM console command, 500
In-Place Upgrade, 16–21
    advantages, 16, **23**
    directory containing NetWare 4.11 drivers, 20, **27**
    disadvantages, 16–17, **25, 452**
    NSS volumes, 69
    post-upgrade procedures, 21, **27, 454**
    pre-upgrade procedures, 19, **25**
    protocol options, 18, **463**
    requirements, 17–18, **22, 23, 448, 459**
    resources, 28
    servers, 16, 21, **22**
    steps, 19–21, **22, 26**
INSTALL.BAT file, In-Place Upgrade, 20, **22**
Installing
    DHCP, **457**
    DNS, 357, **366, 457, 469**
    DNS/DHCP, 330–334
    DNS/DHCP Management Console, 333–334
    FastTrack Server, 371–373, **379, 380**

FTP services, 385–386, **393, 394**
NetWare products and services from GUI, 160
NIAS, 401–404, **408, 409**
Novell Upgrade Wizard, 33–34, **41**
servers, 260, 261
snap-ins, 333, 357
Integrated Drive Electronics. *See* IDE technology.
Integrated Services Digital Network. *See* ISDN.
Internet Packet Exchange. *See* IPX.
Internet Protocol. *See* IP.
Internetworking Configuration utility, 402
IP
    across-the-wire migration, 31, **43**
    DHCP services. *See* DHCP.
IP addresses, 328–330
    configuring IP address objects, 339–340
    distribution to hosts, 329, **344, 445**
IP Gateway software, BorderManager, 423
IPCON console command, **458**
IPCU.NLM utility, 69
IPX
    across-the-wire migration, 31, **40**
    In-Place Upgrade, 18, **24**
IPX gateway, BorderManager, 422
IPXCON utility, 502
IPXPING utility, 502
IRF, 239, 240–241, **248**
    exclusive container administrator, 265–266
    NDS and file system security compared, 243
ISA network boards, 216
ISDN, 399–400

J

Java applets, 158–159, **447**
    adding to NetWare GUI menu, 161–162
    shortcuts, 180, **186**
Java applications, 156–160
    adding to NetWare GUI menu, 161–162
    classes, 158
    hardware requirements, 156–157
    NetWare GUI support, 156, 159–160
    resources, 165
Java AWT standard, 159
JAVA directory, 87

JAVA utility, 502
Java Virtual Machine, loading, 157
JAVA.NLM file, 157, **164**
JAVASAVE directory, 87
Job Details dialog box, 110–111

K

Kernel, NetWare operating system, 142–143, **151**
KEYB utility, 502
Keyboard configuration, 161

L

.LAN, file name extension, 144
LAN drivers, 144
LANalyzer Agent, 419, **432, 457**
LANGUAGE console command, 500
Large Internet Packets. *See* LIP.
Licensing services, **SET** parameters, 496
LIP, 225
LIST DEVICES console command, 500
LOAD console command, 145, 500
Locator object, extending schema for DNS and DHCP, 332, **346**, 357, **467**
Locks, **SET** parameters, 496
Logging scripts, maintaining, 262
LOGIN directory, 85
Low-priority threads, 51

M

MAIL directory, 86, **94**
Mailbox Manager for Exchange, 427
Main menu, ConsoleOne GUI, 170
ManageWise, 418–421
    managing and analyzing network traffic, 419–420, **432, 457**
    inventorying network assets, 420
    monitoring servers, 418–419, **429**
    resources, 437
    virus protection, 420–421, **435**
Manual load printers, 102, 108
Master replica, 279, **285, 449, 451**
Maximum Physical Receive Packet Size setting, 223, **230**
MCA network boards, 216
Memorizing for exam, 443
Memory
    architecture, 204–205, **212**, 213
    cache utilization, 194–196
    failure to recognize, 217
    Java requirements, 156
    monitoring utilization, 196–197

protection, 142, **151**
SET parameters, 496
virtual, 142–143, **151**
MEMORY console command, 500
Memory management, 203–213
    memory architecture, 204–205, **212**, 213
    monitoring memory usage, 208–209
    optimizing available memory, 208
    protected memory, 207–208, **210, 212**
    virtual memory, 205–207
MEMORY MAP console command, 500
Memory pools, 204–205
Message store, GroupWise, 417, **434, 470**
Message transfer system, GroupWise, 416
Micro Channel Architecture. *See* MCA network boards.
Minimum Physical Receive Packet Size setting, 222–223, **452**
MIRROR STATUS console command, 500
Miscellaneous category, **SET** parameters, 496–497
MMPRV, 63
Modify DHCP Options dialog box, 342
MODULES console command, 500
MONITOR utility, 192–197, **198**, 219, 502
    cache utilization, 194–196, **198, 199, 200**
    memory utilization, 196–197
    options, 193–194
    processor utilization, 197
    resources, 202
MONITOR.NLM file, **451**
MOUNT console command, 500
Mouse, Java requirements, 156
MPPP, 400
Multilink Point-to-Point Protocol. *See* MPPP.
Multiple-volume directory structures, 89–90, **93**
Multiprocessor category, **SET** parameters, 496–497
My Server object, ConsoleOne GUI, 171–176, **185**
My World object, ConsoleOne GUI, 171

N

.NAM, file name extension, 144
NAME console command, 501
Name servers, DNS, 355
Name space modules, 144
Names, partitions, 278
NAT, BorderManager, 423
Navigating the console, 147
.NCF file name extension, 147, 149

NCMCON utility, 502
NCP, **SET** parameters, 496–497
NDPS, 21, 98
  printing, 263
NDPS directory, 87
NDS, 49
  backing up. *See* Backing up files and NDS.
  changes, 290–291, **299, 456**
  creating NDS objects, 177
  inconsistencies, 293, **300,** 308–311, **318, 322, 447, 456, 461**
  managing NDS objects, 178–179
  managing with ConsoleOne, 176–179
  queue-based printing.
    See Queue-based printing.
  troubleshooting. *See* Troubleshooting NDS.
  unconditionally removing from server, 298
  versions running simultaneously, 295–296
NDS database, SYS volume, 83
NDS for NT, 424–428, **431**
  Domain Object Wizard component, 426–427
  Mailbox Manager for Exchange, 427
  Novell Client for NT, 427
  resources, 437
  SAMSRV.DLL component, 426, **432, 469**
  snap-ins for NetWare Administrator, 427
NDS Manager, 291–292, **299, 302, 467**
  repairs, 314–316
  troubleshooting, 310–311
NDS partitions, 277–287, **283, 286, 467**
  boundaries, **284**
  managing partition operations, 294–295, **299**
  names, 278
  partitioning process, 278, 280–282
  replicas, 279–280, **284, 285,** 294, **301, 449, 451**
  resources, 287
  rights, **301**
NDS preventive maintenance, 293–305
  backing up, 295
  managing partition operations, 294–295
  NDS versions, 295–296
  replica replacement, 294

  resources, 305
  SYS volume disk space, 296–297
NDS Printer Configuration dialog box, 103
NDS Printer object, **115**
NDS Properties window, ConsoleOne, 178
NDS repairs, 314-317
  DSREPAIR utility, 316–317
  guidelines, 314, **322**
  recovering from crashes, 312, **320, 461**
NDS schema
  extending to include DNS and DHCP objects, 331–333, **345, 346,** 357, **451, 467**
  extending with GroupWise, 415
NDS security, 233–275
  centralized administration, 260–261
  configuring access to network resources, 256–257
  creating container administrators, 263–266
  default rights, 254–256, **267, 268, 269**
  distributed administration, 261–263
  effective rights, 238–239
  FastTrack Server, 377–378
  file system security compared, 243–244
  FTP services, 390, **392**
  guidelines, 257–260
  inherited rights, 239–241
  NIAS, 404–406, **410**
  object rights, 234
  Object Trustees property, 242
  property rights, 234, 235
  resources, 252, 275
  strategies, **274**
  Supervisor object right flow to Server object, 241–242
  trustees, 235–238
NDS synchronization, 261, 290–291, **304, 319, 320**
NETBASIC directory, 87
NetWare Administrator
  configuring print objects, 100–101, **113**
  GroupWise, 415
  path of snap-ins, **346**
  print services quick setup, 106–107, **113**
NetWare Backup/Restore, 125, 129
NetWare Core Protocol. *See* NCP.
_NETWARE directory, 279
NetWare GUI, 156, 159–162
  adding Java programs and applets to NetWare GUI menu, 161–162
  adding support, **163**

background, 161
disk drivers, **164**
installing additional NetWare
   products and services, 160
keyboard configuration, 161
loading, **163**
resources, 165
support for Java applications, 156,
   159–160
video resolution, 160–161
NetWare Loadable Modules. *See* NLMs.
NetWare operating system, 141–154
   kernel, 142–143, **151**
   NLMs, 143–145
   server configuration files, 147–149
   server console, 145–147
   server script files, 149–150
   server startup, **151, 152**
NetWare partitions, 48
NetWare Print Server screen, 108
Network Address Translation. *See* NAT.
Network assets, managing and taking
   inventory of using ManageWise, 420
Network boards, older, 216
Network Information Service. *See* NIS.
Network Interface Cards. *See* NICs.
Network resources, configuring access,
   256–257, **270**
Network traffic, managing and analyzing
   using ManageWise, 419–420, **432**
NI directory, 87, **91**
NIAS, 397–411, **449**
   BorderManager, 422–423
   features and requirements, 398–399
   installing and configuring, 401–404,
      408, 409
   resources, 411
   security, 404–406, **410**
   technologies for remote access data
      transmission, 399–401, **408, 409**
   using, 406–407
NIAS Options screen, 401
NICs, 18
NIS, 385
.NLM file name extension, 143, 144–145
NLMs, **58**, 144–145. *See also specific
   modules.*
   backup and restore system, 122, 125,
      126, 127–128, 130
   loading and unloading, 145

NetWare operating system, 143–145
   unloading, 35, **42**
Nonaggressive mode, suballocation, 51
Novell Client for NT, NDS for NT, 427
Novell Directory Services. *See* NDS.
Novell Distributed Print Services.
   See NDPS.
Novell Education home page, 10–11
Novell Internet Access Server. *See* NIAS.
Novell Storage Services. *See* NSS.
Novell Upgrade Wizard, 30, 32–38, **39**,
   464, 471
   installing, 33–34, **41**
   objects migrated, 36, **43**
   post-upgrade procedures, 38
   pre-upgrade procedures, 34–36, **42, 44**
   project window, 37–38
   projects, 32
   running, 36–38, **39**
NPRINTER utility, 502
NPRINTER.EXE file, 109
NPRINTER.NLM file, 108, 109
NPTWIN95.EXE file, 108–109
NSS File Provider, 63–64
NSS Media Manager Provider.
   See MMPRV.
NSS utility, 502
NSS volumes, 31, 61–80
   advantages, 66–68, **73, 446, 472**
   CD-ROM support, 65, **75**
   consumer, 64, **74, 472**
   creating, 70–71, **72, 77**
   DOS partitions, 63, 65–66, **76, 79**
   file size, 62, 63, **454**
   limitations, 68–69, **75**
   organization of storage space, 62–65
   providers, 63–64, **72, 465**
   recovery from crashes, 66–67
   resources, 80
   size, 62, 63
   storage groups, 64–65, **74, 460**
   transactions, 67
   upgrading using In-Place Upgrade, 69
NSWEB.NCF file, 370–371, **379**
NWBACK32 Backup configuration
   window, 129
NWBACK32.EXE file, 125, **134, 460**
NWCONFIG utility, 70, **72**, 298, 385, 502
NWCONFIG.NLM file, 52
NWPRV, 63–64
NWTAPE.CDM file, 121

O

Object browser, ConsoleOne GUI, 170
Object rights, 234, **245**
    Supervisor object right flow to Server object, 241–242
    trustees, 235–236
Object Trustees property, 236, 242
Objects unknown, NDS database, 309
One-volume directory structures, 89
Organizational Role object, 263, 265, **271**

P

Packet Burst protocol, 224–225, **228**, **458**
Packet filtering, BorderManager, 423, **433**
Packet receive buffers, 51, 222–223, **229**
Pages, memory, 204
Parallel Communication dialog box, 103
Parents
    backing up, 125
    partitions, 282
Partition Continuity window, 310
Partitioning, 261
Partitions, 48. *See also* NDS partitions.
Password Management property, 262–263
Passwords
    changing, 259
    encrypted, 184
    managing, 262
PCI cards, 216
Peripheral Component Interconnect. *See* PCI cards.
PERL directory, 87
PING utility, 502
Plain old telephone service. *See* POTS.
POTS, 399
Pound sign, AUTOEXEC.NCF file, 173–174, **186**
Preemption, kernel, 143, **151**
Preparing for exam, 444
PRI, 400
Primary rate interface. *See* PRI.
Print drivers, 98
Print jobs, 99
Print queues, 99, **455**
    assigning to printers, 104
    creating, 101, **114**
    managing, 110–111
Print server, 100, **114**
    creating, 105
Print Server Print Layout dialog box, 105–106

Print servers
    assigning printers to, 105
    managing, 112
    names, 107, 108, **117**
Print Services Quick Setup (Non-NDPS), 106
Printer Assignments dialog box, 103, 104
Printers, 99–100
    assigning print queues, 104
    assigning to print servers, 105
    connection points, 99–100, **115**
    creating, 101–104
    managing, 111–112
Printing
    NDPS, 98
    queue-based. *See* Queue-based printing.
Processing load, balancing, 143
Processors, monitoring utilization, 197
Profile object, 257, **474**
Program tests. *See* Form tests.
Projects, Novell Upgrade Wizard, 32
Property rights, 234, 235, **246**
    trustees, 235–238
PROTECT console command, 501
Protected address space, **458**
Protected memory, 207–208, **210**, **212**
PROTECTION console command, 501
PROTOCOL console command, 501
Providers, NSS volumes, 63–64, **72**
Proxy Cache software, BorderManager, 423–424, **434**, **462**
PSERVER.NLM file, 100, 107
PUBLIC directory, 85, **91**, **453**
[Public] object
    new servers, 255
    new trees, 254, **267**
    new users, 256
Pure IP, In-Place Upgrade, 18, **24**

Q

.QDR file name extension, 99, 101
QMAN, 129
Questions. *See* Exam questions.
Queue-based printing, 97–118, **446**
    configuring printers, 108–109
    configuring usage rights for users, 112
    managing print services, 109–112
    print drivers, 98
    print queue, 99, 101, 110–111, **114**
    print servers, 100, 105, 112, **114**
    printers, 99–100, 101–104, 111–112

quick setup option, 106–107
resources, 118
starting, 107–108
steps in setting up, **116**
QUEUES directory, 101
QUEUES volume, 99

R

RCONAG6 utility, 502
RCONAG6.NLM file, 173–174, 180, **463**
RCONPRXY utility, 502
RCONSOLE agent, 173–174, 180
RCONSOLE.EXE file, 181
RConsoleJ utility, 180–181, **185**, **188**
  starting from ConsoleOne, 176
RDN, print servers, 107, 108
Read performance, optimizing servers, 220–221, **228**
Read property right, 235
Read right
  new users, 255, 256, **268**
  Object Trustees property, 242
Read-only replicas, 280
Read/write replicas, 279, **285**, **451**
Real Time Data Migration. *See* RTDM.
Recovery, deleted files, 88, **92**
Recovery from crashes, **461**
  NSS volumes, 66–67
  traditional volumes, 66
REGISTER MEMORY command, 217, 227
Relative distinguished name. *See* RDN.
Remote access, NIAS. *See* NIAS.
Remote access to workstations, RConsoleJ utility, 176, 180–181
Remote Console, 181–183, **185**, **187**
REMOTE utility, 502
REMOTE.NLM file, 181, **185**
REMOVE utility, 502
Rename object right, 234, **460**
Repair menu, 310
Replicas, partitions, 261, 279–280, **284**, **285**, **301**, **449**, **451**
  replacement, 294
Required properties, print objects, 100
RESET SERVER console command, 501
Resolvers, DNS, 355
Resource records, DNS, 354–355, 356, **364**, **468**
RESTART SERVER console command, 501
Restoring data
  files and NDS, 131–133, **302**
  steps, **137**
  strategies, 120–125, **138**

Reverse proxy, BorderManager, 423–424
REXXWARE Migration Toolkit. *See* RMT.
Rights. *See also* NDS security.
  Admin account, 258–260
  default, NDS, 254–256, 258, **267**, **268**, **269**, **460**
  effective. *See* Effective rights.
  file system, **245**
  inherited. *See* Inherited rights.
  NDS and file system security compared, 243
  object. *See* Object rights.
  property. *See* Property rights.
  read. *See* Read right.
  required for backing up and restoring, 124–125, **137**
  Supervisor object, 257, 258, 264
  trustees. *See* Trustees.
  turning on, 258
  write. *See* Write right.
RMT, 30, **39**
Root domain, 354
[Root] object
  new trees, 254, **267**
  new users, 256
RootServerInfo Zone object, extending schema for DNS and DHCP, 332–333, 346, 357, **467**
RS232.NLM file, 181
RSPX utility, 502
RSPX.NLM file, 181, **185**
RTDM, 69

S

SAMSRV.DLL file, 426, 432, **469**
SAR object, 339
SBCON, 129
SCAN ALL console command, 501
Scheduling, kernel, 143
Screening routers, 422
SCRSAVER utility, 503
SCSI technology, 219, **226**
Search requests, Web-based resources, 12–13
SECURE CONSOLE console command, 183, 501
Security, **470**
  file system, NDS security compared, 243–244
  NDS. *See* NDS security.
  servers, 183–184
Selected Properties property rights, 237
Self-confidence, 9

Server component, SMS, 125
Server configuration files, 147–149
Server console, 145–147
    commands, 146–147
    loading and unloading NLMs, 145
    navigating, 147
Server management, MONITOR utility. *See* MONITOR utility.
Server object, Supervisor object right flow to, 241–242
Server Preferences page, 374, 375
Server script files, 149–150
SERVER.EXE file, 147–148
Servers
    determining configuration, **458**
    In-Place Upgrade, 16, 21, **22**
    installing, 260, 261
    loading, syntax for, **466**
    managing and monitoring using ManageWise, 418–419, **429**
    memory management. *See* Memory management.
    migrating 3.x servers to NetWare 5, **450**
    monitoring performance, 262
    new, NDS default rights, 255, **268**
    optimization, 231
    planned downtime, 297–298
    security, 183–184
    unplanned downtime, 311–312
Service Location Protocol. *See* SLP.
Service processes, 224
SERVMAN.NLM file, 192–193, **198**
SET console command, 146–147, **227**
SET parameters, 222–224, 493–498
    Maximum Physical Receive Packet Size setting, 223
    Minimum Physical Receive Packet Size setting, 222–223, **452**
    MONITOR utility, 192–193, 196, **198**, 202, **451**
    packet receive buffers, 222–223, **228**
    service processes, 224
Shared data directories, 89
Shortcuts, ConsoleOne, 179–180, **186**
Simple changes, NDS, 290, **299**, **456**
Simulations, 4, 7
SLP, SET parameters, 496–497
SMDR, 127
SMS, 121–122, **135**
    back up process, 127–128
    components and guidelines, 125–127

Snap-ins. *See also specific snap-ins.*
    installing, 333, 357
    for NetWare Administrator, NDS for NT, 427
    path, **346**
Spanning, 48, **229**
    performance improvement, 221
SPEED console command, 501
Splitterless DSL, 400–401
SPXCONFIG utility, 503
SRBs, 51
Start address, 339
START PROCESSORS console command, 501
STARTUP.NCF file, 148–149, 506–507
STARTX.NCF file, 159
Status bar, ConsoleOne GUI, 170
STOP PROCESSORS console command, 501
Storage deposits, NSS volumes, 64
Storage groups, NSS volumes, 64–65, **74**
Storage Management Services. *See* SMS.
Store-and-forward message architecture, GroupWise, 417
Suballocation Reserved Blocks. *See* SRBs.
Suballocation thrashing, 51–52
Subdomains, 354
Subnet Address Range. *See* SAR object.
Subnet Pool object, 340
Subordinate reference, 280, **286**
Supervisor object right, 234, 257, 258, 264, **301**, **467**
Supervisor property right, 235
SWAP console command, 501
Swap files, 206, **211**, **462**
Synchronizing NDS, 261, 290–291, **304**, **319**, **320**
SYS volumes
    creating, 83
    disk space, 296–297, **474**
    NDS database, 83
    requirements for creating, 56, **459**
    traditional volumes, 48, **58**, **69**, **91**
SYSTEM directory, 85
System-created directories, 84–87

T

Target Service Agents. *See* TSAs.
Targets, backing up, 121–122, 125, **134**
TCPCON utility, 503
TECHWALK utility, 503

Test-taking
 basics, 8–9
 strategy, 7–8
Time category, **SET** parameters, 496–497
TIME console command, 501
TIMESYNC utility, 503
Toolbar, ConsoleOne GUI, 170
Tools object, ConsoleOne GUI, 173–174
TPING utility, 503
TRACK ON/OFF console command, 501
Traditional volumes, 47–59
 advantages, 53, **55**
 block suballocation, 50–52, **54**, **58**
 compression, 52, **56**
 configuring, 52–53, **58**
 disk blocks, 50, **57**, **58**
 enabling DS and DC attributes, 49, **54**
 recovery from crashes, 66
 resources, 59
 SYS volumes. See SYS volumes.
Transaction tracking, **SET**
 parameters, 497–498
Transaction Tracking System. See TTS.
Transactions, NSS volumes, 67
Trees
 creating upper levels, 260
 installing servers, 260, 261
 new, NDS default rights, 254, 258, **267**
 removing crashed servers, 312, **321**
Troubleshooting NDS, 308–325, **323**
 examples of errors, 312–313
 inconsistencies, 293, **300**, 308–311, **318**, **322**, **447**, **456**, **461**
 recovery. See NDS repairs.
 resources, 325
 unplanned server downtime, 311–312
Trustees
 NDS and file system security compared, 243
 object and property rights, 235–238, **246**, **251**
Trustees Of dialog box, 236
TSANDS.NLM file, 122
TSA500.NLM file, 122
TSAs, 122, **136**
TTS, 49, 68, 296–297, **303**

U

Ultra IDE technology, 218
UNBIND console command, 501
Unicode, NSS volume support, 68
UNICON, 386–389
 FTP service configuration, 387–389, **459**
 FTP service management, 386, **459**
 starting and stopping FTP service, 389
UNICON login screen, 386, 387
UNICON main menu, 386, 387
UNLOAD console command, 145, 501
Upgrading, 15–28, 261
 In-Place Upgrade. See In-Place Upgrade.
 Novell Upgrade Wizard. See Novell Upgrade Wizard.
 options, 16–17
UPGRDWZD.EXE file, 33–34, **41**
UPS_AIO utility, 503
Usage rights, queue-based printing, 112
User accounts, creating, 262
User level security, NIAS, 406
User objects, new, NDS default rights, 255, **269**

V

VESA_RSP.NCF file, 157
Video
 Java requirements, 156–157
 resolution, 160–161
Video drivers, Java requirements, 156–157
View Server Settings page, 374, 375
VIEW utility, 503
Virtual memory, 142–143, **151**, 205–207
Virtual Private Network. See VPN.
Virus protection, ManageWise, 420–421, **435**
Volumes, 48
 NSS. See NSS volumes.
 traditional. See Traditional volumes.
VOLUMES console command, 501
Volumes object, ConsoleOne GUI, 171–172
VPN, BorderManager, 424, **433**
VREPAIR utility, 66, 503

W

Web-based resources, 9–13
 search techniques, 12–13
Web browsers, FastTrack Server administration, 376
Web server accelerator, BorderManager, 423–424
Web servers, function, 370–371
Windows 3.x
 configuring network printers, 109
 migrating servers to NetWare 5, **450**

Zones **535**

Windows 95/98
    backing up workstations, 122, 130–131, **136**
    configuring network printers, 108–109
Windows NT
    backing up workstations, 122, 130–131, **134, 136**
    configuring network printers, 109
    NDS for NT. *See* NDS for NT.
Workstations
    backing up, 122, **126**, 130–131, **134**
    gathering information using NDS Manager, 310
    remote access, 176, 180–181
    setting up to use DHCP, 340–341
    starting ConsoleOne, 169
Write caches, 196

Write performance, optimizing servers, 220, **226**
Write property right, 235
Write right
    assigning, 257
    new users, 255
    Object Trustees property, 242, **249**

X

xDSL, 400–401, **408**

Z

ZLSS consumers, NSS volumes, 64
Zones
    DNS, 355, **363, 364, 457**
    domain namespace, 355–356

Coriolis Help Center

Here at The Coriolis Group, we strive to provide the finest customer service in the technical education industry. We're committed to helping you reach your certification goals by assisting you in the following areas.

Talk to the Authors

We'd like to hear from you! Please refer to the "How to Use This Book" section in the "Introduction" of every Exam Cram guide for our authors' individual email addresses.

Web Page Information

The Certification Insider Press Web page provides a host of valuable information that's only a click away. For information in the following areas, please visit us at:

www.coriolis.com/cip/default.cfm

- Titles and other products
- Book content updates
- Roadmap to Certification Success guide
- New Adaptive Testing changes
- New Exam Cram Live! seminars
- New Certified Crammer Society details
- Sample chapters and tables of contents
- Manuscript solicitation
- Special programs and events

Contact Us by Email

Important addresses you may use to reach us at The Coriolis Group.

eci@coriolis.com

To subscribe to our FREE, bi-monthly on-line newsletter, *Exam Cram Insider*. Keep up to date with the certification scene. Included in each *Insider* are certification articles, program updates, new exam information, hints and tips, sample chapters, and more.

techsupport@coriolis.com

For technical questions and problems with CD-ROMs. Products broken, battered, or blown-up? Just need some installation advice? Contact us here.

ccs@coriolis.com

To obtain membership information for the *Certified Crammer Society*, an exclusive club for the certified professional. Get in on members-only discounts, special information, expert advice, contests, cool prizes, and free stuff for the certified professional. Membership is FREE. Contact us and get enrolled today!

cipq@coriolis.com

For book content questions and feedback about our titles, drop us a line. This is the good, the bad, and the questions address. Our customers are the best judges of our products. Let us know what you like, what we could do better, or what question you may have about any content. Testimonials are always welcome here, and if you send us a story about how an Exam Cram guide has helped you ace a test, we'll give you an official Certification Insider Press T-shirt.

custserv@coriolis.com

For solutions to problems concerning an order for any of our products. Our staff will promptly and courteously address the problem. Taking the exams is difficult enough. We want to make acquiring our study guides as easy as possible.

Book Orders & Shipping Information

orders@coriolis.com

To place an order by email or to check on the status of an order already placed.

coriolis.com/bookstore/default.cfm

To place an order through our online bookstore.

1.800.410.0192

To place an order by phone or to check on an order already placed.